TRAVELLERS

New Zealand

Second Edition

Cover
Mitre Peak, Milford Sound
(Courtesy Communicate NZ)

Second edition published 1988 by Pacific Tourism Promotions Ltd, C/- The Braynart Group Ltd, 10 Mountain Road, Epsom, Auckland, New Zealand (Private Bag, Newmarket, Auckland, New Zealand). Telephone (09) 392-444. Fax (09) 392-449.

ISBN 0 9597733 2 0

While editorial material covers all the possibilities, the commercial listings are of companies pre-selected by us to ensure that their service was of a high standard. These companies were required to participate upon a strictly factual basis and a charge was made to cover the cost of preparing the material. This has subsidised the cost of the book to you.

All care has been taken to ensure that all information is correct, but we can accept no responsibility for omissions or changes.

The exclusion of any company does not mean that its service is in any way inferior to those listed.

TRAVELLERS

New Zealand

Second Edition

EDITORS:

Gary Hannam and Lesley McIntosh

PACIFIC TOURISM PROMOTIONS

Mts Ruapehu and Ngaruahoe, Volcanic Plateau.
(Courtesy Turangi Scenic Flights)

CONTENTS

A CALENDAR OF EVENTS APPEARS ON PAGES 32, 225 and 231

Introduction

Take three deep breaths of fresh, clean air and start to relax. New Zealand is a reminder of an unspoiled quality of life that many parts of the world will never again know. It offers something to everyone.

Isolated for aeons at the southern end of the vast Pacific Ocean, it is now as accessible as any other part of our ever-diminishing world, and with its small population, offers a rich diversity of sporting, scenic, and cultural experiences.

This book will introduce you to the great range of activities you can enjoy while travelling through New Zealand, whether an overseas visitor or a New Zealander. It has been designed primarily for those travellers who want to make up their own minds about what to do and see – those prepared to allow time out to sample the experiences packed into this small country. There are some major resort areas developed for travellers, but the country also lends itself to exploration off the beaten track. It would be hard to find another country on earth so small that it offers holiday-makers who enjoy cultural diversity and action so great a choice. From a beachcomber's paradise of deserted coast, you can be experiencing the thrill of snow skiing with only two hours' travelling time.

New Zealand is an extraordinary amalgam of physical characteristics that often seem reminiscent of somewhere else, yet remain decidedly and uniquely New Zealand's own – the long, lonely beaches of Northland, the kauri forests where trees take hundreds of years to reach maturity in a complex, sensitive ecological system, the coastal river valleys drowned by the rising seas as glaciers melted creating great bays filled with islands.

The southernmost point in the Pacific's 'ring of fire' turns northward again through New Zealand, on the edge of the Pacific plate, giving rise to a region of intense volcanic and thermal activity in the centre of the North Island. Here a cataclysmic blast 1800 years ago was one of the most violent in human history.

The alps of the South Island are one of the world's great mountain ranges, their valleys carved out by massive glaciers. Some of these glaciers ignored climatic changes and survive as the largest in any temperate zone in the world. In this land of contrasts there are mountains two million years old and mountains 200 million years old, but surely the most outstanding feature of New Zealand's topography is its sheer diversity, concentrated into a relatively small country.

On clean, clear waters – on isolated mountain lakes or in coastal bays dotted with islands – enjoy a huge variety of boating activities: take off on some of the world's wildest rivers in raft or canoe; go boating in a row boat, jet boat, launch, sail boat, or luxury keeler; try windsurfing or para-sailing.

Experience alpine New Zealand – this is a land of superb skiing, especially glacier and heli-skiing, and truly challenging climbing on mountains that produce world-class alpinists.

One of the major appeals of this country is the vast expanses of land, often empty of people. Trails through forests, hills and valleys, across plains, rivers and mountains, alongside isolated lakes and beaches make this a hiker's paradise.

Fishing is a national pastime enjoyed by anyone with a line and the time. In lakes and rivers trout and salmon grow to a great size. There is superb game fishing, especially for striped marlin, on the northeast coast; excellent line fishing from boats and surfcasting from rocks or long empty beaches. Some of the world's finest deep-sea diving provides exciting variety in the rugged bays and islands.

There's no closed season on hunting several varieties of deer, wild pigs, chamois, thar and goats. If your perfect holiday includes a round or two, or much more, of golf, you'll be delighted to learn that New Zealand has more golf courses per head of population than any country in the world; and visitors are warmly welcomed on the country's courses.

For the individual traveller there is still a great deal more to see and do. One traveller may become absorbed in the Polynesian culture of the Maori, whose origins are to be found hundreds of years ago far across the Pacific Ocean. For some visitors the lingering impression is of a volatile place, where the earth's crust is perilously thin; to others it may be the wildlife, particularly the rich unique assortment of birds, or the native flora. All travellers will be amazed at the predominance of bright green pastures dotted with sheep. These animals outnumber the human population many times over and will be one of the first sights you see as your aircraft swoops in towards Auckland or Christchurch International Airport.

Because it developed in isolation from other land masses, New Zealand has a unique plant and bird life.

The closest relatives of New Zealand forest plants are found in other parts of the Pacific and in South America. Seventy-five per cent of flowering native plants are found only in New Zealand, including such beautiful oddities as the white mountain flower known as the Mount Cook lily, which is, in fact, the world's largest buttercup. Strange also is the occurrence of rich, evergreen rainforest, a jungle-like covering rarely found in temperate regions.

The birds of New Zealand evolved in isolation, in a land without predators, so losing the need for strong wings. Best known is the national symbol, the nocturnal flightless kiwi.

Other endemic birds include the impertinent, flightless weka, which will cheerfully raid campsites; the kea, a bold mountain parrot living in the South Island high country; the kaka, a shy bush parrot that lives in the deepest forest and the tui, a bush songbird that lives on nectar, common in forests and gardens throughout the country.

Other bird treats include the yellow-eyed penguin, which can be seen at Taiaroa Head on the Otago Peninsula, the only known mainland Royal Albatross colony in the world (also at Taiaroa Head) and the only readily accessible gannet colony in the world (at Cape Kidnappers).

In this land of contrast even the weather is predictably unpredictable – the country is surrounded by seas and therefore susceptible to sudden changes. Where the sea is close by on both coasts, as in Auckland, there may be clear, cloudless skies one day and torrential rain the next.

In the South Island contrasting weather patterns are accentuated by the Southern Alps. Prevailing winds drop rain on the west coast, creating rainforest thick with ferns, mosses and vines. East of the alps the landscape can sometimes resemble a semi-desert with not a tree in sight.

Travellers in New Zeland should expect such variations as warm, humid, semi-tropical weather or hot, dry weather with little humidity; sudden heavy downpours of rain or drifting mists, and cold, crisp winters. In the simplest terms, pack a sunhat and raincoat because you will need them both.

There is a great diversity in the cities, towns and villages – some with quaint, pitch-roof wooden or stone cottages built over a hundred years ago; some, like Napier, that went through intense development after an earthquake, when art deco was the style of the day; and some such as Twizel that are so new that fifteen years ago the town site was wilderness.

The country's largest city, Auckland, sprawls across a narrow isthmus with dozens of extinct and dormant volcanic cones creating vantage points. The houses and buildings of Wellington, the capital, perch on steep hills spreading up from the closely contained city centre on the harbour edge.

Christchurch, the South Island's largest city, has the gentle, leisured pace of an English country town, enhanced by Gothic-style stone buildings. Dunedin, the fourth major city, has a distinctly Scottish heritage and elaborate, grandiose Victorian architecture.

Other smaller cities include Whangarei, where the forest spills down hills to city perimeters, Hamilton with its prosperity based on the Waikato dairy industries and the Waikato river flowing through its heart, Rotorua with its emphasis on the extraordinary thermal activity and surrounding beautiful lakes, and Nelson, caught between the exquisite, indented coast of the Marlborough Sounds and the sweeping beaches of Tasman Bay.

In travelling around the country, it can often seem at first that there is little for the visitor to do – New Zealanders outside the main tourist centres tend not to proclaim or promote the attractions of their towns, villages and surrounding countryside. But pause awhile and ask. If there's no local information centre, ask in the motel or hotel, at the desk or in shops, restaurants, coffee shops or tearooms. New Zealanders are immensely friendly and justly proud of their country, and you will find them delighted to advise you.

It's not uncommon for New Zealanders to take a visitor under their wing, show them around and invite them home after a chance meeting. But bear in mind also that New Zealanders tend to be reticent people, careful not to intrude – it's up to you to chat to them if you wish.

This same reticence affects the service you will find in hotels and restaurants. What may seem like reluctant or indifferent service is often simply 'different'. If you want something, ask for it pleasantly, don't wait for it to be offered or expect your needs to be anticipated.

Although the people of this country are isolated, New Zealanders have achieved fame in many fields of endeavour – from Sir Edmund Hillary's successful ascent of Mount Everest to Sir Ernest Rutherford's splitting of the atom.

An independence of spirit and natural inventiveness are hallmarks of the New Zelander character.

Settlement

The first Maori settlers arrived in New Zealand about 1,000 years ago from a homeland known as 'Hawaiki', believed to be somewhere in east Polynesia. Maori society is based on a hierarchical system with chiefs, elders and tohunga (priests) heading tribes and sub-tribes. The central marae or meeting place in the communal villages was the forum for elaborate, formal debate – in a system with no written language oratory became a finely polished skill.

By the 1820s the first Europeans began to arrive; traders in flax and timber, sealers, whalers and missionaries. By the 1840s the flow of Europeans was increasing and the pressure on the Maori population was beginning to show. Their culture was increasingly undermined, their land bought for inadequate payment and the people decimated by European diseases such as measles or the common cold.

By the 1860s conflict was unavoidable, in spite of an agreement, the Treaty of Waitaingi, signed in 1840, which ceded New Zealand to the British Crown and guaranteed certain rights to the Maoris. To this day the treaty and its intentions remain a subject of controversy.

Twenty years of bitter fighting between Maori tribes and British troops finally drew to a close in the early 1880s, and the country set about developing itself into a nation.

The Maori people took a long time to recover from the effects of a colonisation that demoralised them, alienated them for their land and undermined their culture. But a resurgence of interest and pride in a unique culture and language has gained momentum in recent years, and those interested in Maoritanga (culture) will find a vital, lively Polynesian culture in New Zealand. It is expressed in song and dance, in weaving and carving.

Maori and European intermarried to an extent that was exceptional in British colonies, and today many New Zealanders have a racial background that is both Maori and pakeha (European).

Although the first European settlers were predominantly British in origin, there were other nationalities who settled various areas. Among the first sealers and whalers, some of whom stayed on, were Americans. Many of the first immigrants were Scots, particularly in Otago and Southland, areas that retain a strong Celtic flavour, but also in Auckland. Waipu Cove in Northland was settled by a group of Scots, not from Scotland but from Nova Scotia.

In the Franklin County area, just southwest of Auckland, the first organised immigration brought many British and Irish settlers from South Africa. The Taranaki centre of New Plymouth was founded by settlers from Devon and Cornwall, the city of Christchurch was a carefully planned Church of England community, and the South Island's west coast attracted the Irish.

Settlers also came from other European countries – the small towns of Norsewood and Dannevirke owe their origins to forest workers from Scandinavia. The tiny village of Puhoi, north of Auckland, retains pride in its origins as a settlement of immigrants from Bohemia, now part of Czechoslovakia. (The Puhoi pub is well worth a detour.) Several villages in the Motueka valley in the Nelson region were founded by German Lutherans.

Yugoslavs from Dalmatia arrived near the turn of the century to dig out kauri gum in the peatlands of the north. Most stayed on, importing brides from their homeland, and their descendants today play a significant part in communities such as Kaitaia, Dargaville and Henderson (west Auckland).

Chinese arrived first as goldminers – traces of their camps are still to be seen in Otago – but most returned to China. Later immigration has boosted the number of Chinese in the community and Indians, from India or by way of Fiji, are yet another significant minority group.

After World War II there was large-scale immigration from Britain, but also a considerable number of Dutch from the Netherlands or from former colonies in South-east Asia.

In the 1960s people from neighbouring Pacific islands, such as the Cook Islands, the Tokelau Islands and Western Samoa, began settling in New Zealand in increasing numbers. It is a continuing story. The people of New Zealand are almost as varied as the country they live in.

How to Use this Book

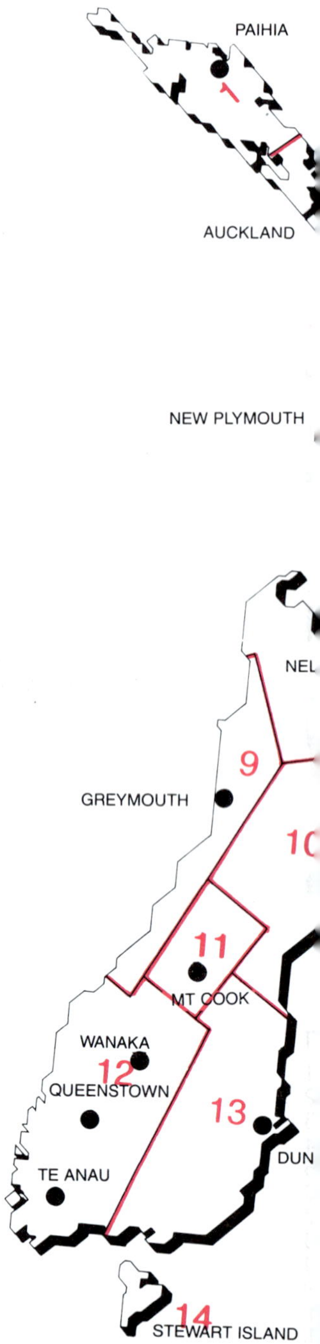

1.

We set out to make a different type of guide-book with a format suited to New Zealand. A holiday here is based on doing things as well as seeing the sights – even if some may require more energy than others – or just relaxing. Our holiday guide presents activities available, a selection from the very active to some ideas for a more relaxing holiday, and a regional touring guide. A number of writers prepared the introductions and, quite separately, the commercial listings were compiled to give factual information and a good selection of facilities, not an overwhelming plethora of detail.

2. THE ACTIVITIES (Pages 16-117)

Each activity is introduced with an editorial review of what is available and a map shows the regional location of each facility. The commercial listings follow, giving details as to when you can do the activity, what to bring and approximate cost. To assist the planning of a tour through New Zealand or to various parts of the country, each commercial listing in the activities sections is cross-referenced to the regional touring Section.

For example:

Fiordland cruises (Sailing and Cruising), is cross-referenced to Region 13 – The Southern Lakes – where more regional listings apply.

Cross-references are also used for commercial listings included in more than one activity or region. Listings from the regional section cross-reference back to the activities sections. To access the cross-references, follow the 'See Also:' notes at the end of each section. The first words apply to either the activity or regional section in which the cross-reference is first mentioned.

3. TOURING IN NEW ZEALAND (Pages 118-135)

Firstly, you are given an introduction to travelling around both the North and the South Islands, then each region is explored in detail. We have created our own definitions of the regions to best serve the holiday-maker. Our main objective is to help you to organise your time. For each region, a regional centre has been selected which becomes the focal point for what to do within one half, one, two and three hours driving time (except for the West Coast, Mount Cook, and Stewart Island). (Detailed road maps required for executing your journey may be obtained from most book shops, vehicle service stations or the Automobile Association in New Zealand.)

The format is similar to the activities sections. An introduction is given to the region, then the regional centre. Listings with details on local sights are provided and activities are cross-referenced to each place so that you can plan your time.

4. THE REGIONAL TOURING GUIDE (Pages 136-264)

For a national transport, accommodation and food guide, refer to this section. Also included are specialist holidays such as rafting trips, adventure holidays and special interest tours. (Accommodation is also presented in the regional guide.)

TOURING REGIONS:

1 Northland
2 Auckland
3 Waikato–Bay of Plenty
4 East Cape–Hawkes Bay
5 Volcanic Plateau
6 Taranaki
7 Wellington
8 Nelson–Marlborough
9 Westland
10 Canterbury
11 Mt Cook
12 Southern Lakes
13 Otago–Southland
14 Stewart Island

REGIONAL CENTRES ●

How to Use this Book

Each region has a map showing the activities available within the time zones from the regional centre. For convenience, map symbols are explained alongside each map together with a quick reference map showing driving times to other regional centres. The maps show the places mentioned in the text rather than all place names, and include the major activities of the area as noted in the listings.

Driving time is calculated at 80 kilometres per hour (50 mph), with a rest break every few hours and consideration taken of the terrain.

Editorial also introduces the main areas outside the regional centre which offer points of interest. Each region has an entertainment, accommodation, food and a travelling around review and guide.

Note:

It is impossible to include all relevant information in one publication, so references for additional information are provided. Additionally, the Public Relations Office or Information Centre is noted for each town. Most have excellent local information.

PLANNING AND BOOKING

1. Many activities require pre-booking of up to three months ahead. Every activity can be booked directly or through a travel agent. Plan what you want to do and check ahead to avoid disappointment.

2. Take note of the seasons for various activities (e.g. except in some parts of the North Island most white-water rafting closes from April until November). See the Sports Calendar for details of hunting and fishing.

3. Each time you use one of the facilities mentioned in this travellers' guide, let the proprietor know, and if there is something we have missed out or something you are dissatisfied with, please write to us.

4. The prices indicated are a guide only, accurate at time of compilation.

5. For overseas visitors: Mid-December and January, Easter and the first three weeks of May are times when New Zealanders take holidays. For skiing, the August school holidays (usually last three weeks of August) means some ski areas are relatively crowded.

TRAVELLERS NEW ZEALAND – THE FILM

For the first time a book is complemented with an entertaining, high-quality film available in any video format.

If the book provides the detail, the 25-minute film captures the spirit of travelling in New Zealand and shows some of the many ways to enjoy this challenging destination.

Send it to a friend or take one home.

Write to: Pacific Tourism Promotions Ltd.
c/- The Braynart Group Ltd,
Private Bag, Newmarket, Auckland.

If you are in Auckland, call us. We would be delighted to hear from you and of any suggestions you may have regarding this book.

NORTH
ISLAND
Kaitaia
Kerikeri
Kaikohe
Whangarei
Dargaville
Great Barrier I
AUCKLAND
Thames
Pukekohe
Huntly
Tauranga
Hamilton
Matamata
Whakatane
Ruatoria
Rotorua
Kawerau
Te Kuiti
Tokoroa
Murupara
Taupo
Gisborne
Taumarunui
Turangi
New Plymouth
Wairoa
Mt Ruapehu
Stratford
Waiouru
Napier
Hawera
Taihape
Hastings
Wanganui
Marton
Dannevirke
Palmerston North
Levin
Masterton
WELLINGTON

SOUTH ISLAND
Motueka
Nelson
Picton
Blenheim
Westport
Reefton
Kaikoura
Greymouth
Hokitika
Cheviot
CHRISTCHURCH
Mt Cook
Ashburton
Haast
Timaru
Waimate
Milford Sound
Wanaka
Queenstown
Oamaru
Alexandra
Palmerston
Te Anau
Roxburgh
Mosgiel
DUNEDIN
Gore
Balclutha
Invercargill
Bluff
Halfmoon Bay
STEWART ISLAND

Travel Notes for Overseas Visitors

Passports

Passports are required by all visitors to New Zealand with two exceptions: children under the age of 16, who are included in the passport of the accompanying parent; and Australian citizens, who do, however, require a passport to re-enter their own country. Passports must be valid for at least six months beyond the intended departure date from New Zealand.

Visas

Visa requirements differ according to nationality, purpose and length of stay. Generally, citizens of the countries listed below do not require a visa or entry permit before embarking for vacation or business visits to this country.
Unrestricted entry for six months:
Australia, United Kingdom, Republic of Ireland, Canada, Belgium, Denmark, France, Luxembourg, The Netherlands, Norway, Sweden, Switzerland.

Unrestricted entry for three months: Federal Republic of Germany, Finland.

Unrestricted entry for thirty days: United States of America, Japan, Tahiti, New Caledonia.

Visa or prior entry authority are required for citizens of the above countries who wish to extend the maximum visit, work, obtain medical treatment or settle in the country.

Entry Procedures

New Zealand maintains three levels of control at all points of entry: immigration, customs and agriculture. Forms are issued to all arriving air travellers prior to landing, and upon arrival passengers will be required to wait while agriculture officers spray the aircraft cabins to ensure that no insects are carried into New Zealand. These sprays are not harmful, but travellers may care to cover their noses with a cloth. Agricultural restrictions are very important to an economy so dependent upon agriculture and horticulture. New Zealand is free from most major plant and animal diseases – it really is one of the last unspoiled lands. To keep it this way, travellers are asked not to bring into the country without declaration: foodstuffs, plants, and plant and animal materials. Please co-operate — it only takes a little of your time to preserve our natural heritage. Goods brought into New Zealand by travellers will not be subject to customs duty or sales tax, provided they are for personal use (your own property) and are taken from the country on departure.

Vaccination Certificates are not required. However, should a traveller fall ill within three weeks of arrival, promptly consult with and advise a doctor of previous countries visited.

Health and Emergency Services

Health insurance is advisable. Most hotels and motels can advise on calling a doctor if required. In emergencies, an ambulance may be called by dialling 111 on the telephone. This number also applies to police and fire services. Chemists (drug stores) are open from 9.00 a.m. to 5.30 p.m. Most cities have 'Urgent Dispensaries', which are open between these hours and throughout weekends (consult the front section of local telephone directory under Hospitals).

Accident Compensation

If any person suffers personal injury through accident, whether visitor or resident, he or she is entitled to compensation for reasonable expenses directly attributable to that accident. This includes medical and hospital expenses, as well as lump-sum payments for permanent incapacity, loss of limb, etc.

Currency. There are no restrictions on the import or export of foreign currencies. However, formal approval should be obtained from the Reserve Bank (through a normal trading bank) for the export of funds. A maximum of $100.00 in New Zealand currency may be exported.

$NZ1.00 = Australian $0.90
$NZ1.00 = United States $0.61

Shopping Hours. Generally 9.00 a.m. to 5.30 p.m., Monday to Wednesday, extended to 9.00 p.m. on either Thursday or Friday, depending on location. Many areas also trade on Saturdays from 9.00 a.m. to 1.00 p.m., or to 4.00 p.m. Generally only dairies (milk, papers and groceries) are open on Sunday.

Goods and Services Tax (GST)

A tax of 10% applies on all goods and services supplied in New Zealand. In many cases, this tax is included in purchase price. Should you be making purchases of goods and souvenirs prior to leaving the country, exemption from this tax may apply upon showing your travel ticket, or through Duty Free shops. Note: GST is to be added to the cost of most of the services listed in this book, unless otherwise stated.

Post Offices. Government owned and operated, controlling the mail, telephone and telex services. Post Offices are highly visible in most towns as major public buildings with their own flag flying. Open from 9.00 a.m. to 5.00 p.m., Monday to Thursday, and till 8.00 p.m. on Fridays.

Telephones. Most parts of New Zealand are on International Subscriber Trunk Dialling (STD) to most countries in the world. Local calls from call boxes cost 20 cents (two 10-cent coins).

Banks. Open from 9.00 a.m. to 4.30 p.m. Monday to Friday. Banks in airports service all incoming and outgoing flights.

Credit Cards. Visa, American Express, Diners and Bankcard

Tipping. Not an obligatory part of any service rendered, usually offered as a bonus where service excels.

Technicalities. Electricity — 230 volts, 50 cycles, alternating current. Most North American direct-current 110-volt appliances will not function unless dual voltage. Most hotels provide a 110-volt socket for electric razors.

Public and School Holidays

Nationwide statutory holidays are as follows: New Year's Day, Waitangi Day (February 6), Good Friday, Easter Monday, Anzac Day (25 April), Queens Birthday (first Monday in June), Labour Day (fourth Monday in October), Christmas Day and Boxing Day (26 December). The main school (and family) holiday period is from mid-December to the end of January. Schools are also closed for two weeks in May and two weeks in August.

Climate

The New Zealand climate is officially described as ranging from subtropical in the north to temperate in the south. It gets neither scorchingly hot in summer nor bitterly cold in winter.

Overall, weather tends to be changeable. You'll need to pack a sweater and a raincoat.

Because New Zealand is "down under" in the Southern Hemisphere, the seasons are the direct reverse of those in the Northern Hemisphere. Summer runs from December to March (New Zealand Christmasses are generally spent at the beach under a sun umbrella), autumn from March to June, winter during July and August, and spring from September to November.

Hikers rest above the Tara Lakes on the slopes of Mount Ngauruhoe, an active volcano in the North Island chain of fire. *(Mal Clarbrough – Dept of Lands & Survey)*

The national and maritime Parks of New Zealand are unique in the world. Nowhere on earth is there such a variety of landforms and experiences within such a small geographical area.

The visitor with a month to spend could go from tropical coastline and islands to volcanic peaks, to snow-covered alps, to southerly fiords in one continuous trip of only 1,000 easy kilometres (620 miles).

The incredible variety of landforms in the parks arises from the country's position at the junction of two of the crustal 'plates' of the earth's surface, which we now know to be constantly moving. The volcanic activity of the North Island parks rises through the crust where one plate is diving under the other, melting as it goes. The result is several active volcanoes and extensive geothermal areas of hot pools of mud or water. The magnificent South Island alps sit astride the collision zone between the two plates, where neither will yield and fold under the other. The collision has pushed the land upwards to a height as great as Mt Cook's 3,764 metres (12,349 feet). Great glaciers still grind the alpine valleys. One of the world's longest glaciers outside polar regions is the 29-kilometre (18-mile) Tasman. Ancient glacial valleys now drowned by the sea created a convoluted fiordland, surrounded by one of the world's great rain forests.

There are ten national parks and three maritime parks. The national parks occupy about eight per cent of the nation's land area. New Zealand was the fourth nation of the world (after the USA, Australia and Canada), to establish a national park system in 1887. The first park, the volcanic Tongariro mountains, was a gift from a visionary chieftain of the first New Zealanders, the Maori. Te Heuheu Tukino IV gave the young European settlement, Tongariro, seat of his ancestral hearth fires, to preserve the land from development. Maori identity is inextricably linked to ancestral land, and the park preserved this for all time.

These parks exist to preserve and protect unique natural features and New Zealand's heritage of native plants, animals and landforms. They also provide for the physical and spiritual recreation of people. Their scenery alone is awe inspiring and breathtaking. Parks are natural areas with a variety of activities available for visitors. Active outdoor holidays of tramping (hiking), climbing, skiing, canoeing, fishing or hunting (in limited areas by permit) can be balanced by relaxed motor touring or resting at facilities provided. Nature study is as near as the doorstep of accommodation, or as far as the feet wish to go. Visitor services vary from park to park. Public transportation is generally readily available.

Though the climate varies considerably through the seasons, the parks are all open year round. They offer different experiences according to season: tramping, camping, boating and fishing are less possible in winter of course, but are replaced by skiing and other winter pursuits. The North Island maritime parks and the thermal areas in and around Tongariro National Park also offer pleasant winter activities of a more temperate nature. Except for the far south or high country, New Zealand's winter is fairly mild by northern-hemisphere standards. Touring and vacationing in winter are definitely reasonable. However, summer is the season for the wide variety of planned and conducted activities.

Mt Cook Lily

The National Parks division of the Department of Lands and Survey administers many resources other than the parks. There are hundreds of scenic, nature, recreational or scientific reserves throughout the country, most open to the public. The nation is criss-crossed by a system of over 100 developed walkways of varying character, in addition to the tracks in national parks. It is possible to walk almost the entire length of the country without setting foot on a paved surface. There is also a system of farm parks throughout the country. These combine New Zealand's unique agriculture – a worthwhile tourist attraction in itself – with nature conservation and recreation. The farming areas are open to public view and include many interesting stock operations, such as sheep herding with dogs, and shearing.

From the coasts to the mountain tops, from top to bottom, New Zealand's great natural bounty preserved for tomorrow's enjoyment beckons the traveller. Uncluttered, sun-kissed, relaxed and friendly times and places await visitors to New Zealand's national and maritime parks, reserves and walkways..

The Whanganui National Park is the newest to be formed, protecting the area inland from Wanganui, the rugged gorges of rainforest surrounding the Wanganui River.
Activities: jet boating, canoeing, climbing, rafting, cruising, tramping, fishing, hunting.

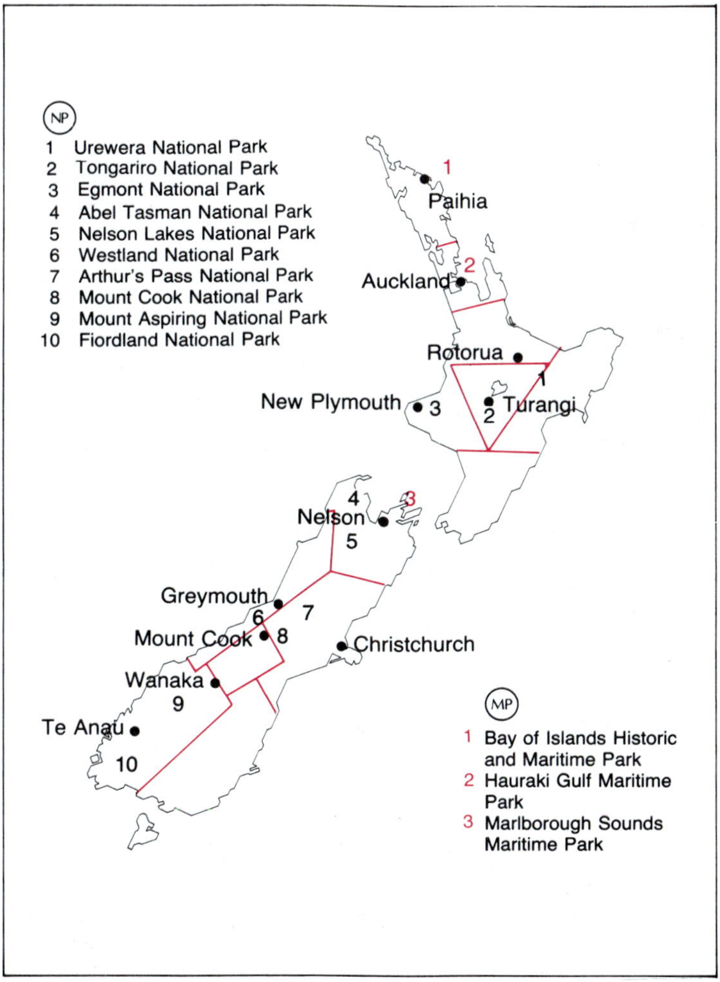

NP MP

The walkways and nature reserves

The highest mountain in Australasia, Mount Cook, rises 3764 metres (12,348 ft) above the Southern Alps of Mt Cook National Park.
(Brian Ahern – Dept of Lands & Survey)

Bay of Islands

There are many Maori pa sites, and famous battles were fought in the Bay of Islands. Waitangi, Russell and Kerikeri also have reserves of historical interest. The Bay of Islands has superb recreational opportunities, warm, dry summers, and unparalleled scenic attractions.

Activities: swimming, picnicking, camping, boating, walking, tramping, fishing, scenic drives, viewing historical features, skin diving, charter-boat trips.

Hauraki Gulf

Public use of the islands varies considerably. Some are so remote and difficult to reach that they cannot be used for recreation. However, their very isolation makes them ideal for the study of New Zealand wildlife in its natural state. Many islands are the home of insects, birds, animals and plants no longer found on the mainland.

Activities: boating, sea fishing, swimming, tramping, camping, nature walks, scenic flights.

A tidal pool on the sandstone beach of Motuihe Island reflects the serenity of the Hauraki Gulf Maritime Park. ***(Tony Lilleby – Dept of Lands & Survey)***

Aerial view of the Coromandel Peninsula. ***(Courtesy Michael Kopp Dept of Lands & Survey)***

National Parks

(NP) (MP)

Tongariro

Three volcanic peaks, Ruapehu (2,797 metres, 9,177 feet) Ngauruhoe (2,291 metres, 7,516 feet) and Tongariro (1,968 metres, 6,457 feet) dominate this park, which is within a day's easy driving from almost anywhere in the North Island. Mt Ruapehu is the North Island's highest mountain and major ski resort. Ngauruhoe and Ruapehu are active volcanoes, and Tongariro, although regarded as dormant, has hot springs gushing out of its upper slopes in the Ketetahi area. Area: 76,198 hectares (188,200 acres).

Activities: skiing, tramping, hunting (red deer, pigs), climbing, sign-posted walks, guided trips, illustrated talks and audio-visual programme in headquarters building, nature programmes in summer.

Children play at the base of a waterfall in Mt Egmont National Park. *(Herb Spannagl – Dept of Lands & Survey)*

Urewera

Urewera National Park has magnificent native forests, lakes and waterfalls. It is rich in bird life. Much of its beauty can be seen from the Rotorua-Wairoa State Highway, which winds through approximately 80 kilometres (50 miles) of bush and lake scenery. Of all New Zealand's national parks, Urewera preserves most strongly the influence of the traditional culture of the early Maoris. Area: 211,777 hectares (523,000 acres).

Activities: tramping, hunting (red deer, pigs), trout fishing, boating, easy sign-posted walks.

Egmont

The almost perfect cone of Mt Egmont (2,518 metres, 8,261 feet) dominates the Taranaki Province. The volcano and the native forest that surrounds it make up Egmont National Park, readily accessible from neighbouring centres and ideal for all mountain activities. Area: 33,532 hectares (82,820 acres).

Activities: skiing, tramping, climbing, easy sign-posted walks, nature programmes in summer, hunting (goats).

Information about the national park system, walkways and scenic reserves is available from many travel agents or New Zealand Government representatives abroad. It is also available directly by mail from the Department of Lands and Survey, Private Bag, Wellington. Telephone: Wellington (04) 735-022.

A tramping party crosses one of innumerable streams in Mt Egmont National Park. The rocks take on rainbow colours from the various minerals spewed out of the volcano. *(Herb Spannagl – Dept of Lands & Survey)*

Marlborough Sounds

A tramper says good morning to New Zealand's native parrot, the kea. ***(David Gregorie Dept of Lands & Survey)***

Rich in history, some of the reserves in the park show evidence of pre-European occupation and others of early European explorers from Captain James Cook to Dumont D'Urville and the early whalers.

The unique blend of a myriad of bays and coves in sheltered warm tidal waters, set against a backdrop of attractive native bush, interspersed with private holiday residences and farm land, makes the park a popular playground for the holiday-maker and tourist.

Activities: fishing (blue cod, tarakihi, snapper), pleasure boating, water skiing, swimming, picnicking, camping, tramping, nature walks, hunting (wild pigs, goats and deer), scenic drives, mail and charter-launch trips, and viewing of historical features – Maori pa and pits.

Abel Tasman

Abel Tasman National Park has numerous tidal inlets and beaches of golden sand. The coastline is rich in history, having been visited by the Dutch explorer Abel Tasman in 1642 and thoroughly explored by the Frenchman Dumont D'Urville in 1827. The granite hills of the park support a wide variety of vegetation from warm-temperate beech forest to shrubland and reverting farmland. Area: 22,370 hectares (55,250 acres).

Activities: tramping, boating, good sea fishing, hunting (pigs, goats, opossums, a few red deer), swimming, walks.

Nelson Lakes

The two beautiful lakes, Rotoiti and Rotoroa, both fringed to the water's edge with beech forest, form the focal point of Nelson Lakes National Park. The surrounding country is rugged, forest clad, and mountainous, rising to over 2,100 metres (6,890 feet). It offers scenery and sport hard to better in New Zealand. Area: 57,450 hectares (142,000 acres).

Activities: tramping, hunting (deer, chamois, opossum), climbing, skiing, swimming, boating, fishing (brown and rainbow trout), sign-posted walks.

Arthur's Pass

A striking contrast between the mountain beech forests and wide river beds of Canterbury, and the mixed rain forests and swift-flowing rivers of Westland, the park is a popular family playground and also attracts naturalists, mountaineers, trampers and casual visitors. Area: 98,408 hectares (243,000 acres).

Activities: tramping, climbing, skiing, hunting (red deer, chamois), guided walks, nature programmes in the school holidays. Evening programmes of slides, films and talks held in visitor centre during school and public holidays.

Totaranui Beach, Abel Tasman National Park, Nelson. ***(Andris Apse Ltd)***

NP MP

National Parks

Westland

Westland National Park rises from just above sea level to more than 3,300 metres (10,827 feet). Its attractions are as varied as its altitudes, ranging from numerous glaciers including the Franz Josef and Fox Glaciers, hot springs, placid lakes, and mountain and lowland bush. Area: 88,753 hectares (220,000 acres).

Activities: tramping, climbing, hunting (red deer, chamois and thar), fishing (quinnat salmon and trout), heli-hiking (helicopter flights onto glaciers for hikers), scenic flights that land on glaciers, easy sign-posted walks, guided trips, nature trips in summer and illustrated talks.

The Hollyford Track winds its way up the distant floor of the old glacial valley of the Hollyford River in Fiordland National Park. ***(Mal Clarbrough – Dept of Lands & Survey)***

Mount Cook

Mt Cook (3,764 metres, 12,349 feet) is New Zealand's highest mountain. More than one third of the park is in permanent snow and glacier ice. One of the longest glaciers in the world, the Tasman is 29 kilometres (18 miles) long and up to 3 kilometres (1.8 miles) wide. The ice at one point is estimated to be 600 metres (1,969 feet) thick. Area: 69,957 hectares (173,000 acres).

Activities: tramping, climbing, alpine skiing, hunting (chamois, Himalayan thar), scenic flights, easy sign-posted walks, guided trips, nature programmes in summer.

Mount Aspiring

The focal point of the park is Mt Aspiring (3,027 metres, 9,931 feet), the country's highest peak outside Mount Cook National Park. The Haast Pass highway passes through the northeast corner of the park, and from the road you can see mountains, river valleys, and forest typical of this remote area. Area: 287,254 hectares (709,500 acres).

Activities: tramping, climbing, hunting, (red deer, chamois and goats), trout fishing, guided trips on Routeburn Track, scenic flights, scenic drives.

Fiordland

One of the world's largest national parks, Fiordland is renowned for its rugged grandeur. The sheer mountainsides, the many beautiful lakes and the fiords make a lasting impression on the visitor. A rare bird, the takahe, previously thought to be extinct, was rediscovered in the park in 1948. The park is also one of the habitats of an even rarer bird, the kakapo. Area: 1,232,000 hectares (3,043,304 acres).

Activities: tramping, climbing, hunting (red deer, wapiti, pig, chamois), fishing (brown and rainbow trout, Atlantic salmon), sea fishing in sounds, scenic flights, launch trips, nature walks, guided trips (Milford, Lower Hollyford and Routeburn Tracks). Permit required to traverse Milford Track unless on guided tour.

Westland National Park. *(Andris Apse Ltd)*

Skiing the Tasman Glacier, Mt Cook. ***(Andris Apse Ltd)***

Take a New Zealand skiing holiday and discover some of the best skiing in the world. From June to October each year there is no better skiing anywhere than in the New Zealand mountains, and for those who delight in spring skiing, the season can stretch into November.

During the northern summer top European ski teams come south to New Zealand for the hard mid-winter racing snow – teams from Canada, the USA, Austria, Italy, France and Norway as well as from Britain and Japan. What draws these top skiers are the same conditions that attract any skier – plenty of good snow, good weather, challenging runs and reasonable costs.

But skiing is far more than a mere escape from high-altitude slush in the northern hemisphere. There is something for everyone, every kind of skiing and all kinds of snow conditions, wrapped up in a country that's smaller than California. As a bonus, there are some features that are unique. It is a new skiing experience.

Just as much snow falls on New Zealand's mountains as on the European alps, and that's a lot of snow, enough to ensure skiable slopes somewhere, even in the mildest winter.

You can ski conventional ski fields (ski areas, as they are also known), or indulge in special alpine thrills such as heli-skiing, glacier skiing (with ski-plane transport), ski-mountaineering or ski-touring. You can ski above mountain lakes, in sight of the Pacific Ocean, on the snow-covered mountain pastures of a high-country sheep station or on the slopes of a live volcano. And all the slopes you ski will be absolutely treeless – just wide open spaces of snow and more snow.

Skiing in the North and the South Island has its own distinct characteristics. On the cluster of volcanoes in the centre of the North Island, skiers can trek to the edge of a steaming crater lake at the summit of Ruapehu (2,797 metres, 9,177 feet) before making a run of several kilometres down a glacier and back to the services of the ski field at Turoa, which offers about 4 kilometres (2½ miles) of continuous skiing from its top lift down to the bottom. Whakapapa, on the northern slopes of Ruapehu, is New Zealand's largest ski field.

In the South Island the chain of the Southern Alps runs for almost 800 kilometres (497 miles), creating an area crammed with peaks, 17 of them over 3,000 metres (9,843 feet), hundreds over 2,000 metres (6,562 feet). With their sharp, steep upper slopes fanning out into wide, gentle valleys, these are classic alps. But unlike the European alps, the mountains rise abruptly from near sea level, giving extraordinary length and angle in proportion to their height.

Most ski fields in these mountains, such as those at Mount Hutt or Porter Heights, are formed in basins, with terrain to suit all grades of skiers – sharp, challenging runs from top ridges drop to an area of moguls to provide exhilarating advanced skiing. Long, more leisurely routes bring intermediates back to base and the wide, undulating slopes of the valley floors are splendid for learners. For a family or group with mixed skiing ability, there is plenty of skiing for all.

If stunning mountain scenery appeals as much as the prospect of good snow, you won't be disappointed – the alpine views are magnificent and varied. In the Mount Cook region, ski in deep powder snow looking down on one of the world's largest glaciers; at Coronet Peak enjoy sophisticated facilities and views of lake and massive mountains stretching to the horizon; at Treble Cone, Cardrona and the Harris mountains near Wanaka, the views are matched only by the diversity of isolated slopes and long runs; at Mount Hutt stand on top of a 2,000-metre (6,562-feet) peak, above a skiing vertical of 650 metres (2,133 feet), and look out across coastal plains to the blue Pacific Ocean – a survey at Mount Hutt has shown the scenery rates highly with skiers, who return again and again.

Overseas skiers revel in the uncrowded ski slopes on New Zealand fields. Crowds – and queues – are the exception, not the rule, so that time and money isn't wasted in long periods of waiting. Skiing is mainly a weekend sport and, as a result, there are crowd-free slopes for mid-week skiers, except during the school holidays in late August.

Even then, weekend and holiday crowds can be compared favourably to weekday crowds on many overseas fields. Most of your time skiing is spent actually skiing.

All the major fields have excellent ski schools, with instructors from Europe, Japan, Canada and the USA as well as New Zealand, so the latest methods from Kitzbeuhl or Colorado are taught on New Zealand slopes.

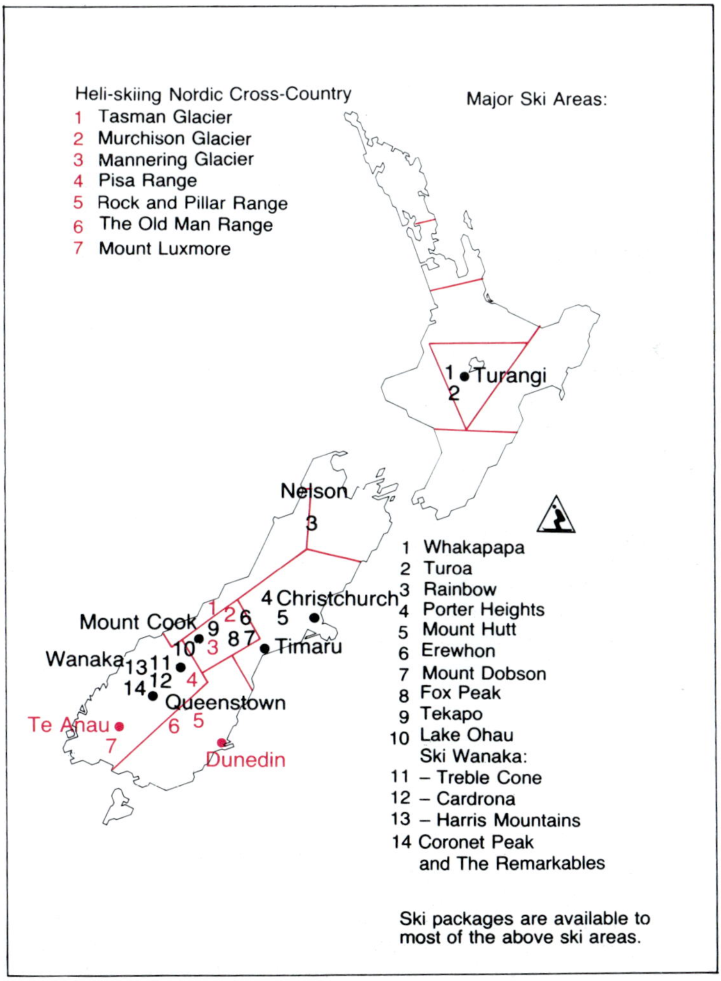

For those who want more than the thrills of downhill skiing from the chairlift, there is fresh powder snow and fresh excitement skiing on glaciers or heli-skiing.

To find glaciers comparable with the 29-kilometre (18-mile) Tasman Glacier, you would need to take an expedition into the Himalayas or Antarctica. The Tasman, however, is minutes away from civilisation, by ski plane that lands skiers and guides on the longest single run in the Southern Hemisphere – 13 kilometres (8 miles) of untrammelled powder snow. Walled in by some of the highest mountains in the country, the fall of the Tasman is mild, through a series of glacial bowls, making it an exhilarating run for intermediate and advanced skiers.

There are steeper, more daring glaciers, such as the Murchison or Mannering, also reached by ski plane or helicopter, and glaciers that extend down to unusually low altitudes where dense rain forest fringes the edges.

Heli-skiing also takes skiers and guides into the enormous, untracked terrain of otherwise inaccessible mountain valleys – so great is the choice that it is possible that you will have the chosen mountain all to yourselves. Ski the Harris mountains near Wanaka (a choice of 30 mountains) and you need never ski the same ground twice.

For those whose skills and ambitions include mountaineering, there is the adventure of ski-mountaineering tours. These take you into the alps for days, with expert guides to minimise the risks and maximise the adventure, climbing and downhill skiing from mountain hut to mountain hut through terrain where Sir Edmund Hillary, the first conqueror of Everest, learned his mountain craft.

Or try the pleasures of traditional Nordic-style cross-country tours, travelling above mountain lakes and into the alps for several days or more.

Heli-skiing in the Ben Ohau Range, Mt Cook Ski Region. ***(Andris Apse Ltd)***

Skiing

Ski Guides (NZ) Ltd
PO Box 177
Wanaka
Telephone: Wanaka 7930 or 7804
Telex: NZ 5636
Owner and Chief Guide: Paul Scaife

Heli-skiing in the famous Harris Mountains (Wanaka) can be enjoyed by strong intermediate and advanced skiers, not just experts! This company pioneered and now regularly skis over 60 different runs on 35 mountains, varying between 2,000 and 4,000 vertical feet (600 and 1,200 vertical metres) on treeless, sheltered basins, mountain flanks and glaciers, all reached by jet-turbine helicopter. Ski in small groups (of your skiing level) with a professional guide, on runs suited to your ability. Snow conditions offer fine powder or beautiful spring corn, depending on month. Season runs July to October. Weather conditions variable, allow extra time to ensure satisfaction. All safety aspects ensured. Bring warm clothing and accessories. Excellent equipment available for hire in Wanaka. Costs on enquiry. Ski weeks, packages and special runs available, plus summer mountain guiding program on request.

Alpine Guides (Westland) Ltd
Main Road
PO Box 38
Fox Glacier
Westland
Telephone: Fox Glacier 825
Chief Guide: Mike Browne

The Fox and Franz Josef névés offer over 5000 hectares (12,355 acres) of skiing terrain from the main divide at 9000 feet to the Chancellor Hut at 4000 feet. The highest ski areas in New Zealand, they receive regular falls of dry powder snow June – December, with spring corn snow conditions common. Alpine Guides offer Ski-adventure alternatives to suit your aspirations, abilities and schedules (advanced skiers only). Access flights, ground transport, guide and specialist equipment, avalanche transceivers all provided, plus hut accommodation and food on overnight tours. You require ski clothing and glasses, skis and boots, and lunch (for day tours). Packs available for hire as is all gear if necessary (from the shop). A delicious lunch can be prepared for you at the restaurant. Bookings essential. Day tour from $315 per person. Overnight tour from $480 per person.

Spring skiing, from late September into November, often brings weather mild enough for T-shirts. The slopes are even less crowded as local skiers abandon skiing to prepare for summer sports. Most likely venues for great spring skiing are Mount Hutt, Mount Cook, Turoa and Whakapapa.

The weather? It is as contrary as anywhere else in the world. As the country is long and narrow, surrounded by ocean, sudden weather changes are a feature of alpine life.

But such is the effect of micro-climates in the mountains that the chances are that when the weather closes in on one field, another field, not too far away, will be open and enjoying good weather.

A skiing holiday needn't be all skiing – you won't find yourself trapped in a mountain resort with nothing else but skiing or snow sports. There are plenty of other activities at hand. Take a break from the snow fields at Turoa or Whakapapa and try bathing in the natural hot pools, horse riding, trout fishing, bush walks or golf. Go spring skiing in the South Island and coincide with the trout and salmon fishing season. At any time, take jet-boat rides on rivers and lakes, play golf, go horse riding – there is always plenty to do.

Because skiers live off the slopes, it is simple to vary a skiing holiday with all the other activities – fish one day, ski the next. The family with diverse interests can go their separate ways on the same holiday, up the mountain or onto the lake as the whim takes them.

Accommodation in hotels, tourist lodges, cabins, self-catering motel units or youth hostels is usually in a village about 30 minutes away from the skiing, with regular skiers' transport provided. On-field accommodation is minimal or non-existent, part of a policy aimed at protecting the mountain environment. Building on the ski fields is limited to essential services such as cafeterias and ski hire.

Those who like to rest their weary ski boots in style after a hard day's skiing will find the most sophisticated comfort near large, well-developed ski fields. Yet even at the smartest hotels the emphasis is on open-fire comfort and friendly bonhomie. The atmosphere is relaxed and welcoming, not haughty and exclusive.

Après-ski is based on the same friendliness, not jet-set high style. Even Queenstown, with a wide selection of hotels and plenty of après-ski diversions such as discos, bars and restaurants, remains a lively small town with the accent on super fun rather than super chic.

Skiing in New Zealand is low on pressure, high on relaxation and friendliness and pleasantly kind to the pocket. On-field skiing costs are about half those of Europe, so your skiing dollar provides twice the action.

Value can be even greater – some heli-skiing rides offer twice the skiing vertical for half the price at popular European venues, and that is a lot of untracked snow. For Australians, a skiing holiday in New Zealand, including airfares and accommodation, can prove cheaper than skiing in Australia.

Whether you settle for one ski field, spread your skiing holiday over several fields or attempt to sample the lot, you will discover that some of the cheapest skiing in the world can also be some of the best.

SEE ALSO:

Climbing: Alpine Guides (Mt Cook).
Tramping: Alpine Guides (Westland).
Lodges: 'The Homestead' (Rakaia), Huka Lodge (Taupo).
Outback Safaris: Alpine Guides (Westland).
Flightseeing: Southern Lakes Helicopters (Te Anau).

Skiing

Turoa Ski Area
12 Clyde Street
PO Box 46
Ohakune
Telephone: (0658) 58-456
24-hr Ski Report: (0658) 58-255
Telex: NZ31377
Facsimile: (0658) 58-992

This major ski area is the second largest in the country, with quad and triple chairlifts, T-bar and platter lifts. Ski runs are up to 4 kilometres (2.5 miles) long and 720 metres (2195 feet) vertical drop. A professional ski school operates through the season; other facilities include ski patrol, mountain transport, creche, comprehensive ski hire, three restaurants and an accommodation booking service. Full rates schedule available – specials for families, students and novices. Ski Warranty offered.

Mount Hutt International Methven
Alpine Tourist Company Ltd
PO Box 14
Methven
Snow reports: Telephone (053) 28-605
Telex: NZ4131
Facsimile: (053) 28-697
Accommodation bookings: Toll Free (053) 28-749

This ski area has become the champions' choice, offering superb skiing, facilities and spectacular scenery.
Promising more than five months per year of consistent skiing, this field is one of two in the Southern Hemisphere offering a 'Money Back Snow Guarantee'. No fewer than ten various lifts cater for all grades of skier and offer 674 metres (2210 feet) of vertical skiing, over some 283 hectares (700 acres). Facilities include a large day lodge (plus kindergarten), cafeteria, sun balconies, extensive equipment hire (beginners to top-flight) and luggage and equipment storage. A full range of instruction is offered including a recreational race department, staffed by five race instructors. Heli-skiing is available. Major credit cards accepted. Accommodation/night life is at foot of the mountain at Methven or Ashburton.

Mount Dobson Ski Area Ltd
PO Box 45
Fairlie
Telephone: (0505) 8039
Owners: Peter and Shirley Foote

Privately owned ski area, between Fairlie and Tekapo. Known for powder conditions, friendly staff, spectacular views, plus easy access. A Doppelmayer T-Bar to 6600 feet (2010 metres), country's longest platter (serves massive learner area), access platter lift, fixed grip tow. Good facilities include canteen, heated day-hut, restrooms, ski patrol, first-aid. Top quality equipment hireage, qualified tuition. Adult Lift Pass from $24; student rates. Uphill transport available.

Tekapo Ski Field
PO Box 7
Lake Tekapo
Telephone: (05056) 852
Owner: Karl Burtscher

Overlooking beautiful Lake Tekapo and snow-covered Godley Peaks (July through September), this field is ideal for families, children, beginners/intermediate skiers. Well equipped with twin-seat Doppelmayer chair and platter lifts, ski instruction programmes (both group and private), excellent hire equipment, canteen and shop, day room, car park, air strip and ski patrol. Closest accommodation is Lake Tekapo. Access by private car and daily bus.

Ohau Ski Area
PO Box 4533
Christchurch
Telephone: (02984) 727
Ski Area: (03) 67-647
Snow Reports: (03) 792-720

Set on the slopes of Mount Sutton and providing great skiing, along with spectacular panoramic views over Lake Ohau and the McKenzie Basin. Staff are friendly and helpful and rates are reasonable. Facilities include canteen, ski school, excellent equipment hireage, professional ski patrol and lift service. The terrain is suitable for all proficiency levels. Comfortable accommodation is available 10 minutes' away at Lake Ohau Motor Lodge (see listing 'Aorangi' Mt Cook Section).

Treble Cone (Wanaka) Ski Area
PO Box 206
Wanaka
Telephone: Wanaka 7443
Contact: Ski Centre
Ardmore Street
Wanaka

Twenty-nine kilometres (18 miles) from Wanaka, this major skiing destination provides stunningly beautiful scenery and exciting sport for all. It is equipped with up-to-the minute Doppelmayer double-chair lift, two T-bars plus three fixed-grip learner lifts, and offers groomed slopes, great powder snow, minimal waits in queues! Services: NZIA Ski School, heli-skiing, professional ski patrol/medical services, ski hire, carpark, cafeteria and two well-appointed day lodges. Major credit cards accepted. Access by private/public transport/heli-taxi from Wanaka township, from nearby ski fields and from Queenstown.

CALENDAR OF ANNUAL EVENTS

JANUARY		
New Years Day (1st)		
Auckland/Northland Anniversary (29th)		*Auckland*
Benson & Hedges International Tennis Tournament	Auckland	*Auckland*
Women's International Tennis Series	Auckland	*Auckland*
Waikato Yearling Horse Sales	Hamilton	*Waikato*
Anglers Trout Fishing Competition	Otorohanga	*Waikato*
Wellington Anniversary (22nd)		*Wellington*
Summer City Festival	Wellington	*Wellington*
Wellington Cup Horse Racing	Trentham	*Wellington*
Tapawera Raspberry Carnival	Nelson	*Nelson*
Nelson Racing Club Summer Trotting Meeting	Nelson	*Nelson*
Blenheim to Picton Walk	Blenheim	*Marlborough*
Wine and Food Festival	Blenheim	*Marlborough*
Kumara Racing Club Golden Nugget Meeting	Greymouth	*Westland*
Southland Anniversary (17th)		*Southland*
FEBRUARY		
New Zealand Day (6th)		
Golden Axe Award	Tokoroa	*Waikato*
National Rodeo Finals	Tokoroa	*Waikato*
Nelson/Westport Anniversary		*Nelson*
Tahuna Beach Carnival	Nelson	*Nelson*
Motueka National 'Cooee' Contest	Nelson	*Nelson*
Kaikoura Agriculture/Produce Show	Blenheim	*Marlborough*
Greymouth Agriculture/Produce Show	Greymouth	*Westland*
Coast to Coast Triathlon (Kumara-Christchurch)	Kumara	*Westland*
Dunedin City Festival Week	Dunedin	*Otago*
MARCH		
Round the Bays Run	Auckland	*Auckland*
The People's Triathlon	Auckland	*Auckland*
Double Brown Ironman Competition	Auckland	*Auckland*
International Track & Field Meeting	Auckland	*Auckland*
Centennary Rowing Regatta – New Zealand Rowing Championships	Lake Karapiro	*Waikato*
Ngaruawahia Regatta – Maori canoes	Ngaruawahia	*Waikato*
Taranaki Anniversary (31st)		*Taranaki*
Biennial Festival of the Arts	Wellington	*Wellington*
Otago Anniversary (23rd)		*Otago*
Scottish Week	Dunedin	*Otago*
APRIL		
Easter Day (1988 – 3rd), (1989 – March 26th)		
National Jazz Festival	Tauranga	*Waikato*
Harbour City 10k Classic Run	Wellington	*Wellington*
Nelson Racing Club Easter Racing Carnival	Nelson	*Nelson*
Youth Production Show Week	Greymouth	*Westland*
Queenstown Triathlon	Queenstown	*Southern Lakes*
MAY		
National Bullfish Duke of Marlborough Contest	Russell	*Northland*
Fletcher Challenge Marathon Run	Rotorua	*Bay of Plenty*
Waikato Winter Show	Hamilton	*Waikato*
Kiwifruit Festival	Te Puke	*Waikato*
The Great Wellington Winter Show	Wellington	*Wellington*
City of Nelson Half Marathon	Nelson	*Nelson*

Continued on page 225

Foothills of the Southern Alps, mid-Canterbury.
Girvan)

Go climbing in the Southern Alps of the South Island and you are in one of the world's great mountaineering areas, where famous mountaineers practise skills that take them to the top of the world in the Himalayas.

For the experts New Zealand is well known. But, it's also a place for the less experienced to learn alpine skills. Alpine guides in main climbing areas provide expert assistance for those unfamiliar with the conditions and terrain or for those who have never tried a climb in their lives. You need only be fit and agile, have a head for heights, a taste for adventure and the desire to test yourself against the tough mountains.

Few places in the world, outside Europe, can offer such a range of climbing so close to civilisation – climbing in New Zealand is an experience, not a major expedition. Even out-of-the-way mountain country can be reached with ease, by jet boat up fast, shallow rivers, by ski plane or helicopter onto snowfields, or by light aircraft onto high-country airstrips, built originally to serve sheep stations or deer cullers. Of course, those who prefer to acclimatise themselves slowly to new terrain and conditions can still take the long way in on foot.

The best-known climbing centre is Mt Cook, an alpine resort village surrounded by the massive mountains of the Mt Cook National Park, including the country's highest mountain Mt Cook 3,763 metres (12,342 feet) and another 140 peaks over 2,000 metres (6,560 feet). Climbing here began in the 1880s, but Mt Cook itself was not conquered until 1894 and has claimed more than 140 lives, so it is not an easy stroll.

The Mt Cook region is an area of spectacular mountain scenery, great glaciers (only the Himalayas and Antarctica have comparable glaciers), deep glacial valleys, sheer mountain faces, sharp ridges, ice, snow and rock – one third of the national park is covered in permanent snow and ice. And there are climbs and high-altitude treks suited to all ability levels.

Sharing a mountainous border with the Mt Cook Park is the Westland National Park, with mountains rising to 3,498 metres (11,473 feet), virtually from sealevel, glaciers and dense, lush rain forests on lower slopes, evidence of the heavy annual rainfall.

Another major centre is Arthur's Pass National Park, on the route across the alps from east to west and right in the middle of climbing country. This is 92,422 hectares (228,282 acres) of snow-covered peaks, forests, rushing rivers and waterfalls. Further south is another area popular with climbers, the 287,319-hectare (709,677-acre) Mt Aspiring National Park. with demanding mountain peaks and gentle valleys. And then there is the immense Fiordland National Park.

North Island mountaineering concentrates on the Tongariro National Park, with short, sharp climbs offering variety on snow, ice and volcanic rock.

But for those serious about a climbing holiday, the South Island provides infinite possibilities, inside and outside the national parks.

The southern mountains are sharp and steep and, because they rise almost from sealevel rather than from high plateaus, they provide a lot more alpine country than their official heights might suggest. Even quite small peaks can often present a major climb.

Perhaps because the mountains are so accessible, the inexperienced sometimes underestimate them. New Zealand mountain conditions can be as tough as anywhere in the world – no one unfamiliar with them should head up into the mountains without a guide or, at least, good local advice, which will be given readily and free. Mountain-safety experts maintain that one of the main causes of accidents involving visiting climbers has been lack of knowledge about terrain, weather and conditions peculiar to New Zealand.

The rock in these mountains is generally less stable than that encountered in other countries, a fact sometimes not appreciated until too late. And for anyone used to weather conditions on large continental land masses, the changeability of New Zealand mountain-top weather can be an unwelcome surprise. The mountains have their own micro-climate, in which cloud, mist or blizzard can sweep in with speed, while the lower slopes bask in sunshine.

Don't take the mountains lightly and, unless very experienced, take a guide. Says one keen climber: 'When you are cold, tired and scared you want someone there to make the right decision.' He climbs every summer, with a guide.

Fortunately for the newcomer, national park rangers will tell you all you want to know about conditions, equipment, routes and guides. All climbing equipment can be bought or hired in main cities or alpine resorts, and guides are based in all the best climbing areas. They will teach correct climbing techniques on rock, snow and ice, awareness of snow and ice conditions, crevasse and avalanche precautions, route finding, an understanding of the weather, and will take you on the climbs best suited to your level of ability.

For those who prefer to clamber underground, New Zealand limestone country hides the kind of caves that cavers dream about.

Expert speleologists have the prospect of exploring the complex system at Mt Arthur, near Nelson, which includes the largest cave in the Southern Hemisphere. Not only has the system yet to be fully explored, it is suggested that at least another 30 years of exploration will be required before the maze is fully charted.

Another region of important caves and unexplored systems lies in the dramatic limestone country at Punakaiki on the South Island's West Coast – territory for the true enthusiast and definitely not for the inexperienced.

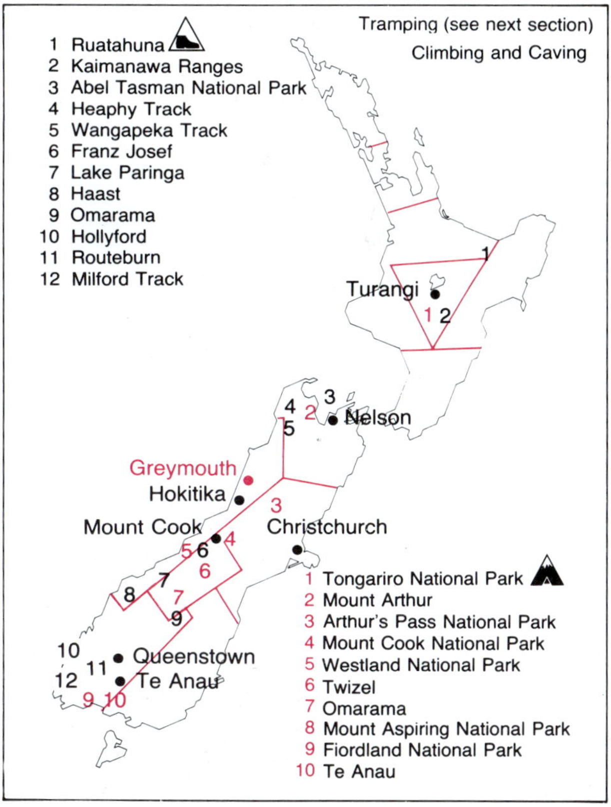

Alpine Guides (Mount Cook) Ltd
PO Box 20
Mount Cook National Park
Telephone: 834
Telex: NZ4187

Within the awesomely beautiful Mount Cook National Park, this sole concessionaire offers a 90-year reputation of leading/teaching experience. Region is renowned internationally for mountaineering and unique ski adventures. June-October: heli-skiing, Nordic skiing, ski touring – day or four/five-day packages. Equipment available. Summer: Climbing school programme. All Guides are exceptional mountaineers/skiers. Courses: 7-14 days (Introductory/ advanced). Also summer coach trips to Tasman Glacier. From $15 to $1,600 depending on requirements.

OTHER REFERENCES:

Alpine Action Adventures, PO Box 123, Turangi.

NZ Mountain Guides Assn, PO Box 20, Mount Cook.

Alpine Recreation Canterbury, PO Box 75, Lake Tekapo.

Mountain Recreation, PO Box 204, Wanaka.

Mt Sebastapol, Mt Cook National Park. *(Andris Apse Ltd)*

Start of the Milford Track, Fiordland.
(Courtesy Tourist Hotel Corporation)

An early morning start. *(Courtesy Air New Zealand)*

Whether you are an experienced hiker who likes to head for the solitude of the hills for weeks on end, or a tenderfoot in search of a soul-restoring interlude, there is a walk to suit you within easy distance of any New Zealand town.

Hiking, rambling, backpacking and trekking are all known as 'tramping' in New Zealand, and heading for the hills is a national pastime. Yet despite this delight in tramping, those tracks and trails are remarkable for their isolation. The reason is simple – there are so few people in New Zealand, and there is so much wilderness.

There are millions of hectares of national parks, forest parks and scenic reserves and only 3 million people. The largest of the 10 national parks, Fiordland, is larger than Yellowstone Park in the USA and so wild parts have yet to be explored.

Trekkers in New Zealand can concentrate on the beauty of the world around them without tripping over hordes of people. Nor do they need to watch for poisonous creatures or dangerous wild animals – there are none. The only precaution to take against wildlife is a good insect repellent – and insects carry no nasty diseases, they are merely a nuisance, not a danger. The birdlife is fascinating, with many species found only in New Zealand (for example: kiwi, paradise duck, weka, blue duck, kaka, morepork, tui, native wood pigeon, kea, rifleman, grey warbler, bush robin).

Walks range from the easy terrain of the national 'walkways' to rigorous trails where mountaineering experience is needed. But for every grade there are guided treks providing a problem-free way to discover the meaning of getting away from it all.

In the North Island these treks might lead across rugged hills with forests of giant kauri trees and flowering rata, through great pine plantations or beside mountain streams where rockhounds may gather gemstones.

They may travel through remote regions of rain, mists and myths, beautiful lakes and wild rivers where rare birds and wild deer live in the dense forest; or to the rim of live volcanoes, amid old lava flows, hot springs, volcanic sands, mountain daisies and buttercups, glaciers and waterfalls.

In the South Island there are limitless opportunities, with seven national parks. Trails lead along deserted golden beaches and high into mountain beech forests and tussock grasslands, along wild, rocky shorelines or into the mountains of the Southern Alps. You can follow packhorse trails to the old goldfields (and try panning for gold) or clamber along ridges surrounded by deep fiords, glaciers, great mountains, bush-fringed lakes and waterfalls that cascade and thunder from the mountain heights.

Here is the famous Milford Track, a three-day walk often described as 'the finest walk in the world' and with good reason. This leads high into the towering mountains, above lakes and by the Sutherland Falls, third highest in the world at 530 metres (1,738 feet). Lesser known, but exciting, are the nearby Hollyford and Routeburn walks.

Guided treks in both islands range from a few hours to two weeks and often combine exciting trails with other activities – rafting, canoeing, jet-boat rides, hunting, trout fishing, bird watching, ski-plane and helicopter rides.

Such trips use organised camps and huts, provide sleeping bags and cooked meals – all you need is clothes and stout walking boots. Everything else is taken care of – some even provide waterproof parkas (you can't have rain forest without some rain).

For novice trampers and families who want to do it alone, the national walkway system is a network of well-maintained, easy paths, where the scenery can be superb. Some walkways cross private land and farms, many are close to cities, most lead through areas of special charm or beauty – through wild meadowlands by a river, along barren cliffs where the Pacific crashes on the rocks below, across hills and valleys thick with tree ferns, among waterfalls, high-country farmland and mountains.

More experienced hikers who want to take to the wilderness burdened with their own heavy backpacks, but free from the organisation of a guided trek, may do so with ease. The New Zealand back country is at the doorstep of every town, often a short bus ride away.

An ideal opportunity for you to relax in the outdoors on various great treks; including the Lewis Pass (3 day) and Arthur's Pass (4 day) – incorporating adventure activities and sightseeing. Spectacular scenery of an untouched wilderness. Group maximum of eight, relaxed and informal. Everything provided depending on requirements. Bring warm clothing and sturdy footwear. Operating October-April, plus Lewis Pass in winter. From $360 (GST inclusive), depending on trek. Group discount available.

New Zealand Treks
PO Box 4523
Christchurch
Telephone: (03) 61-615/ 554-519
Owners: Mary Dobson & Stephen Philip

A combination of launch trip and guided walk, hosted by the Wilsons, makes this 4-day adventure very special. Relax on your 2-hour voyage to Tonga Bay, getting to know your walking companions whilst the skipper gives a personal commentary of historical/geographical interest. Walking track begins at Tonga Bay, through unspoiled native forest, following the coastline of gently curved golden sand beaches separated by rocky granite headlands. Three nights are spent in 'The Lodge' (cottage comforts) at Torrent Bay – fishing, diving, swimming, yachting and boating available (no additional charge). This is an enchanted coast with delightful waterfalls spilling into tranquil lagoons, many native birds, plus dolphins, seals and penguins. All luggage carried for you and meals prepared. Year-through operation. Bring good walking shoes, warm gear and rain wear. Average fitness required. Suitable for all over 10 years of age. Departs Monday and Friday. From $440 (adult), $415 (child).

Abel Tasman National Park Enterprises
Green Tree Road, RD3
Motueka
Nelson
Telephone: (0524) 87-801
Hosts: The Wilson Family

Join a small group of trekkers and explore the South Island's wild beauty. Pat and Christine guide you through pristine podocarp forest and across waving fields of golden tussock in mountain valleys. For the adventurous, traverse high alpine passes above the valley floors. Discover hot pools, hanging glaciers and mountain lakes – never to be forgotten! Company knowledge of the Southern Alps is extensive and reflected in the wide range of treks they offer; from 1-day to 5-day treks, graded from easy (for beginners), to moderate and difficult. Safety considerations are paramount. All you need bring: outdoor mountain clothing, pack, sleeping-bag, waterpoof jacket and boots (all provided if necessary), plus camera. All else is provided. Departures from Christchurch, door-to-door service provided. Minimum/maximum age restrictions are 10 and 60 years (dispensations made). From $80 (day trip), $220 (2 days), $395 (5 days). Special group and children's rates.

Karavan Adventure Treks Ltd
117 Harris Crescent
Christchurch 5
Telephone: (03) 522-177
Owners: Pat and Christine Barrett

Hollyford Valley Walk
Hollyford Tourist & Travel Company Ltd
PO Box 216
Invercargill
Telephone: (021) 44-300
Telex: NZ5737
Facsimile: (024) 83-420

The remote Hollyford Valley, Fiordland National Park, offers varied scenery of unspoiled beauty and real appeal to all. Throughout is prolific native flora, varying from luxuriant fern growth to giant rimu and matai trees. Wildlife includes seal colony, penguins, glow worms and the occasional dolphin or rare white heron. This is your opportunity to see the isolated beauty of this area, through organised and novel adventures. With an experienced guide, tours follow the Hollyford River through to Martins Bay on the West Coast. More than just a walk, this experience includes jet boating and flying. Options: a 4-day, walk in/fly out tour, or a 5-day, walk in/walk out tour. Means of travel is geared towards making your experience even more memorable.
Walk through native forest, by snow-capped mountains and thundering waterfalls, see historic sites of remote pioneers' homesteads and towns, with leisure time for beachcombing, swimming and fishing. Thrill to jet-boat rides through river and lake. (The fly-out tour gives an aerial view of the region, second to none.)
Accommodation is in well-appointed lodges, complete with all facilities. Regularly scheduled tours leave from the Hollyford Road end car park, with courtesy transport from Marian Corner. Public transport: to Marian Corner from Queenstown, Te Anau and Milford, by NZR Road Services. Closest accommodation is Te Anau, 86 kilometres (53 miles) away. Season: October through April. Special group tours May/June by arrangement only. Suitable for ages 7 to 70. A reasonable standard of fitness required. Tour costs are all-inclusive: from $600 (adult), $400 (child). Substantial group concessions (4 or more).

Milford Track
(Head of Lake Te Anau – Milford Sound)
Fiordland National Park
Tourist Hotel Corporation
Telephone:
Auckland (09) 773-689
Wellington (04) 729-179
Christchurch (03) 790-718
Telex: NZ3488

The Milford Track is accepted by people world over as being 'the finest walk in the world'. Thousands take up this 55-kilometre (34-mile) challenge yearly; braving possible torrential rain, conquering a mountain pass, crossing rivers – thoroughly captivated by the magic of this desolate, awe-inspiring region. See splendid scenery; towering rock walls, the thundering Sutherland Falls and bird-filled native forest. Accommodation is provided in rustic but comfortable lodges (hot showers and delicious farm-style cooking), accompanied by experienced guides on each stage of the trek. Service and track itself are administered by the THC. Bring suitable clothing, personal equipment (including camera and film). Adequate fitness levels required. Track is open November through March. From $660 (adult), $475 (child), GST exclusive. Independent walkers may book through THC Te Anau: Telephone: (0229) 7411 or write THC Reservations, PO Box 185, Te Anau. Costs on enquiry.

SEE ALSO:

Skiing Alpine Guides (Westland).
Outback Safaris: Alpine Guides (Westland), Te Rehuwai Safaris (Rotorua), NZ Outdoor Adventure Centre (Rotorua).
River Adventures: Danes Back Country Experience (Queenstown).
Sailing: Fiordland Cruises (Te Anau).
Regional: Westland: Haast Motor Camp (Haast).

Huka Lodge, Taupo.
(Courtesy of Huka Lodge)

A rare combination of luxury, sophistication, seclusion and relaxed informality surrounds guests at exclusive lodges and grand country houses. They cater for the individual wish and whim, organise the activities that interest you and pamper you with superb comfort, food and wines.

Find this leisured holiday style in perfect settings: on a lake shore where bellbirds and tuis sing in the trees by your room; amid acres of smooth lawns and English-style gardens overflowing with flowers; under spreading trees by a swirling river edged with wild broom; on a private island where lawns and trees run down to the lagoon – the 12 metre (40-foot) yacht anchored in the bay is for your exclusive use; in a sprawling sheep station homestead with beach in front and rugged hills behind; in a Victorian mansion set by a remote lake and surrounded by snow-capped mountains.

Log fires blaze in great stone fireplaces on crisp winter evenings; in summer there may be poolside barbecues under shady trees.

Dine on the very best New Zealand fare – sweet fat oysters, baked rainbow trout, smoked marlin, smoked eel, pheasant, wild duck, venison steaks, ribs of sweet baby lamb, rabbit pie, freshly caught crayfish, scallops, blackberry pie, strawberries and thick cream, excellent cheeses.

Enjoy the best New Zealand wines, or those imported from Australia, France and Germany.

Many lodges are furnished with splendid antiques but also provide the important modern comforts. Sleep at night between crisp linen sheets on an antique brass bed – with modern mattress.

Every lodge offers an almost bewildering choice of activities, arranged exclusively for you. One may provide water skiing, windsurfing, line fishing, game fishing, sailing, surfcasting, tramping; another can arrange sailing, trout fishing, tramping, horse riding, golf, tennis, hunting; and yet another might offer hunting, flight-seeing, trout fishing, jet boating, rafting, canoeing, tramping, skiing, climbing and cross-country safaris. Some can offer almost every possible outdoor activity organised just to suit your wishes.

And if you would prefer to do absolutely nothing at all, not even cast a line into the lake or river by your door, there could be no more ideal place to relax in style and tranquility

Some of these are places that international celebrities, visiting royalty and heads of state, film and music stars, choose when they want a holiday away from the public gaze.

Most take very few guests at a time, hence the individual attention, and for those who like or need their privacy protected, this can often be guaranteed.

You can holiday like a prince but not always pay princely prices for this perfection and cossetting.

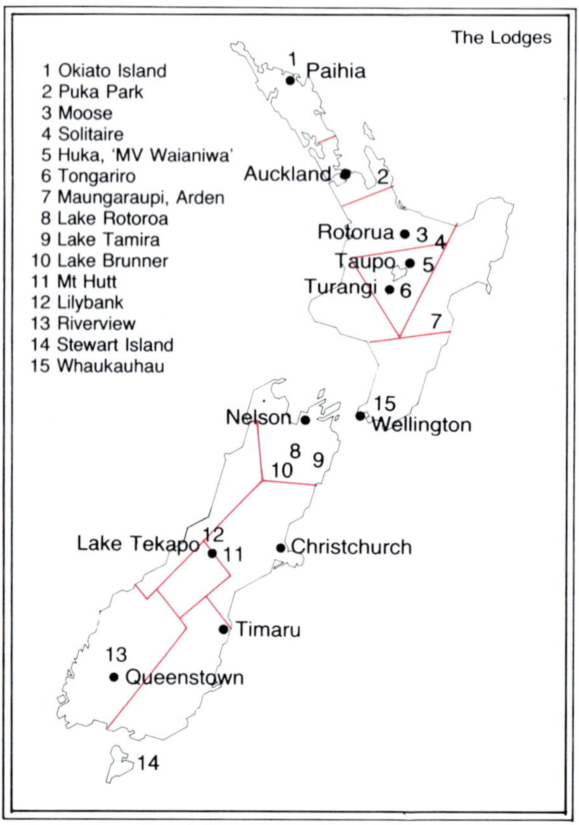

Lodges

Overlooking ocean, Paihia/Waitangi; native forest surrounds. Offers 4 luxury suites (lounge and balcony), personalised service, spa pool, restaurant/cocktail bar. Table features seafood and game. Organises fishing, tramping, scenic flights, sailing. From $200.

Okiato Lodge, Russell
Reservations: NZ Collect
(03) 799-127
(Details/Overseas reservations; see p.131)

On slopes of Mt Pauanui, forest surrounds. Separate chalets/lodge accommodation for 64, including luxury suites. Upmarket restaurant, bar, heated swimming pool. Hosts also speak German. Activities include hang-gliding, golf, tennis, windsurfing. From $245.

Puka Park Resort
Coromandel
Reservations: NZ Collect
(03) 799-127
(Details/Overseas reservations: see p.131)

Nestled in beautiful parkland beside the Waikato River, 300 metres upstream from Huka Falls, the world-famous Huka Lodge offers 17 superb suites with unequalled cuisine and facilities for your total relaxation. Nearby – trout fishing, hunting, horseriding, skiing, golf, jet boating and white-water rafting. Yellow shield member of Relais et Chateaux. Helipad on premises. Tariff includes breakfast, 6-course dinner, evening cocktails and Taupo Airport transfers. From $395 (single), $295 (double) per person, per day.

Huka Lodge
Huka Falls Road
PO Box 95, Taupo
Telephone: (074) 85-791
Telex: NZ63229 HUKA
Auckland Office:
(09) 389-824
Telex: NZ60591 PRIME
Facsimile: (09) 795-807

This diamond embraced by semi-tropical vegetation, perched upon a peninsula, overlooks the hemisphere's finest rainbow-trout lake, dominated by the magnificent Mount Tarawera – a magic setting which appeals to sporting enthusiasts or those desiring a relaxing base. If you like water sports, trout fishing, forest walks, or just time out for your soul, you can count on friendly service in comfort and heavenly surroundings. From $330 per day, meals and open bar, GST inclusive.

Solitaire Lodge
Ronald Road
Lake Tarawera, R.D.5
Rotorua
Telephone: (0973) 28-208
International: (011-64)-73-28208
Telex: NZ2584
Host: Reg Turner

Overlooking Lake Rotoiti, old fashioned elegance with modern luxury. Beautiful secluded grounds, 12 suites, gymnasium, sauna and tennis courts. Hunting, shooting, trout-fishing paradise, plus golf and all activities. Delicious cuisine. Member Relais et Chateaux. From $460 (all-inclusive, single).

Moose Lodge, Rotorua
Reservations: NZ Collect
(03) 799-127
(Details/Overseas reservations; see p.131)

Sumptuous cruise vessel, accommodating 8 with private facilities, saloon, bar, fireplace and full bath! Offers professionally guided fishing charters (everything provided), claybird shooting etc. Charter from $750 per day, plus $75 per person/night.

'MV Waianawa', Taupo
Reservations: NZ Collect
(03) 799-127
(Details/Overseas reservations; see p.131)

Combines gourmet cuisine, relaxing comfort and wide range of activities (close to Tongariro River for superb fishing). Private accommodation of 8 suites, lounge with open fireplace, spa pool and bar. All regional activities organised for guests. From $182.

Tongariro Lodge
Turangi
Reservations: NZ Collect
(03) 799-127
(Details/Overseas reservations; see p.131)

Magnificent, restored 'gentleman's residence', accommodating up to 10 persons. Private suites, snooker/billiards room, swimming pool, tennis court, helipad, superb cuisine and serene environment. All activities/gannet colony safaris. From $165.

Arden Lodge, Havelock North
Reservations: NZ Collect
(03) 799-127
(Details/Overseas reservations; see p.131)

A colonial homestead on a Romney stud sheep station, looking out across Cook Strait to the distant South Island. Provides 2 luxury suites, 2 lodge suites and full amenities. All activities organised. Tourism Award winner. From $240. Winner of RHC 1986 Best Local Cuisine Award.

Wharekauhau Lodge
Featherston
Reservations: NZ Collect
(03) 799-127
(Details/Overseas reservations; see p.131)

Lake Timara Estate
Blenheim
Reservations: NZ Collect (03) 799-127
Details/Overseas reservations; see p.131)

Grand old homestead overlooking lake, spacious English gardens, abundant birdlife, wine-making region. 3 well-appointed suites, swimming pool. Table is local fresh produce. From $176. Winner of RHC 1986 Best Host & Hostess Award.

Lake Rotoroa Lodge
Nelson Lakes
Reservations: NZ Collect (03) 799-127
(Details/Overseas reservations; see p. 131)

A beautiful 19th-century fishing/hunting villa, with 1980s comforts. Idyllic lakeside setting; 9 suites, restaurant and house bar. Renowned fishing area, plus hunting, and walking in surrounding native forest. From $260. Winner of RHC 1986 Best Fishing Lodge Award.

Lake Brunner Sporting Lodge
Mitchells R.D.
Kumara
Telephone: (027) 80-163/ 80-164
Hosts: Marian Van Der Goes and Ray Grubb

The angler's dream – the recluse's paradise – one of our longest established fishing lodges, on Lake Brunner's shores with a backdrop of waterfalls, native rainforest and mountains. The Lodge has been restored to original 1935 glory, native timbers and huge open fireplaces dominate. Eight large, comfortable or deluxe suites with personal, modern facilities have views of lake or gardens, each ensuring privacy. Game foods and secret trout recipes dominate an extensive cuisine, enhanced by medal-winning local and New Zealand wines. Ray serves pre-dinner cocktails in the lounge and guests dine together. Dress is always informal, ambiance is warm. And the fishing? Superb, with 6 river systems, countless streams and 11 lakes, all filled with trout! Professional guides for fishing and hunting onsite, helicopters and boats available. Marian organises escorted, non-fishing activities by request. From $95 (single) Suite, $125 (single) Deluxe Suite, per night. Meals and other activities additional.

'The Homestead'
Mt Hutt Station Resort
No 12 R.D.
Rakaia
(Junction of S.H. 72 & 77)
Telephone: (053) 28-130/ 28-179
Facsimile: (053) 5108
Hosts: Eliza and Robin Quinn

The perfect world to lose yourself in – based on this 8000-acre (3237-hectare) deer/sheep-farming property, equipped with every facility from top-class restaurant to private station aircraft. Situated 90 kms (56 miles) southwest of Christchurch, providing the total holiday from peaceful to adventurous. Accommodation in refurbished original homestead of 1880s or adjoining units. Hunting/fishing safaris, plus organised personal tours. Ski area close by, heli-skiing a speciality. Tariff on enquiry.

Riverview Farm Lodge
PO Box 19
Athol
Southland
Telephone: (02283) 866
Through your agent:
USA: (800) 351-2323
CA (800) 351-2317
Telex: 261-007
Hosts: Liz and Sam Soper

Centrally located in the Southern Lakes, one hour's drive from Queenstown and Te Anau, on S.H. 6 is 'Riverview', a 350-hectare (865-acre) sheep station. This is the heartland for sightseeing, outdoor adventure, trout fishing. Anglers; here is the famous Mataura River at your doorstep (professional fishing guides available). Superbly tasteful, ensuite accommodation of two rooms is complemented by the spacious sitting room with its open fire and selection of books. Liz prepares delicious meals – NZ cuisine of lamb, fresh trout, game, garden fresh vegetables and fruit – barbeques and picnics in summer. Join in farm life or the variety of activities available from here; gliding, golf, sightseeing flights (Milford etc.), shopping in Queenstown. Or simply relax in the rural tranquility of the gardens or swimming pool. From $180 per night (includes meals, wines and farm activities). Reservations essential.

Stewart Island Lodge
Stewart Island
Reservations: NZ Collect (03) 799-127
(Details/Overseas reservations; see p.131)

Secluded, private suites and superb views. Cuisine is freshly caught seafood and game. Beach and bush walks, fishing; launch available to guests for fishing or cruising. From $150. Winner of RHC 1986 Best Outdoor Activities Award.

Horse-trekking on Mt Cardrona, Wanaka.
(Courtesy Gin & Raspberry Stables)

An outback safari is a multi-adventure holiday, available in many guises, but all safaris have one thing in common – they get you far 'off the beaten track' in a way that no ordinary sightseeing trip can ever do.

You can take outback safaris by the day – and return at night to a soft bed, plenty of hot water and a well-stocked bar in the nearest town.

Or you can spend days on the move through high-country tussock, stony river valleys and thick forest, with nights around the campfire.

There is even a kind of stay-at-home safari tour – you are taken into the wilderness to settle down in luxury lodge, cabin or tent and take advantage of whatever adventure appeals most: tramping, four-wheel-drive excursions, horse treks, deer hunting (with rifle or camera), trout fishing, swimming, rafting or canoeing.

Day-trip safaris are as varied as the country's geography: travel in four-wheel-drive vehicles across giant sand dunes to windswept gumlands where turn-of-the-century settlers eked out a living digging precious kauri gum, see the wrecks of sailing ships half-buried in sand on wild surf beaches, and try surfcasting for snapper.

Cross rugged farmland to idyllic bays or travel over treacherous sands where unusual seabirds congregate.

Take hair-raising rides up mountainsides, even through the desolate ash and debris of a volcano that last exploded only 100 years ago.

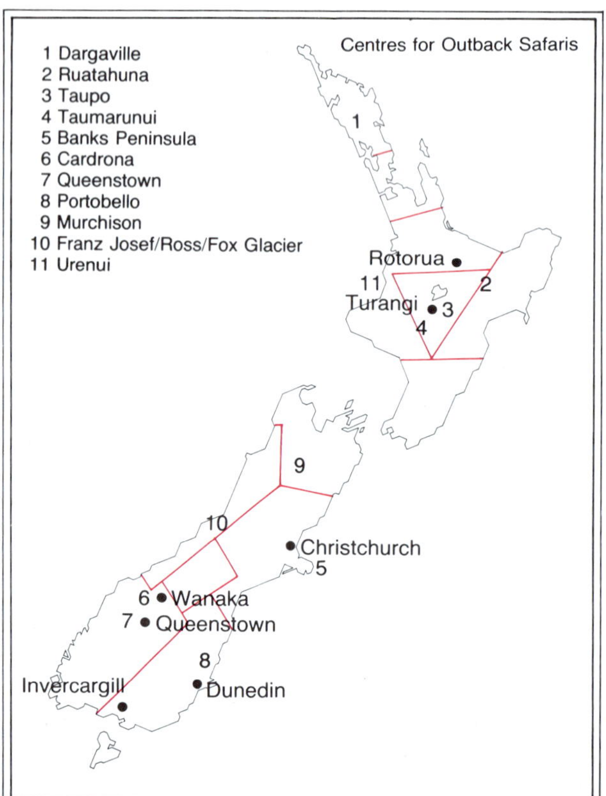

Drive through pine forests, giant kauri forests, dense moss – and fern-filled rain forests or high-country beech forests.

Follow old mining and logging trails into country once accessible only on foot or horseback.

You can do all of these on day safaris or you can extend the excitement into true adventures and spend days in the hills, mountains and forests with time out for hiking, trout fishing, deer hunting, rafting, canoeing or leisurely panning for gold.

For those who don't relish a bumpy journey or sleeping under the stars (even in a tent), there are comparatively sedate outback four-wheel-drive tours, such as a journey through several high-country sheep stations with stops for easy walks and overnight accommodation in hotel comfort.

Set out on a week-long outback safari as the highlight of a New Zealand holiday, or include a safari tour as only one component of an adventure-filled holiday.

'Coaster' meaning up/down as in rollercoaster! Two unique tours: 'South Adventure' – 6-hour four-wheel-drive, coastal tour to historical Pouto Lighthouse, set on wild wasteland. Swim and explore sand dunes. 'North Adventure' – includes Trounson Park, famous Waipoua Kauri Forest, beautiful Kai Iwi Lakes (surrounded by white sand) and 32 kilometres (20 miles) of wild west-coast beach. Champagne and chicken lunch served. Bring swimwear, jacket, walking shoes. From $180 (four people).

Kauri Coaster Tours
PO Box 210
Dargaville
Telephone: (0884) 4425
Host: Bill Fitness

With members of the Tuhoe tribe as guides, explore the dense subtropical rainforests of the Urewera National Park, a park noted for its variety of native flora and fauna, including kiwi whose calls can be heard at night. These remote mountains have also endured as an historical focus of ancient Maori culture and traditions. The Tuhoe people will show you their forests, their ancestral homes and their way of life. Three-, five- and seven-day safaris offered, from November to Easter. All food, equipment and accommodation provided. You will need warm clothes, waterproof gear and sturdy footwear. A good general level of fitness is required. Public transport to Ruatahuna. From $348. Book direct by mail or telephone, through NZTP or travel agent.

Te Rehuwai Safaris Ltd
Private Bag
Rotorua
Telephone: (07365) 65-131
Host: Margaret Biddle

Just off State Highway 3, (Auckland-New Plymouth), stop at Urenui for a great horseback adventure. Whether a novice or an experienced rider, you'll love riding these quarter horses (animals renowned for gentle temperaments and stamina) with big, comfortable western saddles. For 1 hour, a half or full day, trek over a 3,000-acre (1,214-hectare) sheep and cattle farm, through native forest, over winding trails, gaining superb coastal and mountain views of the region, from a high vantage point. Go back in time, riding to an old tree-feller's hut where you'll boil the billy and enjoy lunch, cooked on the open fire. This 'no frills' journey is operated by experienced, knowledgeable professionals who assure you of a remarkable experience and happy memories. Bring sturdy footwear and outdoor clothing. From: $22 (1 hour), $30 (half day), $45 (full day), per person. Available daily, subject to weather. Bookings essential.

Tuahu Western Horse Trails
Upper Kaipikari Road
PO Box 2
Urenui
Telephone: (067) 23-400
Hosts: Bill and Alan Newton

Exciting safaris to suit adventurers! 2-hour challenging trail-bike rides through forest tracks; 5-hour scenic tours – featuring Mount Tarawera crater, forests, lakes, etc; scuba diving, sea fishing (light tackle specialists) for kahawai (sea trout) and coastal holiday safaris. Wetsuit and regulators required, other diving gear provided. Deer hunting, tramping and snow skiing by arrangement. Trail bikes from $66; diving/fishing from $66 per day; scenic safaris from $42 (adult), $18 (child), $99 (family).

NZ Outdoor Adventure Centre (Rotorua)
PO Box 5157
Rotorua
Telephone: (073) 476-174/ 80-623
Telex: NZ60941
Host: Murray Thompson

The country's largest Appaloosa stud offers you a day in the country or farm holiday. View mares and foals, sheep and cattle, enjoy a guided horse trek through native forest, riding Appaloosas (western saddles). Or stay in the large, comfortable farm cottage (bedding/food supplied by arrangement), joining in farm activities – (weaning foals, horse-breaking, shearing, mustering). Treks from $30 per person, Farm stay from $30 ($200 per week). Bookings essential.

Rinestone Appaloosa Stud
Main Highway North
R.D.I.
Taupo
Telephone: (074) 48-291
Hosts: Margaret and Bob Ramsay

Rawhide Holdings
PO Kakahi
Taumarunui
Telephone: (081226) 550
Hosts: Barbara and Rex Taylor

Offering small groups 3-days or more of horseback, tramping or helicopter camping and trout-fishing holiday, through Tongariro State Forest to the beautiful Wanganui River. A personal reputable service, friendly hosts, western saddles, reliable horses, hearty meals with time to relax/fish in the great outdoors. Everything supplied except sleeping bag, personal gear. Operates mainly October-May. From $120 per person. Comfortable home-stays offered (view great leatherwork); from (double) $110 full day; $60 bed/breakfast.

Off Road Tours
435 Rocks Road
Nelson
Telephone: (054) 84-646
Host: David Field

Visit this glorious hinterland in armchair comfort by 4-wheel-drive, to scenic wonderlands inaccessible by conventional vehicle. Watch the sunrise over the ocean (2-hour Breakfast Safari), and explore the beauty of the inland lakes and mountains, their history, wildlife and solitude. Seven exciting safari options, with meals and accommodation provided as required. South Island exploration tours available on request in the luxuriously appointed 'mountain goats'. From $22 (2-hour Safari, per person).

Lake Matiri Horse Treks and Pig Hunts
Matiri Valley Road
PO Box 36
Murchison
Westland
Telephone: Murchison 39-011/ or 18D
Hosts: Lynette & John McKenzie

'Come horse around with us' – 1 and 2-day horse treks on quiet but energetic horses. See beech forests, rivers and waterfalls and Lake Matiri. Catch a brown trout for supper on the 2-day trek! Bring camera, outdoor clothing and sensible footwear. From $65 per person (1-day trek). Lake Matiri Pig Hunts offers you the thrill of the hunt. The skill of the hunter against the cunning of the hunted. Meals/equipment supplied.

Outback safaris

Experience south Westland the natural way, on horseback. Service offers 1 ($60), 2 ($165), 4 ($300) and 12-day ($1,250) safari treks. All meals and equipment provided. Catering for riders of all abilities. Ride down deserted beaches to the roar of the pounding West Coast surf, through lush rainforest, with magnificent views of Mount Cook and the Southern Alps. Camp out under the stars! An adventure where Ruth and Peter have fun watching you enjoy yourself!

South West Saddle Safaris
S.H. 6
Waitaha Valley
R.D. Ross
South Westland
Telephone: Ross 54-182
Hosts: Ruth & Peter Salter

Half-day horse treks on Mount Cardrona or treks of 1 to 4 nights on pack trails through open tussock country of Pisa Range; staying in musterers' huts (elevation 1,500 metres)! Enjoy gold panning, swimming, spectacular alpine scenery. Suitable for confident beginners, minimum age 10 years. Wear sturdy trousers/footwear (bring sleeping bag and overnight gear). Only half-day treks operate Christmas through January. Courtesy transport from Wanaka. Costs on enquiry.

Gin and Raspberry Stables
(Highway 89)
Cardrona RD1
Wanaka
Telephone: (02943) 8152

Horseback riding is for everyone – you don't need to be fit! Abilities and mount preferences are catered to as are treks – from 1 hour to 8 hours in duration. Explore beautiful Banks Peninsula on experienced and quiet horses, enjoying farm activities and delicious food and refreshments. Bring sensible footwear and comfortable outdoor clothing. Treks operate daily depending on weather. Comfortable bunkhouse accommodation available. From $10 (1 hour), $110 (weekend package). Children's rates available.

Overleigh Horse Treks
Overleigh, Port Levy
Diamond Harbour R.D.
Banks Peninsula
Canterbury
Telephone: (03294) 684/697
Hosts: Caroline Craw and Jan Ward

'Waiho Stables'
PO Box 10
Franz Josef Glacier
Westland
Telephone: Franz Josef 747
Host: Susan Miller

Enjoy action-packed, half-day rides on horses/ponies suiting all ages and levels of experience. Susan teaches beginners the basics of safe country riding, and good beginners' horses help to make progress easy. The ride borders Westland National Park, through cattle flats with brilliant glacier and mountain views. Day/overnight trips available to the uninhabited Tasman Sea coast. Safety helmets provided, waterproof stockman's coats for hire. From $30 (GST inclusive), family/Y.H.A. concessions.

Alpine Guides (Westland) Ltd
Main Road
PO Box 38
Fox Glacier
Westland
Telephone: Fox Glacier 825
Chief Guide: Mike Browne

These professional guides offer a range of great tours. Try the Chancellor Adventure: helicopter from Fox Glacier township to the Chancellor Hut, overlooking the glacier. Walk across a snowfield and summit ridge for a magnificent vista of the Southern Alps with Mts Cook and Tasman dominating the skyline. Enjoy lunch at 6526 feet above sea level, before retracing your path home. A delight for keen walkers. Flights, guide, transport and boots provided. Bring lunch (available from base), sunglasses and suncream, plus mountain clothing. From $158 per person. Or take the Saltwater Cycle Tour: using 12-speed mountain bikes, through National Park rain-forests, farmland and coastal flats to Saltwater Forest and the ocean. Time for lunching and studying the nearby bird-filled lagoon, before returning through this beautiful hinterland to township. Suitable all ages. Great value and really enjoyable. Bike, guide and lunch provided. From $60 per person. Both depart 9.30 a.m.

SEE ALSO:

Skiing: Alpine Guides (Westland).
Climbing: Alpine Guides (Westland).
Flightseeing: Southern Lakes Helicopters (Te Anau).
Bicycling: The Bicycle Touring Company (Auckland).
Regional:
Bay of Plenty: Elite Tours (Rotorua).
Volcanic Plateau: Simon Dickie Adventures (Taupo).
Otago: Silverpeaks Tours (Dunedin).

OTHER REFERENCES:

Horseriding:

Activity Holidays, PO Box 975, Tauranga.

Plateau Guides, PO Box 29, National Park.

Hamner Springs Trekking, Hamner Springs.

Hillandale Rides, Dalefield RD1, Queenstown.

Moonlight Stables, PO Box 144, Queenstown.

4-wheel-drives:

Activity Holidays, PO Box 975, Tauranga.

Elite Tours, PO Box 17143, Karori, Wellington.

Action in Marlborough, 59 Lakings Road, Blenheim.

Venture South NZ, PO Box 6053, Dunedin.

Moonlight Lodge, PO Box 72, Queenstown.

Helihikers on the Fox Glacier, Westland.
(Courtesy of Alpine Guides (Westland) Ltd)

Sports calendar

OCTOBER

Spring weather throughout New Zealand. Opening of fishing season in most lakes, streams and rivers. The last runs of fresh spawning fish in the Tongariro River. Harling beginning on Lake Taupo, particularly early morning and evening. Deer are dropping their antlers.

NOVEMBER

The start of summer weather, but often windy. Some good dry-fly hatches, particularly in the South Island waters. Smelting starting in all lakes. Excellent wet-fly fishing and harling on Lake Taupo.

DECEMBER

One of the least crowded months to fish New Zealand waters up until Christmas day. Very good fishing throughout the day on all lakes, streams and rivers. Excellent dry-fly and nymph fishing throughout the country, particularly in mountain streams accessible only by aircraft.

JANUARY

The busiest month of the year with most of the country on holiday. Stream fishing limited to nymphs in many instances, however some good wet-fly fishing beginning at stream mouths. Excellent harling both morning and evening on Lake Taupo, but often deep trolling during the day. Start of the big-game fishing season.

FEBRUARY

Usually the hottest month of the year. Weather very settled for fishing in mountain streams. Fly fishing around the stream mouths is very good, both during the day and at night. Still very good harling on Lake Taupo. Start of the salmon runs in South Island rivers. Deer coming out of velvet.

MARCH

Weather still warm and settled. The last month of good fishing in mountain streams. Good salmon fishing and dry-fly fishing in the South Island. Excellent wet-fly fishing around stream mouths at Lake Taupo, however the good harling is almost over. One of the best months for big-game fishing. The start of the deer-hunting season.

APRIL

Leaves beginning to show signs of autumn. Last month of fishing season in some districts, the first runs of fresh spawning trout in the Tongariro River. The best time for wet-fly fishing around mouths of streams flowing into Lake Taupo. The deer are mating and so the best time for hunting.

MAY

This is the time for catching trophy trout, particularly at Lake Tarawera. Big runs of spawning fish in Taupo rivers. Good stream-mouth fishing in both northern and southern lakes, although deep trolling is now required for boat fishing. The last month to catch that marlin or shoot a deer. The opening of duck season and upland game.

JUNE

The real start of winter. Last month of fishing season in most districts. Excellent fly fishing on the Tongariro River and deep trolling on Lake Taupo.

JULY

For the hardy angler, the Tongariro River offers some of the best fly fishing of the year. Deep trolling on Lake Taupo still very good. Start of the snow-skiing season on most fields.

AUGUST

Often the quietest month of the year for fishing, but most days are cold and clear. Tongariro River fishing well but deep trolling on Taupo is inconsistent. Best month for snow skiing in both islands.

SEPTEMBER

First signs of spring with New Zealand at its greenest. Lots of new lambs and calves. Taupo fishing improving again and opening of fishing season in south Westland and Fiordland for sea-run trout.

It can be done

A remarkable aspect of fishing and hunting in New Zealand is that in the period of just a few hours it is possible to catch a big-game fish, catch a trout and shoot a deer. Patience, persistence and precise planning paid off for Johnnie Boyle on 13 January 1979. After hooking a striped marlin at 10.10 a.m., he landed the 120-kilogram (262-pound) big-game fish at 10.30 a.m. Arriving at Lake Taupo by float-plane alongside Simon Dickie's vessel *Awatea* at 12.30 p.m., it took less than five minutes to hook a trout and by 12.40 p.m. Johnnie was away by helicopter for the third trophy of the 'Big 3'. The deer was shot at 1.25 p.m., giving a total time of 3 hours 15 minutes for all three trophies – a new world record.

(Courtesy Simon Dickie, Simon Dickie Adventures – see FISHING section.)

Bull thar.
(Gordon Roberts)

Red deer in forest interior, Henry River, North Canterbury. *(Gordon Roberts)*

New Zealand offers the hunter the beauty of an unspoiled environment, prolific game animals, magnificent trophies and professional guiding services.

Imagine yourself big game hunting for a magnificent fourteen or sixteen-point trophy stag in isolated unspoiled areas where the air is clear and invigorating and blue sky meets white snow-covered hills and forested mountains, where your escape from crowds and pollution is total. This is your opportunity – here in the hills and mountains of New Zealand – just a few hours' drive, or a short flight from many cities.

In 1986 the government recognised the natural asset that the sport of hunting is to this country and registered the quality guides for the first time. Today when you hunt in New Zealand, you have access to government-registered, professional guides. If the aim and object of your hunting is to bag a trophy, professional hunting operators provide a 'no trophy-no pay' service. Large areas of native forest and mountain wilderness have been enclosed as special game areas and stocked with first-class animals for the overseas hunter whose heart is set on collecting a world-class trophy.

Accommodation is often provided in luxury lodges in these hunting areas. Alternatively, you can take the pioneering route and 'rough it' in outback huts. Wild deer, chamois, thar, goats and pigs are yours for the hunting.

Red deer are the most prolific, most widely hunted game animal in the country, having adapted more than happily to the range of climates and vegetation. Of the other species, fallow deer is the most common. Sika and rusa are more commonly found in the central North Island, wapiti in the South Island and Virginian in Otago and Stewart Island.

Chamois and thar are highly prized hunting animals in their original homelands; both have adapted readily to the New Zealand environment. Released in the Mount Cook region early this century to provide game sport, they have increased to substantial numbers.

Chamois are now found throughout the alpine area in the South Island, and thar generally between Arthur's Pass and Lake Wanaka. Hunting either of these mountain-roaming creatures requires more than just a good eye with a rifle – a good level of fitness is desirable!

Wild goats and pigs were first released into the New Zealand countryside by Captain Cook in 1773, with their numbers subsequently boosted by the escape of domestic animals brought in by pioneer settlers.

As game animals goats are not held in great esteem – they are, perhaps, too easily hunted. But the wild pig is another story. Although descended from domestic pigs, the New Zealand feral pig has more in common – in size, temperament, appearance and taste – with the true wild boar than it has with any farm-bred porker.

Wild pigs are found throughout North Island high country with the Coromandel, Urewera and Tararua ranges favourite hunting areas.

Local information centres and forest park rangers can advise visitors on the best game hunting in their areas and in restricted places such as recreational reserves. Although hunting licences are not needed, permits are often required for particular areas and all guns must be licensed. Permission should always be sought for hunting on private land.

Hunting guides take care of the necessary formalities and provide equipment, accommodation, food and transport, most commonly four-wheel-drive vehicles but also helicopter, light plane, jet boat, horseback, raft or canoe. A hunting holiday needn't be all hunting – a combination of 'huntin' and fishin', whether trout, salmon or sea fishing, can easily be organised for an all-round holiday.

Feathered game is hunted under a different set of rules – the seasons for shooting waterfowl and upland game birds vary with different districts but are usually around late autumn and early winter, April to June. Limit bags and licences apply. (Licenses are available from sporting shops for a few dollars.)

In the marshy wetlands, rivers and lakes there are wild ducks, mainly mallards, black swan, Canadian geese (protected in the North Island) and pukeko (a blue swamp bird). Away from the water are pheasant and Californian quail and, in the South Island high country, chuckor (Indian partridge). Hunting and shooting New Zealand style are not exclusive pastimes of the rich – here the weekend hunter is as likely to be a bus driver as a businessman – and the sports can be as expensive and as organised or as casual as you wish. You can relax at the end of the day in the comforts of hotel or lodge, or return to the simple, spartan base of a Forest Service hut, free of charge.

Bull thar, Murchison Valley, Nelson Lakes. ***(Gordon Roberts)***

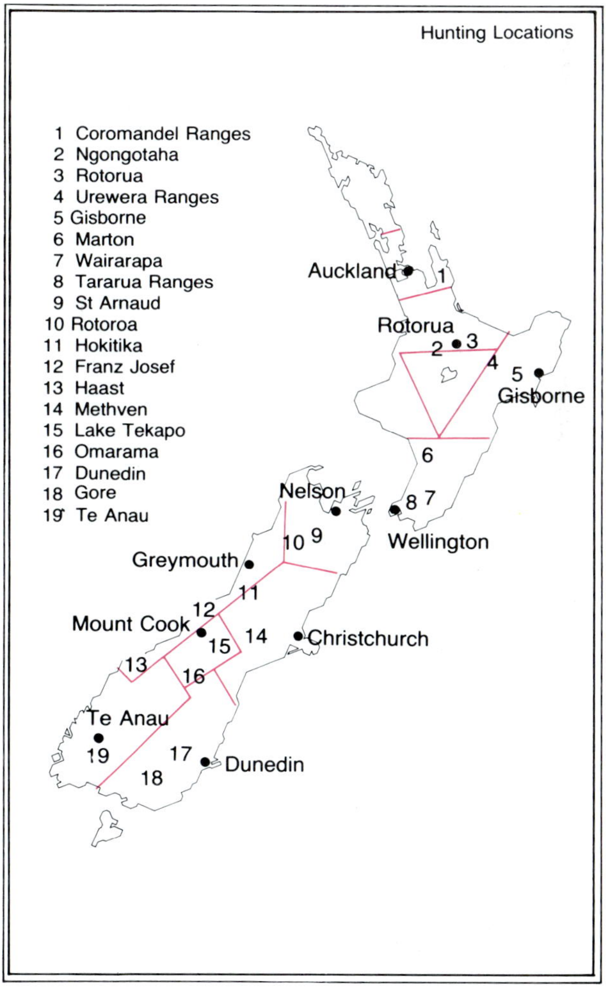

Lilybank Safari Lodge
PO Box 60
Lake Tekapo
Telephone: (05056) 522
Cables: 'CHAMOIS'
Owners: Susan and Gary Joll

This is New Zealand's top hunting lodge with a service rivalling international standards. Lilybank (the first hunting lodge to gain a Government issued Safari Licence), is after 23 years, world-renowned for consistently producing superb trophies of red stag, fallow buck, thar and chamois (no-trophy-no-pay). Gary, a Government registered hunting guide/ President of the NZ Registered Hunting Guides Assn., provides a personal and expert service. Hunts are on foot and horseback, returning to the Lodge each evening where Sue takes over as hostess, serving delicious New Zealand fare featuring game, home grown fresh vegetables, local wines and cheeses. Centrally heated accommodation features private ensuite guest rooms, each centrally heated with all electric facilities, plus gracious dining room and restful trophy room-lounge. For the selective serious trophy hunter Lilybank Safari Lodge is New Zealand's foremost hunting destination. Close to Mount Cook alpine region, 30-minute drive to Tekapo ski area.

MTR Ranch
PO Box 35
Oxford
Telephone: (0502) 24-737
Host: Brian Stanley-Jackson

One-day professional hunting safaris on a private game reserve for fallow deer, red deer, chamois, thar, wild boar and game birds (in season). All outer wear, licences and firearms provided. Transport, outfitters and guides arranged. Be collected from and returned to Christchurch. Especially for those wishing to fit a safari into their existing schedule. Also operating driftboat river-fishing safaris to little known fishing spots. Fishing from $300 per day, Hunting from $1000 per hunt.

SEE ALSO:

Outback Safaris: Lake Matiri Horse Treks.
Lodges: Lake Rotoroa, Huka (Taupo), Solitaire (Rotorua), Riverview (Athol).
Fishing: Mt Thomas Resources (Oxford).
Live with NZ: Repongaere (Gisborne).
Water Adv: Silverpeaks Tours (Dunedin).
Cruising: Fiordland Cruises (Te Anau).
Regional:
Volcanic Plateau: Simon Dickie Adventures (Taupo).

OTHER REFERENCES:

Tarawera Action Adventures, Glenfiddich Heights RD5, Lake Tarawera.

King Country Safaris, PO Box 37, Te Kuiti.

Terry Sleator Safaris, 53 Woodland Road, Opotiki.

Fair Chase Hunt, PO Box 77, Taupo.

Wildlife Safaris Ltd, 48 Gosling Drive, Turangi.

Nelson Lakes Guiding Services, C/- Post Office, St Arnaud.

Westland Guiding Services, PO Box 38, Franz Josef.

NZ Wildlife Safaris, PO Box 4058, Christchurch.

Kiwi Hunting Safaris, PO Box 6074, Christchurch.

Fiordland Travel, C/- Post Office, Manapouri.

Humboldt Hunt & Fish Safaris, PO Box 153, Queenstown.

Viking Safaris Ltd, PO Box 81, Dannevirke.

Hollyburn Park Safaris, Te Tua Road 1 RD, Riverton.

Fishing

Fly-fishing near
Ashburton, Canterbury.
(Bob Girvan)

Fishing in New Zealand can be many different things – sitting in the sun on a rock, wading into an icy glacier-fed river, cruising through an ocean swell surrounded by diving gannets – and each of them will be first rate.

For over 50 years fishing enthusiasts 'in the know' have been travelling to New Zealand for the single purpose of catching fish. They know that New Zealand is the world's finest fishing mecca, and they would be hard pressed to find another place to compare with it.

All types of fishing – deep-sea angling, line fishing, surf casting, trout fishing – are superb, easily accessible, comparatively inexpensive and found amid scenery that ranges from enchanting to awesome.

The visiting enthusiast is never at a loss for local advice – he may find it given free across the counter of a local sports shop or over a beer in a country pub, or he may choose to pay for it in the form of an experienced guide. But he or she will never have difficulty finding out all about tackle, times and fishing spots.

The big-game fish of the Bay of Islands and the rainbow trout of Taupo are well known world-wide. But the excitement of hauling in a 300-kilogram (660-pound) blue marlin in the Bay of Islands or a 4-kilogram (9-pound) rainbow trout at Taupo is only part of the New Zealand fishing story, albeit an important part. What is less well known is that you can fish your way from one end of the country to the other, one way or another.

There is a Sydney businessman who recounts with delight the best, most relaxing fishing holiday he has ever enjoyed – line fishing from a small boat. It went like this: by air from Sydney to Auckland, taxi to the harbour, sea plane to an island bay. Just over four hours out from Sydney and he and his friends had the beach and its cottage to themselves. For a week they lolled about fishing for snapper and then repeated the simple journey in reverse, back to Sydney.

There is an American angler from Maryland who visits New Zealand every year, staying up to two months at a time. He makes his base at Wanaka, a South Island lake heavily stocked with brown trout, but also offering the chance of rainbow trout and land-locked quinnat salmon. Unlike many visitors, he knows about the excellent South Island fishing – 47 lakes all stocked with trout, most of them easily reached and fished by any visitor, and all the adjacent rivers and streams as well.

167kg (367lb) striped marlin caught in the Duke of Marlborough billfish tournament, Bay of Islands, by Neil Campbell. ***(Courtesy Fast Photos, Paihia)***

Big-game fishing

For thrill-of-a-lifetime fishing that needs no prior expertise, take to the sea with big-game fishing – even if you've never caught so much as a sprat, you've got every chance of landing a monster marlin. Game fleet skippers in the Bay of Islands, the acknowledged centre of deep-sea fishing, estimate that 80 per cent of people setting out in their boats have never been fishing before.

You can charter a game-fishing boat by the day, half-day, overnight or longer. If a boat all to yourself is too expensive – although economical by world standards – a share charter system spreads the cost among several people. This brings a day's fishing within the reach of anyone, with time in the game chairs organised by the skipper so that everyone gets the chance of a big strike.

The game fish most likely to take the bait are striped marlin, blue marlin and black marlin, as well as several varieties of shark, broadbill swordfish, blue-fin and yellow-fin tuna and yellowtail kingfish.

The North Island's east coast is studded with game-fishing ports. Paihia and Russell are the best-known departure points, opening the way to the Bay of Islands, considered by experts to be the best striped-marlin fishing ground in the world. The Bay of Islands boasts an impressive number of records for several species of big-game fish – 18 world records and 48 national records at last count.

But there are many other places. Among them are: Whangaroa, a village on one of the world's deepest natural harbours that must also be one of the most beautiful and unspoilt; Tutukaka with excellent rock fishing, line fishing and diving as well as deep-sea fishing; Whitianga on the rugged Coromandel Peninsula; Tauranga and Mount Maunganui for the waters around Mayor Island; Whakatane for White Island.

Game fishing in the South Island centres on the deeply indented Marlborough Sounds, with boats leaving from Picton.

Join the local game-fishing club for a nominal visitor's fee of a few dollars and enjoy the facilities that will certainly include a convivial bar as well as practical assistance with your weighty catch.

Whether you want to have your large fish smoked for eating, mounted or follow the increasing trend to have it tagged and returned to the deep is your choice. Whatever you actually do with the fish, the heady success of landing a big-game fish will remain an incomparable memory.

Trout fishing, Lake Rotorua. ***(Courtesy Brian Colman)***

Trout and salmon fishing

The clear lakes and fast-flowing rivers of New Zealand proved a perfect environment for the brown trout and rainbow trout introduced at the end of the nineteenth century from Britain and California. Here they grow to a size and condition uncommon elsewhere, with little competition for food and vast, unpolluted waters in which to roam.

There are no private fishing waters in New Zealand and so no exclusion from the best stretches of stream or river, nor payment of expensive fishing rights.

The country is divided into 26 fishing districts, each with its own regulations and seasons. Taupo and Rotorua offer year-round fishing, but most other districts open from the beginning of October to the end of April, with local variations. In the Southern Lakes district, for example, river fishing runs to the end of May, fishing in Lakes Wanaka and Hawea until the end of July.

Licences are cheap, a few dollars, and there are special licences for overseas visitors on a fishing tour – you don't need a new licence for each new fishing district.

Trout fishing in either island can be as gentle or as exciting as you wish, although it is always exciting at that moment when the fish strikes.

You can seek out trout by trolling, spinning, dry- or wet-fly fishing. Whether you have spent a lifetime angling or have never seen a trout, guides will organise the best fishing for your abilities – they provide expert local knowledge, tackle, gear and transport.

You can base yourself in a luxury fishing lodge with all the attendant comforts, or more economically in a country hotel or motel.

Fishing for brown trout, Waikaia River, near Gore, Southland. ***(Arthur Bremford)***

Fishing

Enjoy the rural charm of fishing the nearest lake, river or meandering stream, day after day; or take off on a trout- and salmon-fishing excursion through the country (in the South Island, one holiday provides campervan and suggested itinerary). En route, delight in a variety of waters and the full range of New Zealand scenery from mountains to meadowlands, tussock moors, beech forest and subtropical rainforest. You could make trout fishing a casual interlude, a leisurely afternoon's break in a busy schedule.

The pleasure of trout fishing in tranquil surroundings can be combined with the thrills of high adventure: take off by air in helicopter or sea plane to remote back-country areas, skim up-river by jet boat or down-river by raft or canoe, or set off on horseback.

If time is tight and you plan to catch a rainbow trout, shoot a deer and land a marlin with only a couple of days to spare, there are sophisticated operations that will see that you do it all.

Those interested in salmon fishing must concentrate on the South Island, where land-locked salmon are found in lakes and streams, and sea-run salmon converge on river mouths such as the Waimakariri, Rakaia and Rangitata in Canterbury during the November to April season.

Diseases in New Zealand's fisheries and water fowl are relatively unknown. All trout fly-tying material – loose feathers and feathers attached to skin – and used fishing tackle – rods, lines, reels, nets, waders – **must be fumigated by Ministry of Agriculture & Fisheries' inspectors at the port of entry.** Please help keep New Zealand disease free.

Boat, line and surf fishing

Boat fishing needn't be deep sea, of course. The relaxing pastime of line fishing from boats happens wherever a boat can be launched, and there are plenty of places that qualify. Even the treacherous, wild, west coast has long, wide harbours with excellent small-boat fishing – top spots for such fishing on this coast are off the usual tourist routes, places where time seems to stand still in tiny harbour-side settlements such as those on the immense Kaipara Harbour, with its 3,000-kilometre (1,800-mile) coastline, or the long Hokianga Harbour fringed with mangroves.

Line fish from boats in sheltered bays and harbours, particularly in Doubtless Bay (also excellent deep-sea fishing), the Bay of Islands, Whangaroa Harbour, around the Whangaparaoa Peninsula, on the Waitemata Harbour, around the islands of the Hauraki Gulf, both sides of the Coromandel Peninsula, the Marlborough Sounds.

Expect to catch fish such as snapper, yellowtail kingfish, kahawai (Australian sea trout), trevally, hapuku (groper), tarakahi (Australian morwong), blue cod, gurnard, barracouta.

Visit sweeping open beaches on either coast at any time of the year and you will find surf casters in action. Using strong rods and fishing from rocky promontories or wading deep into the surf to cast long lines, surf casters seek the excitement of hooking a fighting fish such as yellowtail kingfish, snapper or kahawai.

You will find surf casters from one end of the country to the other – local sports shops in popular surf-casting areas can supply equipment and many have a rental service.

For surf casters, the Ninety-Mile Beach Surf casting Snapper Competition offers five days of fishing and the promise of prizes – $1,000 for the heaviest fish caught each day and $15,000 to the overall winner (26 February to 2 March 1985 and annually) information from PO Box 71, Kaitaia).

SEE ALSO:

Flightseeing: Floatplanes (Rotorua).
Lodges: Tongariro (Turangi), Huka (Taupo), Riverview (Athol), Lake Brunner, Solitaire (Rotorua), Lake Rotoroa.
Hunting: Mt Thomas Resources.
Outback Safaris: Danes Back Country (Queenstown), NZ Outdoor Adventure (Rotorua).
Diving: Paihia Dive Hire & Charter.
River Adv: Silverpeaks Tour (Dunedin), Alpine Safaris (Wanaka).
Sailing: Fiordland Cruises (Te Anau).
Regional:
Volcanic Plateau: Parklands Motor Lodge (Tauranga), Taupo Lodge (Turangi).
Wellington: Rangitikei River Adventures (Mangaweka).
Otago: Southern Air (Invercargill).

Further Reading:

New Zealand Trout Fishermans Guide: *Rivers and Lakes of the South Island, Rivers and Lakes of the North Island.* George Ferris, Heinemann (NZ) Ltd.

For an introduction to fishing, especially sea fishing, *How to Catch Fish and Where.* Bill Hohepa, Rugby Press. Excellent maps and description of fish.

Fishing

TAUPO! ... The very name is synonomous with fishing, holding as it does the reputation of 'Trout-Fishing Capital of New Zealand'. This is the region's largest trout-fishing outfitting and guiding organisation, with a justified reputation for excellent service. Facilities and services have been developed with a distinctive style, suited to both experienced sportsmen and to escapists, wanting to relax and enjoy one of the world's most enviable holiday environments. Professional guides offer fly and spin fishing tours throughout the region, plus spectacular helicopter safaris for trophy trout. All requirements are catered for; from hiring small row boats for a few hours to chartering sumptuously-appointed cruisers (complete with bathtub and fireplace) for days; including latest tackle, food/beverage/liquor service, hunting and fishing licences. Season open daily, year round. From $60 per half-day, depending on requirements. Company also offers range of hunting, rafting, jet-boating and wilderness tramping tours.

Simon Dickie Adventures Ltd
Boat Harbour, Lakefront
PO Box 682
Taupo
Telephone: (074) 88-115/ 89-680
Telex: NZ60846 FISHING
Host: Simon Dickie

(See SPORTING CALENDAR and BIG THREE record.)

Full range of fishing activities: flyfishing (rivers/Lake Taupo), trolling and spin fishing (Lake Taupo), fly-in wilderness fishing by arrangement. Tuition provided for novices. State of the art tackle provided plus thermal waders, refreshments and transport. Trophy trout a speciality. Member of NZ Professional Guides Assn. Also arranges seasonal skiing and deer-stalking; year-round rafting, horsetreks, flight-seeing. Fishing from $25 per hour depending on requirements, other services on enquiry.

Tongariro Guide Services
PO Box 89
Turangi
Telephone: (0746) 8996/ 8207
Hosts: Brian and Tim McCarthy

Guided flyfishing with a trophy trout expert (winner of 4 I.G.F.A. World Records – brown trout in two finest fly rod classes). For those after that trophy of a lifetime! Everything provided – the best graphite rods to a video of your day's action! Fishing Taupo-Turangi area, year round. International Game Fishing Assn. member; founding member – Sports Fishing Guides Assn. of N.Z. Bring hat/warm clothing. Tuition available. From $50 per hour depending on requirements. Bookings essential.

Lite-Tackle Tours
PO Box 192
Turangi
Telephone: (0746) 7953
Host: Louie 'The Fish' De Nolfo

Join an expert in waters teeming with a variety of sizeable fish. Go big game fishing, December-May, where some 1000 game fish are caught annually including yellowtail kingfish in excess of 45 kg (99 lb) each! Also light tackle fishing for kahawai, snapper, or hapuka (groper). Live aboard 'Ma Cherie', a spacious 40 ft (12 metre) vessel accommodating 6 for game fishing comfortably, with private toilet facilities, well-equipped galley, plus catch refrigeration. Tackle and food available on request. Fish on hourly/daily basis. From $700 per day.

Baker Marine Charters
PO Box 504
Whakatane
Telephone: (076) 70-015
Host: John Baker

Guided float trips for rainbow/brown trout on North Island rivers. Specialised fishing, utilising a combination of air (helicopter, fixed wing) and road transport and purpose-designed inflatable rafts, for access to remote, seldom fished back country. Professionally guided fly fishing packages on trophy trout streams/rivers, ranging from half-day to 5-day camping safaris. Top range equipment and camping gear provided. Trips tailored to requirements. From $560 (1-day float trip for two).

Rangitikei River Adventures Ltd
Main Road
Mangaweka
Telephone: (0658) 25-747
USA: (307) 733-9408
Manager: Tom Kemper

Nelson River Guides
PO Box 469
Nelson
Telephone: (054) 85-095
Host: Vern Brabant

'The Ultimate Challenge' – anglers (both fly and spin fishermen) return annually to fish the Nelson rivers with this specialised service. Catering mainly for experienced anglers (up to 8 people), teaching advanced techniques in a quality fishery – hunting/stalking plus fighting world-class brown trout in difficult waters. Specialise in fly-in fishing to backwaters for trophies. Emphasis on quality/insights into ecosystem. Bring stocking waders, everything provided depending on requirements. From $350 per person/day.

OTHER REFERENCES:

Bay of Islands Sportfishing, PO Box 176, Paihia.
Gamefishing Charters, PO Box 263, Paihia.
Northland Charter Boats Assn, PO Box 133, Russell.
Tutukaka Coast Charter Boats Assn, RD 3, Whangarei.
Northland Fishing Tours, 22 Marana Street, Auckland 10.
Dennis Ward, 6 Manuariki Avenue, Ngongataha.
NZ Game Fishing, RD2, Otorohanga.
Chauffeurlux Services, PO Box 7073, Rotorua.
Bryan Colman, 32 Kiwi Street, Rotorua.
King Country Safaris, PO Box 37, Te Kuiti.
Marc Jackson, PO Box 5, Taupo.
Taupo Fly Fishing Academy, PO Box 1243, Taupo.
Frank Harwood, PO Box 290, Turangi.
Viking Safaris, 106 High Street, Dannevirke.
Clark Reid, 7 Colville Street, Masterton.
Nelson Lakes Guiding, C/- Post Office, St Arnaud.
Westland Guiding, PO Box 38, Franz Josef.
Fair Play Fish Safaris, Racecourse Road, Ashburton.
Kiwi Hunting Safaris, PO Box 6074, Christchurch.
Windwhistle Jets, 2 RD, Darfield.
Mackenzie Country Safaris, 51 Regent Street, Fairlie.
John F. Gemmell, PO Box 197, Hamner Springs.
Mt Hutt Fishing Safaris, PO Box 52, Methven.
Manions Salmon Safaris, PO Box 2, Rakaia.
Tinaka Enterprises, 88 Pages Road, Timaru.
Richard Fraser, PO Box 33, Cromwell.
Geoff McDonald, PO Box 443, Queenstown.
Murray Knowles, PO Box 84, Te Anau.
Paul Miller, PO Box 20, Wanaka.
Fishing Paradise Safaris, 101 Main Road, Clinton.
Peter Cullen, 15 North Terrace, Gore.
Seven Rivers Lodge, PO Box 85, Mossburn.
Hollyburn Park Safaris, Te Tua, No 1 RD, Riverton.

Jet boating. *(Andris Apse Ltd)*

In a land where rivers rush down from the mountains in a steep, wild run to the sea, white-water rafting, canoeing and jet boating are great adventure sports.

Superb rafting rivers throughout the wilderness in both the North and the South Island include some of the world's best. Wild water and rugged scenery combine for the perfect rafting adventure – when Coca-Cola wanted to film an international rafting commercial they chose a New Zealand river, the Rangitaiki.

Canoeists also have plenty of rivers to choose from, calm or wild, with the New Zealand Canoeing Association listing some 1,500 rivers for enthusiasts.

Less strenuous perhaps, but no less exhilarating, are jet-boat rides with passengers carried at high speed through twisting gorges. The jet boat is a New Zealand invention, designed to operate in as little as 10 centimetres (4 inches) of water and incredibly manoeuvrable. Under the control of skilled drivers, jet boats make almost instantaneous changes of direction at high speed, taking river travellers close by rocks and over shallow water in safety. Try the thrills of driving a jet boat yourself in the calmer waters of a lake by hiring a self-drive jet boat.

In comparison with rivers such as the Colorado in the USA, the fall from mountain to sea on New Zealand rivers is sharp. Yet many rivers are surprisingly long, taking tortuous routes to the ocean or lakes.

The Landsborough, one of the top ten rafting rivers in the world, gives 70 kilometres (43 miles) of wild water travelling through remote mountain scenery and falling over 300 metres in the first 25 kilometres (985 feet in 15½ miles). The less turbulent Clarence winds 200 kilometres (124 miles), cutting its way through a wide, high-mountain gorge on a spectacular route to the Pacific Ocean.

Rafting rivers are graded on a scale from one to five, so you know what you are attempting from the start. A grade five is heart-stopping excitement, the most difficult water rafted by commercial operators. Experts suggest a day trip on a grade two or three river for a first-time rafter – rivers such as the glacier-fed Rakaia or the bush-fringed Waimakariri. Then if you want to graduate to more exciting water, look for grade four or five.

Each New Zealand river has its own character, thrills and charm – no one river is quite like another.

Ride the North Island's Wairoa, for example, on a brief breathtaking grade-five rafting run where there is little time to admire the scenery – this is a two-hour hair-raising run with turbulent rapids living up to names such as 'Rollercoaster'. Or try the Motu River, which draws rafting enthusiasts as much by its wild, untouched beauty as by its grade three and four water. Trips on the Motu range from two to six days, camping out in the bush-covered gorge.

Then there's the South Island's Shotover, one of the best-known rafting and jet-boating rivers, with a variety of water as the river swoops and twists down through steep, stone canyons.

Travel the Shotover by raft or jet boat, surrounded by the stark, overwhelming scenery, and discover reminders of gold-rush days, 120 years ago, when the Shotover was described as 'the richest river in the world'. The claim may sound boastful but this was the river where two men went in search of a dog and returned instead with 12 kilograms (26 pounds) of gold scooped from the rocky crevices of the riverbank.

Rafting trips on wild rivers range from a few hours to seven days, with the best companies providing highly skilled boatmen and first-rate equipment. Standards of safety and comfort can be as variable as the rivers, so prospective rafters need to make full enquiries with any operator – rafting companies that belong to the New Zealand Professional Rafting Association must meet certain standards.

The rivers were the first great highways in New Zealand. Since the invention of jet boats and tough, inflatable rafts, the rivers are reverting to routes of adventure, opening up the rugged interior for all groups – from children to grannies, as well as the adventurer. There is something suitable for everyone to enjoy at their own level.

Combine River rafting, jet boating, tramping – plus spectacular Fiordland scenery, unusual vegetation, penguin & seals at the Hollyford valley! These are many combinations.

Raft rivers such as the Landsborough, Hunter, Matukituki, Waiaoto and Kawarau and take time to trek in the surrounding forests and mountains. On some rivers, such as the Mohaka, which flows through beech forest and grasslands, rafts are used for transport on hunting and fishing holidays.

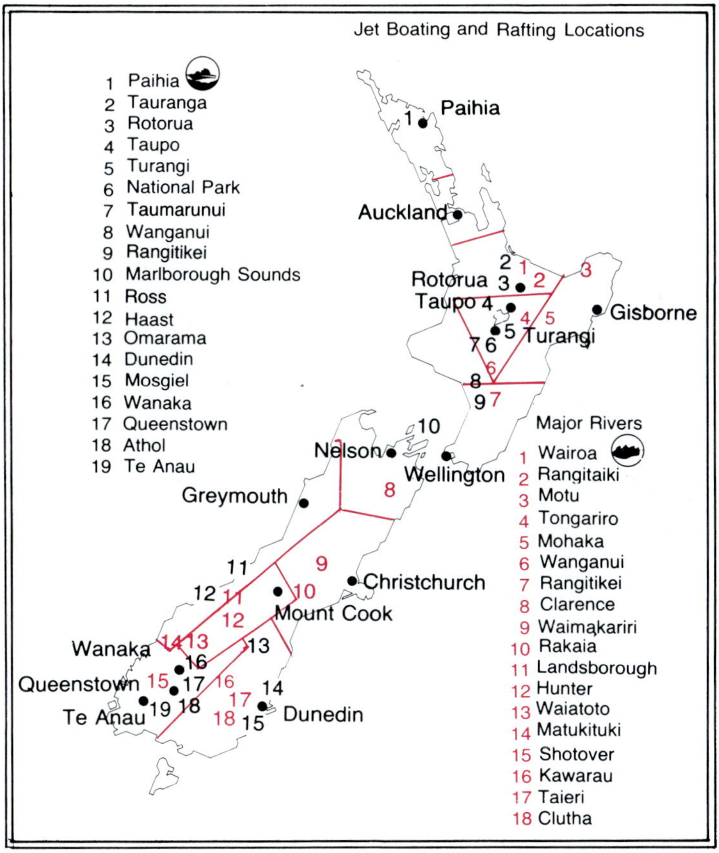

Take off down the rivers of New Zealand by raft, canoe or jet-boat and combine your river adventure with other outdoor activities. On the bush-fringed Wanganui, imbued with Maori and European history, take a canoeing holiday and take time out for swimming, bushwalks, sunbathing and sightseeing or combine a jet-boat holiday with a holiday on a sheep station.

Rangitikei River Adventures Ltd
Main Road
Mangaweka
Telephone: (0658) 25-747
USA: (307) 733-9408
Manager: Tom Kemper

Complete range of great white-water rafting trips: Grade 2 – mild scenic Rangitikei River float for all ages; Grade 3 – medium action, bouncy Tongariro River (13 years plus); Grade 5 adventure trips on the Rangitikei River for ultimate whitewater experience. Reasonable fitness levels required for Grades 3 and 5. Comfort and safety gear provided. Year round fun, company organises diverse activities, including jet boating. Rafting from $13 (adult/1-hour/Grade 2) to $98 (adult/full day/Grade 5).

Twin Rivers Jet (1981) Ltd
PO Box 55
Queenstown
Owners: Geoff Stevens & David Black
Telephones: (0294) 29-747/ 29-347/ 28-641

Experience the excitement and thrills of superb jet boating in the shallows of the Shotover River and the unsurpassed scenery of the Kawarau River – both offering a real experience! The jet-boat trip takes about fifty minutes, both rivers on one trip and real value for money. Courtesy transport is provided from Queenstown to the jetty and return. Allow one and a half hours in total. Light spray jackets and safety equipment are provided. Essential that you wear warm clothing, and bring your camera. Suitable for ages 5 to 75 years, this sport is fun for all and at its best on these great rivers, in the country where the Hamilton Jet was invented. From $38.50 (adult), $22 (child). Group discounts available for 16 or more. Short trip: $27.50 (adult), $16.50 (child).

Whitewater rafting.
(Andris Apse Ltd)

River Adventures

Since 1970 these professionals have shared the stunning Southern Lakes back country with travellers, offering a variety of rafting and adventure trips. Experience the matchless excitement of rafting the white-water of the historic Shotover River or renowned Landsborough. Trips: 3-, 4- and 6-hour trips; overnighters; up to 5-day extravaganzas (including helicopter/camping). Great tramping trips available. All are guided, protective/safety equipment supplied. Costs on enquiry.

Danes Back Country
The Original Rafting Co.
Cnr Camp and Shotover Streets
PO Box 230
Queenstown
Telephone: (0294) 27-318/9
Telex: NZ5678
Owner: Dale Gardiner

Highlight your Wanaka trip with an hour's jet-boat ride – crossing the lake and pausing at Ruby Island en route. Then down the mighty Clutha River, haunt of many large trout, clear water and magnificent scenery. The trip is a scenic one rather than an adrenalin-charge, and fun for the entire family. On the return trip take the opportunity to drive the boat (conditions permitting). Special trips arranged on request – explore the Matukituki River (water levels permitting), take a full-day trip (Robert organises lunch and drinks), or go camping in splendid isolation – camping equipment available. Great fishing is available, Robert supplies trolling gear – you catch your dinner as you enjoy one of the country's loveliest lakes. Life jackets supplied. Wear sensible footwear, weatherproof/warm clothing plus sunglasses. Bookings required. From $30 (adult) $15 (child) GST inclusive. Minimum total fare required of $60 for trip.

Alpine Safaris
PO Box 242
Wanaka
Telephone: (02943) 8446
Host: Robert Murie

Value Tours
Queenstown Ltd
37 Camp Street
PO Box 53
Queenstown
Telephone: (0294) 27-340
Telex: NZ5429
Managers: John Hamilton
& Geoff Hunt

One of the South Island's most experienced rafting companies specialising in river-running tours from half-day to three days duration. A variety of rivers include the LANDSBOROUGH, a premier rafting river – three-day wilderness expedition; the spectacular SHOTOVER with it's 'Tunnel' run, and the big-volume KAWARAU. The company's guides are registered professional boatmen, who return year after year to be part of this experienced team. Tours depart from central Queenstown with all transport provided. Wetsuits, booties and all safety gear supplied. You require a swimsuit or similar, a towel and warm clothing. SHOTOVER and KAWARAU trips depart year around, minimum age 13. The LANDSBOROUGH departs Fridays, October through March, minimum age 15. Book through N.Z.T.P, travel agent or direct. Costs depending on trip. Group and Y.H.A. discounts apply.

Heli Jet Adventures Ltd
PO Box 338
Queenstown
Telephone: (0294) 29-355/ 29-709/23-012
Owner: Ross Marett

Ready for real river excitement? This company combines it all. Go jet boating in a Hamilton Jet down the scenic Kawarau River, or experience the double excitement of vertical helicopter flight in a famous Bell Jet ranger with the thrill of jet boating! Board the 'chopper' at Frankton, whisk past the beautiful Remarkables and skim the surface of the Kawarau River, landing on the riverbank. From here you meet the river at high speed, head-on in the jet boat, and still have a return flight to look forward to. Now if that isn't enough, take the Triple Trip: heli-jetting, and then into wet suits for a white-water rafting thrill. Courtesy coach provided from Queenstown. Protective weather/safety gear provided, but bring a change of warm clothing. Operates year through. All ages enjoy heli-jetting but Triple Trip not suitable for under-15 year olds. From $65 to $110 depending on trip. Book at any travel agent or direct.

SEE ALSO:

Outback Safaris: Danes Back Country (Queenstown).
Tramping: Hollyford Valley Walk (Te Anau).
Flightseeing: Heli Jet Adventures (Queenstown).
Lodges: Riverview (Athol).
Regional:
Volcanic Plateau: Tongariro Outdoor Adventure Centre (Turangi).
Wellington: Rangitikei River Adventures (Mangaweka).
Westland: Haast Motor Camp.

OTHER REFERENCES:

Rafting:

River Rats Rafting Co., PO Box 33-809, Auckland 9.

Aotearoa Adventures, RD1, Whitianga.

NZ River Runners, PO Box 877, Rotorua.

Rough Rider Rafting, PO Box 2392, Rotorua.

Wilderness Voyages, PO Box 580, Rotorua.

Rafting Unlimited (NZ), PO Box 1080, Tauranga.

Plateau Guides Ltd, PO Box 29, National Park.

Kaimanawa Tours & Treks, PO Box 321, Taupo.

Selecta Tours, PO Box 761, Taupo.

Turangi White Water Rafting, 244 Taupehi Road, Turangi.

Sun City Raft Tours, PO Box 216, Motueka.

Rakaia River Raft Company, PO Box 350, Christchurch.

Cycling

Many cyclists believe New Zealand to be one of the best countries for this sport. Road surfaces are good to excellent and traffic ranges from light to very light. New Zealand drivers, while not the world's most courteous, are aware of cyclists. Care is needed in cities and areas of traffic density. The cyclist needs to observe the rules of the road carefully.

Whilst New Zealand is known as a mountainous country, it is usually possible to skirt the mountains, enjoying their majesty from a distance. You can organise your routes so that in the North Island, everything that you cycle is under 1,000 feet (305 metres); in the South Island, you don't need to climb over 2,000 feet (610 metres). The cycling remains within the range of the average recreational cyclist.

The South Island offers rather more challenge to the cyclist than does the North Island. Even so, it remains within the capabilities of people of reasonable fitness; it is unnecessary to be an experienced cyclist to enjoy a cycling holiday in New Zealand. If you like, join a bicycle tour and have a support van available to give you a ride, should you need it! These vans also transport your luggage and equipment.

New Zealand-wide, van-supported cycle tours, with a variety of routes, giving maximum cycling and scenic enjoyment. The company's extensive experience ensures a trouble-free holiday. Tours start in main centres and towns (connecting transport arranged as required). Bring sleeping bag and personal effects. Top-line bikes are supplied, as are meals and accommodation en route. Tours operate October through May; suitable for all, reasonable fitness preferable. From $800 (6 days, GST inclusive).

The Bicycle Touring Company
6A Joval Place,
Manukau City
PO Box 23-215
Auckland 6
Telephone: (09) 278-9387
Telex: NZ63139 PRPARTS

OTHER REFERENCES:

New Zealand Pedaltours, PO Box 49039, Auckland.

Tararua Outdoor Recreation, Gorge Road RD, Otaki.

Cross-Country Rentals, PO Box 6003, Christchurch.

Rent-a-Bike NZ Ltd, 82 Worcester Street, Christchurch.

Canoeing:

Venturetreks Ltd, PO Box 37-610, Auckland 1.

Outdoor Pursuits Centre, Private Bag, Turangi.

Kahutara Canoes, RD1, Featherston.

Tararua Outdoor Recreation, Gorge Road RD, Otaki.

Canoe Safaris (NZ) Ltd, 678 Tremaine Street, Palmerston North.

Baldwin Canoe Adventures, PO Box 198, Wanganui.

Canoe Safaris, PO Box 467, Queenstown.

Jet Boating:

King Country Safaris, PO Box 37, Te Kuiti.

Aniwhenua Jet Boat Tours, PO Box 626, Whakatane.

Viking Safaris, PO Box 81, Dannevirke.

Pipiriki Jet Boat Tours, RD6, Wanganui.

Bell Waimakiriri Services, Main North Road, Kaiapoi, Christchurch.

Waiau Gorge Jets, 41 Woodbank Road, Hamner Springs.

Trail Blazer Safaris, 11 CRD, Oamaru.

Kawarau Jet Service, PO Box 168, Queenstown.

Rapid Travel Jet, 42 Moana Crescent, Te Anau.

Waitemata Harbour, Auckland. *(Courtesy Air New Zealand)*

With thousands of kilometres of coastline indented with bays, coves and harbours, and dotted with islands, taking to the sea is second nature for New Zealanders.

It has been estimated that there is one boat for every 15 people in the country and some 'boaties' consider that estimate to be very conservative.

For visitors this national obsession means there will be plenty of opportunities to get off dry land and experience the country from the sea. Make friends with a local (that's not difficult) and the chances are you will be invited out in his boat. New Zealanders love the sea and love to introduce others to the delights of their coastline.

Charter boating began in a small way around 1975, long after charter cruising was well established in centres such as the Greek Islands and the Caribbean. It is still low key, remaining a personal, friendly operation. The people in the charter-boat business are there because they love sailing – they have turned their passion for the sea into their livelihood.

Operators find overseas visitors like to be treated as guests rather than tourists. Get away on a luxury keeler and it will probably be crewed by the owner and his regular crew, not owned and operated by a large, impersonal company. Even the largest bare-boating company has a fleet of about 20 boats, compared with 150 or so in Mediterranean operations.

For sail-yourself holidays, otherwise known as bare-boating, you and your friends or family are the skipper and crew but everything else, right down to the can opener, is supplied.

Yachts larger than 12 metres (40 feet) are usually available only with skipper and crew – understandably owners are reluctant to commit a $250,000 luxury yacht for bare-boat cruising. But the skipper will certainly be an experienced blue-water sailor who will know how to make the very most of your cruise.

Smaller yachts can also be hired with a crew – splendid for those who lack the experience to take the helm themselves. It is also possible to have a skipper aboard to teach the necessary skills until you feel ready to take over yourself.

Flotilla sailing is another variation, a compromise that allows bare-boats to sail themselves under the guidance of a lead ship and so explore far from the home port, cruising around isolated offshore islands..

Cruising New Zealand is not coconut palms and tropical heat. The summer temperatures are similar to the northern Mediterranean, with pleasantly hot days and warm evenings. New Zealand's east-coast sailing grounds reveal mile after mile of fine golden sand, unspoiled wooded islands and thousands of nautical square miles of unpolluted cruising water.

Sail away in the Bay of Islands, the best known area for bare-boating, and you can wend your way around 522 kilometres (365 miles) of coastline and 144 islands in the broad, sheltered bay, relax on tree-shaded sandy beaches with not a soul in sight and feast on the fish you have caught. And all for around the same price as a hotel room.

Other charter centres include Auckland's Hauraki Gulf with 1,200 nautical square miles of cruising and 100 islands, Lake Taupo where you can sail off to a deserted bay and fish for rainbow trout, and the Marlborough Sounds, deep bush-fringed sheltered waters at the northern end of the South Island.

Charter sailing is only one of many cruising opportunities – there are boating variations to suit anyone's taste, time and pocket.

Day cruises and sundowner cruises on board large skippered yachts give a taste of the sea for those on a tight time schedule.

Sailing and cruising

There are holidays afloat on less conventional craft such as an old kauri schooner that takes passengers island hopping in the Hauraki Gulf. The comforts are not up-market but the cruise is great fun. At the other end of the sophistication scale are luxury motor-launch holidays that pamper guests while they sightsee, sunbathe or try deep-sea fishing.

Sightseeing launch trips operate from almost every town with wharf access to sea or lake. Some offer chicken and champagne lunches aboard or picnic barbecues on beaches.

The best-known sightseeing cruise is probably the Bay of Islands' Cream Trip, delivering mail and supplies to outlying islands and following a route once taken by launches collecting cream from island dairy farms.

The many others include: harbour launch cruises and casual ferry-boat rides from Auckland to nearby islands; regular summer launch trips from Tauranga to Mayor Island, place best known for the adjacent deep-sea fishing, but also an unspoilt, bush-covered island that hides two volcanic lakes and masses of native birds; and excursions through the deep, almost roadless sounds that form the coast at the northern end of the South Island.

Take a launch trip along the coast of Abel Tasman National Park, with granite cliffs, sandy bays and bush-covered islands. Or combine a launch trip there with a guided trek along the shore.

Down in the deep south the lakes abound with boat trips. There's a one-day excursion on Lake Wakatipu aboard an old-time lake steamer that calls in at an isolated sheep station. At Lake Te Anau you glide through glow-worm caves in a small boat. At Lake Manapouri, a deep, dark lake of brooding beauty, a launch trip down the lake links with another down a spectacular fiord.

Spend several days at Doubtful Sound, living on board a cruising launch, amid the majesty of the remote fiords, and discover the history of Cook's visit and the tragic lives of later settlers.

No matter where you are in New Zealand the sea or lakes are not far away, whether you want to spend an hour or two or a week or two afloat.

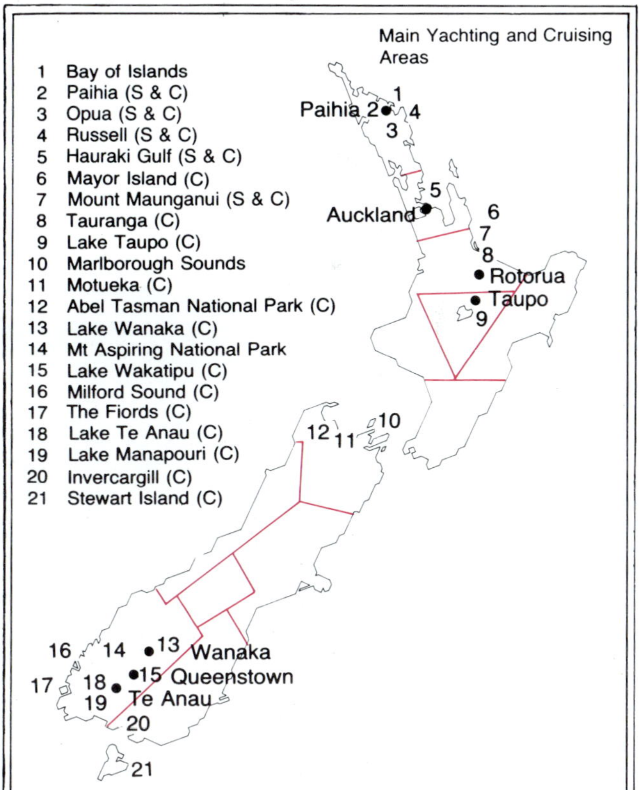

Seclusion in the Bay of Islands. *(Courtesy Rainbow Yacht Charters)*

With a splendid cruising area from the Bay of Islands to Whangaroa, some 900 kilometres (559 miles) of secluded bays, islands and inlets, are yours to explore. Rainbow offers the largest fleet of yachts and motor cruisers in the country. Your alternatives:
INDEPENDENT BAREBOATING: From 7.7-metre to 12-metre range of yachts, 9- and 11-metre motor cruisers; accommodating 4-6 persons. Boating experience required by at least one person. Boats are fully equipped for overnight cruising. From $130 per day (6-metre sail), $270 per day (9-metre cruiser).
CREWED AND SKIPPERED CHARTER: 'Shalimar', 14-metre centre cockpit cutter, offers luxury – two private double or twin cabins accommodating up to six guests (crew quarters are separate). A fast and beautiful ocean-going yacht. From $180 per person, per day. All food, wine, skipper and crew supplied. Prices all-inclusive.

Rainbow Yacht Charters
C/- Post Office
Opua
Bay of Islands
Telephone: (0885) 27-821
or Auckland (09) 389-419

Explore the myriad of beautiful islands and bays in the Hauraki Gulf Maritime Park aboard one of Rainbow's fleet of yachts or launches, from the gateway city of Auckland. For bareboat or skippered charters, bring friends or family and enjoy fishing or just relaxing in the splendid isolation of deserted beaches and bays or visiting shore-side restaurants and bars. Providoring by request. Contact Rainbow for your complete boating holiday requirements.

Rainbow Charters
PO Box 8327
Symonds Street
Auckland
Telephone: (09) 389-419
North America (800) 722-2288, (800) 227-5317

Sail your dreams! Cruise the waters, visiting the islands of the truly magnificent Hauraki Gulf Maritime Park – a national treasure covering some 1,500 sq. nautical miles. Adventure or tranquility, the choice is yours, aboard a modern sailing yacht or launch. Government-approved vessels range from 20 to 42 feet (6 to 13 metres). Cruise under your own command or with a qualified, friendly skipper. On-going holiday options are available for this experience of a lifetime! Costs on enquiry.

South Seas Yacht Charter Ltd
PO Box 38-366
Howick, Auckland
Telephone: 534-2001
Cables: MARCONSULT-NZ
Hosts: Brian & Vivienne Whiteman

Totaranui Beach, Abel Tasman National Park, Nelson.
(Andris Apse Ltd)

Sailing and cruising

A superb sailing experience awaits you on a luxury 52-foot (16-metre) cruising yacht, skippered by a qualified master. Specialising in a personalised service to small parties, John provides everything, and will be delighted to discuss requirements, suitable itinerary, catering, etc. Carillion is available for special occasions including film-making – offering luxury accommodation in separate cabins for overnight cruising, taking additional guests (up to 10) for single day excursions. Cost on enquiry. Other bareboat charters available.

Carillion Yacht Charters
PO Box 31-114
Auckland
Telephone: (09) 397-633/ 500-503
Host: John Hare

SAILING HOLIDAYS, for the cruise of a lifetime on your own skippered, ocean-going yacht in the famous Hauraki Gulf, Bay of Islands and coast, amongst a myriad of islands and bays – sailing, sightseeing, shore adventures, sports fishing, swimming, diving and relaxing. Anne and John know these waters intimately. Three days and over from $150 (per day/guest). Includes first-class meals with wine. Private cabins; bring only personal effects. Major credit cards accepted.

Sailing Holidays
Anderson Road
R.D.1
Kaukapakapa
Auckland
Telex: NZ2901 POLAND SEEK
Hosts: Anne and John Poland

High safety standards and a wealth of experience, plus a fun-loving skipper and hostess; ensure that your sailing holiday will be an unforgettable experience! A personal, friendly service caters to your requirements, from collection from motel or airport to meals. Bring a positive mental attitude and a pair of soft-soled shoes, plus personal effects. Whether a scheduled day cruise meeting new friends, an overnight cruise, or a private charter, Jane and Ian guarantee you a wonderful time with the invitation to add your name to the long list of delighted 'sailors' in their visitor's book! 'Seika' is a fast, sensitive ocean-cruising yacht, featuring roomy accommodation, sophisticated stereo system and hot shower! Learn sailing tips as you go or simply relax. Overnight from $125 (per day/person), Day Charter from $660 (12 persons) and lunch. Alcohol catered additionally.

Seika Charters Ltd
15 Marina Heights
Bucklands Beach
Auckland 5
Telephone: (09) 577-405/ 573-529
After hours: (09) 534-5031
Facsimile: (09) 577-936
Hosts: Jane and Ian Walker

Charter Link New Zealand
Auckland – Marlborough Sounds
Queenstown – Bay of Islands

Charter Link New Zealand offers the widest range of charter boats available in the country, throughout prime cruising areas, in national maritime parks environs, where cared-for wilderness and unspoiled waters are yours to enjoy. Charter Link has the involvement of established charter professionals, priding themselves on their personal flexible service and modern well-maintained vessels. All requirements catered to; tuition available as part of cruise and learn option. This service is fully guaranteed.

Charter Link New Zealand – Bay of Islands
(Freedom Yacht Charters)
Matauwhi Road
PO Box 34, Russell
Telephone: (0885) 37-781
USA: (800) 262-8872
Telex: NZ2583

Sail yourself or retain a skipper and cruise the famous Bay of Islands, living and sailing on a modern, fully equipped cruising yacht. Enjoy the freedom, the fishing, the beaches and clear water of the bay, for as little as $150 per person per week! Adventure holiday or sedate family sail – the choice is yours. Everything supplied except food. From $665 per week (off-season rate) for five-berth Bonito 22.

Charter Link New Zealand – Auckland
PO Box 82-111,
Highland Park
Auckland
Telephone: (09) 535-8710
Telex: NZ21057 INTCOM CFYC
Facsimile: (09) 792-103
Hosts: Elizabeth & Russell McClue

'Let us suit your dreams' – cruise Auckland's beautiful Hauraki Gulf; over 1,500 nautical square miles of sailing encompassing over 60 islands with safe anchorages, beautiful beaches, park walks to explore, unspoiled native flora and fauna and historical sites. Enjoy our clean, modern, well-maintained and appointed vessels and services of our caring personnel. Bareboat or skippered charters on yachts/launches. All types of catering. Also exciting coastal cruising on fully crewed, blue-water vessels.

Charter Link New Zealand – Marlborough Sounds
PO Box 246,
Picton
Telephone: (057) 36-591
Telex: CPO NZ3470
Hosts: Millie Pickering, Gavin Taylor, Gaynor Boese

The Marlborough Sounds offer scenic beauty unsurpassed. Historic sites, fishing, diving and boating, barbeques on the beach, peace and tranquillity; for a perfect holiday on the water. The 1,475 kilometres (885 miles) of coastline with sheltered bays, licensed lodges, hotels, homestays, food and fuel supplies for your convenience. Tramp the native forest tracks, dive for scallops or crayfish, explore sunken wrecks. Cruise the Marlborough Sounds – New Zealand's best kept secret!

Charter Link New Zealand – Queenstown
PO Box 1669, Dunedin
Telephone: (024) 741-109
Telex: NZ5406 REMPAR
Facsimile: (024) 772-948
Host: Mike Holloway

The shining beauty of New Zealand's mountain lakes provide some of the finest sailing and recreational experiences available worldwide today. The Queenstown and Wanaka resorts border famous lakes, offering miles of sailing adventure challenge and excitement, and there are three other lakes to choose from as well! Charter Link Queenstown will take you to this area of absolute splendour – enabling you to experience what the rest of the world only dreams of.

Fiordland Cruises Ltd
C/- Post Office
Manapouri
Telephone: (02296) 609
Owners: Cliff and Irene Barnes

Until recently, only the fit or fanatical could penetrate Fiordland's rugged bush, deep glacial fiords, towering snow-capped mountains and spectacular waterfalls. Now you can explore this awesome beauty and isolation, on 2- and 6-day cruises – learning early history in fiords where Captain Cook anchored, seeing natural wonders and animal life. Cliff knows the area thoroughly. Or simply relax or go tramping, deerstalking, fishing and beachcombing. Enjoy the comfort and camaraderie of a motel afloat, with four two-berth cabins, dining/living area, flush toilet and shower. Everything is provided, even rifle permits. All you require is warm and comfortable clothing, waterproof coat/footwear and camera. Dining and private charters a speciality. Cruises depart regularly during summer season and by arrangement remainder of year. From $273 to $1145 plus special rates.

Sailing and cruising

SEE ALSO:

Tramping: Abel Tasman National Park Enterprises (Motueka).
Regional:
Northland: Whangaroa Harbour Cruises, Fullers Northland (Paihia).
Auckland: Fullers Auckland.
Bay of Plenty: Delta Tours (Hamilton).
Otago: Southern Air (Invercargill/Stewart Island).

OTHER REFERENCES:

Bay of Islands Yacht Charter, PO Box 51, Okaihau.

A Place in the Sun, PO Box 78, Russell.

Te Aroha Great Adventure Cruise, PO Box 338, Auckland.

Auckland Harbour Cruise Co., PO Box 3730, Auckland.

Mercury Bay Yacht Charters, PO Box 80, Whitianga.

NZ Yacht Charters, PO Box 2360, Tauranga.

Challenge Charters, PO Box 1251, Taupo.

Sunset Yacht Charters, PO Box 294, Taupo.

Kaimanawa Tours & Treks, PO Box 321, Taupo.

Taupo Lake Adventures, PO Box 5, Taupo.

Nelson Charter Yachts, PO Box 874, Nelson.

Marlborough Sounds Charters, PO Box 284, Picton.

Benmore Charter Services, PO Box 4, Otematata.

Southsail Yacht, PO Box 1669, Dunedin.

Air Safari's flightseeing the Grand Traverse in the Southern Alps. *(Andris Apse Ltd)*

Take to the air and the contrasting landscapes of New Zealand can be seen at their very best – snow-covered mountains, grassy plains, arid semi-desert, thick rain forest, steaming volcanoes or tranquil lakes. Some flights can encompass all of that in less than two hours.

There is flight-seeing from airports, large and small, all over the country. From lakes and bays you may take a novel flight-seeing trip in an amphibian, taking off and landing in a flurry of water.

Fly over islands in the Bay of Islands and the Hauraki Gulf or over the active, steaming volcano, White Island. Fly to deserted bays on small islands, into long sheltered harbours, onto the dark, deep waters of fiords far away from roads. Fly over forests and mountains to land on high, remote lakes.

Or fly direct to lake or beach resort and land almost at the doorstep of your hotel – amphibians land on floats and then trundle up the beach on wheels.

In South Island mountain country small planes take off from airfields to land, with outsize skis, on snowfields and glaciers – a unique style of transport for sightseers and skiers. You don't simply fly over the mountains, you fly among them, at times breathtakingly close. Remind yourself ski planes have been making these mountain tours for more than 25 years.

From the North Island town of Rotorua, fly over the moonscape colours of the steaming thermal areas, over lakes and forests, the Tongariro mountains and the barren dark Rangipo Desert, on an excursion that takes only 90 minutes.

Use small aircraft, float planes, ski planes and helicopters not just for spectacular sight-seeing but as a fast way in to an adventure holiday – hunting, fishing, trekking, rafting, jet boating and skiing.

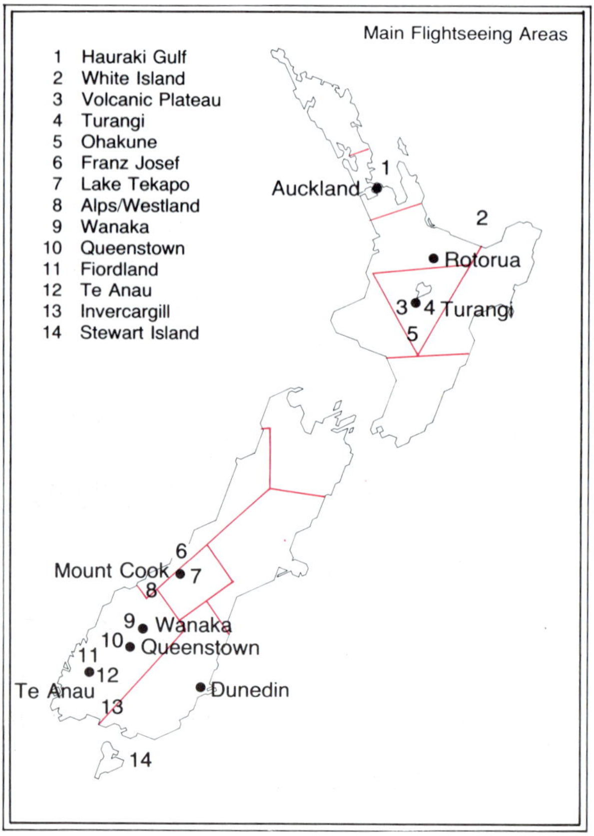

For flights that take you exactly where you want to go, when you want to go, charter your own plane and pilot, whether on a short trip to a fishing spot or a country-long tour from Kerikeri to Queenstown.

It's possible to charter an aircraft even in out-of-the-way places, as small towns often have an airstrip and aero club. Club members are hobby pilots, but many clubs also run charter services with licensed commercial pilots and have planes for hire for those qualified to fly themselves.

Naturally, each club has regulations governing the use of its hired aircraft, which limit the scope of private pilots wishing to fly over unknown territory – the club wants its planes back in one piece. But for those who meet the New Zealand requirements, fly-yourself excursions are a great possibility.

Flying schools are often attached to aero clubs. Take a cheap trial lesson and find out if flying is the hobby skill for you.

Gliding clubs also operate from club fields, for example, the excellent facilities at the Matamata field, and Omarama in the Mount Cook Ski Region.

Flightseeing

If you want to take to the air in the simplest fashion, floating on the winds with a hang-glider, New Zealand is an ideal place to try. With its open countryside, cliffs, hills and mountains and sea-borne breezes, it is not difficult to discover the perfect hang-gliding conditions.

Flight historians now believe that a New Zealander, Richard Pearse, was probably the first man to fly, taking to the air on his back-country farm several months before the Wright brothers. (See a replica of his machine in Auckland's Museum of Transport and Technology.)

See and do more by air! More sights, destinations, fishing, lakes, rivers – more of everything beautiful – in and around Rotorua. Take off and land on water; circle active volcanoes; go trout fishing on lakes inaccessible by road. Combine float plane/jet boat trip for the thrill of a lifetime. Sightsee Rotorua, take fly/fishing excursions (plus guide/equipment); fly/lunch excursions on Rotorua's lakes. Operates year round and fun for all. From $27 (10-minute flight).

Floatplanes of Rotorua
Downtown Lakefront
PO Box 640
Rotorua
Telephone: (073) 84-069
89-984

This service offers a variety of scenic flights through the wonders of the Volcanic Plateau, starting from a ten minute joyride around the southern shores of Lake Taupo, the world-famous Tongariro River and Turangi township, through to two fifty minute flights – one taking in the many colourful volcanic lakes, National Parks, extinct craters, the continuously active Mts Tongariro, Ngaruahoe and Ruapehu – and more. The second flight covers Lake Taupo, Taupo township, the Waikato River (longest river in New Zealand), beautiful Huka Falls, the steaming Wairakei Thermal Region. Flights are also available into the beautiful Kaimanawa Forest Park (for hunters, fishermen and trampers). Operates year through. Courtesy transport from Turangi township available. From $10 to $120 per hour. Book direct or through Government Tourist Bureau.

Turangi Scenic Flights
PO Box 260
Turangi
Telephones: (0746)
7870
Hosts: Cam and Kris
Shepherd

Hover over the craters of Mount Tarawera, which erupted less than one hundred years ago, the sparkling Blue and Green Lakes, the incredible Waimangu Thermal Region, and many more highlights of this spectacular area – from the armchair comfort of a Bell Jet Ranger helicopter. Full in-flight commentary is given through complimentary headsets. Charters, photographic and special-interest flights arranged by request. From $20 per seat.

The Helicopter Line
PO Box 631
Rotorua
Telephone: (073) 59-477
or 479-810

Bring camera and extra film for the sheer grandeur of the 'Grand Traverse' scenic flight around Mount Cook's massive ice and snow fields, through the Main Divide to the West Coast and the Franz Josef, Fox and Balfour Glaciers. Fifty breathtaking minutes of flight through spectacular alpine scenery. Hourly departures daily from Lake Tekapo and Glentanner Park subject to weather, in modern 7- to 15-seater aircraft. From $85 (adult), $50 (child).

Air Safaris and Services
(NZ) Ltd
PO Box 21
Lake Tekapo
Telephone: (05056) 880
or Mt Cook (05621) 855

This company offers the greatest New Zealand flightseeing experience, passing over the superb mountains and glacier regions of the Southern Alps. From Wanaka, fly direct to Milford Sound to connect with the launch cruises down the fiord or choose your trip from a wide variety of scenic alpine flights including Mount Cook and Mount Aspiring, year around, weather permitting. From (adult) $90 (child) $60 for 45 unforgettable minutes. Book direct or through Wanaka Information Centre (7277).

Aspiring Air (1981) Ltd
PO Box 68
Wanaka
Telephone: (02943) 7942
or (02943) 7943
Afters hours (02943) 8054

Southern Lakes Helicopters Ltd
PO Box 156
Te Anau
Telephone: (0229) 7167/7067/7467
Owners: Richard & Janey Hayes

Take off in a helicopter – circle world-famous Mitre Peak and plummeting Sutherland Falls – step onto massive glaciers or snow for champagne breakfasts/picnics! Fly in/walk out (Milford/Kepler tracks – when open); take a hunting/fishing safari flight to remote regions for wapiti, red or whitetail deer, or rainbow trout! Go heli-skiing through untouched powder snow with qualified guide. Maximise your time – access rugged Fiordland easily. From $50 (scenic flight), charters on enquiry.

Southern Air Ltd
(Invercargill Airport)
PO Box 860
Invercargill
Telephone: (021) 89-129

Links Otago and Southland with beautiful Stewart Island less than 20 minutes away from Invercargill by air. Stewart Island is an historic fishing community, set in an environment offering wonderful flora and fauna. Amid breathtaking scenery, tramp, fish, hunt, scuba dive, swim and sightsee. Return flights daily to Stewart Island from Invercargill.

Flightseeing, White Island, Bay of Plenty. (Courtesy The Helicopter Line)

SEE ALSO:

Outback Safaris: Danes Back Country (Queenstown).
River Adventures: Silverpeaks Tours (Dunedin).
Tramping: Hollyford Valley Walk (Te Anau).
Regional:
Auckland: Sea Bee Air (Auckland).
Mt Cook: Lake Ohau Lodge.
Volcanic Plateau: Taupo Air Services.
Westland: Alpine Guides Westland (Fox Glacier).
Otago: Southern Air (Invercargill).

OTHER REFERENCES:

Great Barrier Airlines, Domestic Terminal, Airport, Auckland.

Marine Helicopters, PO Box 257, Papakura, Auckland.

Mercury Airlines, PO Box 44, Whitianga.

Air Hamilton, Airport Terminal, Hamilton.

White Island Airways, PO Box 7118, Te Ngae, Rotorua.

The Helicopter Line, PO Box 631, Rotorua.

Manawatu District Aero Club, PO Box 9004, Palmerston North.

Associated Air, PO Box 1594, Paraparaumu.

Capital Helicopters, PO Box 21025, Wellington.

Float Air, PO Box 7, Picton.

Glacier Helicopters, PO Box 33, Fox Glacier.

Garden City Helicopters, PO Box 14147, Christchurch.

Alpine Guides (Mt Cook) Ltd, PO Box 20, Mount Cook.

Air Wakatipu, PO Box 194, Queenstown.

Southland Air Charter, PO Box 1171, Invercargill.

Diving at the Poor Knights, Northland.
(Courtesy Sportsways Aqualung Centre)

New Zealand is surrounded by sea, has an irregular, indented coastline and many islands. Put it all together and you have one of the longest coastlines of any country in the world.

The country stretches through latitudes from subtropical to subantarctic, offering a range of diving experiences that includes discovering huge sponges and lacy corals in the surreal underwater world of the Poor Knights in the north and cavorting with seals in the south.

Visiting divers enthuse about the clarity of the unpolluted waters and the variety and abundance of marine life.

Diving in New Zealand can be separated into game diving for lobsters, clams and fish, which takes place all around the country, and adventure diving, of interest to overseas divers in search of excitement.

Top of any list is the Bay of Islands and Poor Knights, a marine reserve with over 50 diving spots and served by a large fleet of dive boats. The water here is sharply clear and alive with subtropical and tropical fish such as groper, parrotfish, red pigfish, yellowbanded perch, Sandager's wrasse, stingrays, sunfish, conger eels, dolphins and all kinds of sharks. Less mobile sights include black coral trees, brightly coloured sponges and gorgonian fans. An added novelty is fish so friendly they hang around to be handfed by divers.

The diving opportunities at the Poor Knights are both strange and spectacular. You can see a mix of tropical and subtropical fish, kelp and coral side by side, rocky cliffs that continue below the surface, underwater tunnels, pinnacles and archways of giant proportions.

The Poor Knights are special and spectacular, but there are many other diving excitements. There's the magnificent Whangaroa Harbour where giant crayfish are common and sharks rare; the Cavalli Islands where subtropical species include bluefish, goldribbon groper, bonito and flying fish; Cape Brett with rugged, varied terrain – reefs, guts, canyons – and sea life ranging from tiny reef fish to marlin and bronze whaler sharks.

From Tutukaka, a whole coast of diving opens up. Boats leave from here for the Poor Knights, but the long mainland coast also offers excellent diving. For a diving fanatic, Tutukaka makes a good base.

Within easy distance of Auckland by car is the village of Leigh, the take-off point for dive boats heading to the Mokohinau Islands, where the flora is similar to that of the Poor Knights, and monster crayfish, kingfish and groper can be found.

Preparing to dive, Bay of Islands. ***(Courtesy Paihia Dive Hire and Charter)***

Right by Leigh is a marine reserve and research area around Goat Island. Marine life here is fully protected but recreational divers are allowed ready access and the result is a remarkable experience – crowds of fish that show no fear and flock after divers to be hand fed. Blue cod, maomao, leatherjacket, kelpfish and snapper all cluster around.

The rocky headlands, deep inlets and islands of the east coast of Northland, and the warmer waters (20 – 22°C), make the area a main attraction for adventure divers. As one goes south the water temperature drops – by almost 15°C – and the emphasis is more on game diving.

Boats from Whitianga and Tairua on the Coromandel Peninsula give access to the peninsula's east coast and many islands. The wild terrain that waits under water – steep cliffs, sharp pinnacles, reefs and caves – echoes the wild terrain of the land above. The species of fish and flora are just as varied, from scallops to marlin, black coral and sunfish.

The Bay of Plenty lives up to its name for divers with boats leaving from Tauranga, Mount Maunganui and Whakatane.

The main destination from the first two ports is Mayor Island, long known for deep-sea fishing. As the tip of a dormant volcano, Mayor Island provides an undersea world of rugged, unpredictable terrain that attracts plenty of marine life. As well as common fish such as snapper, yellowtail kingfish and John Dory, there are demoiselles, bonito, sponges and corals.

Kapiti Island, within easy reach of Wellington is washed by warm currents and is an attraction for divers. The island's underwater reefs, rocks and caves attract an extraordinary range of fish from the ubiquitous snapper through to skipjack tuna, albacore, dolphins, orca and sharks.

In the South Island the deeply indented Marlborough Sounds produce over 100 kilometres (60 miles) of coastline, most of it inaccessible except by sea and most of it attracting a marvellous variety of sea life – shipwrecks and scallops are specialities.

The Otago Peninsula is one of the best areas for diving in colder waters, with common southern fish such as butterfish, red cod, blue cod and moki. Here too are kelp forests and the chance to watch seals underwater. It is also an area frequented by white pointer sharks, an advantage or disadvantage depending on how you care to view a chance encounter.

Compared with some popular diving spots in other countries, sharks are a minor danger. Says one keen diver: 'Shark attack is about as likely as being hit by lightning down there. It is the least of our worries.'

Diving in New Zealand is a year-round sport, although summer is the most popular time. Wet suits are essential for winter diving and are usually worn at all times of the year. Bring your own gear for a diving holiday or hire equipment from well-stocked local suppliers. You will find excellent dive shops in all main cities and on popular diving coasts, and also plenty of air-filling stations.

The best diving season is January through to May; from October to December a heavy plankton bloom turns the water a milky green.

With marine life that includes tropical, subtropical, temperate and subantarctic species, there is a lot of diving waiting in New Zealand waters.

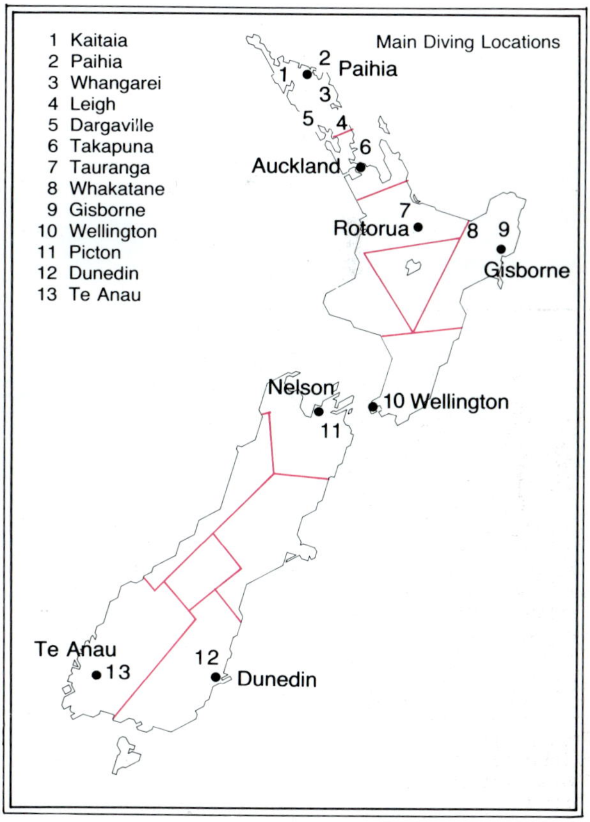

Baker Marine Charters
PO Box 504
Whakatane
Telephone: (076) 70-015
Host: John Baker

Experience spectacular, year-round diving around an active offshore island volcano, with excellent visibility and abundant fishlife. Featuring White Island, Whale and Motihi Islands plus an active underwater vent just 4 miles (6.4 km) from Whakatane! Live aboard 'Ma Cherie', a spacious 40 ft (12 metre) launch, accommodating eight comfortably, with private toilet facilities, hot shower and well-equipped galley. Dive equipment available on request. Dive on hourly/daily basis. From $700 per day.

SEE ALSO:

Cruising: Fiordland Cruises (Te Anau).

OTHER REFERENCES:

Paihia Dive Shop, PO Box 210, Paihia.
Tutukaka Charters Ltd, RD3, Whangarei.
Chris Neill, 7 Tahuna Pl, Onerahi, Whangarei.
Peter O'Brynne, 72 First View Avenue, Auckland 6.
Ron Blake, 69 Gladstone Road, Auckland 9.
Tauranga Dive Centre, PO Box 885, Tauranga.
Dianne & Ken Gulley, PO Box 34, Havelock.
Southern Marine Charters, PO Box 246, Picton.
Gem Resort, PO Box 85, Picton.
Fiordland Cruises, C/- Post Office, Manapouri.
Southern Charter & Marine, PO Box 176, Bluff.

Fish schooling, Poor Knights, Northland. *(Courtesy Sportsways Aqualung Centre)*

Wherever you are, in city, town or village, there is a golf course nearby. New Zealand has over 400 golf courses – more per head of population than any other country in the world.

Auckland has 17 courses within easy reach of the city, Christchurch has 12.

And the courses, like the rest of the country, are seldom crowded. Only at peak times are popular courses under pressure and golf, in New Zealand's equable climate, is a year-round sport.

The courses are as varied as the country and the top courses are superb. There's Titirangi, in Auckland, designed 50 years ago by the famous Scot, Dr Alister McKenzie. Set amid large trees, Titirangi is a beautiful course that makes the most of the gently sloping countryside.

Wairakei is a course that Arnold Palmer said everyone should play and Peter Thomson described as the best in New Zealand. It is certainly exciting, and cleverly designed as a testing course for both advanced and average golfers. And it is a public course, with no club membership, open all the year round.

If you are planning an action-packed holiday, the Wairakei course is in the centre of the North Island, close to trout fishing, boating, trekking, rafting, hunting and the Ruapehu ski fields.

Other top courses include two near Wellington – Paraparaumu, an excellent championship course in the Scottish links tradition, and Heretaunga, an elegant course set in a parkland of streams and trees.

Selected Golf Courses

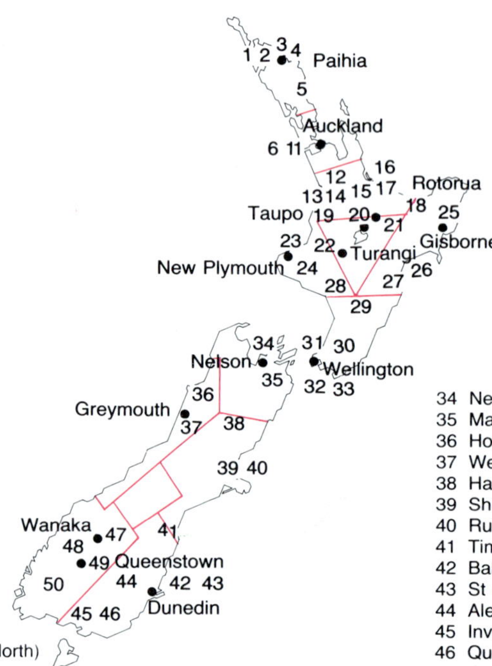

1 Ahipara
2 Kaikohe
3 Kerikeri
4 Waitangi
5 Whangarei
6 Chamberlain
7 Grange
8 Manukau
9 Muriwai
10 Remuera
11 Titirangi
12 Hamilton
13 Waitomo
14 Cambridge
15 Okoroire Springs
16 Mount Maunganui
17 Tauranga
18 Whakatane
19 Te Awamutu
20 Wairakei
21 Arikapakapa (Rotorua)
22 Chateau Tongariro
23 New Plymouth
24 Inglewood
25 Poverty Bay
26 Hastings
27 Napier
28 Wanganui
29 Manawatu (Palmerston North)
30 Masterton
31 Paraparaumu
32 Heretaunga (Wellington)
33 Miramar (Wellington)
34 Nelson
35 Marlborough (Blenheim)
36 Hokitika
37 Westport
38 Hamner Springs
39 Shirley (Christchurch)
40 Russley (Christchurch)
41 Timaru
42 Balmacewan (Dunedin)
43 St Clair (Dunedin)
44 Alexandra
45 Invercargill
46 Queens Park (Invercargill)
47 Wanaka
48 Queenstown
49 Arrowtown
50 Te Anau

Golf

Dunedin, a city settled by Scots, naturally has excellent golf courses – Balmacewn, founded by the Otago Golf Club in 1871, is a championship course with many fine holes; St Clair is a course set spectacularly amid pine woods on the coast.

Some good courses are renowned for their setting as much as for the golf they offer. At Waitangi play on a beautifully kept course in a historic area, looking out over the blue waters of the Bay of Islands. At Queenstown the setting is a knock-out, with a backdrop of spectacular mountains – jet-boat transport on the lake from town to course gives quick and novel access.

That's only nine golf courses – there are about 390 more, such as those at Ahipara or Muriwai on reclaimed sand dunes alongside pounding surf beaches, the pleasant course and rural charm at Kerikeri, the excellent Arikikapakapa course at Rotorua, with a background of thermal steam and geysers, the splendid Shirley course at Christchurch, the Miramar course right in the centre of Wellington.

Some courses are public, owned and maintained by the local town council, government tourist department or similar authority, with unrestricted access for anyone; others are club courses with private membership but these all have access for non-member golfers – the conditions vary with each club. Almost all welcome visitors. Some may limit visiting players to weekday golf, others simply charge non-members a higher green fee.

But wherever you play in New Zealand you will find green fees amazingly cheap by world standards — no more than a few dollars. A $5 fee might even include hire of a trundler (motorised carts are not used on New Zealand courses)

SEE ALSO:

Auckland: Chamberlain Golf Course.
Bay of Plenty: Wairakei International Golf Course.

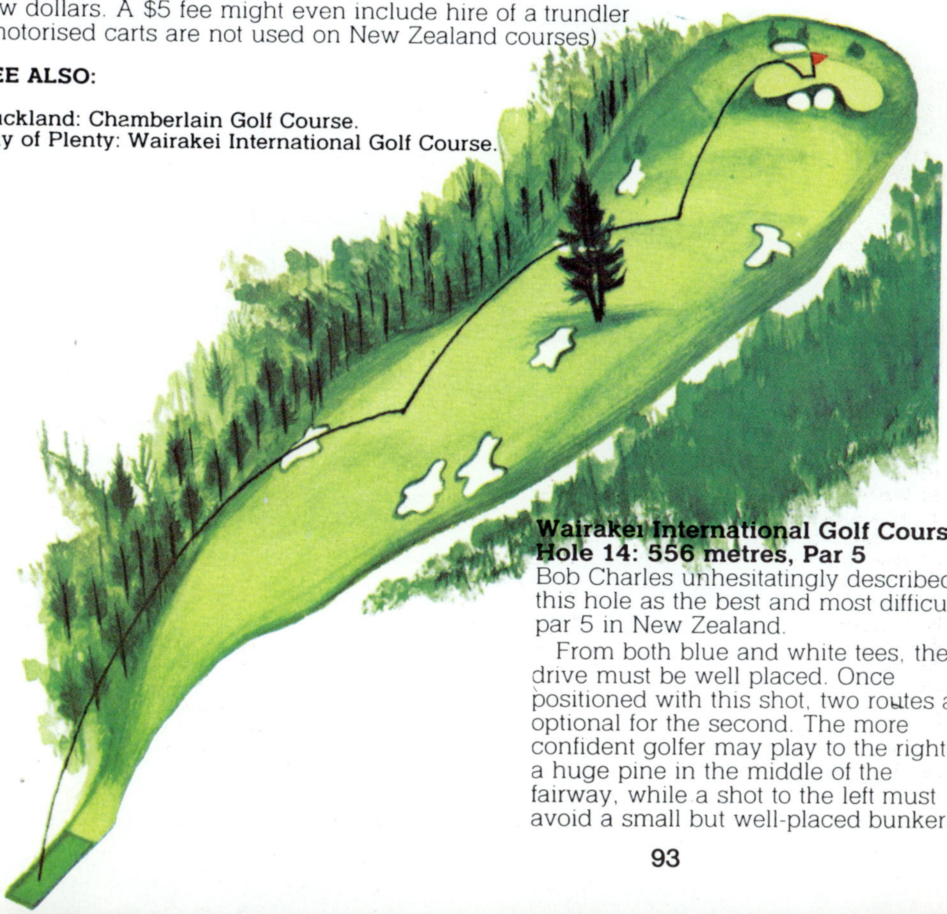

Wairakei International Golf Course
Hole 14: 556 metres, Par 5
Bob Charles unhesitatingly described this hole as the best and most difficult par 5 in New Zealand.

From both blue and white tees, the drive must be well placed. Once positioned with this shot, two routes are optional for the second. The more confident golfer may play to the right of a huge pine in the middle of the fairway, while a shot to the left must avoid a small but well-placed bunker.

In Touch with History

History is recorded not only in the dry stuff of manuscripts and books. It lives on in towns and in the countryside, and in New Zealand carved even in the hills. By looking around we can see the past and explore it. From the marks that have been made on the land, we can find out which people at various times in past centuries have come to New Zealand, from where they came, and when.

One Tree Hill, Auckland. (Courtesy Air New Zealand)

History of the Maori

Most New Zealanders have grown up believing in the Maori myth of Kupe, the Polynesian discoverer of Aotearoa, and of a great fleet, that followed 400 years later in 1350 A.D.

Modern scholarship has shown that early historians erred by uncritically unifying Maori tribal traditions into a national one. Each tribe has its own distinct whakapapa (genealogy) tracing their traditions back through the generations to a founding canoe. In the Taranaki Museum may be seen the traditional anchor stone of Tokomaru, the canoe of Te Atiawa people, as well as the greenstone adze, Potamawhiria, with which the canoe is believed to have been carved. Separate tribes tell separate Kupe legends. The National Museum in Wellington displays the large pierced stone said to be the anchor of Motahorua, Kupe's canoe. Only 30 years ago the Maori people of Hokianga placed a sacred white obelisk in the shadow of Whiria Mountain Pa beside the road near Opononi to mark Kupe's embarkation point for his return to Hawaiki. Auckland Museum's new Maori court will show a prized pearl-shell lure, evidence that the earliest voyagers came from an eastern Polynesian homeland. Also on display is a unique carved door lintel from Kaitaia clearly showing Eastern Polynesian influence.

Twentieth-century archaeology has traced New Zealand's earliest settlement back to at last least 1000 A.D., when the Maori camped in bays and river mouths, hunting inland for the huge flightless bird, the moa (see a reconstructed moa at the National Museum). In rock shelters they scattered bones of rats, fish and birds, some of which, like the moa, are now extinct, and drew with black charcoal and red ochre on the rock walls. (Visit the Timpendean Rock Shelter at Weka Pass in Canterbury to see a famed early rock-art site).

Canterbury Museum has a display of finds from the ovens and rubbish dumps of the important Wairau Bar moa-hunter settlement in Marlborough, which was occupied perhaps 800 years ago. From the summit of Auckland's Mt Eden, a later pa site, you may look out at distant Motutapu where an early Polynesian settlement was buried by the ash from the firey birth of the nearby triple-peaked Rangitoto in the fourteenth century.

By 1350 the big bird was becoming rare and the South Island Maoris increased their forgaging for fern roots and smaller birds. Kumara and taro, brought from eastern Polynesia, flourished in the North Island's warmer valleys, encouraging a more settled lifestyle, which gave dominance to the northern tribes. Visit Rewa's kainga (unfortified village) at Kerikeri and you will see simple whare puni (sleeping houses) made of the reed raupo, and pataka (food storehouses) typical of the eighteenth-century Classic period of Maori culture. From the reconstructed village look out across the now peaceful inlet to Kororipo Pa, from which the chief Hongi launched musket raids on the almost defenceless southern tribes. Near to the pa may be seen the historic Stone Store, together with New Zealand's oldest mission-period building, Kemp House.

The more permanent lifestyle resulted in an increase in inter-tribal fighting and the development of fortified hilltop villages or pa, to which the people retreated in times of danger. The carved war canoes joined the whare runanga (meeting house) as one of a tribe's most treasured possessions. See Te Mata o Hotoroa in Wanganui Museum, and the huge canoe Te Toki a Tapiri at Auckland Museum, saved from being burned following the wars of the 1860s.

The Auckland isthmus with its steep headlands, islands and volcanic cones was especially densely populated, with probably 3,000 to 4,000 inhabitants in pre-European times. The flanks of mountains like Mt Eden, Mt Wellington and One Tree Hill, though now bare of their wooden palisades, are carved with broad terraces and steep scarps, signs of their former occupation. At Turuturumokai Pa near Hawera in Taranaki the deep trenches and underground passages made it a formidable stronghold. Ruapekapeka in Northland was so strongly fortified against the British that it took 20 men to uproot a single post after its capture. Its largely underground refuges served as a model for trench warfare in World War I.

At Auckland's west coast beach, Piha, climb the 100 metre (330-foot) Lion Rock, once an island pa but now accessible at all tides, and look south across the bay to Taitomo (Camel Rock), protected on three sides by sheer cliffs. Both were used as refuges during the intertribal conflicts of the eighteenth and early nineteenth centuries.

The first European explorers and missionaries brought potatoes, iron implements and axes, helping Maori farming to expand, but they also brought guns. The early 1800s saw much bloodshed and changing of tribal boundaries as well as skirmishes with visiting Europeans who came to loot for kauri spars, seals and whales and to 'save souls'.

It was this period too that saw the development of elaborate meeting houses beside the marae, the open space where tribal matters were discussed. Te Hau ki Turanga in the National Museum was built in Poverty Bay in the 1840s and is considered the finest example of a carved meeting house. Hotunui at Auckland Museum was carved in 1868. Also at Auckland is Hotunui Pukeroa, the gateway figure from a Rotorua pa. Stripped of the ubiquitous rust-red paint used in the late 1800s, it reveals its true colours – white, red, black and green.

The Waitangi Meeting House beside the Treaty House in the Bay of Islands has no name. It belongs to the Maori people as a whole, its carved figures representing heroes and ancestors of all the main tribes.

The Bay of Islands represents a turning point in New Zealand history, for it was here that the missionaries set up headquarters and here that the first town, Kororareka, now Russell, began as an untidy village of shanties, stores and pubs. Across the Bay from here in 1840, the British Government and Maori chiefs signed the still-controversial Treaty of Waitangi at the Georgian-styled Treaty House. Above the present town of Russell (formerly Kororareka) looms the flagstaff that Hone Heke, one of the first Maori signatories to the treaty, cut down repeatedly in frustration when he saw the promises of the document not being honoured.

SEE ALSO:

Outback Safaris: Te Rehuwai Safaris (Rotorua).
Regional:
Northland: Whangaroa Harbour Cruises (Whangaroa), Northern Wairoa Museum (Dargaville).
Auckland: Pounamu Ventures (Auckland).
Bay of Plenty: Ohaki Maori Village (Te Kuiti).
Wellington: Wanganui Regional Museum.

Historic Places

Travellers in New Zealand can visit historic places owned or administered by the New Zealand Historic Places Trust from Kerikeri in the far north to Waikouaiti in Otago.

Beside the Stone Store in the Kerikeri basin stands New Zealand's oldest wooden building, Kemp House, built in 1822 for the Anglican Mission established there by Samuel Marsden. Constructed with hand-made nails and a kauri shingle roof, the house was home from 1832 to the blacksmith-missionary James Kemp, and generations of Kemps lived there till it was handed to the nation in 1974. The Kemps also ran the Stone Store as a shop. It still operates today.

Inland from the Bay of Islands, at Waimate North, is New Zealand's second oldest surviving house, once part of a thriving Selwyn-founded mission farm. Built in 1831-32 by Maori workers, it stood in the centre of a large Maori population and it was the place where the great Ngapuhi chief, Hongi Hika, had his cultivations. In its heyday the mission was a busy village with a mill, English crops, pigs and poultry. But the farm was uneconomic and during the war in the north in the 1840s all the buildings, fences and gardens suffered badly while British troops were stationed there. The mission house escaped serious damage and has been returned to its original condition. Even the green walls one missionary wife called 'dismal' have been repainted to the original colour.

Waimate Mission House, Waimate North. ***(Courtesy Historic Places Trust)***

The Catholics founded missions too, and Pompallier House, named after New Zealand's first Catholic bishop, still looks out over the bustling Russell Harbour. The 1841 house is a substantial pisé-de-terre (rammed earth) structure with two-foot-thick walls and light, airy verandahs. For eight years Pompallier House served as the mission printery and published religious books in the Maori language. The original Gaveaux press was later used by the Maori King Movement in the Waikato, but was returned by the Maori Queen as prize exhibit for the present museum in the house.

Hurworth, New Plymouth. ***(Courtesy Historic Places Trust)***

Hurworth, near New Plymouth in Taranaki, is the plain timber house of Harry Atkinson. He arrived in 1853, took up 80 hectares (200 acres) of bush land and sawed his own timber for the modest house he built. From this beginning he went on to become Sir Harry, and premier of New Zealand four times.

Pompallier House, Russell. ***(Courtesy Historic Places Trust)***

From early in the nineteenth century European whalers tracked their prey in New Zealand waters. In 1842 a Scot, Robert Fyffe, established a shore-based whaling station and whaled on the Kaikoura Peninsula in Marlborough. His brother George built the home that is all that remains of the enterprise. Fyffe House is in many respects a typical early weatherboard

Alberton, Auckland. ***(Courtesy Historic Places Trust)***

cottage, but the whaling background is built into the house. The piles of one wing, still visible at the back of seats under the verandah, are large whale vertebrae, and the house's pink hue comes from a paint mixture of whale oil and red and white lead.

In Auckland the history of Ewelme cottage shows how extensively Auckland has sprawled in 120 years. Built in 1864 on the open fields of Parnell, Ewelme was city home for Vicesimus Lush, vicar of coastal Howick. The journey is now made through unbroken suburban housing. The land wars of the 1860s did not reach Auckland so the cottage was a refuge for the Lush family from the more vulnerable Howick. The house remained in the family for over 100 years and was altered little in that time. The family preserved an extraordinary amount of the ordinary paraphernalia of a Victorian household; even early carpets and wallpapers survive to be admired.

Much grander Auckland houses are Alberton in Mt Albert and Highwic in Newmarket, both dating from the same period as Ewelme. Highwic, with its expansive view and sweeping lawns, was built in early English style for a prosperous stock and station agent, Alfred Buckland. Successive extensions accommodated his 21 children. Behind the grand ballroom and lavish dining room, a clutter of kitchens comprise the work area.

Another successful settler was Allan Kerr-Taylor, who invested profit from his 220-hectare (550-acre) farm in forestry and gold mining. As his fortunes grew so did his house, from a simple gabled farmhouse to an ornate mansion featuring towers and balconies that reflected Kerr-Taylor's Indian birthplace. Alberton was a great social centre, host to dances, archery parties and hunts. A team of servants, living more austerely in spartan attic rooms, serviced the family's luxurious lifestyle.

Industry too had its place in Victorian New Zealand. The Trust has cleared the scrub and gorse hiding the Brunner Industrial Site in the Grey Valley on the west coast of the South Island. Here coal was mined and coke, fire-bricks and other products were manufactured from the 1860s to the 1940s.

At Totara Estate near Oamaru you can visit the birthplace of New Zealand's export meat industry. This is where the stock for the first shipment of frozen meat was killed and dressed; the carcasses were then taken to Port Chalmers where the refrigerated sailing ship *Dunedin* waited to take her historic cargo to Britain.

The Lyttelton Time-ball Station, erected in 1876, enabled sea captains to check the accuracy of their chronometers. Stations like this existed in ports all round the world, but few survive in working order, as Lyttelton's does.

Further south at Oturehua in Otago the Trust operates a rural engineering works. In 1895 Ernest Hayes manufactured pollard cutters (pollard was a bran mixture used for poisoning rabbits), while his wife Hannah cycled the countryside, returning with farmers' orders that turned this into a flourishing farm-equipment business. The smithy is still operational.

Antrim House in Wellington's Boulcott Street is home for the Historic Places Trust. Appropriately it's a historic house itself.

Timeball station, Lyttelton. ***(Courtesy Historic Places Trust)***

Ewelme, Auckland. ***(Courtesy Historic Places Trust)***

Hayes Engineering Works, Oturehua. ***(Courtesy Historic Places Trust)***

SEE ALSO:

Regional: Wellington: Kawana Mill (Wanganui), Old St Pauls (Wellington).

Historic Places

Bulldozers and cranes are the tools of the demolition trade, ripping into central Auckland's Victorian remnants and earthquake-prone Wellington's shakey core. But the new plate-glass and steel structures still jostle buildings that have escaped the wrecker's hammer. Take a look above the verandahs in any New Zealand city and you'll find the stone or wood pediments and cornices of the older city. Some are preserved, like Auckland's Custom House and Wellington's old Government Buildings, the largest wooden building in this hemisphere. But observant visitors will discover many for themselves.

From Antrim House in Wellington, get written guides for walks that will take you through historic Thorndon, the wharves and Aro Valley.

In Auckland the City Council operates free guided tours that show you the old Custom House, old Government House, and Auckland's original shoreline. Take yourself up Victoria Street West and see the pillars and verandahs of an earlier town.

Follow on to Victoria Park Market on the site of the old city incinerator and you'll be standing on the reclaimed shore of Freemans Bay, the wharves distant behind motorway fly-overs and cricket pitches. A little further on Renall Street preserves a narrow slice of nineteenth-century Auckland, artisans cottages stacked against each other down a hill.

Dunedin's Public Relations Office has a city walk that shows you the grand facades of historic buildings, the railway station and the police station. Dunedin's Pacific Street in Roslyn is worth a visit to see some historic houses, as are London Street, Maori Hill and upper High Street.

Increasing industrialisation brought people to the cities and jobs, and each family wants its quarter acre. The suburbs of Auckland's Massey and Wellington's Porirua contain acres of low-cost housing. Distinctive blocks of identical homes, the older ones with tiled roofs and high windows, are part of the state housing schemes first instituted by the Labour government after the depression of the 1930s to house New Zealand families. Orakei has older state houses; Mangere has modern developments.

Urban drift has brought what is called the 'new Maori migration' as Maoris leave depressed rural areas for city jobs. A Maori Affairs crash housing programme in the 1960s created the South Auckland suburb of Otara. In Rotorua tours can include an overnight stay at a marae. South of Matamata (on the Tauranga road) stop for fresh pikelets and tea at Te Omeka Marae, a rural marae that functions as a community centre for local people. Notice the symbols of the Ratana Church on the front of the building. Arepa and Omeka were the prophet Ratana's two sons, named after the Greek letters, alpha and omega, the beginning and the end.

Away from the larger cities, many small towns reflect the history or hint at the future. Walk down the enormously long main street in the old gold-mining town of Thames and note the many splendid Victorian pubs in fine condition; or Oamaru's Thames Street with its distinctive white limestone commercial buildings, the courthouse, gaol, stable, banks, and the Brydone Hotel.

To bring you into the 1980s, visit Kawerau, east of Rotorua. Kawerau was carved out of the bush and bracken to service the huge Tasman Pulp and Paper mill started in 1953. In 30 years the population has grown to over 8,000 people, but the mill downwind to the east still dominates the town with its mountain of logs and chips.

In Touch with History

Between the cities and the towns, wander off the main highways; the landscape is much the same as it was 50 or 100 years ago, except that the farm bike has replaced the horse.

Travel on to country roads with untidy verges thick with rank grass, gorse and wild flowers. Occasional bursts of rambling roses are legacies of colonial settlements. Drive past farmyards cluttered with oil drums and farm machinery, both functioning and dead. Corrugated iron characterises the New Zealand landscape, invariably rusty or bearing the faint markings of long-ago paint. Corrugated iron is used in New Zealand for everything from house roofs to water tanks to warehouses and houses. See one of the largest corrugated-iron buildings in the South Island at Dunedin – John McGregor's Engineering and Boilermaking firm.

Note also the miles upon miles of barbed wire, taut and gleaming, or sagging and dotted with white tufts of sheep wool.

SEE ALSO:

Regional:
Westland: Shantytown (Greymouth).
Otago: Olveston (Dunedin).
(NOTE: Museums are listed under the For a More Relaxing Holiday section.)

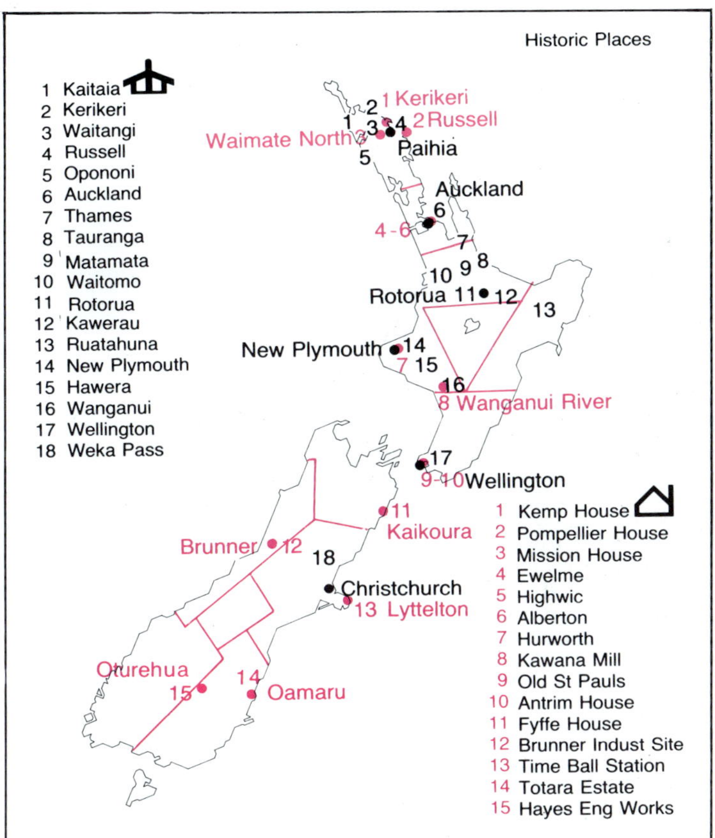

Down on the farm. *(Andris Apse Ltd)*

New Zealand supports around 3 million people, 10 million cattle and 60 million sheep. Ask any visitors for their lingering impressions of the country and the answer will inevitably include 'sheep', along with 'mountains, lakes, rivers and friendly people'.

Sheep are everywhere, even in city parks, and cows, responsible for the famous rich butter, graze wherever there is lowland pasture. You can't miss noticing either.

But visitors who want more than a passing glimpse of life 'down on the farm in New Zealand' can gain a close-up view by visiting a farm or taking a farm holiday.

You can discover why this land is one of the best, most efficient, agricultural producers in the world by making day visits to farms. Tour a dairy farm with its highly mechanised milking system – cows are milked by machines that deliver the milk to holding tanks, from where it is syphoned into large tankers for transport to factories.

You can visit a high-country sheep station where a shearer can remove the wool from 300 sheep in a day. Tour a deer farm where deer are bred for velvet and venison. Learn that the ubiquitous kiwifruit is the product of carefully tended vines growing in rich soil in a subtropical climate. Tour vineyards, large and small, and take the opportunity to sample the products. See some of the world's largest man-made forests where *Pinus radiata* romps to maturity in 25 years. Take a look at stud farms with prize cattle, sheep or racehorses.

Visitors with a special involvement in a particular aspect of agriculture can arrange to visit a government research station. In the midst of the Waikato dairying country, the largest such research centre has five dairy farms and concentrates on soil fertility, weed control, irrigation and animal health. Nearby is the world's largest milk-processing plant, which can cope with 1,688,000 litres (375,000 gallons) a day.

To see the latest in farm equipment and expertise, join the 75,000 visitors to the annual three-day National Field Day at Mystery Creek, near Hamilton, in June. The innovations range from earth-moving machinery to electric fencing, the stock from prize bulls to prize rabbits. It is one huge farming market that attracts farmers from as far afield as Europe, North America, South America, the Middle East and Asia. Even if you're not shopping for the latest tractor, Mystery Creek is worth a visit.

In a farming country there is always something going on somewhere. There are special tourist displays such as Rotorua's Agrodome or Queenstown's Cattledrome, but you can also find the real rural New Zealand at a show day, an agricultural exhibition, sheepdog trials, shearing contest or sale day. Catch the rumbustious atmosphere of sale day in country towns such as Feilding, where animals are herded into the stockyards to be sold at auction.

Get a taste of rural life at an Agricultural and Pastoral Society Show – every farming community has an annual A & P Show. In small towns the show is a festival of rural living, an annual fair where the best local breeds and produce are on display, children parade their pet lambs and calves, riders and horses compete for prizes in the show ring and farmers' wives compete for prizes with cream-laden cakes and jars of preserves.

The biggest A & P Show is a city show, the annual Easter Show in Auckland. For an excellent large country fair, the Hastings A & P Show in October is hard to beat.

In the hill country and mountains, sheep such as hardy Merino are bred for their wool. On lowland farms, Corriedale, Romney and cross-breeds are fattened for meat, which will find its way onto tables throughout the world.

Down on the farm

Dairy farms are found from Northland to Southland, but the main dairying areas are the Waikato and Taranaki in the North Island. Beef cattle too are found everywhere but are most common on the hills of the North Island, run together with sheep.

Less traditional farms include angora goat farms, deer farms, rabbit farms and fitch farms. Forest farms combine grazing stock with commercial pine forest. Farm parks are working farms, often on the coast, giving free access to the public, such as the Cape Colville Farm Park on Coromandel Peninsula. This farm concentrates on breeding Hereford cattle, is fringed with sandy bays and beaches and allows some camping.

With an excess of fresh clean air, water and soil, all kinds of crops thrive in a variety of climates – from avocados to cherries, asparagus or apricots.

There are subtropical orchards concentrated around Kerikeri in Northland and Te Puke in the Bay of Plenty, growing sweet oranges, mandarins, kiwifruit, tamarillos, avocados, persimmons and babacos. Stone and pip fruit such as apples, peaches and plums are grown everywhere, but the main commercial orchards are found around Auckland, Hawkes Bay, Nelson and Central Otago. Almost every area has its specialist crop – asparagus in Hawkes Bay, garlic and grapes around Blenheim, oranges in the north, blackcurrants and apricots in the south. If you are driving around and see P.Y.O. signs, they mean 'pick your own'. Either buy produce fresh at the orchard gate or even cheaper and lots of fun,pick your own.

Wakelin's Agtour
Haruru Falls Road
R.D. 1
Paihia
Telephone: (0885) 27-054
Manager: Kristeen Jones

Known as New Zealand's Farming Showcase, Wakelin's comprises five working, Land Corporation-owned farms. Take a guide for maximum benefit to see this 700-hectare (1,729-acre) station of Saanen and Angora goats, Santa Gertrudis and NZ Angus cattle, Perendale sheep; red, wapiti and Moluccan rusa deer. The cycle of seasons offers different features of farming life (spring – birth of lambs, kids and calves; summer – shearing sheep and goats). See the yoghurt/cheese factory, displays, shearing demonstrations, tractor hay rides, farm dogs working, goat milking, and pets like 'Sooty' the cow. Enjoy scenic views, walks, picnicking and summer swimming. Highly commended farming introduction for all the family and special interest groups. Travel rugs, skins, natural cosmetics, goat yoghurt and cheeses sold at shop (Visitors Centre). Please telephone for further information or to book a guide. From $3.50 (adult), $1.50 (child) – no guide. Special rates for family groups.

The Agrodome
Riverdale Park
Western Road
PO Box 634
Ngongotaha, Rotorua
Telephone: (073) 74-350

In lush pastureland; this huge timber building houses a permanent agricultural exhibition. 60-minute stage show is rated best of its kind world-wide, featuring top ram breeds. A multiple-language commentary benefits all. Learn about wool, view shearing demonstrations and sheep dogs working. Relax in Cottage Cafe for morning/afternoon teas/light lunches; browse in Sheepskin Shop. Shows daily: 9.15 a.m., 11.00 a.m., 2.30 p.m. From $5.50 (adult), $2.75 (child), GST inclusive. Concessions, group/family rates.

Otuiti Deer Lodge
Main Road (S.H. 3)
R.D. 3
Ohaupo
Telephone: (071) 296-430/ 296-888
Host: Neville Johnson

Just 10 kilometres (6 miles) south of Hamilton, one of the country's premier red deer parks. By arrangement only. An elite herd bred from red deer in England's Warnham and Woburn Parks, Austria's Rossleg Park, Yugoslavia and Hungary, including a direct son of 'Leopold', commonly regarded as the finest red stag in the world. Tour in the lodge vehicle, inspecting stock and learning of farming and handling techniques. Costs upon booking. Please telephone for appointment.

Expo Cattledrome
Skippers Park
R.D.1
Queenstown
Telephone: (0294) 29-759

Only show of its kind in the world – an amazing live stage act offering wonderful family entertainment. Selected cattle star, portraying New Zealand's beef/dairy industry, multi-language explanations. Touch the animals and experience the thrill of hand-milking a cow! Shows held daily, 9.30 a.m. and 2.30 p.m. (check times June-August, usually one show daily). Bring your camera. Bookings unessential, unless large party. From $5.30 (adult), $2 (child). Discounts for large groups on application.

SEE ALSO:

Lodges: Riverview (Athol), Wharekauhau (Wairarapa).

Drovers and cattle.
(Andris Aspe Ltd)

Living with New Zealanders

NZ

One of the best ways of getting to know the country is to stay with the people. Not only do you meet one family, but they may also introduce you to their friends and different ways of life.

Decide on a farm holiday and you won't find yourself on a 'dude' farm but on a real, working farm. Paying guests stay in farmhouses that offer high standards of comfort; houses vary from rambling, colonial charm to modern, sophisticated design. You live with the family, get to try your hand at farmwork if you wish and enjoy typical hearty farm fare – cooked breakfasts, rich roasts of lamb, mutton or beef, and between-meal sustenance of scones and sandwiches. It is a great way to experience New Zealand life, and for those with particular farming interests it offers the chance to gain some first-hand knowledge.

The farms may also offer contact with history – an old goldmine, magnificent old machinery, small country settlement or an old pub. And there are different types of farms all over the country: beef, sheep, dairy, horticultural; farms in the lowland, the high country, near towns or in the outback.

'Homestays' is the term given to urban accommodation with New Zealand families. Host families from many walks of life invite you to their homes, which range from some of the great historic houses of New Zealand to modern suburban houses.

Living with New Zealanders is an excellent way to learn about local social and political issues, sports and the arts, or, if you have a special interest, to meet others so inclined. Most home host organisations can arrange for special interests if given sufficient time. Out of this contact come friendships that sometimes last many years, and a real insight into the lives of some New Zealanders.

BED AND BREAKFAST NEW ZEALAND STYLE can book all the best 'bed and breakfasts' in New Zealand. Every year, they travel the length and breadth of New Zealand meeting the wonderful people who make staying in a private home, farm or 'bed and breakfast' the experience of a lifetime! One of the attractions of our country is the friendliness of its people. Staying with New Zealanders in their homes as you travel around is a great way to make the most of your visit, as well as enjoying the comfortable, friendly, relaxing lifestyle of the locals. They're sure to know the best shopping, the best sightseeing, the best way to help you enjoy your holiday. Each host family – whether farm, city or country dwellers – provides quality accommodation and delicious home-cooked meals. Those 'bed and breakfasts' not providing dinner will tell you the best local eating places. Wherever you want to explore – scenic coastal routes, high country farming areas, lakes, river valleys – this company will reserve your accommodation, or provide you with a 7-night (or more) 'Go as you please' Bed and Breakfast package, with or without rental car. To make the most of your stay, please be prepared to give us some information about yourself – age group, interests, smoker or not – whatever is important to you, and while the company won't guarantee a perfect match, they'll try to find the folks you're most likely to like! The majority of hosts you could never meet other than through this agency service and the information they hold is comprehensive, so trust them to make a great choice for you. B & B from $55 (share twin/double), full farmstay from $154 (share twin/double), half-price for children under 12 years. If you're in New Zealand, credit card bookings handled over the telephone.

Bed & Breakfast – New Zealand Style
(NZ Home Hospitality Ltd)
PO Box 309
Nelson
Telephone: (054) 82-424
Telex: NZ3914
Facsimile: (054) 69-519
Auckland Office:
(09) 479-7568
USA: (800) 854-3413
Canada: (416) 863-0799
(604) 687-4004
Owners: Dulcie and Allan Carson

Wairoa Farm Stays
PO Box 36
Paihia
Northland
Telephone: (0885) 27-379
Host: Dorothy Bayly
(Overseas guests only)

This elegant country home overlooks stretches of secluded coastline, private beaches and green farmland. Just 8 minutes' drive from Paihia, stay and enjoy dinner, bed and breakfast in gracious surroundings. Spacious lawns/gardens are full of birdlife, excellent facilities include spa bath and tennis court. Enjoy daily life of a modern sheep/cattle farm or relax in peace, walking or fishing (Dorothy will cook your catch for you!). Upwards of $65 person/day. Bookings essential.

Ryan Farmstays
Tower Road
R.D.1
Matamata
Telephone: (0818) 25-770
Hosts: Val and Morgan Ryan and neighbours

Stay with families in a community renowned for its hospitality, delicious home-cooked meals, and spacious homes and gardens. Renowned too for its outstanding kiwifruit, dairy, beef, deer, sheep and thoroughbred farms. Watch racehorses in training, craftworkers in studios. Enjoy forest walks in the Kaimai Ranges, golf, fishing, mineral hot pools and seeing historic places. All-inclusive $100 per day. Group discounts. Transport from airport and day tours to Rotorua, Waitomo and secluded beaches organised.

'Farmhouse Bed and Breakfast'
Albert Road, Tokomaru, R.D.4
Palmerston North
Telephone: (063) 298-868
Hosts: Marilyn and Em Turney

Cosy cottage stay and friendly hospitality. Rural peace and farmhouse meals – homemade and homebrewed! Well-appointed facilities, accommodates up to four. Reasonable rates from $45 per night (meals included). Children's rates.

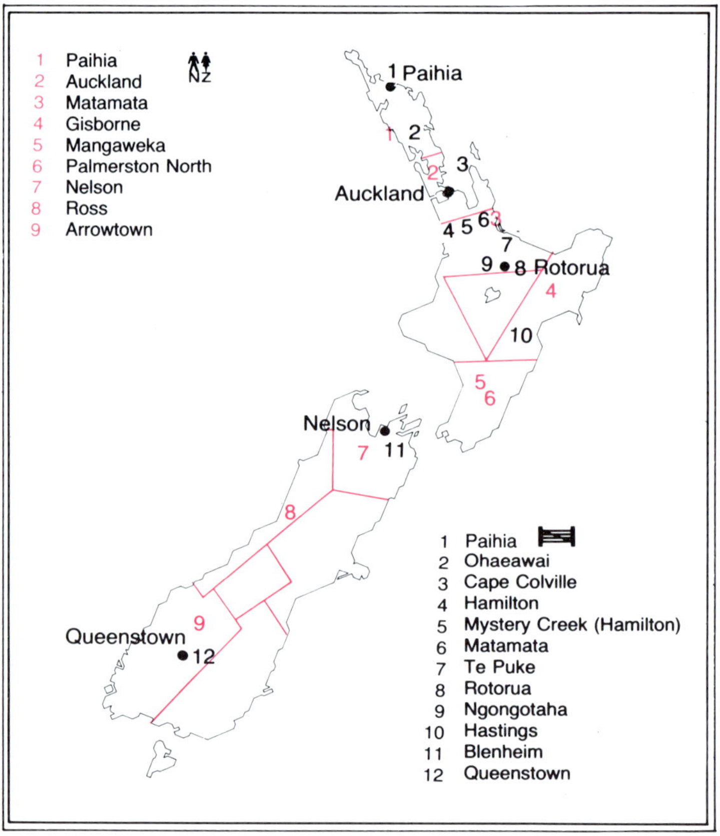

Living with New Zealanders

This lovely home is designed for gracious living, with stunning lake views. Offering small numbers of guests privacy, peace and pampering in the finest New Zealand tradition. Meals as required, featuring New Zealand gourmet delights and wines. Tours available for personal sight-seeing, fishing, hunting, golf or skiing. Comforts include – personal bathrobes, fresh fruit and flowers in rooms, indoor mineral pool, billiard room and open fires. From $75 (single), $95 (double), breakfast included.

Koha Lodge
50 Koha Road
Taupo
Telephone: (074) 87-647
USA: (800) 351-2323
(303) 223-6771
Hosts: Pat Gluyas and Lindsay Turner

Enjoy out-going hosts and tranquillity on this mixed farming property, 18 kilometres (11 miles) from Gisborne. Beautiful old homestead set in established English gardens, with swimming pool and tennis court. Spacious, private accommodation with ensuite facilities. Dine in formal dining room enjoying tastefully prepared New Zealand cuisine. Visit winery boutiques, beaches, Maori meeting houses; enjoy native forest walks, mineral pools, golf or trout fishing. From $120 person/day, meals/wine inclusive. Groups welcome. Book direct or through NZTP.

'Repongaere'
Lavenham Road
PO Box 116
Patutahi, Gisborne
Telephone: (079) 27-717
USA: (800) 443-3623/
(303) 223/6771
Hosts: Midge and Michael Dods

Experience farm life with hotel comfort. Farmhouse accommodation includes spacious double bedroom, ensuite bathroom (with sunken bath) and private verandah; or twin bedroom. An excellent cuisine is offered with good New Zealand wines. Rest, play tennis on the court, horse ride, swim in the river or roam the farm on foot. The area abounds with activities – Sue and David will arrange trout fishing, white-water rafting, tramping, canoeing and heli-skiing (in season) for you (cost exclusive). Or just relax in the peaceful country – the choice is yours. German and French are spoken by friendly hosts who enjoy sharing this unique lifestyle. Situated 12 kilometres (7 miles) from Mangaweka. Drive or be collected from the train at Taihape, bus at Mangaweka or Palmerston North Airport. From $45 (single), $75 (double) – bed and breakfast; $25 (campervans); $25 (dinner).

'Mairenui Holidays'
Ruahine Road
Mangaweka
Telephone: (065) 825-564
Germany: (05766) 1778
Hosts: Sue and David Sweet

Throughout the beautiful Nelson region, renowned for mild climate and long sunshine hours, Pat provides a personal service, arranging quality home/farmstays. Preferences are noted and matched carefully with hosts of similar interest. Facilities are ensuite or shared. A holiday for all seasons, everything from fishing and skiing, to hunting and gold-panning. Special interest tours organised – golf, arts/crafts, etc. Bed/Breakfast from $45; Dinner, B/B from $65; Farmstays from $75, children half-price.

The Friendly Kiwi Home Hosting Service
195 Moana Avenue, Nelson
PO Box 5049, Port Nelson
Telephone: (054) 85-915
Telex: NZ3509 FRIENKI
Host: Patricia Jones

Stay on this cattle and sheep farm bordering a beautiful reserve, 12 kilometres (10 miles) south of Ross. Bed and breakfast accommodation (from $22), campervan facilities (from $5 per van and $5 per person). Facilities for disabled.

Fergusons Farm Stays
State Highway 6
R.D. Ross, South Westland
Telephone: Ross 54-125
Hosts: Jocelyn and Jim Ferguson

Stay on this sheep and crop farm, enjoying country hospitality, clean mountain air and superb scenery. A self-contained flat sleeps four in warm comfort, with fully-appointed kitchen and conveniences. Close to all major lake resorts but offering peace and quiet. Join farm activities, play tennis and walk the hills. Guided tours offered for great fishing, golf or winter skiing at three nearby major ski areas. From $68 (double) per night.

'Royalburn Farm'
Crown Terrace
PO Box 54
Arrowtown
Telephone: (029420) 573
Hosts: Jane and Michael Burdon

OTHER REFERENCES:

Farmhouse & Country Homes, PO Box 31250, Auckland.
Hospitality Haere Mai, PO Box 56-175, Auckland.
NZ Farm Holidays, Private Bag, Parnell, Auckland.
Rural Tours New Zealand, PO Box 228, Cambridge.
Town & Country Home Hosting, PO Box 143, Cambridge.
Sam Horrocks Kiwi Hospitality, RD 2, Ngaruawahia.
Farmstay Ltd, Rotorua, PO Box 630, Rotorua.
Farm Hospitality Service, Mt. View Road, Raetihi.
Selecta Farm Holidays, PO Box 761, Taupo.
Okaihau Vacations Farmstays, Settlers Way, Okaihau.
New Zealand Host Homes Ltd, PO Box 60, Russell.
New Zealand Travel Hosts, 279 Williams St, Kaiapoi, Christchurch.
Rural Holidays, PO Box 2155, Christchurch.
Queenstown Home Hosted Holidays, Lake Hayes RD2, Queenstown.

Apsley House, Ohaeawai, Bay of Islands. *(Courtesy Apsley House)*

For a more relaxing holiday

Whale Bay, Whangarei. *(Courtesy Ron Monton)*

If you want to holiday at a more sedate pace, or you need a restful breathing space, New Zealand offers many choices. In these small islands interesting sights and experiences are never far away.

For tired limbs, soak in a hot mineral pool. You can often hire a private pool and loll in the steamy water with friends. There are well-known pools in Rotorua, and at Waiwera and Parakai north of Auckland. But try Hauraki Hot Springs on the flat plains farmland at Miranda; Morere, south of Gisborne, where you can also picnic in a pleasant bush reserve; Te Puia on the East Coast Road; Okoroire under its sheltering plane trees in the Waikato. You'll need a spade at Hot Water Beach on Coromandel Peninsula. Dig your own bathing hole in the sand at low tide; adjust the temperature by digging deeper.

In the South Island, Hanmer Springs in North Canterbury was once a fashionable spa, the thermal pools reputed to ease arthritis and skin diseases. At Maruia Hot Springs on the Lewis Pass Road, you can take the waters while admiring a spectacular setting of bush and snow-covered hills.

In warmer weather the beaches beckon. In Wellington and Auckland there are splendid clean beaches right in the city; try especially tree-fringed Thorne's Bay on Auckland's North Shore, good for swimming at all tides. But a little further afield New Zealand has hundreds of beaches from well-populated resorts to untouched gems fringed with scarlet-flowered pohutukawa and plume-headed toitoi. East coast beaches have golden sand and even surf. On the west coast the iron sand is black or the beaches are pebbly, and the sea surges in across the Tasman in rolling breakers. Most of the popular beaches are patrolled by surf clubs.

Visit the fishing village of Makara, west of Wellington, or take an impromptu lunch of french bread and smoked fish roe to Auckland's dramatic west coast beaches from Karekare to Muriwai. On a good day take towel, togs (bathing suit) and a book and idle the day away.

Literature

Reading fiction will open to you the world of New Zealanders. All towns of any size will have a library and bookshops. In fact, New Zealanders buy more books per head of population than any other nation. Browse through them and look for New Zealand authors.

Katherine Mansfield was part of the same literary set as Virginia Woolf and Vita Sackville-West. Read her short stories 'At the Bay' and 'The Garden Party' for memorable scenes of middle-class colonial life.

The traumas of growing up in the early years of this century are the subject matter of two autobiographical novels: Robin Hyde's *The Godwits Fly* and Labour politician John A. Lee's *Children of the Poor*. Ronald Hugh Morrieson's novels of small-town New Zealand, *Pallet on the Floor* and *The Scarecrow*, have been made into films and have made him into a cult figure for a younger generation. And Maurice Gee creates heroes of 'ordinary' New Zealanders in *Plumb* and *Meg*. Read Barry Crump's on-the-road type novels, especially *A Good Keen Man*. Try Maurice Shadbolt's collection of short stories *The New Zealanders*. In *Smith's Dream*, C. K. Stead takes us into a near future where riot police and US soldiers battle ordinary citizens, turned guerillas.

Two New Zealand authors are currently enjoying international recognition. Janet Frame's novels explore the inner world – *State of Seige* and *Living in the Maniototo* – and experiences in mental institutions – *Faces in the Water*. The first volume of her autobiography – *To the Is-Land* – has been much praised. Sylvia Ashton-Warner is internationally acclaimed as an educationalist and a writer. Her novel *Spinster* tells of a young woman teacher in a small New Zealand school; it was filmed starring Shirley MacLaine.

Younger writers who are making a mark include Sue

McCauley, whose *Other Halves* examines the pleasures and pain of a love relationship between a European woman and a younger Maori man; and Maori writer Keri Hulme, creator of the epic novel *The Bone People*.

Other Maori writers specialise in short stories, especially Wiiti Ihimaera, who in *Whanau* and *The New Net Goes Fishing* looks at rural Maori life and the effect of the shift to industrial cities. In *The Dream Sleepers* Patricia Grace paints evocative pictures of Maori family life and the clash of traditional Maori and modern European values. Ihimaerá and D. S. Long have co-edited an anthology of Maori writing; called *Into the World of Light*, it represents a range of Maori writers.

Small children will delight in two recent picture books: Patricia Grace and Robyn Kahukiwa's *The Kuia and the Spider* and Miriam Smith and David Armitage's *Kim and the Watermelon*.

Films, Music and Theatre

If you like seeing rather than reading, look in daily paper's entertainment pages for recent New Zealand movies that may be playing. There's a small but active industry here; an exhibit at the Film Archive in Wellington traces the industry's development.

In the entertainment pages look too for gigs featuring local musicians. At concerts, open-air soundshells (in the summer) and in pubs you'll hear everything from rock to country and western. Maori music might be heard on the hit parade, or featured at Maori or Polynesian festivals and cultural events. See too the New Zealand Symphony Orchestra, playing different venues around the country.

At live theatre you could see a local production of overseas work by anyone from Shakespeare to Caryl Churchill, or catch a New Zealand play. In Auckland visit the Mercury; in Wellington, Downstage and Circa; in Christchurch, the Court; in Dunedin, the Fortune; and in Hamilton, the Founders Theatre.

The Fine Arts

At the Founders also admire the Ralph Hotere mural. You'll notice murals also in other places you visit. At Auckland Airport waiting in queues is brightened by huge 40-metre (120-foot) long murals. The Beehive in Wellington is dominated by John Drawbridge's mural, and enormous woven wall hangings. Auckland University's School of Architecture, the new Arts/Commerce block and the Medical School all feature stunning wall art. Artist Robin White painted the Otago Peninsula and healing words on her mural at Otago Medical School; Pat Hanly uses the spectrum of colours on a festive theme to adorn the new Christchurch Town Hall.

If you want to see something smaller, visit public art galleries in all the centres. Most have collections that include colonial artists like John Kinder and John Gully, important twentieth-century artists like Frances Hodgkins and Rita Angus and contemporary artists like Toss Woollaston, Colin McCahon, Selwyn Muru, Gretchen Albrecht and Tony Fomison. Look out for the Lindauer Maori portraits at Auckland, Len Lye's kinetic sculptures at the Govett Brewster in New Plymouth, the Edith Colliers at the Sargeant in Wanganui, Colin McCahon's Northland panels and the Rita

Maori carver at work, Maori Art's and Craft's Institute, Whakarewarewa, Rotorua. *(National Publicity Studios)*

Angus collection in Wellington, early New Zealand water colours at the Bishop Suter in Nelson and famous Goldie Maori portraits in Dunedin.

Private dealer galleries exhibit the latest paintings and prints of contemporary New Zealand artists. A print showing landscapes or social life by Stanley Palmer, Marilynn Webb, Nigel Brown or Fassett Burnett can be bought at a reasonable price and will hold special memories of the country. In Auckland visit Denis Cohn, RKS and New Vision; in Hamilton, Centre Gallery; in Wellington, Janne Land, Gallery Legard, Peter McLeavey and next door, Louise Beale; in Christchurch, Brooke Gifford; and Dunedin, Red Metro and the Bosshard. Have lunch or supper at the City Limits Cafe in Wellington or The Last and First in Auckland and you'll see the latest work of young artists.

The Art of the Maori

Public museums show examples of Maori art from incised domestic gourds and ancient heirloom greenstone hei tiki, to soaring carved meeting houses and canoes to seat a hundred warriors.

Spears, adzes, even fish hooks of stone, bone, wood and jade were brilliantly finished, polished and carved with spiral and other symbolic patterns. The whare runanga (meeting houses) have carefully chiselled support and facing posts, painted rafter patterns and tukutuku weaving on the walls. All designs have special meaning to the tribe who created them, celebrating ancestors and spiritual roots, and each whare runanga is named. Pataka, or elevated store houses, are also elaborately decorated.

Maori weaving created treasured ceremonial cloaks of dog skin, gleaming kiwi and kaka parrot feathers, and korowai (cloaks) decorated with black-dyed tags. At Ohaki Maori village near the Waitomo caves, visit a weaving centre built by the family of Rangimarie Hetet and her daughter, Digger Te Kanawa, to show their skill at weaving flax korowai. Visitors

Lake Hayes, near Arrowtown, Southern Lakes. *(Andris Apse Ltd)*

can see all parts of the weaving process and feel the flax in their hands.

Crafts

In craft shops watch out for beautiful traditional woven kits made from harakeke (flax).

Rotorua is the home of the Maori Arts and Crafts Institute at Whakarewarewa, where you can see a Maori carver working. Also see a carver at work at Rotorua's Ohinemutu village on the lakeside, next to Tama-te-kapua, an outstanding whare runanga containing carvings of passengers on the ancestral Arawa canoe.

Moko or facial tattoos were very beautiful, but most old people bearing them have died – see them in photographer Marti Friedlander's book *Moko*. If you want to know about Maori mythology, look for *Wahine Toa*, in which writer Patricia Grace and artist Robyn Kahukiwa reinterpret Maori myths, emphasising strong women mythological figures and explaining Maori symbolism.

See superb examples of traditional Pacific art at Auckland and Dunedin's museums.

New Zealand is renowned for its pottery, which ranges from delicate translucent porcelain to chunky earthy stoneware. For something special visit the Hereford Fine China Studio in Hamilton, where figurines and miniature animals are made by skilled craftspeople.

The Dowse Art Gallery in Lower Hutt has a permanent collection of pots giving an overview of New Zealand pottery. Craft shops in cities and suburbs sell pots, but look also in country and seaside settlements for potteries set up by escapees from the city. Northland, Coromandel and Nelson have attracted many such alternative lifestylers.

Fine china at the Hereford Fine China Studio, Hamilton. (Courtesy Hereford Fine China)

Museums

Inside still, visit museums, large and small, public and private, to learn about New Zealand's Maori and colonial past and its natural history. All over New Zealand are pioneer villages, recreations of Victorian shops and streets, restored houses and specialist museums. You'll find museums specialising in the army (Waiouru), clocks (Whangarei), kauri timber milling (Otamatea at Matatoke, Northland), steam engines (Tokomaru), gold mining (Shantytown, Greymouth; Coaltown, Westport), native plants (Otari at Wellington), agriculture (Brayshaw, Blenheim), shipwrecks (Waitangi), cars (Queenstown), and the only major gallery of rugby memoribilia going back to the 1870s (Palmerston North).

Scenic Drives and Picnics

Ask at the local Automobile Association for scenic routes that will present spectacular views of coast, countryside and cities. Auckland's Scenic Drive takes you high above the city through native bush. From Christchurch drive round the five Signs of the Takahe or over the Cashmere Hills to Lyttelton via Taylors Mistake and other beautiful beaches. Drive round Wellington's sombre hill-locked harbour to the bays, where you'll see a plaque marking Katherine Mansfield's house. Go to the top of Bluff Hill and look beyond the aluminium smelter at Tiwae Point to Awarua Lagoon and Foveaux Strait beyond. From Tauranga's The Minden, you can see from East Cape to Coromandel in the west.

Combine a picnic with a drive. Most towns and cities have domains or botanic gardens where you can spread a rug and bring out the thermos and sandwiches. Very beautiful are Ashburton Domain with its massive trees and Christchurch's Botanic Gardens. On the Avon feed the ducks with lunch scraps then slide along the river in a hired punt.

Further out of town, bush reserves and beaches offer auspicious spots for an idyllic outing. Sit on the sun-baked rocks at McLaren Falls near Tauranga. Out of New Plymouth see the spectacular sight of conical Mt Egmont mirrored in the water at Lake Mangamahoe. Near Blenheim picnic on the Wairau Bar opposite an ancient moa-hunter site. The Otago Peninsula has many fine picnic places with the added attractions of an aquarium, pa sites, lighthouses, soaring cliffs, an albatross colony and a castle to be seen on the way. For something quite different, try the world's first timber maze at Wanaka.

Also visit the graveyard at Otakou Maori Church, the last resting place of three great South Island chiefs. Churchyards often have much to tell of New Zealand's past from historic events to domestic tragedies – small children died of influenza, young men drowned while whaling. At Christ Church in Russell, see the graves of the Ngapuhi chief Tamati Waka Nene, members of the family of the first honorary US consul, Clendon, and *Hazard* crew members killed in a clash with Hone Heke's men in 1845. At Waimate North see the graves of early missionaries and settlers as well as carved wooden Maori headboards seen only in Northland. At Queenstown cemetery see a plaque commemorating Chinese goldminers and at Otemataha Military Cemetery in Tauranga, sited on an old pa, read inscriptions the graves of Maori and Pakeha dead from the Gate Pa and Te Ranga Battles.

For a more relaxing holiday

To experience mainstream New Zealand social life, lean on the bar at the local pub or tavern with a handle of beer. You could try the carpeted, revamped lounge bar of one of the trendier hotels, then cross the road to where it's linoleum and formica tables for 'serious' drinking. There could be a game of darts or billiards in progress, or the radio or television giving the latest sports scores or racing results.

New Zealanders watch sports as much as they play. You can join the local crowds and maybe see some of the best sportsmen and women in the world – runners like Allison Roe and John Walker or world-famous All Black rugby players – and the sleekest, fastest horses. Enter Auckland's Ellerslie raceway through an avenue of towering phoenix palms. Further south visit Te Rapa at Hamilton, or Riccarton at Christchurch. Trotting is the specialty at the Alexandra Park Raceway in Auckland and Trentham in Wellington.

In the winter wrap up warmly and go to a rugby game – the major parks are Eden Park in Auckland, Athletic Park in Wellington, Lancaster Park in Christchurch, Carisbrook in Dunedin. In the summer watch a sparkling game of one-day cricket. All year round, watch wet-suited surf-board riders waiting like seagulls for the right wave at Piha near Auckland, Raglan west of Hamilton, and the golden Mt Maunganui.

Then there's polo at Clevedon and annual events like Auckland's yachting regatta and Round-the-Bays run.

New Zealand is a water-bound land, with cities and towns clinging to the shores of glistening bays and harbours studded with islands. To see Auckland's harbour take a ferry to the historic marine suburb of Devonport, to lovely Waiheke Island or the more distant Great Barrier Island. In remote areas join a rural mail and stores run. Nose into silent coves and nudge up against weathered jetties on the famed Bay of Islands Cream Trip or the Queen Charlotte Sound Mail Run in Marlborough.

SEE ALSO:

Museums:

Northland: Captain Cook (Russell), Wagener (Houhora), Far North Regional (Kaitaia), Northern Wairoa (Dargaville), Claphams Clocks (Whangarei), Northland Regional (Whangarei), Otamatea Kauri (Matakohe).

Auckland: War Memorial (Auckland).

Bay of Plenty: Waikato Museum of Art and History (Hamilton), Waikino Pioneer (Waikino), Firth Tower (Matamata).

East Cape: Gisborne Museum and Arts Centre.

Wellington: Wanganui Regional, Manawatu (Palmerston North).

Westland: West Coast Historical (Hokitika).

Otago: Otago Early Settlers (Dunedin).

Historic Parks and Vintage Engine Museums:

Wellington: Tokomaru Steam Engine.

Canterbury: Ferrymead (Christchurch), Plains Vintage Car (Ashburton), Pleasant Point Railway (Timaru).

Southern Lakes: Queenstown Motor, Matuku Engine (Te Anau).

Arts & Crafts:

Bay of Plenty: Perrin Cottage (Hamilton); Lichfield Pottery (Putaruru).

Nelson: Bishop Suter Art Gallery (Nelson).

Westland: Hokitika Craft, Hokitika Gifts.

And Different:

Auckland: Kelly Tarlton's Underwater World (Auckland).

Bay of Plenty: Diamond Hot Pools (Waingaro).

Canterbury: Barker Wines (Geraldine), DB South Island Brewery (Timaru)

Bay of Plenty: New Zealand Maori Arts and Crafts Institute (Rotorua).

Christchurch: Geocraft Tours (Christchurch).

For a country that stretches 1,600 kilometres (1,000 miles) from north to south, with only 3 million people, the transport system is surprisingly well developed. While the cost sometimes may be higher than the heavily patronised routes of Europe or North America, the traveller has a good choice of alternatives.

In organising travel, remember that it takes longer to drive distances in New Zealand than might be expected. For example, the 657 kilometres (394 miles) between Auckland and Wellington takes 11 hours to drive (at legal speed limits with meal stops allowed), compared to 8½ hours for the 725 kilometres (435 miles) between San Francisco and Los Angeles.

Roads, however give access to the remote corners of the country, by car, campervan or scheduled bus service. When you run out of road try a horse or helicopter, or walk.

More limited in scope is the passenger rail service between Auckland and Wellington. A daylight journey on the main trunk line (13 hours) is very picturesque. Part of the track, known as the Raurimu Spiral, at the edge of the Waimarino Plateau, is an engineering feat of international note. Here the land rises 215 metres (700 feet) in 5.5 kilometres (3½ miles). To overcome the steep gradient, an ascending spiral in the form of a circle, three horseshoes and two short tunnels was constructed, increasing the distance to 11.5 kilometres (7 miles) – and thus reducing the gradient.

Branch lines operate from Wellington to New Plymouth, and Wellington to Gisborne. The New Zealand Railways (NZR) also run a car and passenger ferry service across Cook Strait and an intermittent passenger ferry service across Foveaux Strait.

The South Island main trunk runs from Picton to Christchurch and Dunedin. A branch line runs from Christchurch to Greymouth. NZR also runs an extensive scheduled bus service.

Scheduled bus services and regional touring services offer a comfortable and relaxed way of seeing some of the scenic areas of New Zealand. Large companies like Newmans, Guthreys, Mount Cook Lines, Fourways Pacific and H & H operate nationally, with many regional tours, for example Newtons (Dunedin), Pacific Tourways (Christchurch). Local tours, for example, out of Queenstown, can provide relief from driving in the high country.

Air travel connects most cities and towns in New Zealand and makes it possible to move quickly around the country.

In four to five hours, given changes of planes, it is possible to fly from remote Fiordland to Auckland by scheduled service. Three tiers of service exist: a national carrier (Air New Zealand), sub-national carriers (Mount Cook Line and Ansett (NZ)), plus a variety of small regional airlines that often operate charter aircraft and flight-seeing services.

Given the geological and scenic diversity in the country, air travel, especially by small plane, should not be missed. And there is a wonderful variety of aircraft as well: Boeing 737, Fokker F-27 Friendship, Hawker-Siddeley 748, Nomad, Islander, Cessnas 180/185s (ski planes), Banderantes, Piper Navaho, Metroliners, Cessna 402/Titan, Grummon Widgeons.

Touring in New Zealand

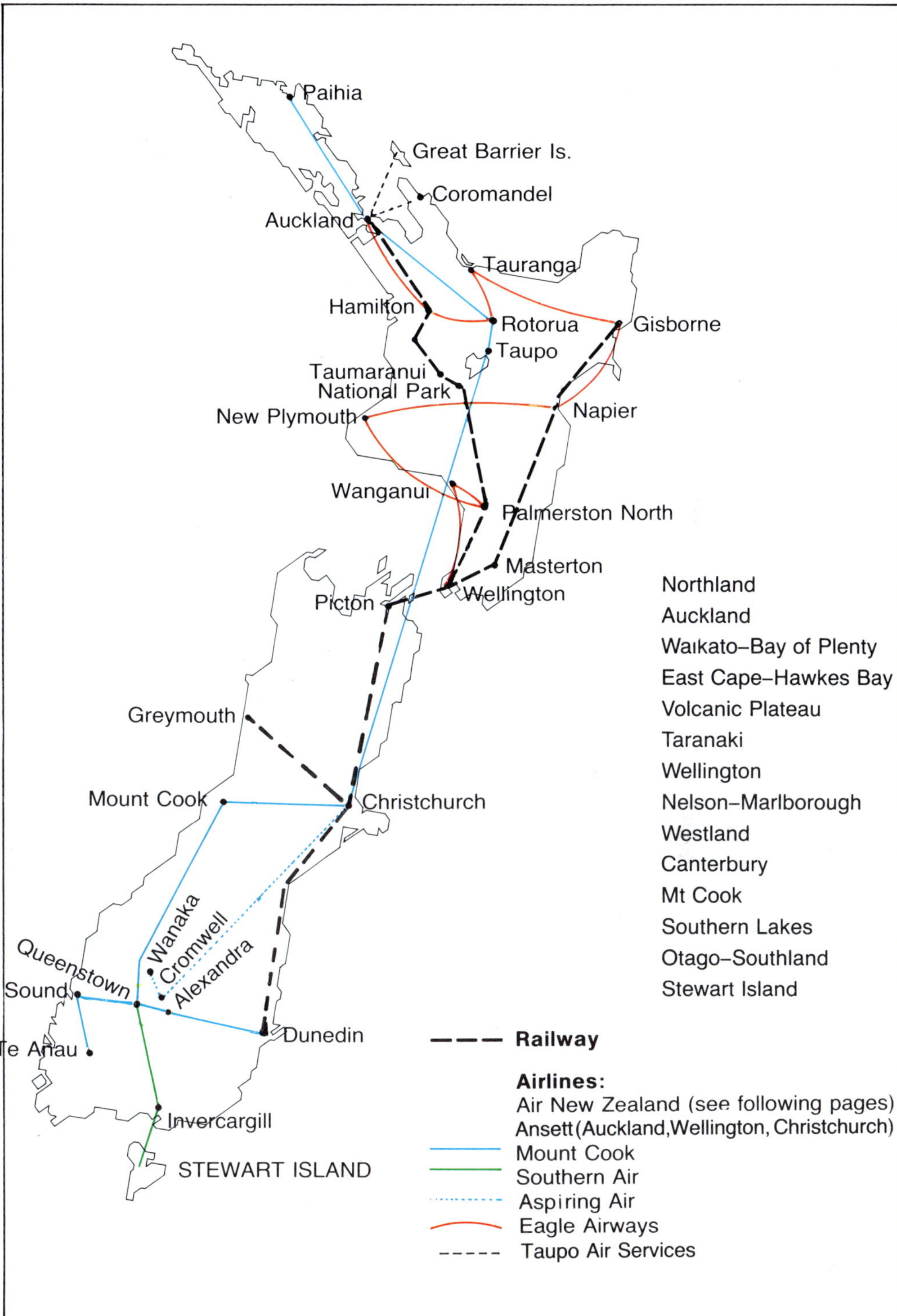

Getting about with air new zealand

Your time in New Zealand can be organised (especially useful if your stay is short) or casual and spur-of-the-moment so you can visit all places at leisure. Air New Zealand operates to 24 cities and towns from the far north to the deep south, and you can connect with rental cars (fly/drive), chauffeur cars, mini-buses, intercity buses and air-conditioned super coaches for regional guided tours. Roll-on, roll-off vehicle and passenger ferry boats operate between the North and South Islands.

Air New Zealand treats its guests to everything they are accustomed to receiving from the world's best airlines. The welcome as you step aboard your Air New Zealand aircraft reflects not only the pride in the presentation of a commercial service, but pleasure that you have chosen to discover and share our South Pacific paradise.

Any day of the week, Air New Zealand makes at least 220 flights between the 43 airports and 16 countries in its network. Twenty-three of these airports are in New Zealand and the others are spread between Australia, Fiji, Western Samoa, New Caledonia, Norfolk Island, the Cook Islands, Tahiti, North America, Tonga, Singapore, Hong Kong, Japan, West Germany and Britain. Air New Zealand has offices in each of these countries and in other major cities throughout the world.

In October 1987, Air New Zealand added Dallas to its existing North American ports of Honolulu and Los Angeles. Frankfurt became the airline's second European destination in the same month.

Boeing 767s and 737s operate on the main routes within New Zealand as well as to some South Pacific island destinations. Fokker Friendships link provincial centres with the main cities. The longhaul international sectors are flown by Boeing 747s and 767s.

The Koru

This symbol used in Maori art is shown on the tail of all Air New Zealand aircraft. The design symbolises the uncurling of native fern fronds, and also signifies continual growth and rebirth. It was first seen on the prows of early Maori canoes that navigated the vast reaches of the Pacific Ocean centuries ago.

Air New Zealand First Class

Fly first class on Air New Zealand and you'll be a very special passenger. First-class comfort, first-class service, first-class surroundings are made totally enjoyable by crew dedicated to ensuring your journey is pleasant and relaxed. There is a first-class menu of gourmet dishes and connoisseur's wines. On the Boeing 747s a sheepskin Recaro sleeper seat awaits you. There are just four rows of Recaro sleeper seats, with each row staggered to give a feeling of privacy.

First-class passengers also enjoy easy check-in facilities and access to Air New Zealand V.I.P. lounges at most airports and baggage is tagged 'first-off' for easy retrieval at your destination.

Air New Zealand Pacific Class

For a little more than the normal economy fare, appreciate the extra space, relaxed atmosphere and special service of Air New Zealand's unique Pacific Class on Boeing 747 and 767 aircraft. On the 747 aircraft Pacific Class is located on the upper deck, reached by an easy access stairway. There are much wider than normal sheepskin-clad seats with special inflight service to match. Pacific Class travellers also enjoy special check-in facilities and access to Air New Zealand V.I.P. lounges at most airports and baggage is tagged 'first-off' for easy retrieval at your destination.

Touring in New Zealand

Air New Zealand Economy Class

'Economy class' can often be a label for second-class. Not with Air New Zealand. Every passenger is special. To make your flight enjoyable, there's Air New Zealand's renowned in-flight service, carefully prepared and presented meals, plus a wide selection of wines.

As with First-class and Pacific Class fares, normal economy fares allow you maximum flexibility. You can book at any time without penalty. There is no minimum stay requirement. Your ticket is valid for one year from commencement of your journey and if you decide to amend your travel plans, any portion of travel unused is fully refundable.

Children

Children under 12 years pay only 50% of the adult international fares while infants under 2 years, not occupying a seat, pay only 10% of the adult fares (limited to one infant with each accompanying adult). With domestic fares, children under 15 years pay only 50%. Children under 4 years, not occupying a seat are not charged. Infants under 2 years are not charged.

Accommodation

Organise your travel and accommodation together with one telephone call! Refer Hotpac listing in this section.

Air New Zealand domestic and international routes.

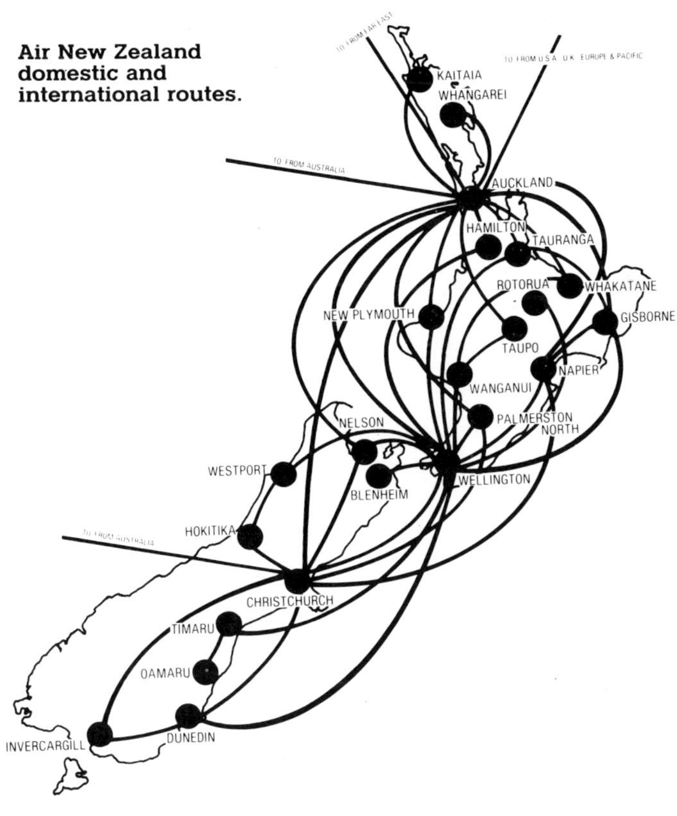

Driving in New Zealand

Driving Licences

A current licence and/or an international licence are acceptable. Minimum age for rental-car hiring is 25 years. Front seat belts must be worn by law ($25.00 fine otherwise). In built-up areas speed limit is 50 km/h (30 mph); on open road and motorways, 80 km/h (50 mph). LSZ means Limited Speed Zone, in which the maximum is permissable only when conditions are ideal. If there are children, pedestrians, heavy traffic or bad weather, 50 km/h prevails. This sign is shown on the outskirts of towns and cities.

Traffic Officers (Ministry of Transport)

Traffic Officers enforce the speed limit and deal with accidents. They are separate from the Police Force and neither carry weapons. Report all accidents to the Ministry of Transport.

Petrol

High-octane gas is about NZ$ **4.30** per gallon (**96** cents per litre). No discounting, same price countrywide.

Maps and Driving Aids

The Automobile Association (AA) provides an excellent road-map and accommodation-guide service. Free reciprocal membership privileges are offered to members belonging to equivalent overseas organisations. Check with the telephone directory in each town or city for the local AA address. AA Head Office: corner of Lambton Quay and Willis Street, Wellington, P.O. Box 1053. Telephone: (04) 851-745.

Motor Homes

Now becoming a popular way to explore the back roads of New Zealand taking your accommodation with you. With few restrictions on where you can go and where you can stop, the wilderness can really be yours to enjoy – by a lake or near the beach.

There are more than 450 motor camps in New Zealand and, except at the peak summer season (December through February), there is no need to pre-book. Facilities generally include washing machines, dryers, showers and superettes. The average tariff is $3.00-$7.00.

Droving sheep on the Mt Cook Rd, Mackenzie Country. *(Andris Apse Ltd)*

Touring in New Zealand

Cars and motor homes

Avis Rent A Car is New Zealand's largest rental car company with more than 100 branches and service agents throughout New Zealand. A wide range of late model vehicles to choose from, ranging in size from small sedans and hatchbacks to large automatic sedans and station wagons. Also available are comfortable 10-seater Mini Coaches, perfect for the larger family or group. The spacious interior means plenty of room for luggage as well as ensuring travel comfort. All vehicles at competitive rates including unlimited mileage. To reserve your Avis Rent A Car in New Zealand, or for more information, write or telex direct or contact any Avis Worldwide location or NZ Tourist and Publicity Office.

Avis Rental Cars
22 Wakefield Street
Private Bag
Auckland
Telephone: (09) 792-545
Telex: NZ2543

AVIS

Avis offer late-model 2-, 4- and 6-berth Motorhomes, well-appointed with cassette radio/stereo, gas cooker, battery/electric refrigerator and all cooking equipment and bedding. Avis Motorhomes are designed so that they can be plugged into mains voltage at any of over 300 well-equipped and sited camping grounds and caravan parks, throughout New Zealand, as well as being able to operate on battery when 'off the beaten track'. Avis Motorhomes are comfortable 'homes away from home' and a great way to see New Zealand. All are supplied with a comprehensive map directory. To reserve your Avis Motorhome in New Zealand, or for more information, write or telex direct or contact any Avis Worldwide location or NZ Tourist and Publicity Office.

Avis Motorhomes
105 Neilson Street
Onehunga
PO Box 13-314
Auckland
Telephone: (09) 642-168
Telex: NZ2543

AVIS

Drive yourself in the right direction with Henderson Rental Cars! Choose your car, van, mini bus, 20-seat coach, 4-berth motorhome or four-wheel drive vehicle for your great New Zealand venture from a great range of all types of late model vehicles. Rates are better than competitive and value is assured. Service points and replacement vehicles are available throughout the country. For your convenience, Henderson Rental Cars will deliver your vehicle to you and collect it again, anywhere in the central Auckland area! All vehicles are well maintained and provided with thoughtful extras such as a map of Auckland, with maps for every area of your New Zealand travel; ski racks for skiers; child restraint seats if required for the safety of little ones; plus AM/FM radios (tape cassette decks in latest models) for your added enjoyment. All major credit cards are accepted.

Henderson Rental Cars Ltd
9 Dora Street
Henderson
PO Box 21-012
Auckland 8
Telephone: (09) 836-8089
Telex: NZ21580
Facsimile: (09) 32-659

This company specialises in motor caravan rental, providing a wide range of top-quality and well-maintained vehicles including 2-berth pop-tops, economical 4-6 berth diesel and luxury 6-berth (with shower/toilet) units. A special feature offered exclusively, is a tape tour programme – your personal tour guide on cassette, giving you history, Maori mythology, places of interest and some little-known spots often missed by travellers. These cassettes cover a variety of routes, taking in New Zealand's main attractions. They are complimentary and can be retained for use with your movies or slides. All vehicles are fully equipped with bedding, cooking equipment and utensils, and heater. They are available for pick-up from either Auckland or Christchurch and one-way hires are available at no extra charge. From $350 per week.

Rainbow Adventure Vans
PO Box 43-235
Auckland 6
Telephone: (09) 275-8944
After hours: (09) 657-338
Telex: NZ63120

Maui Tours of New Zealand Ltd
100 New North Road
Private Bag
Auckland
Telephone: (09) 793-277
Telex: NZ60109
Facsimile: (09) 371-450

Operating New Zealand's most modern fleet of campervans, ranging from 2-berth 'campas' to the pride of fleet, the Maui 6-berth deluxe. Vehicles come fully equipped with cooking utensils, bedding, and additional extras such as microwave ovens and outdoor furniture! The luxuries of home and more! There's no better way to experience the scenic splendour of this beautiful country, with a company guaranteeing holiday satisfaction. Rental stations located at Auckland and Christchurch, open daily, year round.

Newmans Rentals Ltd
PO Box 22-413
Otahuhu, Auckland
Telephone: (09) 275-0709
Telex: NZ2662
Christchurch Office:
Telephone: (03) 535-800

MOTOR HOME HOLIDAYS: Newmans offers a wide range of excellent motor homes, comfortably accommodating, 2, 4, or 6 people, depending on your personal requirements. These modern, easy to drive vehicles are superbly appointed, with lots of storage for your clothes and equipment, and other thoughtful touches for your comfort – like chains and a ski gear compartment if you're off to the snow-covered slopes! Feel right at home in the great outdoors – by the beach, native forests and mountains, or use New Zealand's many excellent motor camp facilities. This is the ideal way to independently see New Zealand, stopping wherever you want for as long as you like. Offices in U.S.A., Japan, Canada and U.K.

Guthreys New Zealand Tours Ltd
126 Cashel Street
PO Box 343
Christchurch
Telephone: (03) 793-560
Telex: NZ4243
Facsimile: (03) 790-175

Guthreys

This company offers a full range of great holidays. You may use self-drive rental cars, motor homes or 8-seater mini buses. Options are offered of either fixed itineraries, self-planned or Freewheeler Tours, utilising superior or budget style hotel and motel accommodation. Motor homes sleeping up to six persons are available from either Auckland or Christchurch. Offices in Sydney, Melbourne, Perth, Los Angeles, Vancouver, Tokyo and London for your booking convenience.

Bus travel – Scheduled and Regional

Newmans Coachlines Ltd
PO Box 39-462
Auckland
Telephone: (09) 399-738/ 31-149
Telex: NZ2478
Facsimile: (09) 389-811
Telegrams/Cables: 'Newcoach'
Christchurch: Telephone (03) 795-641

TRAVEL NEW ZEALAND WITH NEWMANS COACHLINES: With a fleet of modern coaches and a renowned reputation for reliability, Newmans operates regular daily services between many towns in New Zealand. For visitors, Newmans Coachlines are an ideal, flexible and inexpensive way to enjoy more of the country. No comfort is lacking, coaches are air-conditioned and each seat has its own especially comfortable sheepskin cover. Drivers are friendly, informative and helpful. Reservations may be made at any Newmans office or travel agency.

Newmans Tours Ltd
PO Box 3719
Auckland
Telephone: (09) 31-149
Telex: NZ2478
Facsimile: (09) 389-811
Telegrams/Cables: 'Newcoach'
Christchurch: Telephone (03) 795-641

GREEN DOMAIN COACH HOLIDAYS: Superior and Deluxe coach holidays offer top quality coach tours where the emphasis is on luxury accommodation and a high standard of service and quality. These holidays incorporate all you want to see and do in either one island or both the North and South, and are fully escorted by a driver/courier, who packs every kilometre with interest and amusement. Some holidays include farmstays or home stays (staying overnight in New Zealand homes, enjoying local hospitality). Offices in: U.S.A., Japan, Australia, Canada and U.K.

Touring in New Zealand

NEWMANS 18-35 COACH HOLIDAYS: If you're between 18 and 35 and feel like putting real adventure into your life – take off around New Zealand with Newmans! Join a group of singles and couples and go boating, riding, flying, skiing, dancing, drinking, laughing, singing ... plus loads more! You'll stay in cabins, hotels, castles, and a Maori marae (meeting place). Travel in style – Newmans coaches have great stereo sound and are really comfortable. Available year through for sun and fun. Snow adventures are seasonal. Offices in: U.S.A., Japan, Australia, Canada and U.K.

Newmans Tours Ltd
PO Box 3719
Auckland
Telephone: (09) 31-149
Telex: NZ2478
Facsimile: (09) 389-811
Telegrams/Cables: 'Newcoach'
Christchurch: Telephone (03) 795-641

With offices in Sydney, Melbourne, Perth, Los Angeles, Vancouver, Tokyo and London for your booking convenience, this company offers an extensive range of fully-escorted coach tours, covering the length of New Zealand. With a reputation for excellent service, itineraries range from 4 to 19 days with regular, fixed departure dates, throughout the year. A superior standard of accommodation and meals are provided. Comprehensive sightseeing with entrance fees included in costs.

Guthreys New Zealand Tours Ltd
126 Cashel Street
PO Box 343
Christchurch
Telephone: (03) 793-560
Telex: NZ4243
Facsimile: (03) 790-175

Guthreys

Specialised Tours

The first independent holiday without having to drive! Tours tailored to your needs, fully flexible with emphasis on personal service. Why drive yourself? Using quality scheduled coach travel, please yourself when you leave! Staying at motor lodges or live with New Zealanders, hosts welcome you en route with assistance and sightseeing advice. From 3-day Bay of Islands/Rotorua to full 13-day New Zealand adventures, or plan your own itinerary! From $269 (GST inclusive).

Go New Zealand Holidays
Level 2,
155 Karangahape Road
PO Box 68-440, Newton
Auckland
Telephone: (09) 795-520
Telex: NZ60898
Facsimile: (09) 795-520

The country's National Tourist Office and the obvious contact for all travellers. NZTP TRAVEL specialises in custom-tailored individual and group travel. Through modern technology, NZTP TRAVEL has instant access to virtually all aspects of travel within New Zealand and overseas. Whether you wish to travel on a fixed itinerary or go as you please, NZTP TRAVEL is the place to go before you go places!

Head Office: NZTP Travel Office
Private Bag
Wellington.
Telephone: (04) 728-860
Telex NZ3491

NZTP Travel Office	**Queenstown**
Auckland	**Sydney**
Rotorua	**Brisbane**
Wellington	**Melbourne**
Christchurch	**London**
Dunedin	**Los Angeles**

In addition to coach and fly/drive tours, Guthreys offers a full range of camping, skiing, adventure and special interest holidays. 'Footloose 18-35' camping tours operate October to May, staying in cabins and chalets, with regular departures from Auckland and Christchurch. The skiing season runs from June through November, and Guthreys features tour packages to Turoa (Mount Ruapehu), Mount Hutt, Mount Cook, Wanaka, the Remarkables and Coronet Peak (Queenstown), with several grades of accommodation and travel by coach, rental car or motor home. Adventure packages include hiking, back-packing, climbing, white-water rafting, canoeing, jet-boating, trout- and salmon-fishing and scuba-diving. A special interest department will plan any type of tour to suit your requirements, specialising in planning conferences and conventions. Offices in Sydney, Melbourne, Perth, Los Angeles, Vancouver, Tokyo and London for your booking convenience.

Guthreys New Zealand Tours Ltd
126 Cashel Street
PO Box 343
Christchurch
Telephone: (03) 793-560
Telex: NZ4243
Facsimile: (03) 790-175

Guthreys

Self Drive Holidays
Mutual Holidays
(Division of the Mutual Group)
22 Wakefield Street
PO Box 5913
Auckland
Telephone: (09) 792-495
Telex: NZ2804
Facsimile: (09) 370-269

If you prefer a packaged holiday of New Zealand that includes accommodation and self-drive car and require flexibility with time and places you choose to visit, then Mutual Freewheel Holidays are the answer. A wide range of Fixed Itinerary Holidays are also available, ranging in duration and covering the North, South or both main Islands. All holidays offer a wide choice from three grades of accommodation – standard, quality or superior, and all tours include discount admissions to some of the country's top attractions. Mutual Holidays use New Zealand's largest rent-a-car company, Avis Rent A Car, giving a choice of vehicle size (including mini buses) with Unlimited Mileage. For more information, including a wide range of complimentary, attractive, four-colour brochures, write or telex direct or contact your nearest New Zealand Tourist & Publicity office.

Newmans Tours Ltd
PO Box 3719
Auckland
Telephone: (09) 31-149
Telex: NZ2478
Facsimile: (09) 389-811
Telegrams/Cables: 'Newcoach'
Christchurch: Telephone (03) 795-641

SELF-DRIVE HOLIDAYS: A Self-Drive holiday is a holiday tailored for your own special requirements. Explore where you want, see and do what interests you, stay as long as you please. Newmans offers you three great Self-Drive ways to tour New Zealand: 1. Freewheeler Holidays: flexibility with no itinerary 2. Prebooked Holidays: totally preplanned leave it all up to Newmans 3. Individually Selected holidays: describe your ideal holiday to Newmans and Newmans will plan your adventure of a lifetime! All Self-Drive holidays offer three styles of accommodation: hotel, motor inn or motel and a range of vehicle sizes. Whatever your choice, Newmans will help you to plan your adventure. Offices in: U.S.A., Japan, Australia, Canada and U.K.

Budget and Backpackers Accommodation Group
c/- Rainbow Lodge
Titiraupenga Street
Taupo
Telephone (074) 85-754
or c/- Avon View
208 Kilmore Street
Christchurch
Telephone: (03) 69-720

A recent phenomenon is the appearance of this group of budget-priced hostels and hostel-style lodges. Throughout New Zealand, these privately owned and operated enterprises offer an opportunity for the long-term, self-sufficient traveller to make the economies in accommodation expenses that a prolonged and active visit may demand. Premises and atmospheres vary almost as much as locations: Northland to Southland, Central City to Rural Retreat, Crackling New to Nicely Mature – but each has an understanding of travellers' needs, and each provides all that's needed to shelter, refresh, feed and inform the inveterate traveller. All for $13 per night or less (GST inclusive)! Blue and white "Budget and Backpackers Accommodation" brochures, which list all participating establishments and give further details, are available throughout New Zealand at entry points and Information Centres, or direct from Rainbow Lodge, Taupo; or Avon View, Christchurch.

Rainbow Adventure Holidays
PO Box 8327 Symonds Street
Auckland
Telephone: (09) 389-419
North America
(800) 722-2288
(800) 227-5317
(See listings in Sailing section.)

Discover the 'real' New Zealand – combining action with sightseeing the way YOU want it! Through the regionally based 'Discover New Zealand' Kit, Rainbow organises whatever you want – superb sailing adventures, skiing, fishing, diving, tramping. A choice of transport from cars to campervans is available and a range of accommodation from private farms to deluxe hotels can be prearranged or chosen as you go. Costs vary depending upon your personal requirments. Enquiries direct in New Zealand or U.S.A.

Touring in New Zealand

Specialised Holidays

SPECIALIST INTEREST TOUR AND INDEPENDENT TRAVEL: This team of very experienced operators challenge you to name it and they'll organise it! Whatever your special interest – be it farming, photography, arts/crafts, gardening, history, Maori culture, mountaineering or whatever – Silver Fern Holidays is proud to introduce you to their services, and to New Zealand – our 'world in miniature'. Silver Fern will design a trip for you guaranteed to delight, arrangements are detailed to suit your requirements. They'll arrange your travel, from flights to a chauffeur-driven limousine or yacht; welcome you on arrival, organise transfers, accommodation – including home-hosted or farm stays with New Zealanders, sight-seeing and adventures. Professional escorts provided if required. If you have time constraints or would prefer to join others in a coach or group tour, Silver Fern Holidays offer a variety of wonderful tours of our country.

Silver Fern Holidays Ltd
PO Box 206
Auckland
Telephones:
Auckland – (09) 798-764
Vancouver – (604) 6849-722
Seattle – (800) 3259-667
USA – (800) 3685-252

'Listen to New Zealand'. You've organised your car or campervan for your great New Zealand adventure and you are ready to set off on the road. Not quite! Don't start without this superb set of easy listening cassette tapes, for you to play as you tour. They provide entertaining and informative insights about the areas you're travelling through – history, accommodation and things to do and see. The set of four cassettes covers the country from north to south and is an excellent travelling complement to this book, plus providing a reminder of your trip to keep at home. Set comes complete with a Holiday Planner sheet, detailing audio information and assisting you in daily planning. From $24 (plus $2.40 GST for NZ residents) and overseas airmail postage from $5.60. Order direct by mail or telephone.

South Pacific Tourist Services
PO Box 11-023
Dunedin
Telephone: (024) 42-373/ 44-884

Mts Ruapehu and Ngaruahoe, Volcanic Plateau.
(Courtesy Turangi Scenic Flights)

Accommodation

At the top of the scale are the luxury hotels that provide all the style, comfort and services expected of top international hotels – places such as the Sheraton in Auckland, the Hyatt Kingsgate in Auckland and Queenstown, and in Rotorua, the Parkroyal in Wellington, Noah's Hotel in Christchurch, the Queenstown Travelodge on the shore of Lake Wakatipu. Find hotels of this standard only in major cities or favourite tourist destinations.

Tourist Hotel Corporation, or THC, hotels are state-owned, luxury hotels in places of special tourist interest, often remote.

Find THC hotels at Waitangi, where the modern complex spreads along the shore looking out on the Bay of Islands; at Waitomo, near the caves, in a rambling Victorian country hotel; at Rotorua, right by steaming geysers and with an emphasis on Maori entertainment and culture; at Wairakei, set in 1,620 hectares, (4,000 acres) of parkland, including one of the best golf courses in the country; at Tokaanu, on Taupo's southern shore, with an emphasis on trout fishing; in the elegant splendour of the THC Chateau Tongariro on the lower slopes of Mt Ruapehu.

In the South Island there's the THC Hermitage, focal point of Mt Cook village, with balconied rooms looking out towards the mountain; the THC Milford Hotel on the shore of Milford Sound with views of Mitre Peak; THC Te Anau sits in a spreading parkland of lawns and trees on the edge of Lake Te Anau; balconied rooms at THC Wanaka look out past pines, firs and poplars and over Lake Wanaka; THC Franz Josef is surrounded by mountains and thick bush, and adjacent to the glacier that forces its way through the rain forest.

Also offering top accommodation are the exclusive, small, family run lodges, country resorts with first-class standards of comfort, service and informal sophistication. Activities here are organised to suit the individual's wishes and most specialise in fishing and hunting. Sites are usually superb, in garden seclusion on lake or river edge. (See the Lodges section.)

As well as a good range of up-market hotels, cities usually have modest, moderately priced hotels near the city centre, places such as the DB Royal International in Auckland, the Grand Establishment in Rotorua, St George in Wellington, the Clarendon in Christchurch, the Mountaineer Establishment in Queenstown. The Vacation Inns provide an excellent standard of accommodation in most of the main tourist centres, as well as in more remote areas such as Te Anau.

In country towns old hotels that have seen grander days often provide bargain accommodation for those trying to stretch their travelling dollar – expect to find a comfortable, simple room, usually with private bathroom, but without telephone or television (there will be a 'television lounge' for the use of guests). Some such hotels are privately owned; most will be brewery owned, by the DB or Lion chain. Both chains have some very smart hotels, such as the high-class DB Rotorua, and a good range of moderate hotels, but the budget-watching traveller should remember the small-town hotels – expect good plain cooking in the dining room and find lively hotel bars that are a local meeting place.

Hotels all have a licence to serve liquor, with a house bar for guests and public bars. A 'tourist licensed' hotel will be licensed to serve liquor to guests only – no public bar. A 'private hotel' has no liquor licence but can often provide good, economical accommodation – guest houses and private hotels are similar in style and function.

A 'motor inn' might also be labelled a 'motor hotel', 'motor lodge' or 'serviced motel' – generally anticipate modern quality accommodation, especially well suited to car travellers. At many you park your car by the entrance to your room. Expect a licensed restaurant and a house bar.

Motels are a feature of New Zealand travel – most motel units are, in fact, small self-contained apartments, with separate bedroom(s), bathroom, sitting/dining room and fully equipped kitchen. There's everything necessary for self-catering, from toaster to oven dish. Instant tea, coffee, salt, pepper and milk are provided – you must cook your own meals, make your own beds, but for a moderate price you have, in effect, got a suite.

Motels are usually small, family-run concerns, with six to 12 units, and so provide an individuality not found in major accommodation chains.

Travellers on a shoe-string budget will find youth hostels in main cities and towns and at prime tourist destinations. Camping grounds are prolific, on the outskirts of cities and towns, but particularly along the coasts and by lakes. Most also offer simple cabin accommodation. Take to the hills and mountains in National Parks and Forest Service Parks and you will find a unique system of 'huts', strategically placed in the remotest territory. Some provide the simple basic needs of shelter; others are large and modern with extra comfort, such as cosy armchairs to pull up around the huge stone fireplace. National Park huts charge a few dollars a night, Forest Service huts are free.

Air New Zealand Ltd
Hotpac
Accommodation

The Hotpac reservation system arranges accommodation and a wide range of tour and leisure products throughout New Zealand – the simple way to pre-arrange your holiday. With a copy of Hotpac's brochures you can access your complete New Zealand travel requirements. Designed for use by Air New Zealand passengers, Hotpac's 'The Good Night Book' accommodation brochure contains in excess of 500 hotels, motels and motor inns worldwide. The New Zealand section covers all accommodation options from luxury hotels to budget-priced guest houses. Included are over 100 of the popular motor lodges of New Zealand properties – well appointed, quality units with the majority offering kitchen facilities. Save with Hotpac rates.

Hotpac also assists with planning your leisure time. The 'Go As You Please' Holiday Planner is designed so Air New Zealand passengers can access some 200 tour and leisure products throughout New Zealand. Firstly – select your competitively priced rental car or motorhome (ranging in size and types), then book any number of leisure activities to enjoy during your journey through the country. These cover a vast range of interests, from city tours and cruises to forest walks and live theatre, farm stays to flightseeing and fishing – something for everyone! Again, the Holiday Planner provides a price saving over walk-in door rates.

Air New Zealand reservations staff or your travel agent can advise availability, rates etc, and make your Hotpac reservations when booking your Air New Zealand flights, issuing you with pre-paid Hotpac vouchers before you leave for handing to the hotel or tour/leisure operator on arrival. Air New Zealand offices are located in Canada, U.S.A., Japan, Singapore, Hong Kong, United Kingdom and Europe and throughout Australia and the Pacific Islands.

Flag Inns Ltd
PO Box 3654
Auckland
Reservations:
Telephone: (09) 799-444
Facsimile: (09) 396-239
Telex: NZ2602
Singapore: 732-9388
London: (01) 930-0909
USA – CA (213) 277-9037
USA – TOLL FREE (800) 624-FLAG

FLAG INNS

A warm welcome awaits you whenever you stop at a Flag Inn. More than 50 motor inns throughout New Zealand fly the Flag – it's a symbol of guaranteed friendly hospitality and a consistently high standard of service.

Flag Inns are owner-operated so each has its own special individuality and charm, while sharing the same standard of excellence. From world renowned resorts like Rotorua and Queenstown, through glaciers like Franz Josef and Fox, to warmly accommodating cities like cosmopolitan Auckland and the garden city of Christchurch, Flag Inns give you New Zealand. The Flag service can even take care of planning your accommodation itinerary.

Flag Inns' computer booking system operates throughout New Zealand and the South Pacific, so all you need do is choose whether to plan in advance or book as you go along.

THC

THC WAITANGI RESORT HOTEL, Telephone: (0885) 27-411 Telex: NZ 2200
THC WAITOMO RESORT HOTEL, Telephone: (0813) 88-227, Telex: NZ 2905
THC ROTORUA INTERNATIONAL HOTEL, Telephone: (073) 81-189, Telex: NZ 2427
THC WAIRAKEI RESORT HOTEL, Telephone: (074) 48-021, Telex: NZ 2223
THC CHATEAU TONGARIRO RESORT HOTEL, Telephone: (081223), 809, Telex: NZ 2213
THC TOKAANU RESORT HOTEL, Telephone: (0746) 8873
THC THE HERMITAGE, Telephone: (05621) 809, Telex: NZ 4308
THC GLENCOE LODGE, Telephone: (05621) 809, Telex: NZ 4308
THC MOUNT COOK MOTELS AND CHALETS Telephone: (05621) 809,Telex NZ 4308
THC FRANZ JOSEF RESORT HOTEL, Telephone: 719, Telex: NZ 4367
THC WANAKA RESORT HOTEL, Telephone: (02943) 7826, Telex: NZ 5636
THC TE ANAU RESORT HOTEL, Telephone: (0229) 7411, Telex: NZ 5335
THC MILFORD SOUND RESORT HOTEL, Telephone: (02298) 6, Telex: NZ 4300

Tourist Hotel Corporation

1 WAITANGI
On the shores of the Bay of Islands and set in the grounds of the Waitangi National Trust.

2 WAITOMO
Set amid the green rolling hills of the lush King Country.

3 ROTORUA
Overlooking legendary Whakarewarewa with its abundance of thermal activity.

4 WAIRAKEI
Opposite the two Wairakei Golf Courses and near to the Huka Falls.

5 TOKAANU
A small fisherman's hotel at the southernmost end of New Zealand's largest lake – Lake Taupo.

6 CHATEAU TONGARIRO
Mountain resort hotel on the slopes of Mount Ruapehu, highest peak in the North Island.

7 THE HERMITAGE
High up in the Southern Alps in a small mountain village.

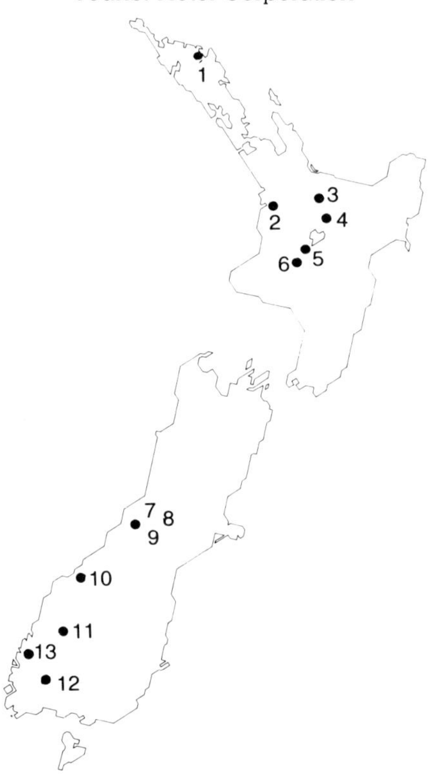

8 GLENCOE LODGE
An economy priced hotel, Glencoe Lodge has grand views of surrounding mountains and glaciers.

9 MOUNT COOK MOTELS AND CHALETS
Superb views of the surrounding mountains and glaciers.

10 FRANZ JOSEF
Located on the perimeter of Westland National Park with a grand view of mountains, glaciers and sub-tropical bush.

11 WANAKA
On the shores of Lake Wanaka with superb views of the Lake and surrounding mountains.

12 TE ANAU
Within views of Lake and mountains, Te Anau Hotel is on the doorstep of New Zealand's largest National Park, Fiordland.

13 MILFORD SOUND
New Zealand's most remote Hotel is located deep in Fiordland National Park at Milford Sound – views of the mile high Mitre Peak and the Sound itself.

Touring in New Zealand

With just one call, organise a superb first-class New Zealand holiday, staying at any of 20 individually operated retreats throughout the country. These are intimate lodges for a select few, and are personally hosted by the owner.

A Retreat Holiday makes possible a style of New Zealand living tailor-made for people whose needs are different and whose tastes are for the unusual. Even in well-known resorts, Retreat Holidays offer secluded preserves like Arden Lodge, near Havelock North, or a first-class homstead on a sheep station, overlooking the wild southern Pacific Ocean. There are lakeside and riverside resorts – for example, an Edwardian mansion nestled on the shore of an alpine lake. Each of them offers the full variety of activities available in New Zealand or the most peaceful and restorative holiday imaginable.

Whatever you require, a Retreat Holiday is an excellent way to experience the magic that is New Zealand in a first-class manner. See the Lodges Section and Regional Listings for a full description of these properties.

Assistance is provided with itineraries and travel advice. A RHC video brochure and compendium is available on request.

Retreat Holiday Company Ltd
Head Office: Regent Building
Cathedral Square
PO Box 4026
Christchurch
Telephone: (03) 799-126 or 799-127
Telex: NZ 40051 RHC HOT
Facsimile: (03) 795-769

AUCKLAND: Retreat Holiday Co. Ltd, Tamaki House, 70 Anzac Avenue, PO Box 80-090, Auckland 7, Telephone: (09) 796-743, Facsimile: (09) 32-639.

AUSTRALIA: RHC International, Retreat Holiday Co. Ltd: BRISBANE, Qld 4000, GPO Box 365, 1st Floor, 150 Edward Street, Telephone: (07) 229-4445, Telex: AA 40472 ATTN BR 146, Facsimile: (07) 229-8812: MELBOURNE Vic 3001, GPO Box 974 H, Telephone: (03) 690-8429, Telex: AA 30625 ATTN ME2406.

USA: RHC International, Retreat Holiday Co. Ltd, 3652 MacArthur Boulevard, Suite 310A, Santa Ana, CA92704, USA. Sales Office: (714) 540-0428, Reservations: (CA) telephone (800) 238-9875; (USA) telephone (800) 228-8345, Telex 495-3090 SPAC U1.

SINGAPORE: RHC International, Retreat Holiday Co. Ltd, 135 Cecil Street, 04-01 LKN Building, Singapore 0106, Telephone: 224-5454, Telex: RS42421 SIMSHI, Facsimile: 2-241-628.

JAPAN: RHC International, Retreat Holiday Co. Ltd, 50-6 Jingu-Mae, 5 Chome Shibuya Ku, Tokyo 150, Telephone: (03) 4-987-636, Telex: 2-325-325, Facsimile: (03) 4-985-403.

EUROPE: RHC International, Retreat Holiday Co. Ltd, West Germany; PO Box 1849, AM 44 NR.33, 6740 Landau, Telephone: (06341) 82-960/84-327.

AUSTRIA: RHC International, Retreat Holiday Co. Ltd, Peregringasse 2, A-1090 Vienna, Telephone: (0222) 316-735, Telex: 116-156, Facsimile: (0222) 343-485.

RETREAT HOLIDAYS IN THE SOUTH PACIFIC EN ROUTE: The Retreat Holiday Company is affiliated to R.H.C. INTERNATIONAL, which also offers exciting stopover possibilities: Island Resorts of The South Pacific (nine island resorts on five islands through Tahiti).

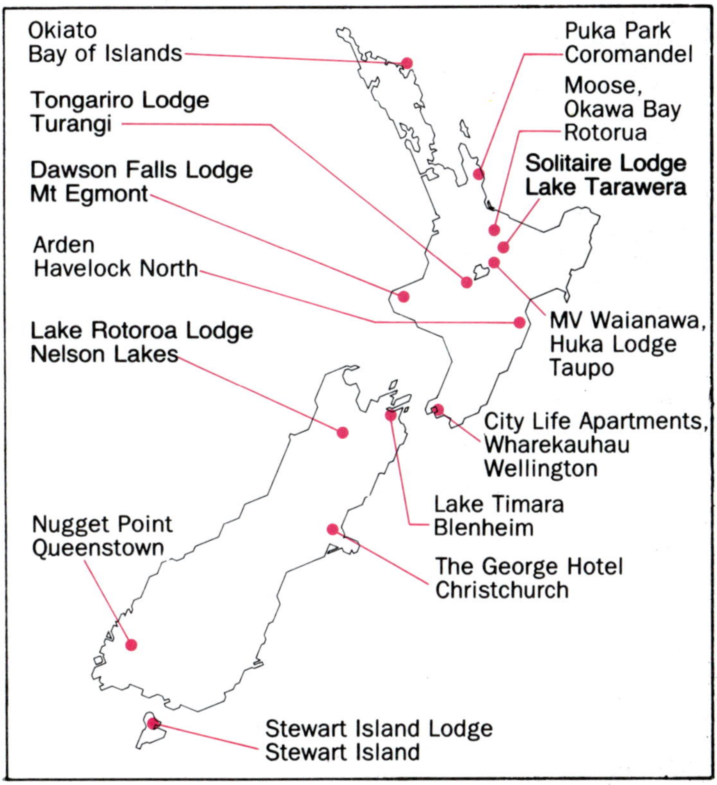

To make the most of eating in New Zealand, – to enjoy world-class gourmet delicacies at relatively low cost – it is a matter of knowing what to look for and how to find it.

Food

Surrounded by seas, there is an abundance of first-rate fish and shellfish – snapper, red snapper, tarakahi, hapuku, blue cod, orange roughy, John Dory, flounder and sole are all excellent white fish.

Fish smoking using aromatic manuka wood is a tradition in New Zealand. Smoked snapper roe is a true gourmet delight, spread on brown or rye bread, with a dash of lemon juice and a dusting of black pepper. Other smoked pleasures are smoked eel, smoked marlin and smoked salmon, but don't neglect the more prosaic smoked snapper, smoked trevally and smoked mullet.

The famous New Zealand crayfish is an exquisite luxury, known elsewhere in the world as rock lobster, spiny lobster or crawfish. It is usually sold ready cooked, which too often means over cooked. Realise that any restaurant prepared to get live crayfish and cook them on the premises is probably also fussy about correct cooking. For a perfect summer picnic buy a cooked crayfish from a good fish shop or local fisherman (in seaside towns and villages there are often well sign-posted backyard sales).

Two kinds of mussel are widely available – a small, blue-lipped mussel and a large green-lipped mussel. Both are equally delicious and usually well presented in restaurants. They can also be bought pickled in brine for picnics or snacks.

There are three varieties of oyster – small, sweet rock oysters, large Pacific rock oysters and the rich, distinctive Bluff oysters dredged from Foveaux Strait. Oyster connoisseurs will want to try the Bluff oysters, in season between March and August.

And then there's the tuatua, a relative of the famous toheroa, but more readily available, generally served in a creamy soup or as fritters but also wonderful simply steamed open in the shell.

Try also the whitebait, a tiny delicacy, unlike any other whitebait except that caught in the river mouths of Tasmania.

Game-food specialities to seek out are venison and wild pork; and don't pass up any opportunity to taste sweet spring lamb.

Given a climate that ranges from subtropical to almost subantarctic, local fruit and vegetables cover a wide range, and tropical fruit are flown in from the Pacific islands to the north. If you want fruit and vegetables very fresh, pick your own (P.Y.O.) in road-side gardens – a very popular phenomenon new in most major towns.

Local cheeses to try are cheddar (especially South Island mature cheddar), Epicure, Cheshire, Havarti, Colby, Blue Vein and Feta. There's good local Camembert and Brie as well.

In main centres, and a surprising number of minor ones, specialist food shops and delicatessans carry a full range of imported and local food – great places to select food for outdoor eating. In main cities find the best French bread and croissants outside France (one French baker in Christchurch sends fresh croissants by air daily to Australia). Other specialist breads include excellent wholegrain and farmhouse-style loaves – try Vogels bread, it really is a bread sensation.

Many New Zealand honey sources are unique and so provide unusual delights for honey connoisseurs. These include pale gold kamahi and tawari, light amber rewarewa, sweet, delicate pohutukawa and the rich, aromatic-ling heather honey. Bush honey is a dark, rich blend originating from forest flowers.

Touring in New Zealand

Where to eat? Starting at the bottom of the scale are the fast-food eateries, including the ubiquitous Kentucky Fried Chicken, Pizza Hut and MacDonalds. The traditional fast-food standby is fish and chips – ask a local where the best fish and chip shop is to be found or choose one with the longest queue (if the locals are prepared to line up for their order, the results should be worth it). Try meat pies – best from places proclaiming 'home cookery' or 'baked on the premises'.

Coffee shops provide good snack meals and poor coffee. If you relish good coffee, drink tea instead; or try the delicious apple juice. Also find milk bars, distinctly 1950s in style, using rich creamy milk in the milkshakes.

Dining out in the cities of Auckland, Wellington or, to a lesser extent, Christchurch, offers a sophisticated range of possibilities. Also find plenty of pleasant choice in tourist-oriented towns such as Rotorua, Taupo and Queenstown.

Restaurants are either licensed to sell wine or BYO (meaning bring your own wine). The latter are usually smaller and more informal but the quality of cooking may well be better than that of an elegant, more expensive establishment.

Off the beaten tourist track, where time and trends move more slowly, first-class stylish cooking can be hard to find although eating treats can turn up anywhere – an imaginative little restaurant with a superb tuatua soup or simply the best meat pie ever, wrapped in layers of light flaky pastry. Look for old-fashioned farm-style cooking and try mammoth morning and afternoon teas. Helpings are always large.

In a country that's small, with excellent communication systems, food is transported quickly from its source at one end of the country to a table at the other. You can dine on fresh Hawkes Bay asparagus in Queenstown or just-picked Nelson cherries in Auckland, but make the most of delectable produce by concentrating on specialities in their region of origin.

The standard of restaurants changes continually. For a selection of restaurants, read local newspapers and magazines like *Metro* (Auckland) and *Cosmo* (Wellington). Diners Club publish a restaurant guide (available from their offices in Auckland, Wellington and Christchurch), which covers a good selection of restaurants through the country (but not all). Each year, Diners Club conduct the 'Restaurant of the Year' competition, voted for by consumers. The Diners Club 'Restaurant of the Year' and top ten restaurants for 1983, plus progress results for 1984, in order of popularity are:

1983
Wheelers, Auckland
Bacchus, Wellington
Bonapartes's, Auckland
Bronze Goat, Auckland
Rogues, Auckland
Orsini's, Auckland
La Scala, Dunedin
Aorangi Peak, Rotorua
Camelot Room, Regency Hotel, Christchurch
Plimmer House, Wellington

1984
Rogues, Auckland
The Sign of the Takahe,
Camelot Room, Regency Hotel, Christchurch
Antoines, Auckland
Coachman, Wellington
Wheelers, Auckland
Jules, Auckland
Olivers, Tauranga
Paul Revere, Christchurch
Gainsborough House, Hamilton

Take home the culinary secrets of some of these chefs, or select your restaurant from the recipes offered by 50 chefs from around the country in *The New Zealand Restaurant Cookbook*, by Michael Guy and Digby Law (Lindon, 1983).

There's a distance of little more than 800 kilometres (500 miles) from Cape Reinga, in the far north of the North Island, to Wellington, the capital city that looks out towards Cook Strait and the South Island. But don't be misled – it may take longer than you think to travel around in New Zealand.

The North Island's main route, State Highway 1, runs almost all that distance, through major cities and towns, from Kaitaia, near magnificent Ninety Mile Beach, through hills and valleys to Northland's commercial centre of Whangarei, and south to Auckland, occasionally brushing by the coast.

From Auckland the highway leads straight into the heart of the Waikato dairylands, the city of Hamilton and the leafy town of Cambridge, continuing on to the Central Plateau – a region of thermal springs, geysers and vast Lake Taupo. Crossing the bleak desert lands east of the live volcanoes of Tongariro National Park, State Highway 1 descends into hill pastures and plains to the city of Palmerston North, a prosperous agriculture-oriented city surrounded by rich farmland. The highway then veers west to the coast, following the strip of lowland between rugged hills and sea before winding its way over windswept ridges to Wellington.

To explore the variety of the North Island, to discover the diversity of North Island life, diverge from the highway onto side routes and by-ways, and link up with other main North Island routes – one following the Pacific coast to the east, the other the wild Tasman to the west.

State Highway 2 branches off south of Auckland and leads down through coastal cities and towns, – such as Tauranga, Gisborne, Napier and Hastings – through forests, farms and orchards and by sheltered bays and long ocean beaches.

State Highway 3 swings away to the west just south of Hamilton, taking a route that leads near the Waitomo Caves and through to New Plymouth, Mt Egmont National Park and along the coast to Wanganui on the banks of the romantic, unspoilt Wanganui River. The route links up again with SH1 at Palmerston North.

A fourth state highway, SH4, leaves SH3 to run through the rugged King Country to Taumaranui, to the Central Plateau west of the Tongariro mountains, to link with SH3 again at Wanganui. And SH5 branches in a loop from SH1 to lead to Rotorua, then to Taupo and then away again to Napier and SH2.

These main routes are all two- or four-lane highways and all sealed, although road-surface conditions vary with topography.

Driving the North Island can be an adventure in itself, discovering how sparsely populated the countryside is, that little roads always lead somewhere, that traffic can be so light that drivers exchange a friendly wave as they pass.

Roads wind and intertwine between the three major routes, opening up fascinating possibilities when choosing a touring itinerary. Make the most of a countryside where the next turn of the road may open up entirely new vistas, where the small towns en route may offer as much, or more, than the main centre ahead.

Take these back roads and don't expect ideal road conditions – some will be excellent, wide, smooth-sealed roads, some narrow well-sealed lanes, others loose-metal winding hill roads.

Provincial highways bear double numbers such as 22 or 41; others are simply 'secondary roads'.

Between SH1 and SH2, east of Hamilton, for example, take provincial highways and secondary roads that spread out in a net across dairy pastures and horse-racing stud farms, through tiny villages that consist of little more than an aging community hall and rural school.

At Mangaweka head up into the hills on Provincial Highway 54 to reach Palmerston North by way of hill farms and great views over wide winding river valleys.

Take Provincial Highway 35 around the East Cape and be amongst the first in the world to greet the morning sun.

North Island Touring

The sea dominates Northland. From the sheltered bays of the east and the long sweeping beaches of the west, the sea reaches deep inland with harbours, inlets and tidal creeks thick with mangroves.

The north is great hills, gentle green valleys, long single-lane bridges over mangrove inlets, native cabbage trees (a species of palm lily), scarlet Caribbean flame trees and the giant kauri that grows to a height of 50 metres (165 feet) with a girth up to 15 metres (50 feet). It is a warm place of sudden contrasts, stony hill country that struggles to support sheep, cattle or goats, rolling green pastures where Friesian or Jersey cows graze, hillsides of white-flowering manuka scrub and occasionally pink-flowering manuka. There are dark green forests where the wild white clematis splashes over the treetops, vast peat swamps, mountainous sand dunes and lush subtropical orchards where tamarillos and oranges hang like bright globes, sheltered by high bamboo hedges.

History here stretches back over the centuries to the first Maori settlers. Legend has it that Northland was their first landfall – at Taipa in Doubtless Bay over 1,000 years ago. Many Northland communities today are predominantly Maori, and ancient pa sites, the fortified villages used in tribal warfare, can be seen as terraced hills. Ancient artifacts and tools used by the region's early fishermen and moa hunters can be seen in the museum at Kaitaia and the Wagener Museum at Houhora.

New Zealand's earliest European settlements also grew up along the edges of the bays and rivers, first with the arrival of sailors, who felled the tall kauri trees for spars for their sailing ships, and then with the missionaries, who arrived to preach the gospel and teach reading, writing, arithmetic, European agricultural methods and Victorian values.

Reminders of the mission days linger in many places, especially in the serene charm of Waimate North, the brooding isolation of Mangungu, the Kemp House and Stone Store at Kerikeri, the Williams Memorial Church at Paihia.

Kauris dominated the forests that grew over the hills and valleys of Northland – most of the forests have long gone, the trees felled for timber or burned to clear the ground for farming and digging kauri gum, the fossilised gum that made high-quality varnish.

See stands of kauri in the 9,000-hectare (22,000-acre) Waipoua Forest, in the Puketi Forest where the rare kokako bird lives in the forest canopy, in the Omahuta Kauri Forest, in the Ngaiotonga Scenic Reserve and in the small but superb Trounson Park.

The country's oldest town, Russell, began life as Kororareka, a wild settlement dubbed 'the hellhole of the Pacific', where whalers and seamen sought rowdy solace in the grog shops. Original buildings line the sea shore in today's tranquil town, now a major game-fishing port.

Further north is Whangaroa, a place to buy fresh oysters from the farms in the upper reaches of the harbour, drink in the harbour-side pub where commercial fishermen and game fishermen gather, and explore by boat the unspoilt, romantic outer harbour, still inaccessible by roads.

At Mangonui the town spills down the hill to the harbour, where buildings stand out over the water on stilts. At a small aquarium on the wharf giant packhorse crayfish and rare fish can be viewed. On the west coast harbour of Hokianga are Rawene and Kohukohu, once bustling timber towns but now villages of quiet charm and old buildings. A car ferry crosses the inlet.

In the far north the prosperous centre of Kaitaia began as a mission station, but owed much of its early development to the navigable Awanui River. Nearby Ahipara, a Maori settlement and small beach resort, was once larger than Kaitaia when gum from the rich gumfields was shipped out from Ahipara

Bay. About 80 hectares (200 acres) of the gumlands have been kept as a special reserve where visitors can envisage the harsh life of Yugoslav gumdiggers, whose descendants now form a significant part of the population in the far north.

In the south the region's only city, Whangarei (pop. 40,179), owes its growth to the deep sheltered Whangarei Harbour, able to handle the world's largest oil tankers.

Roads came late to this region and the towns and villages relied on the sea and rivers for transport and communication. Don't be afraid of travelling down a gravel road to discover your own private cove.

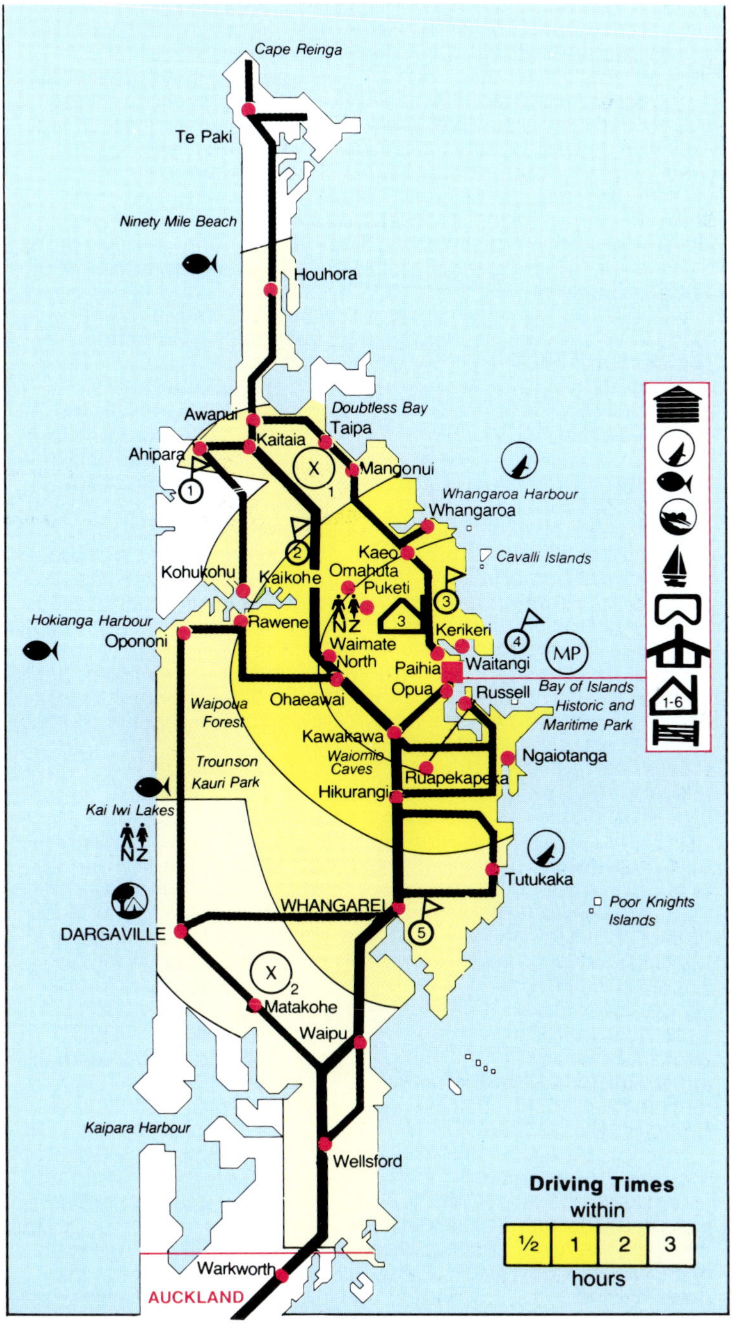

NORTHLAND

National Parks
Bay of Islands Maritime & Historic Park.

Lodges
Roberton Island.

Outback Safaris

Fishing
Big Game

Other

River Adventures

Yachting/Cruising

Diving

Golf
1. Ahipara; 2. Kaikohe; 3. Kerikeri; 4. Waitangi; 5. Whangarei.

History
1. Kemp House; 2. Stone Store; 3. Waimate Mission House; 4. Pompellier House; 5. Waitangi Treaty House; 6. Ruapekapeka Pa.

Down on Farm

Live with NZ

Local
1. Far Northern Museum; 2. Otamatea Museum.

Paihia

The holiday town of Paihia spreads along the foreshore, looking out across the Bay of Islands. Motels and hotels range from modest to luxury, tours leave for all parts of Northland, and down at the wharf side boats wait for the visitor.

Take off on the water on a launch trip around the bay or on a game-fishing expedition; hire a jet boat, sailing dinghy or row boat; charter a yacht with skipper or arrange a bare-boating holiday; take a barbeque cruise or a dinner cruise around the islands; rent a surf-cat or windsurfer; arrange a ski-tow boat for an afternoon's water skiing or take a water taxi service to an isolated island bay for a picnic, fishing, diving and swimming – the boat will return at a pre-arranged time. (Arrange similar boating pleasures across at Russell if you wish.) Take a scenic flight from Paihia and capture it all.

There are 144 islands and hundreds of coves, bays and beaches in the Bay of Islands, and nearly every one of them has a perfect spot for a picnic. Most islands are uninhabited so you may find not only a bay to yourself, you may find a whole island. Camping is allowed on Urupukapuka Island and others.

Back in Paihia, walk along the waterfront to find history, modern shops and motels clustered together on a short stroll. The Williams Memorial Church stands on the site of an 1823 mission station; a nearby Norfolk pine was planted by a missionary's wife in 1835. Walk towards Waitangi and pass the Waitangi National Marae, where Maori chiefs gathered in 1840 before crossing the river to sign a treaty acknowledging British sovereignty of New Zealand. (See In Touch with History section p.89).

The Treaty of Waitangi was much later adopted as the symbol of the birth of the nation. But these days the annual Waitangi Day celebrations at Waitangi are likely to be the occasion of demonstrations and protests that the treaty was a 'fraud'. Although initially seen by the British as a way of keeping the peace, the treaty was never ratified and protesters consider many of its provisions were never honoured. Many Maori leaders never signed it, and the slightly different meanings of the Maori and English versions caused considerable confusion over the years.

By Waitangi River bridge a three-masted barque is permanently moored – aboard is a shipwreck museum with intriguing displays of treasure retrieved from the deep.

Over the bridge is Waitangi, an area of 570 hectares (1,400 acres) centred on the Treaty House, built in 1833 on a headland overlooking the bay. There is also a Visitors Centre (with audio-visual displays on the Treaty of Waitangi), a Maori meeting house with carvings from many North Island tribes (a meeting house usually has carvings only from its own tribe) and, on the shore, a 36-metre (120-foot) ceremonial war canoe.

From Paihia take a passenger ferry or jet-boat taxi across to Russell to walk through a town of historic charm. Find old colonial buildings including elegant Pompallier House, the police station and jail, an 1835 church bearing musket-shot holes from a siege.

Also in Russell is the Captain Cook Memorial Museum with a 7-metre (23-foot) replica of his barque *Endeavour* and displays of local history. At the headquarters of the Maritime Park on The Strand audio-visual displays detail the Bay of Islands in the past and today.

Above the town is a hill where Ngapuhi chief Hone Heke four times cut down the British flagstaff before attacking the town in 1845.

Bay of Islands Community Public Relations Office Inc.
Marsden Road, Paihia
P.O. Box 70
Telephone: Paihia (0885) 27-426

1 Northland

Northland, with its favourable climate and fertile land and coast, was a centre of Maori population and thriving agriculture. However, coinciding with the arrival of the Europeans, inter-tribal warfare raged. The Maori population retreated under attack to massive fortresses called pa, built mostly on easily defensible high points and coastal headlands. The remains of pa sites, recognisable by their ridges, terraces and levelled hilltops, are mostly on private property, but at Ruapekapeka, 16 kilometres (10 miles) south of Kawakawa on State Highway 1, earthworks clearly show the huge scale of fortifications.

Ruapekapeka was the scene of the final battle in 'Heke's War', when 1,600 British troops under Governor Sir George Grey bombarded the palisades. Hone Heke achieved lasting fame by repeatedly chopping down the Russell flagpole as a political protest. His father-in-law, Hongi Hika, the leading warrior chief of the North's Ngapuhi tribe, returned from England in 1821 armed with 300 muskets and a suit of armour (a gift from the king). During Hongi's bloody incursions on enemy tribes, thousands were slaughtered before Hongi himself was shot when he forgot to wear his armour. Muskets and disease introduced by the Europeans reduced the Maori population dramatically from an estimated 150,000 when Captain Cook arrived in 1769 to just over 42,000 by 1896.

Entertainment. – The Bay of Islands in January shows a hint of its wild colonial past – holiday-makers converge on the bay for summer revelry that centres on the old Duke of Marlborough pub, Russell. With summer yacht racing and game fishing contests right through into autumn, the Bay of Islands is Northland's liveliest spot. Elsewhere the pace is slower, and small-town activities can include highland bagpipes at New Years Day (Waipu), Yugoslav folk dancing (Kaitaia and Dargaville), rodeo, agricultural fairs, arts and crafts festivals, or a beer and a game of darts in the pub.

Cruising in the bay. *(Courtesy Rainbow Yacht Charters)*

Kerikeri Stone Store.
(Courtesy Air New Zealand)

Around Paihia

By road from Paihia visit Kerikeri, where rich soil and warm climate combine for an area of subtropical orchards – tour orchards and taste unusual fruit. Down by the tiny harbour is New Zealand's oldest building, a wooden mission house built in 1822, and the Stone Store, the first stone building, built in 1833. There's also an authentic reconstruction of a Maori village of pre-European times nearby.

The charm of Kerikeri attracts artists and craftspeople – music, arts and crafts thrive in Kerikeri and it is a village where quality handcrafts can be bought.

Nearby are the historic Kororipo Pa reserve, the impressive Rainbow Falls and the Fairy Pools. A range of sporting/recreational activities offers including a championship golf course, yacht club headquarters, a nightclub and numerous restaurant facilities. A range of accommodation is available, from camping and caravan parks, motels and guest houses to a hotel.

Yet another mission site awaits visitors at Waimate North. The house, built in 1831, has idyllic surroundings of wide lawns, old-fashioned English flowers, huge trees. Next to the house is the Church of St John the Baptist, built in 1871. Wander through a graveyard with wooden headstones and wild flowers under spreading oaks, the oldest planted in 1824.

And see the giants of the native forest, the kauri trees, in the Puketi Forest to the west of Kerikeri or in the Ngaiotonga Scenic Reserve east of Russell. For more splendid kauris, travel further afield to the vast Waipoua Forest.

Kawakawa has the oddity of a railway line running down the main street. Of greater interest nearby are the Waiomio Limestone Caves, with stalactites, stalagmites and a great gallery of glow worms, and Ruapekapeka Pa, a huge intensely fortified pa, with fortifications well preserved and spectacular views.

Travel around Northland by car to reach out-of-the-way places independently rental cars are available in main centres such as Paihia, Kaitaia and Whangarei. Fly from Kaitaia, Kerikeri and Whangarei to Auckland on scheduled services and charter flights from Paihia, Kaikohe, Dargaville, Kerikeri, Kaitaia and Whangarei. Use scheduled bus routes operated by N.Z.R. Road Services for economical wandering, or choose from the many coach tours.

Kerikeri citrus orchards.
(Courtesy
Air New Zealand)

1

Northland

Let Fullers (originators of the world-famous Cream Trip) introduce you to their Bay of Islands. Relax on a coach trip to Cape Reinga where spirits depart; tour Ninety Mile Beach; cruise in armchair 'supercat' luxury to the bay's beautiful islands; dine at Zane Grey's restaurant at Otehei Bay; catch a ferry from Paihia/Russell; view an unsurpassed underwater world from 'Nautilus'!

Fullers Captain Cook Cruises
PO Box 145
Paihia
Telephone: (0885) 27-421
or Auckland, telephone
(09) 394-901

These beach-side, architecturally designed luxury suites cater to comfort, with panoramic views. Two minutes from bus, wharf, shops, restaurants and facilities, yet secluded. Features include family units, honeymoon suites, private hot spa pools and in-house video, plus laundry and children's facilities. Use the dinghy, have a barbeque or continental breakfast in bed. Off-peak rates and discounts available. Book in advance in summer. From $90 per night (twin/double). Extra person $10 per night.

Abel Tasman Motel
Waterfront, Marsden Road
PO Box 51
Paihia
Telephone: (0885) 27-521
Telex: NZ63111
Host: Colin Routley

Centrally located on the waterfront and just 100 metres (300 yards) from Paihia wharf and village, this is an ideal base for exploration of the region. All rooms are well appointed with private facilities and suites additionally feature spa baths, cooking facilities and a view over the Bay. The Reef Restaurant (overlooking the water) serves breakfast and à la carte dinners. Suites from $150, rooms from $95 (single). Off-peak rates apply June-September.

Autolodge
Marsden Road
PO Box 28
Paihia
Telephone: (0885) 27-416
Telex: NZ21730

Owned by Russell's inhabitants – their contribution to preservation of one of our most historic areas – relics reflect Maoris, early pioneers, whalers/traders, missionaries, deep sea fishing. Open 10.00 a.m. to 4.00 p.m. From $1.50 (adult), .25c (child).

Captain Cook Memorial Museum
York Street
Russell
Telephone: (0885) 37-701

Take a tour through this major sub-tropical orchard in the 'Orangemobile', gliding past kiwifruit, tamarillos, tangelos, oranges and other fruit trees, enjoying the comprehensive commentary on orchard operation. Refreshments (plus fresh juices), crafts, souvenirs available.

The Orange Centre
Bulls Road
Kerikeri
Telephone: (0887) 79-397
Hosts: Lesley and Snow Emanuel

Very popular; friendly and informal, succulent New Zealand seafoods, delicious local fruits/vegetables, complemented by cocktails, entrées, desserts and wines. Open daily from noon. 'NZ Food Specialists'. Bookings essential.

Spokes Restaurant
Hub Mall, Kerikeri
Telephone: (0887) 79-700
Hosts: Ivan and Roger Harding

In Bay of Islands heartland, set amongst sub-tropical garden acreage twixt town and stone store. Six free-standing cottages with private patios, saltwater pool, spas, game/fitness rooms, in-house video, plus barbeque areas.

Colonial House Motel
170 Kerikeri Road
PO Box 37
Kerikeri
Telephone: (0887) 79-706
Hosts: Edith and Dick van der Scheer

Northland's Fiord Cruise – on one of our loveliest harbours, accessible only by boat! DAYTIME: Late September-April, 2 (2-hour) cruises daily – 10.15 a.m. and 2.15 p.m., departs Whangaroa jetty. Commentary details history of the area. Beverages available, order lunch day before. Wheelchair access; reservations unnecessary, ring Kaeo for times/other months. From $20 (adult), group discounts.
EVENING/OVERNIGHT CRUISES: Relaxed cruising, wining, dining; licensed vessel accommodates up to 14 persons in olde worlde charm with personal service. Bookings required. From $30 per person.

Whangaroa Harbour Cruises
Operations:
Telephone: Kaeo 132S
Administration:
PO Box 7085,
Wellesley Street
Auckland
Telephone: (09) 371-503
Facsimile: (09) 793-836

North to Kaitaia and Cape Reinga

Far North Community Public Relations Office
Commerce Street
Kaitaia
Telephone: Kaitaia 171

From Kaitaia, the main commercial centre for the farming and tourist area, visit the many beach hideaways the Far North has to offer.

Try the local seafoods at the Albatross Restaurant at Ahipara, situated at the foot of Ninety Mile Beach; take a tour to Cape Reinga and see Spirits Bay, where the souls of the Maori depart this world. The beaches at Doubtless Bay, Cape Karikari and up to Houhora offer tranquility far from the crowded city. Houhora has the Wagener Museum, showing the history and collections of the Wagener family. The homestead was built by the Subritzkys, forebears of the Wageners and descendants of the Polish Royal House of Sobieski, who came to Houhora in the 1860s.

South from Kaitaia take the back roads to Kohukohu, the car ferry across the Hokianga Harbour to Rawene and down to Opononi. Read Maurice Shadbolt's short stories *The New Zealanders* to capture the essence of this area.

Far North Regional Museum
South Road
PO Box 94
Kaitaia
Telephone: Kaitaia 892

A well-kept, progressive museum, with displays covering the history and development of the Far North. Colourful exhibits include excellent photographic records illustrating this unique region. Learn about early Maori settlement, Kaitaia's mission station, the de Surville anchor and other maritime relics, plus aspects of pioneering life. Helpful staff provide assistance and background information on kauri gum digging and Ninety Mile Beach before you tour to Cape Reinga and the gumfields. From $2 (adult), 50c (child).

The Wagener Museum
Houhora Heads
Northland
Telephone: Houhora 850
Owner: W.E Wagener

New Zealand's largest privately owned collection – amazingly diverse. Encompasses Victoriana, antiques, Maori history/archaeology, natural history, conchology, arms/weaponry, carts, toys, fantasy. Lives musically and mechanically. Entertaining, educating and communicating.

Adriaan Lodge Motel
PO Box 114
Ahipara
Telephone: Ahipara 888
Hosts: Lynn and Graeme Neville

Situated in spacious grounds, overlooking magnificent Ahipara Bay, southern end of the famous Ninety Mile Beach and Shipwreck Bay. Comfortable and well-appointed 1- or 3-bedroomed units offer sea views. A splendid secluded retreat.

Albatross Licensed Restaurant
PO Box 114
Ahipara
Telephone: Ahipara 888
Hosts: Lynn and Graeme Neville

Provides excellent dining, delicious seafood a speciality. Just a 10-minute drive from Kaitaia, overlooking famous Ninety Mile Beach. Dine in luxurious surroundings while you watch the sun setting over the bay. Medium price range.

Ninety Mile Beach Holiday Park
Waipapakauri
PO Box 71
Kaitaia
Telephone: (0889) 77-298
Hosts: Jean, Tony & Brljevich Family

New Zealand's northernmost holiday park, 18 kilometres (11 miles) north of Kaitaia and an ideal base for wonderful northern beach adventures, plus fishing, surfing and yachting. Well-appointed cabins, van and tent sites accommodate all your requirements. Friendly atmosphere and facilities include modern ablution block and kitchen, mini-store, colour TV, video games and trampoline for children. Speciality is delicious roast lamb on the spit from the licensed dining room. Range of costs available.

Whangarei Public Relations Office
Forum North, Rust Avenue, Whangarei
Telephone: (089) 481-079

Northland

1

Accommodation. – Excellent hotel or motor-inn accommodation is available in Paihia, Waitangi, Russell, Kerikeri, Whangarei and Kaitaia. Motel units, with fully equipped kitchens for self-catering, are in all main towns and along the coast, sometimes right on almost-deserted beaches. Old-fashioned hotels, many now renovated, provide bargain accommodation in towns that have shrunk to villages – expect a comfortable bed, often a private bathroom, but no television or telephone in the room. Youth hostels can be found at Kerikeri, Kaitaia, Whangaroa, Opononi, Whangarei, with private hotels at Paihia. Camping grounds for those with tents or campervans are almost inevitably near the sea.

Food. – Surrounded by the sea, seek out the freshest fish and seafood such as snapper, hapuka, flounder, crayfish. Try smoked marlin in the region where marlin is caught. The shellfish tuatua is prolific on Northland beaches – try soup or fritters with tuatua straight from the shell, not the can. Also look for huge Pacific oysters or small sweet local rock oysters on the east coast. In the Bay of Islands sample fresh fruit, juices or preserves of goldfruit, tangelos, mandarins, tamarillos, passionfruit, babaco and kiwifruit.

SEE ALSO:

NZ Historic Places: Pompellier House (Russell), Kemp House (Kerikeri), Waimate Mission House (Waimate Nth).
Lodges: Okiato (RHC)
Sailing/Cruising: Charter Link NZ Bay of Islands, Rainbow Yacht Charters.
Down on Farm: Wakelins Agtour.
Live with NZ: Wairoa Farm Stays.
National Parks: Bay of Islands Maritime and Historical Park.

Apsley House, Ohaeawai, Bay of Islands. ***(Courtesy Apsley House)***

South via Hokianga & Dargaville to Auckland

Much of the land of the Hokianga lies idle, and there are visible signs of deterioration. For a long time land there was cheap and bought up by absentee owners and speculators. Communal ownership of Maori land once discouraged development, but Maori owners are now returning to settle on land previously used only for holidays and weekends.

While farmers' children leave for the city life, in the past 10 years a strong community of 'alternative lifestylers' have been attracted by the Hokianga's peacefulness, isolation (nearest towns Dargaville and Kaitaia are an hour's drive) and untamable vitality. On small farms and communes, these new settlers have built interesting houses – look out for their craftwork and delicious honey at roadside stalls. Forestry is now beginning to change both established and alternative lifestyles.

Local Government Centre, Hokianga Road, Dargaville. Telephone (0884) 7059

A town that was once one of the busiest ports in the country, when kauri timber and gum were loaded at the riverside onto sailing ships, the tiny port on the Wairoa River sees little commerce today. But the town makes a good base for exploring the wild west-coast beaches such as Bayley's Beach and Glink's Gully, and the Waipoua Kauri Forest. Travel out to the historic lighthouse on the Kaipara Heads and catch glimpses of old shipwrecks in the drifting sands, try surf casting from the beaches, visit the tiny perfect Kai-iwi Lakes, with white silica-sand beaches rimmed with pines.

Northern Wairoa Museum
Harding Park
Dargaville
Telephone: (0884) 7555

Adjacent to a Maori pa, housing Maori and pioneering artefacts, early kauri furniture, local maritime records and history plus masts of the 'Rainbow Warrior'. Includes the spacious Lighthouse Restaurant complex (see listing). From $2 (adult), .50c (child).

The Lighthouse Restaurant
Mt Wesley
Mahuta Coast Road
Dargaville
Telephone: (0884) 7133
Host: Gary Burnett

Dargaville's newest fully licensed restaurant catering for tourists and casual diners, 7 days and nights. Set in parklike grounds adjoining the Maori and Maritime Museum, with panoramic views over Dargaville and the northern Wairoa River. Dine and dance evenings, enjoy a light or à la carte lunch – indoors or at a picnic table in these lovely grounds. View the 'Rainbow Warrior' masts in the doorstep. Large groups welcome. Closed Good Friday.

Parkview Motel
36 Carrington Street
Dargaville
Telephone: (0884) 8339
Hosts: Gillian and Frank Grover

Quiet location close to town centre. Excellent facilities include solar-heated swimming and swirl pools, restaurant, laundry and car wash. Self-contained and comfortable twin, double and family units. From $52 (single), $60 (double).

Otamatea Kauri & Pioneer Museum
(Off State Highway 12)
Matakohe
Northland
Telephone: Paparoa 37-417
Curator: Merv Sterling

Superb museum (between Paparoa and Ruawai) built as tribute to pioneers, and nationally important for the 'Story of the Kauri' and unique kauri gum collection (over 1,500 pieces). The history is told with photographs, models, wall timber, early furniture (plus kauri bath!) and industry tools. Picnic amongst living kauris; refreshments available. Souvenir shop specialises in kauri/wooden novelties. Open daily 9.00 a.m. to 5.00 p.m. (closed Christmas Day). From $3 (adult), .50c (child). Group rate applies.

SEE ALSO:

Outback safaris: Kauri Coasters Tours.

South via Whangarei to Auckland

Explore the fine native forest walks, golf courses, art galleries, museums and meandering natural harbour. There are choices in dining and entertainment, and local repertory and operatic groups offer regular entertainment. Check programmes at Forum North, civic and cultural heart of the city.

The beaches are famous, from the awesome power of Ocean Beach, a surfers paradise, to tranquil beaches dotted along the harbour (Matapouri and Whale Bay are the better known). The twin areas of Ngunguru (a tidal estuary where shellfish are abundant) and Tutukaka (centre for deepsea/line fishing charters, and dive trips), are only a 30-minute drive from the city. The area is rich in Maori and European history, well-documented in collections at the Northland Regional Museum, plus places of historical interest including the Clarke Homestead at Maunu and Devil's Causeway at Taurikura. Parahaki is an historically important area; a choice of walks leads to the war memorial on the summit; view Maori earthworks, a waterfall, even an old goldmine en route. Or drive to the top for panoramic city and coastal views. Whangarei is rich in a variety of parks and walkways. For the most active, Mount Manaia presents a challenge, while others enjoy a quiet stroll through Mair Park or explore the mangrove boardwalk.

Whangarei
Public Relations Office
Whangarei City Council
Forum North, Rust Avenue
Private Bag
Whangarei
Telephone: (089) 481-079

Clapham Clock Museum is justifiably world renowned. The late Mr Archibald Clapham spent years collecting items with clockwork mechanisms. The museum is open from 10.00 a.m. to 4.00 p.m. weekdays, 10.15 a.m. to 3.00 p.m. weekends and public holidays.

Clapham Clock Museum
The Rose Gardens
Water Street
Whangarei
(089) 483-993

This pool complex is adjacent to the Town Basin, a haven to many overseas yachts. The recently completed complex offers a tepid pool, spas and sauna, while in summer, the outdoor Olympic, diving and children's pools operate.

The Ted Eliott Memorial
Pool Complex
Ewing Road
Whangarei
(089) 487-957

A truly spectacular setting for a holiday resort, just 29 kilometres (18 miles) from Whangarei, set in splendid isolation on the top of a peninsula, commanding breathtaking views of the Pacific Ocean (from Poor Knights Islands to Hen and Chicken Islands) and Tutukaka harbour. Thirty fully self-contained units – from studio to executive (3-bedroomed) suites. Amenities include swimming pool, heated spa pool, full-sized tennis court, children's play area, games room, modern laundry and barbeque. Close to safe and private beaches, surfing beaches and boat moorings. The area is well-known for superb game and line fishing and diving, all readily accessible from this resort. Summer months from $100 (double), off-peak rates from $70 (double), GST inclusive.

Pacific Rendezvous Motel
Motel Road
Tutukaka, R.D. 3
Whangarei
Telephone: (08933) 847
Hosts: Peggy and Tony Potts

Colonial architecture with comfort and elegance, overlooking the Hatea River, close to shops, facilities, golf courses and local scenic attractions. Sixty rooms offer a range of excellent accommodation from luxury suites to single rooms, all with in-house video and mini-bars. The first-class licensed restaurant is well known, complemented by house bar. Amenities include guest laundry and ample car parking. Major credit cards accepted. From $54.50 (single, GST inclusive).

Settlers Motor Hotel
Hatea Drive
Whangarei
Telephone: (089) 482-699
Telex: NZ2258

Superb camping facility set on a peninsula in 26 acres (10 hectares) of reserve. Two minutes' walk, to ocean beach. Family oriented, 150 powered van sites, 150 tent sites and full amenities. Up to 15 years old free; from $8 (tent site), $9.50 (van site).

Ruakaka Reserve
Beach Road
Ruakaka
Telephone: (089) 27-590
Host: Jean & Alby Vallantyne

Auckland may be the country's most populated region, but for those who wish to escape the city the surrounding area provides extraordinary opportunities with its islands, beaches, hills and valleys.

Centred on a narrow isthmus of dormant and extinct volcanoes, the region of Auckland sprawls out from the city over the hills and countryside. This is a region of people – about a quarter of New Zealand's population lives in this area – yet it feels more like a series of villages with a small city centre than a major metropolis.

The suburbs spread out in a vast web from the commercial centre on the edge of the Waitemata Harbour, through vineyards and orchards to the hills of the west where houses nestle in the native bush; along the beaches and tiny bays to the north and east and across green fields to the south.

At first glance it is a homogeneous collection of houses and trees strewn over hills and valleys, thinning at the green perimeters where the true countryside takes over. Yet the suburbs, the outlying country towns and villages all have their own distinct characteristics throughout the region.

Travel to the north of the region, through the pretty riverside town of Warkworth to the village of Leigh, where fishing boats and dive boats gather in the inlet. In a spectacular marine reserve along several kilometres of the shoreline divers can hand feed fish. Surfers head over the hill to the long, beautiful beach at Pakiri. From nearby Sandspit, boats leave for Kawau Island, where visitors can see through a grand mansion, once the home of a governor, Sir George Grey. Bush walks lead over a rugged, roadless island – walk quietly and you may find wild wallabies sharing the track.

Reach most islands of the Hauraki Gulf from Auckland City's harbour front – there are about 100 islands out there. Ferries, yachts, launches or sea planes open the way to the islands, right out to the furthest and largest of them, Great Barrier. This covers 28,000 rugged hectares (70,000 acres) and has a population of less than 500. Closest to the city is Rangitoto, an uninhabited, sharply defined volcano, formed a mere 800 years ago.

Safe, sheltered swimming beaches indent the coast of the gulf. Some, such as Snells Beach, Algies Bay, Waiwera, Orewa and Manly, are dense with holiday cottages and permanent homes, but also offer village shopping amenities. Others such as Wenderholm and Mahurangi Heads are special reserves where the natural beauty of the shoreline is unmarked by any buildings. All are popular but never crowded – an important distinction.

Aerial view over Westhaven marina and the harbour bridge. *(Andris Apse Ltd)*

At Waiwera natural hot springs have been tapped and turned into an elaborate complex of hot-water swimming pools, with private dip pools and giant water slides – barely a towel's throw from the beach. Also find natural hot-water swimming to the west at Parakai, near Helensville.

The beaches of the west coast are wild and treacherous, favourites with surfers and those who like invigorating surf swimming – surf life-savers patrol the black-sand beaches of Muriwai, Piha and Karekare, ensuring visitors know the safe places to swim and surf.

Between the city of Auckland and the closest west-coast beaches rise the Waitakere Ranges, high forest-covered hills, threaded with walking tracks. Once dominated by kauri forest that was milled out last century, the bush remains thick enough to get lost in if you stray from the tracks. Stands of kauri remain in the hills, and an information centre on the Scenic Drive near Titirangi details the history, the walks, the flora and fauna of the ranges.

To Bombay at the south of Auckland the hills rise again,

rich, volcanic soils in the south west providing a patch-work of market gardens. To the south east there are more bush-covered hills, dipping down to pretty east-coast bays, the home of riding schools and the mini-estates of the wealthy.

Travel on towards the Coromandel Peninsula, across the edge of a flat plain where deep ditches border the road and divide the fields, and boulders keep river levels above the surrounding land. Ahead looms the extraordinary contrast of the sharp, raw splendour of the peninsula.

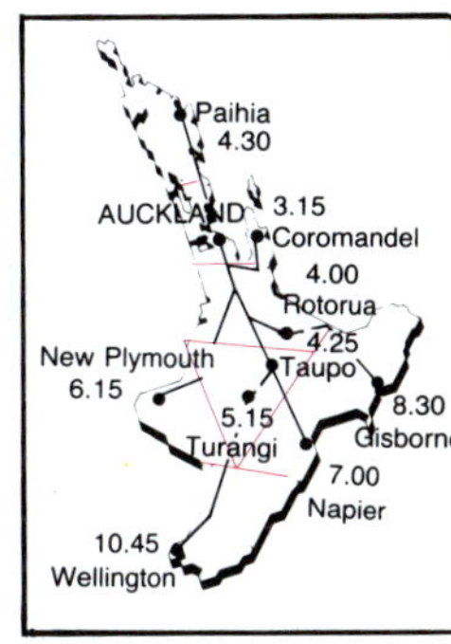

Travel around by car in Auckland. Fly by amphibian aircraft to islands or bays on the east coast, and fly on small land craft to Whitianga or Pauanui. Public buses, run by the Auckland Regional Authority, serve some beaches and villages outside the city limits. N.Z.R. Road Services buses have a regular service through the Coromandel from Auckland. Take tours, with a wide variety to choose from.

AUCKLAND

National Parks
Hauraki Gulf Maritime Park.

Lodges
Ellerton.

Fishing

Yachting/Cruising

Flightseeing

Diving

Golf
1. Muriwai; 2. Chamberlain; 3. Grange; 4. Remuera; 5. Titirangi; 6. Manukau.

History
1. Ewelme Cottage; 2. Highwic House; 3. Alberton; 4. Mt Eden – Pa site; 5. One Tree Hill – Pa site.

Live with NZ

Local
1. Museum; 2. Zoo.

Sailing at Takapuna Beach. *(Courtesy Air New Zealand)*

Auckland is a city of views. From hilltops and ridges you can look down to the Waitemata Harbour on the east coast and the Manukau Harbour on the west. At the narrowest point there is scarcely more than a kilometre between the two coasts.

Generations of Maoris heaved and dragged their large and small canoes over these portages from harbour to harbour as a shortcut during wars or on fishing trips. Being surrounded by good locations for pa and two good harbours, Auckland was coveted by a number of Maori tribes. Although numbering up to 4,000 people in pre-European times, European guns and disease drastically reduced the Maori population before Auckland was founded in 1840.

About 900,000 people live in Auckland, mostly in single-storey houses each with its own garden – there is little high-density living. Drive to the top of One Tree Hill or Mt Eden and see houses and gardens spreading out through the valleys in an area the size of greater London. Filled with trees, freshened by sea breezes and showers, Auckland has little of the hazy pollution that plagues many cities.

For other perspectives of the city, drive around the Waitakere Ranges through thick native forest, or cross the harbour by bridge or ferry to Devonport and the twin cones of Mt Victoria and North Head.

On the North Shore residents relish a casual lifestyle in beachside suburbs. Visit beaches such as Takapuna, Cheltenham, Milford or, on the city side, minutes from the centre, swim at Mission Bay, Kohimarama, St Heliers.

Down at the waterfront find boats and sea planes that will whisk you away out to the islands of the Hauraki Gulf for fishing, sailing or sightseeing.

Back in the city, discover the many beautiful parks. Albert Park in the city centre is distinctly Victorian, with flowerbeds and band rotunda. The Auckland Domain ençompasses woods where daffodils grow, unusual trees, cricket grounds, tropical glass house, ponds and statuary. Cornwall Park merges with One Tree Hill into more than 120 hectares (300 acres), where sheep and cattle graze under old oaks, olives and Norfolk pines. A huge Edwardian-style afternoon tea taken at the kiosk provides an unusual time warp.

Old buildings also emphasise the city's Victorian origins. Down town is the old Customhouse. Further afield see through grand mansions, Highwic and Alberton, and the charming cottage, Ewelme Cottage and Kinderhouse (see the History section page 94)).

Auckland Region Visitor Bureau (Inc.)
Aotea Square
299 Queen Street,
Auckland
P.O. Box 7048
Telephone: (09) 31-889

A style of architecture known as 'Selwyn' dominates early Church of England buildings – find this romantic Gothic style in Parnell, especially the tiny St Stephens Chapel, at All Saints' in Howick and St Andrew's in Epsom.

Stroll or bus to Orakei state-housing suburb, one of the areas where the state has housed low-income families. Over 70 years ago the first town-planning conference sponsored a competition for the design of a garden suburb. Orakei has been developed almost along the lines of the prizewinning model.

Discover the large ostentatious homes of Paritai Drive on one side of the valley and the unpretentious state houses of the Orakei marae on the other. Facing Okahu Bay, find the roughcast and brick houses with terracotta tiled roofs and Georgian proportions. Influenced by the English garden suburb, they represent the idealism of the 1930s.

Entertainment – Find out when the Auckland Philharmonia plays by watching the ads in the back of both Auckland daily papers. Unearth jazz, blues and rock by reading the *Auckland Star* on Thursdays when there's a special entertainment and gig guide. For jazz music check out Delmonico's in the Hotel De Brett. Rock lovers jam into the Galaxy and the Gluepot. Those wanting a more sophisticated cabaret atmosphere should try Club Casa Blanca, Club 21, Club Mirage, Retro or Brandys.

Auckland boasts several theatre companies. For stimulating inventive productions, visit the Mercury or Arena Theatre at night, or the New Independent, a theatre group that specialises in lunchtime shows. The Maidment Arts Theatre in the university grounds often features theatre, recitals and dance. Limbs Dance Company delights audiences there regularly.

Do not miss getting a copy of *Metro* magazine – one of the country's best. The Metrolog pages of the magazine give the most comprehensive entertainment guide and good reviews of restaurants are also provided. See too the Dining Entertainment Guide in the free, weekly *Auckland Tourist Times*, which is distributed nationally to hotels, car-hire firms, and tourist booking offices and "What's On", in Friday's *Auckland Star* newspaper.

A view from North Head across the Waitemata Harbour to the downtown area of Auckland city. *(Andris Apse Ltd)*

Parnell Village, Parnell. (Courtesy Air New Zealand)

Museums detail the past. The imposing War Memorial Museum in the Domain has a splendid display of Maori and Pacific Island artifacts, and at Western Springs the Museum of Transport and Technology is a stunning collection of everything that whirrs, from music boxes to Lancaster bombers.

Adjoining the technology museum is the zoo, with an international collection in park-like gardens, and your chance to see the strange kiwi bird in a special nocturnal house. More animals? On the western outskirts of the city, at Massey, is a lion park – great fun for children, with camels that insist on being hand fed, a small water slide and a moated fort with paddle boats.

More spectacular youthful fun can be found in the complex at Rainbow's End, where there are water slides, bumper boats mini racing cars. This is in the south at Manukau City (administratively Auckland splits itself into eight cities and many boroughs).

For more grown-up pleasure, tour the vineyards of the western suburbs where grapevines spread over the gentle lower slopes of the Waitakere Ranges. Small or large, the vineyards welcome visitors and there is the opportunity to discover how good New Zealand wines can be. Some vineyards have pleasant outdoor restaurants where you can linger under a canopy of vines.

Browse through markets: at Nelson Street and Victoria Park Markets find the fun and bargains of any big city bazaar; at the Mill discover a concentration of quality crafts; and out at the Otara Shopping Centre carpark each Saturday morning there's a distinctly Maori and Pacific Island market, where raw shellfish, melons, taro, rewena and kumi kumi are sold along with more durable wares.

In the city find further evidence that Auckland is the world's largest Polynesian centre in Karangahape Road, and also Ponsonby, where chic boutiques are side by side with shops selling cheerful island cottons and food such as yams, taro and green coconuts.

Over 60,000 Polynesians live in Auckland; more Niueans, Tokelauans and Cook Islanders live here than in their own islands. Large Samoan and Tongan communities also bring vitality to city life.

For up-market, sophisticated shopping, visit Parnell and find exclusive fashion boutiques, excellent pottery, glassware, jewellery, wood crafts, books, antiques, hand-made sweets. If you long for pastrami, Parma-style ham, pumpernickel or simply a good cup of coffee, you should find it here.

There is far more variety in Auckland than that first glance might imply.

Highwic house, Epsom. *(Anthony Henry Photography)*

2

Auckland

Accommodation – Auckland city has a full range of accommodation, from luxury hotels at one end of the scale down to youth hostels. You can choose according to your pocket and inclination. Outside the city, motels offer the traveller the best accommodation, often right by beautiful beaches. Find youth hostels also on Great Barrier Island, Waiheke Island and Opoutere Beach on the Coromandel. Well-serviced camping grounds, many with cabin accommodation as well, exist throughout the region. Four huts provide free overnight accommodation in the Coromandel Forest Park, and there are several camping areas in remote bays on farm parks on the Coromandel Peninsula.

Food – Eat as well as you wish and spend as much or as little as you wish in the city's proliferating restaurants. You can dine elegantly with fine china, fine silver and the best French-style cooking or in casual, bistro-style informality. Ethnic restaurants offer Greek, Lebanese, Italian, French, Japanese, Chinese, Indonesian, Indian, Thai and Vietnamese cooking.

To sample the best of local produce, look for sea food such as snapper, orange roughy, John Dory, smoked snapper roe, crayfish, mussels, squid, whitebait, oysters. Find baby lamb cooked to pink perfection or large venison steaks. Local fruit and vegetables are superb when well presented – globe artichokes, zucchini, kumara, nectarines, melons, strawberries, kiwifruit. Travel out of town and the standards vary wildly – you may find an exciting little restaurant in a seaside township, you may find fish and chips. Picnic on delicious fare – buy freshly cooked crayfish from a fisherman, peaches and melons from a roadside stall and you have the basis of a perfect picnic.

The Auckland City Art Gallery boasts one of the most notable public art collections in New Zealand. Occupying a fine building in the French Chateau style, it possesses excellent collections of historical European art, contemporary international prints and New Zealand art, past and present. The gallery is superbly situated in a central city location; the bustling heart of the city on one side, the green slopes of Albert Park on the other. It opened its doors to the public in February 1888 with a fusion of the private collections of Sir George Grey (a former Governor of New Zealand), and James Tannock Mackelvie, a once prominent New Zealand merchant. While those collections are still a feature, the city's own holdings have grown and expanded to the point that they are without rival in New Zealand.

Auckland City Art Gallery
Cnr Wellesley and Kitchener Streets
Auckland
Telephone: (09) 792-020
After Hours: (09) 792-069

The Auckland Racing Club is New Zealand's premier thoroughbred racing club, and its track and facilities at Ellerslie have won a worldwide reputation.
The Club races on more than 30 days during each racing season and attracts the highest class fields drawn from horses from throughout New Zealand. Summer meetings include the prestigious New Zealand Derby and the D.B. Auckland Cup. In winter, jumping events are programmed, including the Nescafe Steeplechase, held by many to be the best event of its kind in the world.
Ellerslie Racecourse's facilities are excellent, with full food, beverage and betting services. Also to be enjoyed are the famed grounds and gardens. Only 5 minutes' drive from the city centre, these are a must for every visitor to Auckland, even when races are not being held.

Auckland Racing Club Inc.
Ellerslie Racecourse
Greenlane Road
Auckland
Telephone: (09) 544-069
Facsimile: (09) 548-680
Secretary/General Manager: Richard Benson

Kelly Tarlton's Underwater World
Tamaki Drive
Orakei
Auckland
Telephone: (09) 580-603/585-175
Telex: NZ 2553 SEATECH

The largest aquarium of its kind in the world with acrylic viewing tunnels running for 120 metres (394 yards) – introduces a world only divers normally see – where huge stingrays lazily flap, sharks veer and schools of stunningly coloured fish dart through the water all around you, behind viewing glass! Minutes from the city centre along the waterfront, ample parking and facilities for the disabled. Refreshments and souvenirs available. From $3 (child), $6.50 (adult), GST inclusive. Group concessions.

Sea Bee Air Ltd
Mechanics Bay
PO Box 1971
Auckland
Telephone: (09) 774-406
Telex: NZ21253 SEA BEE

Unique opportunity to experience the thrill of water take-offs and landings in amphibious aircraft from Auckland's downtown shoreline! Daily services operate to islands in the beautiful Hauraki Gulf – Great Barrier, Waiheke, Pakatoa, Kawau and the Bay of Islands further north. Specialising in flight seeing, photographic charters, trips to thermal, scenic, skiing and fishing destinations as per requirements, New Zealand-wide; using Grumman amphibians, fixed wing aircraft and helicopters. From $33 per person depending on requirements.

Shalom Home Tours
36 Allenby Road
Papatoetoe, Auckland 6
Telephone: (09) 278-7756/799-412
Hosts: Helen and David Levin

Helen and David conduct your tour of Jewish sites, explaining the Jewish heritage of Auckland, plus general sightseeing. This special Jewish interest tour includes a meal in their home. From $60 per person.

Vacation Inn, Logan Park
187 Campbell Road
Greenlane Auckland
PO Box 17-042
Auckland
Telephone: (09) 661-269
Telex: NZ2781
Facsimile: (09) 396-063

This comfortable low-rise hotel offers conference facilities, private spa pools, heated outdoor swimming pool, excellent restaurant and bar facilities and well-appointed rooms with in-house video. Situated midway between city and airport, in peaceful surroundings adjacent to a major Auckland park popular with joggers. From $105 (single). Major credit cards accepted.

Clevedon Woolshed
Main Road
Clevedon
South Auckland
Telephone: (09) 2928-615
Owner: Judy Donovan

Pure wool and New Zealand crafts in the country. Just 30 minutes' pleasant drive southeast of Auckland city, in the heart of Clevedon Village, set amongst beautiful farmland, discover an exciting range of pure wool products – excellent quality knitwear, innovative fashion garments, weaving, sheepskins, yarn and toys. See also superb examples of New Zealand crafts – pottery, woodware and glassware – made by talented local craftspeople. An innovative and everchanging shop and well worth a visit.

SEE ALSO:

National Parks: Hauraki Gulf Maritime Park.
Lodges: Puka Park (RHC) (Coromandel).
Sailing/Cruising: Carillion Yachts, Charter Link NZ Auckland, Rainbow Charters, Sailing Holidays, Seika Charters, South Sea Yacht Charters (Auckland).
Bicycling: The Bicycle Touring Company.
NZ Historic Places: Ewelme Cottage, Alberton, Highwic (Auckland).

Auckland

Auckland is yours to enjoy – seeing and experiencing insights into a city guaranteed to delight, providing many memorable moments! Take an aerial birds-eye view of this vast, sprawling metropolis and its stunning coastlines; maximise your shopping time superbly; taste excellent wines, and explore our native rainforests and beaches. There are friendly, personalised tours for small groups, sharing what makes this city special, on half-day, full-day, evening or custom-designed tours. Our members are professionals, each providing the specialist service you see below.

Auckland Tourist Industry Association
Telephone: (09) 797-748

SHOPPING SAFARIS for designer hand-knits, sheepskin and leather goods. FASHION TOURS for clothing, shoes etc. Factory and warehouse outlets, lowest prices but tops in quality! All plus sightseeing and fun by mini-coach. From $15.40, book direct.

Julie Steele's Shopping Tours
PO Box 3262, Auckland
Telephone: (09) 397-442

Fascinating tour, taking you through West Auckland wine-making heartland, known for its European heritage in producing finest vinifera varieties. Taste the wines and learn, enjoying a delicious lunch. From $59 per person (GST inclusive).

Wine Tours
Auckland
Telephone: (09) 398-670

Visit unique natural attractions with Auckland's outdoor specialists. Explore the Waitakere Ranges, rainforest and spectacular West Coast beaches. Visit a nesting gannet colony or take a 2-day tour to the Coromandel Peninsula.

Outdoor & Natural History Tours
Bush and Beach Ltd
Auckland
Telephone (09) 779-029

This Maori company stresses individuality, natural environment and Maori life-style, with warm, friendly Polynesian/Maori guides. Half-day tour Auckland. Full day: Rotorua cultural & lifestyle, also Bay of Islands. Details/costs on enquiry.

Tainui Travel & Tours
Auckland
Telephone: (09) 796-743
Telex NZ60112
Fax: (09) 32639

Bring friends and take to the sky! A great way to appreciate Auckland, bordered by the Pacific Ocean and Tasman Sea; beaches, countryside and Hauraki Gulf. Great fun, from $29 per person for 30 minutes.

Capt Al's Fantasy Flights & Grand Rural Land Tours
Telephone (09) 298-5067/ 299-6456
A.H. (09) 502-511

This relaxing tour includes Kelly Tarlton's Underwater World of wonderful deep-sea creatures, the waterfront, and Heritage Park – demonstrating New Zealand life, plus live Maori concert. From $48 (includes transport/admission), $24 (child). Reservations essential.

Sunday Tours
Auckland
Telephone: (09) 398-670 (24 hours)

HAERE MAI (Welcome)! A superb Maori cultural experience awaits you at Auckland's Memorial Museum; indigenous art is complemented by Maori songs/dances plus meet the performers. Two shows daily; a guaranteed highlight of your visit.

Pounamu Ventures Ltd
Auckland
Telephone: (09) 836-7876

Design tours to suit, from short Auckland adventures to full New Zealand expeditions! Personalised, friendly service; relaxed, enjoyable environment, great viewing; travelling in comfortable 12-seater mini-coaches. Competitive rates with airport/hotel transfers included.

Custom Tours
East Coast Bays Transport Ltd
Auckland
Telephone: (09) 478-8257

A day tour of ALL of Auckland's diversity – city/suburban attractions, native rainforest, countryside, beaches. Meet Aucklanders, watch craftspeople work, taste local wines, feed Angora goats! City hotel pickup/return, to 10 people. Inclusive cost.

That Other Tour
Auckland
Telephone: (09) 686-638 (24 hours)

Walkways, Parks and Reserves

Walkways

The Auckland Isthmus – where only 9 kilometres (5½ miles) separate two oceans – is latticed with sign-posted walkways.

Urban Area: The Coast To Coast Walkway

This is a great way to get to know Auckland. Linking both harbours, it is a permanent route through parks, gardens, past historic barracks and buildings to the summits of both Mt Eden and One Tree Hill. Starting from Queen Elizabeth Square, the total distance of 13 kilometres (8 miles) takes about four hours, and a guide map is available from the Auckland City Council Visitors and Convention Bureau.

Nature and Historic Walks

Aucklanders and visitors can explore the city with experienced guides provided free by the city council. Sunday walks in the Domain (nature and historic walks leave at 1.30 p.m. from museum steps) go all year round, other walks summer only (November to the end of May). Leaflets available from the city council or the Visitors Convention Bureau, Aotea Square. Other walks, most of which take two hours, explore markets, galleries, historic places, the suburb of Parnell, theatres, àrts and crafts, and architecture and leave from a variety of gathering points.

The Waterfront Walk

There are other mapped walks you can follow on your own, taking from 15 minutes to two hours, along the beautiful Auckland waterfront from the Harbour Bridge to Mission Bay. Brochures from the Visitors Bureau have maps and points of interest.

Devonport and North Head

Cross the harbour by ferry to quiet Devonport. The historic North Head Reserve is a short waterfront walk away past yacht moorings and quaint old houses. North Head, once a volcano, was an old military fort built in 1885 and further strengthened with successive 'Russian scares'. In World War I it was an internment camp, in World War II its gun emplacements protected the channel and city.

The Point England Walk

The Point England Walk, about 8.7 kilometres (5½ miles), takes about three hours. Take a bus to the end of the

Pastoral scene in Cornwall Park *(Andris Apse Ltd)*

waterfront, Tamaki Drive to St Heliers. From there walk to Achilles Point for harbour views. Hugging the shoreline, the walk passes two ancient pa sites, an old volcanic crater and 600-year-old pohutukawa trees before descending to the Tahuna-Torea nature reserve, bird sanctuary and sand spit. (Tahuna-Torea is well worth a visit on its own – take a Glendowie or Glen Innes bus from the city terminal. A thoughtful walk right round takes just over an hour.) The walk continues through greenways and reserves to St John's Ridge for panoramic views of the isthmus, Rangitoto and the Tamaki Estuary.

Parks and Reserves

Within driving distance of Auckland are many large parks, bushlands and farms open to the public. Auckland Centennial Memorial Park is the largest of the Auckland Regional Authority's 10 regional parks, and is a reminder of the heavily forested landscape that greeted the first Europeans. Within its 8,400 hectares (20,000 acres) of forest are many nature trails, peaceful picnic stops and varied coastlines. Stands of kauri and a profusion of other native trees and plants, as well as relics of the kauri sawmills and steep bush railway, are only 40 minutes drive from the city centre. Stop at the Information Centre on the Scenic Drive, 5.5 kilometres (3½ miles) from Titirangi, for leaflets, displays and information. From there join the identification trails (20 minutes, 40 minutes or 75 minutes) to numbered stations giving plant and forest information, the story of the forest's regeneration, growth, maturity and decay. There are also over 185 kilometres (115 miles) of walking and tramping tracks in the park and Waitakere Ranges (maps from the information centre).

Muriwai Beach Regional Park

Muriwai Beach Regional Park has wild surf and west coast scenery 45 kilometres (28 miles) from Auckland. For good views take the Mitchelson Track on the main hillside overlooking the beach. The Maori Bay Track follows the cliffs to a disused quarry with unusual lava rock and views of an island bird colony.

Parks and Reserves

Tawharanui Regional Park

Tawharanui Regional Park, 90 kilometres (55 miles) from Auckland, is a coastal and marine park. A three-hour walk along the beach shows historic Maori terraces and pits; a one-hour walk along clifftops offers views of Kawau and Little Barrier Islands.

Wenderholm Regional Park

Wenderholm Regional Park is a favourite family picnic spot with an old-world charm, 48 kilometres (30 miles) from Auckland. It features walks through coastal bush, where native wood pigeons and tuis can be seen feeding on berries and flowers. Visit the historic Couldrey House.

Long Bay Regional Park

Long Bay Regional Park is only 25 minutes from Auckland (26 kilometres or 16 miles) and can be reached by a regular bus service. A coastal walk leads to two smaller bays.

Shakespear Regional Park

Shakespear Regional Park, at the tip of the Whangaparaoa Peninsula (56 kilometres or 35 miles from Auckland) has a regular bus service from the city terminal. Sign-posted trails through a wooded stream valley emerge into open paddocks at the Park's summit, with views of the gulf and Auckland. Swamps are homes for pukekos, waders and an Australian green frog.

Omana Regional Park

Omana Regional Park, on the east coast 42 kilometres (26 miles) south of Auckland city, between Beachlands and Maraetai, was once a profitable kauri gum-digging area. Perendale sheep and Hereford cattle now roam the paddocks, open to the public. A perimeter walk passes an old Maori pa site.

Waharau Regional Park

Waharau Regional Park, 70 kilometres (44 miles) from Auckland on the Firth of Thames, is coastal forest, with some abandoned farms gradually reverting to forest. Walking tracks (4-5 hours, 1½ hours, 1 hour or 30 minutes) are colour coded and sign-posted.

Awhitu Regional Park

Awhitu Regional Park, 90 kilometres (55 miles) from Auckland, is on the southern shores of the Manukau Harbour, and is another Auckland Regional Authority farm. It includes tidal mudflats and birdlife – featuring the migratory godwit and pied oystercatcher, the rare fernbird and banded rail.

The Regional Botanic Gardens

The Regional Botanic Gardens, 23 kilometres (14 miles) south of Auckland, just off the motorway at Manurewa, has informative and attractive walks specialising in plants growing best in the Auckland region.

Hunua

Brochures about the regional parks can be obtained from the Auckland Regional Authority or the Visitors Bureau. In the Hunua Ranges in Auckland's water-catchment area, walking tracks link dams and reservoirs (information from the ARA Water Department, Moumoukai Depot, phone 292-5870).

Hauraki Gulf Maritime Park

The Park was established in 1967 with the aim of protecting a range of islands and island groups situated off some 250 kilometres (155 miles) of the Northland and Coromandel coastline. There are 47 islands in the Park and one mainland reserve, making up a magnificent collection of reserves, having important wildlife, conservation, scientific and historic values as well as providing a wide range of recreational opportunities. From the clear, sub-tropical seas surrounding the rugged outer islands to the sheltered deep green waters of the inner gulf, you will find an amazing variety of landforms. Volcanic islands of black lava only hundreds of years old, contrast with islands of sedimentary rock that were formed millions of years ago. Scheduled cruises ply the peaceful waters of the inner gulf daily, providing fascinating trips to these beautiful, sunny islands. These are places where you can picnic, swim, walk and explore, experiencing both the natural and human history of the Hauraki Gulf.

Wenderholm Reserve near Waiwera. *(Andris Apse Ltd)*

Rangitoto Island	Dormant for only 250 years, the youngest of Auckland's volcanoes, Rangitoto, emerged from the sea about 800 years ago. Today, more than 200 species of native plants can be found on the island. Tracks, built from crushed lava by prison labour during the 1930s, go around the island and to the summit, with its World War II defences and magnificent views of Auckland and across the Gulf.
Motutapu Island	Of sedimentary rocks, millions of years old, this island is home to numerous archaeological sites, including major Maori pa sites. Maori people were living on Motutapu while Rangitoto was erupting and footprints have been found in the ash of the last eruption. The island is linked to Rangitoto by a narrow causeway at Islington Bay. Home Bay, a 3-hour walk from Islington Bay via the island's highest point is a popular camping area on the island.
Rakino Island	Rakino is a much older island (about 130 million years old), most of which is privately owned, with reserves and a walking track from wharf to summit for great views.
Motukorea (Browns Island)	A short trip for boaties, the island lies off the mouth of the Tamaki Estuary. Early Polynesian settlers lived on the island from about 1300 AD and developed three defended pa sites by 1820.
Motuihe	With two beautiful sheltered beaches on both sides of a narrow sand bar, Motuihe has been a popular picnic area since the 1930s. Swim, picnic, sunbathe or explore the fascinating intertidal rock pools. Walking tracks run over the island, which like Motutapu is run as a farm park. From the wharf to Calypso Bay return is about 2 hours; around the island, about 3 hours.
Kawau Island	Kawau Island is the site of Mansion House, once the home of New Zealand's Governor, Sir George Grey. Grey bought Kawau in 1862 and converted an old mine manager's house into a mansion. He introduced a variety of exotic trees including Brazilian palms, Indian rhododendrons, Mediterranean olives and English oaks, while also importing zebras and antelope and other wild animals. The house and gardens have been restored to their former glory, whilst on the walks through the park, you can still see the wallabies, kookaburras, rosellas, parakeets and peacocks that remain.
Great Barrier Island	With long beaches and pounding surf along its eastern coastline and sheltered anchorages in the west, Great Barrier Island has a wild beauty, loved by its inhabitants and treasured by visitors. Find a well-established bird population, including kaka, kokako, brown teal duck, and black petrel. The birds thrive in the absence of predators, and the forests thrive, due to the absence of deer, wallaby and possums. Part of the island is privately owned, the balance being held by government agencies as reserves. An excellent walkway system links bays to other reserves and camping grounds. See old gold, silver and copper mines; whaling stations, kauri dams and hot springs. Main residential area is at Tryphena, where there is also accommodation.

See the Hauraki Gulf and its islands through both regular scheduled cruises and special charters. Luxurious, fast supercruises run daily from Auckland to Kawau Island, Rangitoto and back, with time to relax and enjoy. Or see Rangitoto, with a coach tour on the island. Island hop on commuter services or take a harbour cruise with refreshments/meals provided. Services also run to Great Barrier Island and Coromandel Peninsula. Check with Fullers for schedules and options.

Fullers Captain Cook Cruises
PO Box 448
Auckland
Telephone: (09) 394-901
Facsimile: (09) 370-636

South to Coromandel

Gold is the history of the Coromandel peninsula. A brief but wildly successful gold rush began in 1867, with one mine producing more than a ton of gold in one month in 1871. The town of Thames became a boom town, with a hotel on every street corner – many of the buildings remain, some still as hotels. Find historical reminders of the gold-rush days in the towns of Thames and Coromandel and in the hills where guided walks lead through old mine shafts and tunnels.

The peninsula is a favourite with hikers – more than 30 major tramping tracks and many short walks lead deep into the ranges throughout the Coromandel Forest Park. Track information can be obtained from an information centre in Thames' Queen Street or from the Forest Park headquarters in the beautiful Kauaeranga Valley.

Rock hounds who can recognise semi-precious gemstones in their raw state find the peninsula New Zealand's most productive area. There's agate, jasper, onyx, carnelian, chalcedony, amethyst, quartz crystal, sinter and chert to be found in the streams and along the beaches. Polished stones and jewellery can be bought at crafts shops, which often sell excellent potttery as well – some of New Zealand's best potters have chosen to live on the peninsula and sell their work locally.

The peninsula is the southernmost limit of kauri forests. The forests were ravaged in the early nineteenth century, but some splendid ancient trees survived and can be reached today by well-defined tracks. Through much of the forest the kauri trees are regenerating in their natural environment.

But it is the beaches, perhaps even more than the hills, that make Coromandel a spectacular and special area. Long golden beaches with rolling surf, tiny perfect bays surrounded by gnarled pohutukawa trees, great rocky promontories where the sea crashes in.

Every beach has its own charms and character: Hahei, with its pink-tinged sands, ancient pa sites and excellent diving; Hot Water Beach, where hot springs seep through the sand at low tide and swimmers can leave the sea to scoop out hot pools in the sand; Whitianga, where dive boats and game-fishing boats congregate in a deep, sheltered harbour; Pauanui, a long golden beach where a carefully designed holiday town nestles in the pines.

Information Centre
Kapanga Road
Coromandel
Telephone: (0843) 58-598

Stay at this lovely historical hotel. Enjoy personal friendly service, comfortable accommodation (40 persons) and licensed restaurant! This is your chance to have fun discovering 'Whodunnit' on an 'Agatha Christie-type' weekend, or join in a 'Trivial Pursuit' weekend, interesting capers all organised for your entertainment. Barbara also arranges personalised tours of the adventure-filled, scenic Coromandel Peninula. Central to Thames and all facilities. From $30 (single, share facilities), $45 (single/own bathroom).

Brian Boru Hotel
200 Richmond Street
Thames
Telephone: (0843) 86-523
Telex: NZ2630
Facsimile: (0843) 89-760
Host: Barbara Doyle

This is a wide region of forests, hills, plains, river valleys, lakes and marshes. Around Rotorua is extraordinary thermal activity, where subterranean heat bursts through the earth's thin crust with geysers, hot springs, boiling mud and steaming fissures.

Boiling mud, Rotorua. ***(Andris Apse Ltd)***

On high ridges, giant ferns grow under a shady canopy in forests of tawa, rimu and totara. Across former wastelands, man-made forests of pine march in straight lines as far as the eye can see. Down in the gentle valleys, willows, elders and poplars edge streams, hedgerows of box and hawthorne divide rich green pastures. In remote gorges of the Waikato River, huge hydro-electric stations straddle the river creating long, tranquil lakes.

To the west towards Waitomo, where sheep and cattle graze on hill farms, there's steep limestone country with peculiar outcrops and deep caves. To the east on the warm coast from Katikati to Te Puke are subtropical orchards crowded with kiwifruit vines, orange and avocado trees.

Travel from the north toward the remarkable volcanic area of Rotorua and discover en route great wetlands (Whangamarino is 10,000 hectares (24,700 acres) of wild swamp sheltering 50 species of birds), marshy lakes where mists lie low, rich dairylands and lush pastures where great racehorses are bred. Find out about dairying around Hamilton; visit stud farms around Cambridge and Matamata.

Find too memories of fierce battles between British troops and Maori defenders in the land wars of the 1860s. Riverside communities from Mercer to Cambridge began as garrison towns at the end of the war in 1864. At Meremere there's a terraced hilltop where the Maoris halted the British advance for three months; at Rangiriri a plan of a battlefield is displayed in a tiny cemetery where British soldiers were buried. History of the land wars is well displayed in the Waikato Art Museum in Hamilton, where there's also a famous 140-year-old war canoe.

By the riverbank at Ngaruawahia travellers can sometimes see great ceremonial canoes moored by Turangawaewae Marae, a splendid complex of buildings and home of the Maori queen.

Travel to the west of the region into the limestone country that contains the Waitomo Caves and glide on a punt through underground caverns studded with thousands of glow worms. Nearby at Otorohanga a bird park concentrates on native birds, featuring the kiwi. Not far away too is a specially created village demonstrating traditional Maori crafts – authentic, unusual souvenirs can be bought.

Travel east to the coast for long ocean beaches and orchards of kiwifruit, feijoas, tamarillos, oranges and avocados, around the city of Tauranga and the kiwifruit 'capital' of Te Puke. Here, at Tauranga and Whakatane, game-fishing boats leave for offshore islands.

Discover also more memories of bitter fighting in the land wars, at Tauranga's Gate Pa battleground, and visit an elegant early mission house, 'The Elms', surrounded by spreading lawns and gracious gardens. At Whakatane discover a town rich in pre-European Maori history and legends, where archaeological excavation has revealed settlement stretching back for centuries. Inland in the southern part of the region, immense forests of pine cover the country. Planting began on unproductive land before World War I, was increased in the 1930s and by the 1940s the pine forest of the central North Island was the largest man-made forest in the world. Tour the giant pulp, paper and board mills at Kinleith, Kawerau, Whakatane. At Kawerau, underground energy is harnessed with deep bores, providing natural steam for the milling process.

3

Waikato – Bay of Plenty

Travel around by car rented in Rotorua, Auckland, Hamilton, Tauranga. Small planes flit around the region from the airport in Rotorua or from Lake Rotorua for amphibian flights. As well as the ubiquitous N.Z.R. Road Services buses, there are coach services travelling out of Rotorua to various points, operated by Mt Cook and Newmans. Many tours are available from Auckland, especially through Newmans and Guthries.

WAIKATO/B.O.P.

National Parks
Urewera National Park.

Tramping

Lodges
1. Solitaire Lodge;
2. Muriaroha.

Outback Safaris

Hunting

Fishing
Big Game

Other

River Adventures

Flightseeing

Diving

Golf
1. Matamata; 2. Okoroire Springs; 3. Hamilton; 4. Cambridge; 5. Mount Maunganui; 6. Tauranga; 7. Waitomo; 8. Arikikapakapa.

History
1. Rotorua; 2. Ohaki Maori Village.

Down on Farm

Live with NZ

Local
1. Pioneer Museum; 2. Waikato Art & History Museum; 3. Clydesdale Museum; 4. Firth Historical Museum; 5. Kiwi House & Native Bird Park; 6. Waitomo Caves.

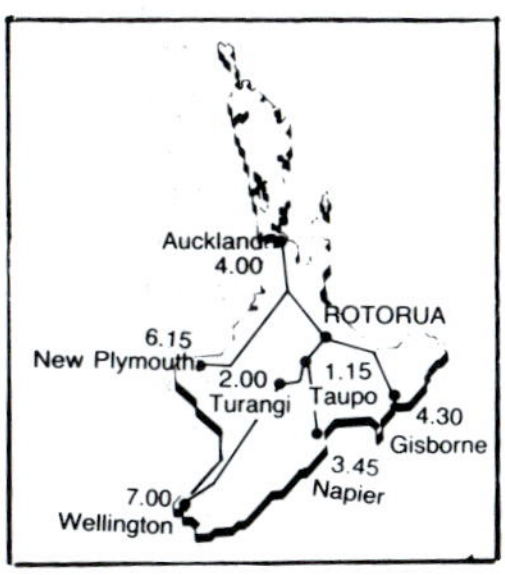

Driving Times
within

½	1	2	3

hours

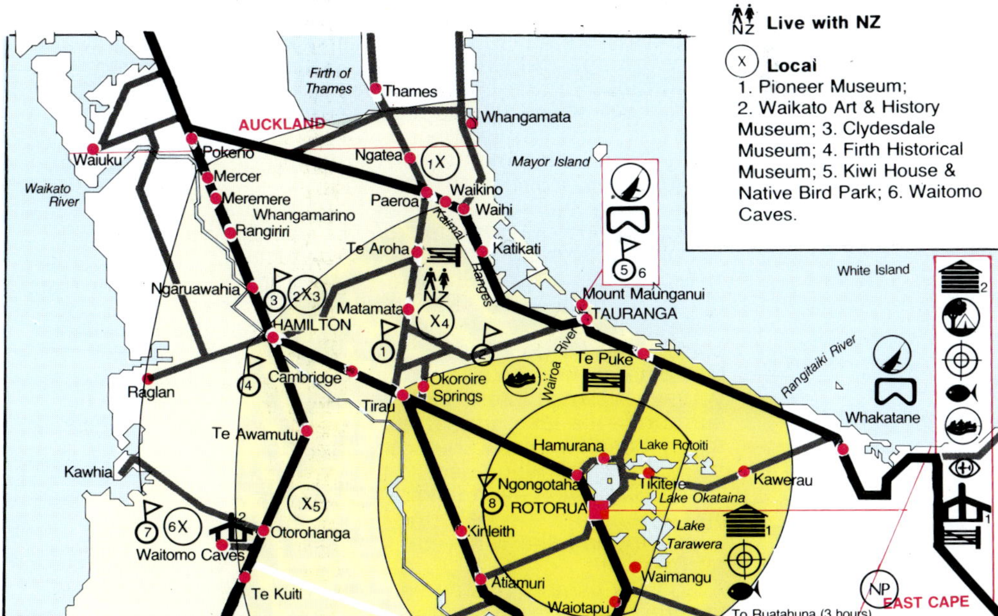

Rotorua is one of New Zealand's best-known tourist centres for the simple reason that there is so much to see and do – the area is crammed with unusual sights, experiences and spectacular scenic surprises.

Maori pa entrance, Ohaki Maori Village (near Waitomo Caves)

Visitor Information Service
NZTP Travel Centre
Cnr Fenton & Hauhapa Streets
Rotorua
Telephone: (073) 85-179

Rotorua

For a start, the whole town seems to be steaming. Steam pours up, not just in the areas of intense activity, but in backyards, along pavements, on golf courses. The smell of sulphur hangs heavy on the air – not the balmiest of perfumes, but one soon gets acclimatised and ceases to notice it.

To see thermal activity at its fuming best, visit concentrations of erupting geysers, boiling mud and multi-coloured silica terraces: at Whakarewarewa, Maori villagers use the hot water for bathing, cooking, washing and heating; at Waiotapu the thermal area includes over a hectare of rainbow-hued terraces; at Waimangu there's a 4-hectare (10-acre) boiling lake and also the startling colours of a turquoise lake backed by blood-red cliffs; at Tikitere (also known as Hell's Gate) fiercely boiling pools contrast with picturesque warm waterfalls.

If you want more evidence of subterranean violence, take a four-wheel-drive tour to the crater of Mt Tarawera. In 1886 the mountain, believed extinct, erupted with sudden devastating force. Ash and volcanic debris were strewn over 16,000 square kilometres (617 square miles), three Maori villages were obliterated and 153 people died. There's a fast way to the mountaintop – by small aircraft that lands on the crater rim.

Take flight-seeing trips from Rotorua over the thermal areas, lakes, forests and mountains and over White Island, the constantly active volcano off the coast near Whakatane (a round trip over White Island takes little more than an hour).

In the nineteenth century Rotorua was a spa town where visitors sought the invigorating, curative, hot mineral waters. The Elizabethan-style Tudor Towers in the Government Gardens was once a magnificent bath-house, and is now a complex of art gallery, museum and restaurant.

Rotorua's waters have been claimed as a remedy for many ailments, from rheumatism to skin complaints. Whether or not you wish to test the health-giving properties, there are plenty of opportunities to enjoy a good hot swim.

Should you tire of all the hot-water springs, visit cool freshwater springs in pretty parkland settings at Rainbow and Fairy Springs, Taniwha Springs, Paradise Valley Springs, Hamurana Springs. All have sparkling springs, streams and trout pools where monster trout, as big as 10 kilograms (22 pounds), crowd in the clear water. Each has its own special charms such as a magnificent fernery or grove of redwoods, ancient pa site or native bird aviary.

And then there are the lakes. Take a launch cruise to Mokoia Island on Lake Rotorua, an island imbued with a romantic love story. There are 4 kilometres (2½ miles) of bush walks on the island. Also hire a jet-cat, speed boat or children's mini-jet for self-propelled fun on the lake.

Cruise Lake Rotoiti where holiday cottages dot idyllic bays surrounded by dark bush. Take a cruise on perfect Lake Okataina or hire a boat and explore the unspoilt lake shores yourself – dense forest dominated by giant tree ferns surrounds the lake, unmarked by roads or buildings. Secluded sandy beaches spread out from under the ferns; ancient pa sites, birds and wild deer hide in the bush.

The Blue and Green Lakes, side by side, are actually blue and green, and can be found on the way to serene, bush-fringed Lake Tarawera, spreading under the shadow of Mt Tarawera.

Go trout fishing, even if you have never held a rod before. Fishing guides provide all the equipment and take you to the best fishing places on lakes or streams.

Rotorua is also a centre of Maori life and culture. At Whakarewarewa find the Maori Arts and Crafts Institute, a prestigious centre of traditional carving and weaving, and Rotowhio Model Pa, a reconstruction of a pre-European fortified village. At Ohinemutu Maori Village on the lake edge there's an outstanding Maori meeting hourse, Tama-te-kapua, built in 1878, with some magnificent carvings dating back to 1800. A concert of traditional songs and dances is held regularly in the meeting house. Similar performances are held at several hotels and theatres in Rotorua, often combined with a 'hangi', food cooked Polynesian-style in a pit of steaming stones. (In Rotorua nature simplifies the cooking process.)

Entertainment. – In Rotorua the Maori concert and 'hangi' dinner is a novel variation on theatre and dinner. Dine and dance is a feature of some restaurants and hotels provide pop, jazz or rock entertainment. Around a region obsessed with horses, discover country race meetings, polo, show jumping, hunt club meets (no foxes, they chase hares) and sales of yearling thoroughbreds (in Hamilton). In Rotorua there's the Agrodome, a vast agricultural entertainment with 17 breeds of sheep, some of which perform a song and dance routine! And there are A & P Shows – in Rotorua (late January), Te Puke (mid-February), Whakatane (early March). Tauranga has highland games in January, A & P Show in February and an orange festival in August. And at Ngaruawahia in mid-March at Turangawaewae there's a special kind of Maori regatta with a grand parade of huge ceremonial war canoes, canoe races and performances of songs and dances by many tribes.

Rotorua thermal area.
(Andris Apse Ltd)

Southwest via Te Kuiti & Waitomo Caves

Te Awamutu

Home of the outstanding Otawhao Meeting House on the college campus, and the Waipa Kokiri Centre where Maori carving and other arts and crafts skills are taught. Public Relations office, opposite the Rose Gardens, will arrange tours. Take time out to visit the District Museum.

Otorohanga

Again, this area is rich in Maori history, proudly bearing the name 'King country'. Before the advent of the European, about 4,000 Maori people lived here, growing crops on the fertile river flats. They allowed the main trunk railway to be built through the area on the condition that no liquor was introduced with it. The area remained 'dry' until 1955, when liquor licenses were first granted.

Otorohanga Kiwi House & Native Bird Park
Alex Telfer Drive
Telephone: (08133) 7391

It can be difficult and sometimes impossible to identify many New Zealand birds in the wild. The breeding and display centre at Otorohanga offers natural surroundings and a chance to see some of New Zealand's rarest birds. View kiwis in their nocturnal habitat. A guide (and graphic display) explains this strange ancient genus, of which the large spotted, little spotted, and the North Island brown kiwi species are kept at the park. A huge dome-shaped aviary, complete with native rainforest, is the home of native birds including bellbird, tui, pigeon, red-fronted parakeet, yellow-fronted parakeet, pied-stilt, shoveller, scaup, grey teal ducks and silvereyes. The rarest are two breeding pairs of saddlebacks. The park also holds New Zealand's living fossil – the tuatara. Two species of rare New Zealand ducks are on display – breeding pairs of the two blue ducks and brown teals.

Marokopa Falls, King Country. *(Andris Apse Ltd)*

3

Waikato – Bay of Plenty

Te Kuiti

In Te Kuiti, find one of the finest examples of a Maori meeting house still in daily use. 'Tokanganui-anoho', the beautifully carved headquarters of the Maniapoto tribe, a gift from Te Kooti to the Maniapoto who gave him sanctuary during the land wars in the latter part of last century.

Waitomo

A fascinating natural phenomenon of millions of tiny, luminous glowworms in stalactite caverns, stalagmite figures and limestone formations. Three main caves have handrails and walkways for viewing and boats take the visitor floating on an underground river through the galleries of glowworms in the roofs and walls of the caves.

Tours are hourly for the Glowworm Cave and several times daily for the Ruakuri and Aranui caves. Also in the area, find the beautiful Mangapohue Natural Stone Bridge, and the Marokopa Falls, a 30-metre (98-foot) cascade.

Ohaki Enterprises
(near Waitomo Caves)
Ohaki Maori Village and Walks
PO Box 123
Te Kuiti
Telephone: (0813) 86-610
Hosts: The Te Kanawa Family

Ohaki was set up as a family enterprise in order to build a centre dedicated to the preservation of the weaving skills of 95-year-old Mrs Rangimarie Hetet (MBE, CBE) and her daughter Mrs Digger Te Kanawa. Because very few people still practice this ancient art form, using authentic materials and techniques, these women have become renowned internationally. Away from tourist routes, members of this family guide visitors around the model village. Some visitors spend a day, listening to stories of pre-European Maori life, watching the weaving, joining in the family life, taking native forest walks (half to three-quarters of an hour duration) and marvelling at the work display which includes several priceless feather cloaks.

North to Auckland

Matamata

In the heart of the rich Waikato pastures, Matamata is surrounded by farms – dairy farms, sheep farms, cattle farms and race-horse stud farms. Go to the races for first-class country racing meetings.

The Firth Tower and Historical Museum were part of the huge Firth Estate which was subdivided in 1904. The Homestead and village includes an old post office, church, school, historical and railway displays.

Matamata Public Relations Assn. Inc., Hetena Street, Matamata, P.O. Box 93. Telephone: (0818) 7260

The grassy airfield at Matamata is one of the best known venues for gliding in the North Island, making use of conditions created by the almost-flat plains and the Kaimai Ranges rising immediately to the west. Drive to the Kaimai Lookout on a ridge of the ranges for a view stretching out across the Waikato as far north as Auckland's Bombay Hills.

Raglan

Highway 23 from Hamilton takes you to the west coast town of Raglan, an important seaport during the Waikato wars, but today a peaceful resort enjoying an excellent climate. Raglan is world renowned for its surfing beaches; Ocean Beach, Manu Bay (famous for its left-hand break), Whale Bay and Indicators. There are ample opportunities to get off 'the beaten track' and enjoy this ruggedly beautiful coastline. Visit the Raglan Pioneer District Museum, go sea fishing or surf casting, visit the spectacular Bridal Veil Falls (off the Raglan-Te Mata Road). Good accommodation is available.

Port Waikato

From Raglan northwards on Highway 22, see Port Waikato where the mighty Waikato River reaches the ocean and visit the Diamond Springs hot pool complex at Waingaro. This road joins up with State Highway 1 near Auckland and is an interesting alternative route north.

Diamond Hot Springs Waingaro Springs, off S.H. 1 Private Bag Ngaruawahia Telephone: (071) 254-761

This unique oasis invites you to relax and rejuvenate in soothing, thermal mineral pools. These sparkling pools are filtered and chlorinated with temperatures (32-42 degrees Celsius) adjusted hourly to suit the weather. Included in the 4.5 hectares (11 acres) of parkland, are New Zealand's longest open hot water slides, private mineral spa pools, bumper boats, deer park and extensive picnic/barbeque areas. Come for a day's outing or use the Holiday Park deluxe van sites and motel units.

Via Huntly on State Highway 1

Huntly is the centre for a large farming community and the largest coal producer in the country, more than 300 million tonnes of which lies buried under the ground. On the western bank of the Waikato River at Huntly see New Zealand's largest power station. Make an appointment and take a tour of this dual-fuel powered plant (Telephone: (0817) 89-590) or stop and view it from the many picnic and rest areas on the eastern side of the river.

North End Motel S.H.1, Huntly North Telephone: (0817) 88-298 Hosts: Lorraine and Tom Peden

With swimming pool and off-street parking, this establishment offers 16 well-appointed and self-contained units, some sleeping up to 4-5. Cooked and continental breakfast available, plus pool table. Credit cards accepted. From $60 (double).

'Pitstop' Roadhouse 160 Great South Road Huntly Telephone: (0817) 89-995 Hosts: Janine and John Reid

Excellent refreshment stop with ample parking. Licensed restaurant, cafeteria and fast-food service, plus souvenir shop and restrooms. On Waikato River and overlooking largest dual-fuel power station in the Southern Hemisphere. Closed Christmas Day. Reasonable prices.

3

Waikato – Bay of Plenty

Hamilton

'The Fountain City' borders the mighty Waikato River and is set in the heart of one of New Zealand's richest agricultural areas; it is also the junction of all major highways in the central North Island.

Hamilton was named after Captain John Fane Hamilton, who was killed in action at the Battle of Gate Pa Near Tauranga in 1864. Organised European settlement began that same year with an advance party of one hundred men who set up redoubts on both banks of the river, establishing two distinct settlements which became one town in 1877.

Until the arrival of the main trunk railway, the town depended on paddle steamers plying the river, for trade. Today, the licensed floating restaurant, the MV 'Waipa Delta' paddle steamer and a tourist launch cruise the river. Visit the Hamilton Gardens off Cobham Drive. Take a stroll along the riverbanks, to Hamilton Lake or through Jubilee Bush. A variety of good dining out is available as is evening entertainment; the Drury Lane Theatre restaurant, the Left Bank Theatre and the Arts Centre, all providing live entertainment. Check the Hamilton Founders Theatre for any national or international touring shows.

Organisations such as the Dairy Herd Improvement Centre of New Zealand and the Ruakura Research Centre, leaders in agricultural research, are centred here. The city is world famous for its field days held at Mystery Creek in early March, June and November. These attract crowds in excess of 130,000 people annually and are a great way to see the development of agricultural, industrial and sporting activity in New Zealand, and also to meet with people from all over the country. The area is also famed for its thoroughbred horse studs, some of which may be visited by appointment.

Hamilton City Council
Public Relations Office
Barton Street north,
Hamilton
P.O. Box 1100
Telephone: (071)
386-444

Dairy herd, Waikato.

(Courtesy Air New Zealand)

Rick Lewis and Associates
Perrin Cottage
Main Road North
R.D.8
Frankton, Hamilton
Telephone: (071) 493-973/ 299-870

Perrin Cottage is home to Hereford Fine China, unique in the Southern Hemisphere, stunningly beautiful fine bone china models of birds, animals and figurines equal to the world's best. (See photograph on page 111). One-off pieces have been presented to royalty. During your visit, you can purchase arts and crafts and wool garments in addition to the china. Light meals and Devonshire teas are available for your enjoyment. Open daily, 9.30 a.m. to 4.30 p.m.

Waikato Museum of Art and History
Cnr Victoria & Grantham Streets
Hamilton
Telephone: (071) 386-533/ 386-606

Opened in October 1987, the new Waikato Museum of Art and History is the principal museum in the Waikato. Built by the Hamilton City Council, the seventeen public galleries present a wide range of changing exhibitions, interestingly augmented by regular lecture series, films, demonstrations and audio-visual productions. A major feature of the museum is the magnificently restored and decorated war canoe 'Te Winika', gifted to the people of Hamilton by the Maori queen, Te Arikinui Dame Te Atairangikaahu. The innovative architecture of the museum provides visitors with unequalled views of the mighty Waikato River. The museum is complemented by a licensed restaurant and a museum shop. Open daily, 10.00 a.m. to 4.30 p.m., closed Christmas Day, Boxing Day and Good Friday. Admission is free.

M.V. 'Waipa Delta'
River Road
Memorial Park
P.O. Box 1534
Hamilton
Telephone: (071) 394-419

Welcome aboard MV 'Waipa Delta', New Zealand's finest paddleboat. The tourism award-winning 'Waipa Delta' is a fully licenced floating restaurant, cruising the picturesque Waikato River. The daily schedule includes 1½-hour Morning Tea (10.30 am.), Luncheon (12.30 p.m.) and Afternoon Tea (3.00 p.m.) cruises, plus fabulous 3-hour Moonlight Dinner cruises (7.00 p.m.). A magnificent smorgasbord is served on luncheon and dinner cruises. Live entertainment nightly. Your captain will give a colourful commentary during each cruise.

Hilldale Zoo Park
(8 kilometres from city centre)
Brymer Road
Hamilton
Telephone: (071) 386-720

Well signposted from Te Rapa, on State Highway 1 from Auckland, these 14 hectares (35 acres) of developed zoo complex contain an extensive display of native/introduced birds, parrots and waterfowl. See zoo animals in a setting where deer, llama, wallabies and even a camel will eat from your hand! Species include pumas, jaguars, zebras, South American peccaries, and loveable otters. A farmyard contact area delights children with donkeys, pigs/piglets, sheep, goats, rabbits and pigeons. Don't miss seeing the New Zealand keas with their brilliant plumage and cheeky manners! Tearooms are open during summer months. A barbeque area is available; bring and cook your own lunch. Open daily (except Christmas Day) 9.00 a.m. to 5.00 p.m. From $2.75 adults, $1.10 children. Group discounts available.

Hamilton Centennial Pools
Minogue Park
Garnett Avenue, Te Rapa
Hamilton
Telephone: (071) 494-389

Not far from the city centre, find one of the most modern competition and recreation swimming complexes in Australasia – open all year round with fully air-conditioned indoor facilities. The indoor heated pool complex consists of: 50-metre x 21-metre (8 lane) competition pool, dive pool and tower, 25-metre x 11-metre learners pool and toddlers pool. It provides spectator seating for 1,000, numerous dressing rooms, meeting rooms, a conference room and well-appointed cafeteria. Outdoors, in lovely surrounds, are the lido and toddlers pool, with picnic and barbeque areas available. The outdoor pool is available October to March (weather permitting). Additional attractions include a double hydroslide, play area with trampolines, 9-hole putting green and shop. Admission is inexpensive. Towels, swimming costumes and clothes lockers available for hire.

Waikato – Bay of Plenty

With rural outlook or views over swimming pool and gardens, this well-appointed accommodation offers all facilities including in-house video. Choice of double or executive suites. Excellent restaurant service. From $50 (weekend rate per person).

DB Glenview Motor Hotel
Cnr Resthills Cres and Ohaupo Road
P.O. Box 8039, Hamilton
Telephone: (071) 436-049
Telex: NZ63307

Historical delights – restored gasoline stationary engines (both local and imported), used from late 1800s till circa 1925, in cowsheds, woolsheds and for driving other machines. Collections of cream separators, vacuum pumps, polished gum, mineral rocks and gem stones (cut and uncut). Learn of the gold days in the Victoria Gold Battery from 1895 to 1925. Open Sunday to Friday, 9.00 a.m. to 4.00 p.m. From $2 adults (GST inclusive), children free. Restrooms available.

Waikino Pioneer Museum
Poland Street
Waikino
Telephone: (08163) 5974/6970
Host: Peter Davison

Hamilton South via Putaruru

Putaruru

Known as New Zealand's Camellia town, Putaruru is a pleasant little community town developed around today's major timber industry. Visit the Timber Museum for the history of the local forest area, the Tapestry Weaving Centre behind the Borough Council building and Lichfield Pottery on the main highway. There are five trout-fishing streams near Putaruru plus the hydro lakes of Arapuni and Waipapa.

See an excellent range of hand-crafted pottery by many New Zealand artists, from domestic wares (casserole dishes, salt/pepper sets, etc.) to novelty items, such as miniature cottages (great lamp bases), bells, large pots, planters and vases. See range of home-made perfumes in pottery containers. Margaret works in the adjoining workshop and is happy to explain pottery-making process.

Lichfield Pottery
State Highway 1
Putaruru
Telephone: (0814) 26-898
Hosts: Margaret and Doug Salmon

Hamilton South via Tokoroa

Tokoroa

People from over forty different national origins have made their homes here, giving Tokoroa a multi-culturalism unmatched by most similar sized towns, thus the range of arts, crafts, and cultural activities is wide. Book a tour through the huge pulp and paper mill at Kinleith, by telephoning the Public Relations Office at New Zealand Forest Products Ltd. (Telephone: (0814) 61-999). Visit the famous totara tree, thought to be the oldest in the country at some 1800 years old!

Rotorua Southeast to Whakatane

Take Highway 30 from Rotorua through to Whakatane via the lakes, the Kawerau pulp mill and Awakeri hot springs, or the beautiful coastal route via Highways 33 and 2. The Bay of Plenty was so named by Captain Cook after having been well provisioned on his first visit to New Zealand. Whakatane is one of the principal coastal towns, where in AD 1150 the great Polynesian explorer Toi Te Huatahi landed in search of his lost grandson, and was reputed to be the landing place in the 14th century of 'Mataatua', one of the Great Migration canoes.

In Whakatane see the sacred Pohaturoa Rock, and an original Maori canoe, and visit the Museum in Boon Street.

The coastline is superb; the active volcano, White Island, steams off-shore and golden beaches stretch for miles. Visit Ohope Beach and Otarawairere Bay, stroll along the walkways to the site of Toi's Pa or one of the largest stands of the native pohutukawa trees in the country, a magnificent sight when in full bloom around Christmas time.

Whakatane Public Relations Office
10 Commerce Street
Whakatane
Telephone: (076) 86058

Visitor Acitivity Centre
Corner Fenton and Amohau Streets
PO Box 640
Rotorua
Telephone: (073) 70-555

Where to go, What to do and How to do it in Rotorua! Make this your first port of call on arrival in Rotorua. The Visitor Activity Centre provides information on all activities, accommodation and restaurants in the area. They will book everything for you or simply give you their considered advice and assistance. For your convenience, a free shuttle bus runs from the Centre to main hotels and motels hourly. The Centre is open from 7.00 a.m. to 8.00 p.m. every day of the week. Relax in comfort in the coffee shop, use the free local telephone, have your precious films developed quickly, watch free and informative videos, browse in the souvenir shop. A 24-hour tourism information machine completes this comprehensive facility, created to help you to make the most of your visit.

Rainbow Springs
Fairy Springs Road
PO Box 25
Rotorua
Telephone: (073) 479-301
Owner: Max Martin

A major attraction – Wildlife Wonderland features nocturnal kiwihouse, native walkthrough aviary, underwater trout viewing, deer farm, aquarium and vivarium. Shopping complex provides quality souvenirs, Maori crafts, fur and woollen garments. Delicious light luncheons in Springs Cottage Restaurant. Rainbow Farm adjoins with shows daily at 10.30 a.m., 1 p.m. and 2.30 p.m., plus wagon rides by giant Clydesdale horses. Umbrellas provided, wheelchair available. From $2 (child), $6 (adult), family discount. Farm prices same.

Elite Tours Rotorua
Tumunui Tourist Complex
Highway 5
PO Box 1502
Rotorua
Telephone: (073) 82-727/ 70-555
Facsimile: (073) 87-832

Highly skilled, profficient ex-military personnel show visitors a Rotorua region few locals know. Take morning/afternoon tours of Rotorua's key attractions or tour Mount Tarawera's summit, which violently erupted only 100 years ago! For more excitement, learn to parachute in one day or take adventure excursions where anything goes. Elite takes you fishing, hunting, snorkelling, climbing or tramping; whatever your sporting interests – they'll provide a day to remember! From $33 depending on requirements.

Accommodation. – In Rotorua the range covers every possibility. Large luxury resort hotels overlook lake or steaming geysers, exclusive fishing lodges shelter in the seclusion of bush by lake or stream. The city is crammed with motels, grand, average and humble – many in all categories have private hot mineral pools. Budget travellers find accommodation in simple motels, old hotels that have seen better days, an excellent youth hostel, cabins at camping grounds on the edge of town. Elsewhere in the region find a choice of excellent quality motels and motor inns in Hamilton and Tauranga, a charming old THC hotel at Waitomo. Along the coast from Waihi to Ohope, motels and well-serviced camping grounds serve the beaches. Find youth hostels also at Te Aroha by the high Kaimai Ranges, at Tauranga and nearby Mt Maunganui, at Whakatane, Hamilton and Otorohanga. Off the beaten tourist track the choice narrows – accommodation often caters for the utilitarian needs of foresters, hunters and trampers.

Food. – In Rotorua dine on ordinary 'international' cooking, special New Zealand fare, plain home-style cooking or every kind of fast food. Catch a rainbow trout and a hotel or restaurant kitchen will cook it for you. Look for New Zealand specialities such as lamb, venison, wild pork, avocados, tamarillos and, of course, kiwifruit. (Buy kiwifruit by the kilo from the orchard gate in Te Puke.)

3

Waikato-Bay of Plenty

'Nau mai haere mai', welcome to our world! The New Zealand Maori Arts and Crafts Institute, incorporating the Whakarewarewa Thermal Reserve, invites you to catch a glimpse of the excitement of Rotorua – the heart of Maoridom. 1,001 memories await you at this world, as you watch the tohunga whakairo (master carver) teach trainees the prestigious art of their tupuna (ancestors). Experience the friendly warmth of the guides as they transform flax into clothing. Whakarewarewa is New Zealand's best known thermal area, featuring the mighty Pohutu Geyser, with other geysers in close proximity and a tremendous variety of thermal activity. Over 500 springs in the reserve vary from cold to violently boiling cauldrons. Some are brilliantly clear, others 'plop' with mud.

New Zealand Maori Arts & Crafts Institute
Hemo Road
PO Box 334
Rotorua
(Enquiries welcome)
Telephone: (073) 89-047

Created with Mount Tarawera's 1886 eruption, this 15-kilometre (9-mile) volcanic valley is full of colourful thermal beauty. View the Emerald Pool, the Waimangu Cauldron, Ruaumoko's Throat; see the Lake Rotomahana bird sanctuary and take a cruise to view the Steaming Cliffs and the red mountain crater. Walking tracks are signposted (multi-lingual maps available); a coffee shop provides light meals and souvenirs. Valley package (includes launch) from $10.50 (adult), $5.50 (child).

Waimangu Thermal Valley
Rotorua-Taupo Highway
Waimangu

Unsurpassed panoramic views overlooking Rotorua. Fifteen minutes' scenic drive from city centre or short helicopter flight. Winners of New Zealand Lamb Cuisine Award, menu features finest local produce, enhanced by a wine list including many New Zealand medal winners. Attentive service in elegant surroundings of the Mokoia Room, evening reservations essential.

Aorangi Peak Restaurant
Mountain Road, Rotorua
Telephone: (073) 70-046
Hosts: Shirley and Bill Barry

Set in 2 acres of spacious grounds, quiet yet close to city centre. Modern, self-contained, centrally heated units plus laundry, heated swimming pool, private thermal pools, children's play area and shopping centre opposite. From $60 (double).

Motel Cleveland
113-119 Lake Road
Rotorua
Telephone: (073) 82-041
Hosts: Shirley and Barry Haywood

Facility offers 40 deluxe rooms, appointed with minibar and in-house video. Facilities: 24-hour room service, restaurant/bar, gymnasium, sauna, spa/pool, courtesy coach, tennis courts. Water sports, para flying, fishing, sightseeing organised. From $120.

Okawa Bay Resort
Lake Rotoiti
Reservations: NZ Collect (03) 799127
(Details/Overseas reservations; see p.129)

Features individual log cabins, tourist cabins, dormitory lodge and van sites. Facilities include a unique building for campervans (with own cooking, washing facilities, dining room and lounge); heated, filtered swimming pool, hot plunge pools, games/TV rooms, camp store, laundry and drying rooms and refrigerated lockers. 5 minutes' drive from the city centre, close to Whakarewarewa, opposite the Arikapakapa Golf Course. Choice of ensuite or share facilities.

Rotorua Thermal Motor Camp
Old Taupo Road
Rotorua
Telephone: (073) 88-385

SEE ALSO:

Lodges: Moose (RHC) (Rotorua), Solitaire (Rotorua).
Outback Safaris: Te Rehuwai Safaris, NZ Outdoor Adventure Centre (Rotorua).
Flightseeing: Floatplanes Rotorua.
Down on Farm: Otuiti Lodge (Ohaupo), The Agrodome (Rotorua).
Live with NZ: Ryan Farmstays (Matamata).
Fishing/Diving: Baker Marine (Whakatane).

Captain Cook monument, Gisborne. *(Courtesy Air New Zealand)*

This is a region of distinct and dramatic contrasts. In the north the few roads twist and wind over hills of primeval forest and around the coast to reveal one of the most spectacular coastlines in the country, with beautiful bush-fringed coves and long empty beaches. Tiny communities, often little more than a hotel, general store and church, cling to the coast.

It is a place apart, where time can move very slowly, where children ride to school on horseback, where drivers stop while a large flock of sheep pass by.

The Urewera and Raukumara ranges, with mountain beech on the highest hills and almost impenetrable forest reaching down into the valleys, formed the character of the East Cape, enforcing an isolation on the inhabitants. European influence came to the Cape, making less impact on the Maori way of life than in many other parts of the country.

Travel the coast road between Opotiki and Gisborne for 335 kilometres (208 miles) and discover idyllic picnic spots and camping places by sandy bays, long beaches and rocky inlets that can be completely deserted. Find settlements that were once busy whaling stations, see simple, beautiful Maori churches and elaborately carved meeting houses, and quench your thirst in the most easterly pub in the world (at Te Araroa or Tikitiki – both claim the distinction).

Wander through general stores that might have escaped from a 'western' – bare board floors, old shop counters, everything on sale from sunhats, lanterns, haberdashery, food and fishing lines.

Take the overland road from Opotiki to Gisborne through the spectacular Waioeka Gorge, a wild and sparsely populated area. A route recommended only for the adventurous and competent driver, in fine weather and with a sturdy, reliable vehicle, is an old coach road through Motu and Toatoa, from Matawai to the coast. It looks like an hour's drive on the map, but it will take half a day and will take you back 50 years in time.

At Gisborne you are in the commercial centre of Poverty Bay. Realise that the name is a misnomer as you pass by vineyards, orchards, cornfields and prosperous sheep farms. Captain Cook made the mistake after his first landing in New Zealand here in 1769, but the bay enjoys the irony. Gisborne enthusiastically commemorates Cook's historic landing with memorials on Kaiti Hill and on the shore below.

In the deeply indented Hawkes Bay, there is another rich coastal area patch-worked with market gardens, orchards and vineyards. Sheep stations spread into the high hills behind the bay, farms that have often remained with the same family for several generations. Màny pioneer sheep farmers built grand, elegant houses, colonial versions of English country houses with sweeping driveways, croquet lawns and English trees.

The English 'county' lifestyle mimicked by the early run-holders lingers on among their descendants around Hastings and Havelock North and the small towns to the south – tweed, cavalry twill and cashmere sell well here, and horse show-riding is a popular pastime.

Perhaps the most spectacular 'sight' of the region is the excursion to Cape Kidnappers, the world's only mainland gannet colony, where about 15,000 gannets congregate from late July to February each year. The setting here is dramatic, with sheer barren cliffs dropping into the ocean in a series of sharp-edged hills. The area is open to the public from the end of October, when egg-laying and hatching is over.

East Cape – Hawkes Bay

Travel around independently by car – rent a car in Gisborne, Napier or Hastings; railway runs between Gisborne, Napier and Hastings, heading south through the region towards Wellington. N.Z.R. Road Services, Newmans and Hawkes Bay Motors provide bus services. Flight-seeing trips available from Gisborne and Napier.

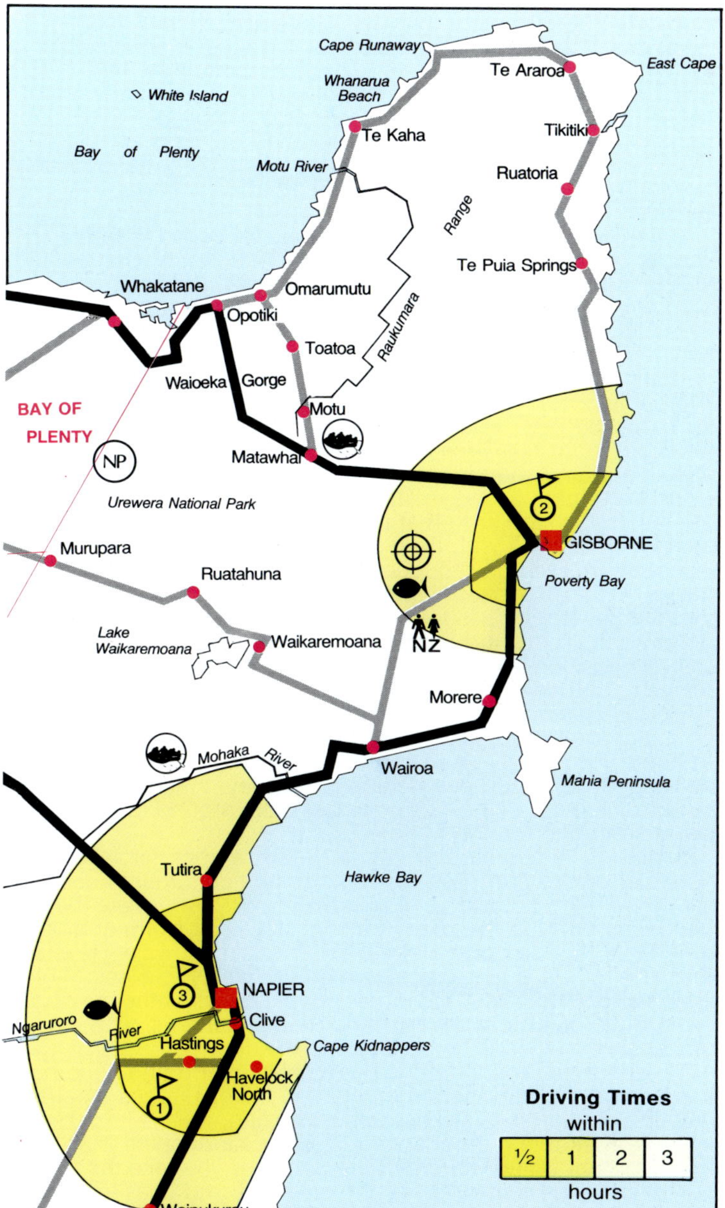

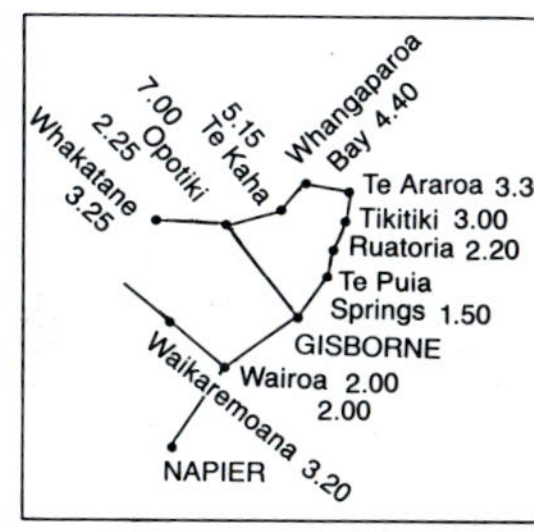

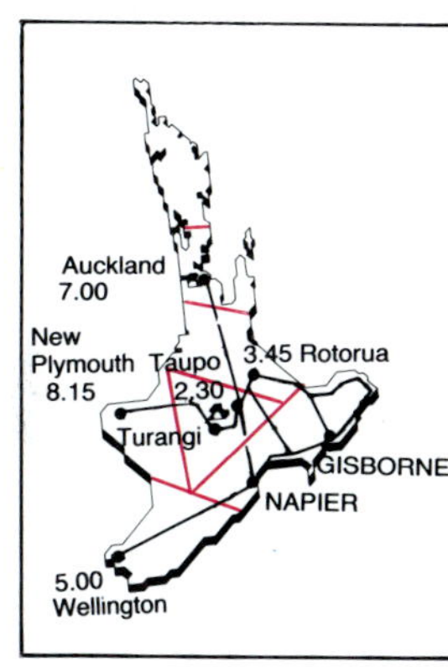

EAST CAPE

National Parks
Urewera National Park

Hunting

Fishing

River Adventures

Golf
1. Hastings; 2. Poverty Bay; 3. Napier.

Live with NZ
1. Y-Wury Station.

Napier/Hastings

The main centre for Hawkes Bay, Napier makes an excellent base for travel in the surrounding region.

The city owes its present appearance to a massive earthquake that shook the area back in 1931 on a hot February morning. Almost every building in Napier and neighbouring Hastings was destroyed or badly damaged when the towns were reduced to rubble in less than five minutes. Cliffs collapsed into the sea, a lagoon lifted itself out of the sea to create 3,340 hectares (8,250 acres) of new land and 258 people died.

If disasters on a grand scale fascinate you, visit the city museum where photographs and contemporary newspapers detail the devastation. The museum also houses an excellent collection of Maori artifacts from the moa-hunter period.

The city today, almost completely rebuilt immediately after the earthquake, is a celebration of 1930s Art Deco architecture. Walk the streets of the small City and absorb the styles, in particular hotels such as the Masonic, the Provincial, the Central and the Rothmans Building and the Municipal Theatre.

Along the sea front is the Marine Parade, edged with tall Norfolk pines. Here find an aquarium, oceanarium, marineland with performing dolphins, roller-skating rink, gardens, paddling pools, illuminated fountain, a kiwi house.

On Bluff Hill look out along the coastline of Hawkes Bay and also find cottages that survived the earthquake. Botanic gardens spill down the hillside and not far away is the Centennial Rock Garden featuring native shrubs and plants. For more gardens, visit the Kennedy Park Rose Garden, which has more than 3,000 rose bushes.

Hastings Public Relations Office
Russell Street North
Private Bag
Hastings
Telephone: (070) 60-205

Take a tour of the vineyards, independently or organised. Vines were first planted in Hawkes Bay in the 1850s, in a climate that is similar to that in the best grape-growing areas of Europe. Combined with the Poverty Bay vineyards around Gisborne, this region produces most of New Zealand's wine grapes. Vineyards near Napier and Hastings range from large commercial enterprises to small family-run wineries. The country's first vineyard established by the brothers at a Catholic mission is here. Another, the first commercial vineyard, still uses the original cellars.

Around Hastings there are tours of local industries – this is the major food-processing area, with the largest cannery in the Southern Hemisphere and frozen-food plant. Discover where the ubiquitous frozen pea begins its journey, to turn up on dinner plates from North Cape to the Bluff, around the Pacific Islands and even in the Middle East.

Hastings is a similar size city to Napier, a commercial and industrial centre based on the region's horticulture, but also a city of parks and gardens, old English trees. From there the road leads through the pretty town of Havelock North and up to Te Mata Peak for one of the most dramatic views of Hawkes Bay. The hill rises abruptly above a river valley to a height of 1310 metres (4297 feet) giving sweeping views of the curving coast, the orchards, vineyards and market gardens, with the hills of sheep stations spreading into the distance.

Travel out into the foothills around Napier and find winding rivers in valleys lined with Poplars and Silver Birches – perfect riverside picnic spots are not difficult to find.

Napier Public Relations Office,
Marine Parade,
Napier.
Telephone: (070) 57182

The remarkable gannet colony at Cape Kidnappers is an essential item on an itinerary here, whether you take the safari four-wheel-drive tour or brave the elements and tides and approach along the beach independently.

4

East Cape – Hawkes Bay

Entertainment – On the East Cape, head for the nearest pub – one way or another it will be entertaining. Find a little more sophistication in Hawkes Bay and Gisborne, though no less fun. Annual events include the excellent Hastings A & P Show in October and at Easter in Hastings the unusual spectacle of highland games with bagpipes, highland dancing, tossing the caber and even hurling-the-haggis contests.

SEE ALSO:

National Parks: Urewera National Park.
Lodges: Arden (RHC) (Havelock North).
Fishing/Diving: Baker Marine (Whakatane).
Live with NZ: Repongaere (Gisborne).

Cape Kidnappers, Napier.
(Courtesy Air New Zealand)

North to Gisborne & Opotiki

Just north of Napier on the coastal route (Highway 2) to Gisborne, is the Lake Tutira bird sanctuary, originally part of a sheep station owned by Guthrie-Smith, an early conservationist. Guthrie-Smith meticulously documented the spread of weeds and pests in his book *Tutira, The Story of a New Zealand Sheep Station.*

Nearer Gisborne, take a break at Morere Springs – bathe in the curative waters and picnic in the 200 hectare (500 acres) bush reserve.

If you're feeling tired on arrival at Gisborne, reflect on the stamina of Elizabeth Colenso, a missionary who walked to Gisborne for the birth of her child. It took 11 days in the 1840s.

Gisborne

Gisborne Community Public Relations Inc., 209 Grey Street, Gisborne P.O. Box 170 Telephone: (079) 86-139

The first Europeans to step ashore landed on Kaiti Beach in 1769. A series of unfortunate incidents led to the death of six Maoris, after which Cook named the area Poverty Bay, 'because it afforded us no one thing we wanted'. Others who followed Cook found the reverse, establishing orchards and vineyards on the rich flats around Gisborne. New Zealand's first winery was founded here by French Brothers of the Society of Mary to produce altar wine. Other links with Gisborne's past can be found in the local museum, where local craft work can be purchased. To the north stretch a string of beaches, excellent for swimming and fishing.

The trip around the East Cape combines spectacular coastal scenery with a sense of the past. Maori culture flourishes, the isolation is splendid. See highlights of Highway 35.

**Pinehurst Manor Restaurant
4 Clifford Street, Gisborne
Telephone: (079) 86-771
Hosts: Donna & Johann Tschurtschenthaler**

Exposed timbers in 19th-century manor – superb setting for excellent dining. Blackboard menu of fresh international cuisine, prepared by Austrian chef (prepares your catch on request). Seafood/venison specialities. Closed most Sundays. Reasonable prices. BYO licence.

**Gisborne Museum and Arts Centre
18-22 Stout Street
Gisborne
Telephone: (079) 83-832**

Illustrates the history of this area, including an internationally recognised historic photographic collection. Great exhibitions, a restaurant, souvenirs and information. Open Tuesday-Friday, 10.00 a.m. to 4.00 p.m.; Sundays, 2.00 p.m. to 4.30 p.m. From $2 (adult), .50c (child).

Opotiki

Sheltered from cold southerly winds and with some of the highest sunshine hours in the country, Opotiki offers an all-year-round interest. The sea, the rivers, the mountains, history and horticulture offer a great variety of things to do. Opotiki is not a tourist mecca, but an isolated escape from the world, where one spends time joining in with the locals – fishing, boating, sailing, swimming, rafting, jet boating or just walking.

Long an area of Maori Settlement, the Europeans established occupation for fishing and whaling. Tribal warfare decimated the local Maori tribes, especially after the Ngapuhi of Northland obtained muskets in the 1820s and raided the area. The pressures of European settlement led to open warfare.

Accommodation – Motor inns, hotels and motels in Gisborne, Napier and Hastings especially. In out-of-the-way places, find old hotels that can offer bargain accommodation and old-fashioned roast dinners. There are motels and camping grounds along the East Cape coast as well as opportunities for camping wild. At Whanarua Bay, one of the prettiest on the coast, 160 hectares (400 acres) have been reserved for holiday-makers. Youth hostels are at Gisborne, Tutira (a sheep farm near Napier) and Clive, near Napier.

Food – Look for fresh fish and shellfish such as paua, mussels, tuatua, pipis and crayfish around the cape. Getting it cooked to perfection may be more difficult – this is not haute cuisine territory. From Gisborne through Hawkes Bay enjoy fresh fruit and vegetables – apples, peaches, melons, avocados, grapes and, around Hastings especially, the best green asparagus in the country. Dine and wine well in Hawkes Bay.

Maori carving on the pataka at Te Araroa School, East Cape. *(National Publicity Studios)*

Gisborne to Opotiki

via East Coast Highway 35
From Gisborne:
326 km (202 miles)

Highway 35 – Gisborne to Opotiki – is one of the lesser-known roads of New Zealand. It combines spectacular coastal scenery with a sense of the past. Maori culture flourishes. The isolation is splendid, and remember – if you want any information, ask a local.

Tatapouri
From Gisborne:
5 km (3 miles)

Good fishing and fresh crayfish are often available for sale. Commercial deep-sea fishing boats call here and take out parties; also a deep-sea fishing club. On the seafront is a licensed hotel.

Tolaga Bay
From Gisborne:
14 km (9 miles)

The streets of the town are named after Captain Cook's crew, who cast anchor here in 1769. The distinctive Tolaga Bay Inn is 'Old English', both in architecture and hospitality.

The best-situated campsite on this coast is about three kilometres south on the beach at the end of the bay.

Tokomaru Bay
From Gisborne:
55 km (35 miles)

Named after another of the great canoes. A township developing into a holiday resort – a tavern, motels, campsite and caravan park.

Te Puia Springs
From Gisborne:
91 km (57 miles)

An oasis of thermal activity plus hotel, a hospital, a small settlement and a tiny lake.

Ruatoria
From Gisborne:
102 km (64 miles)

Ruatoria, with a charm of its own, is the centre of the great Ngati Porou tribe. Sir Apirana Ngata, a Maori statesman, lived here. The town offers banking and a full range of facilities.

Tikitiki
From Gisborne:
128 km (80 miles)

Tikitiki contains much of interest to the student of the Maori. The people here are descendants of the legendary Whatonga and Toi, the first to establish themselves in this fertile valley.

Above the township on the flat Pukemaire Hill are clearly defined trenches dug in 1864 during the land wars, superimposed on the older earthworks of the pre-European era.

Do not miss the Anglican Church at Tikitiki. Built in 1924 to incorporate Maori design, it led to a resurgence of Maori arts and crafts in the area.

Te Araroa
From Gisborne:
147 km (92 miles)

Here stands the world's largest pohutukawa tree and the Kawa Kawa Hotel, very well appointed and run on the best lines – a welcome surprise in this remote place. (In front of the hotel is a landing strip for light aircraft.)

A delightful side trip is the road to the world's most easterly lighthouse at East Cape.

Hicks Bay
From Gisborne:
174 km (108 miles)

A sudden and dramatic change in landscapes greets the traveller in this lovely bay, named after a crewmate on Cook's ship, *Endeavour.* Hicks Bay marks the start of the large sheep and cattle stations that extend along the East Coast far to the south and for many miles inland.

Lottin Point
From Gisborne:
183 km (114 miles)

The serenity of quiet bays contrasts with rocky coastline and pounding seas. Good fishing for both skindiver and surfcaster.

Whangaparaoa (Cape Runaway)

It is here that the two famous legendary canoes landed from Hawaiiki – the Tainui and the Arawa. Kumaras were supposedly introduced into New Zealand here. An old pa and meeting house are nearby. Good beach and fishing.

Waihau Bay
From Gisborne:
216 km (134 miles)

A rock-strewn bay where you will find a well-appointed private hotel, Post Office, store and deep-sea fishing club. Good fishing, swimming at nearby Oruaiti Beach.

Whanarua Bay
From Gisborne:
227 km (141 miles)

One of the prettiest bays on the coast, with several small secluded beaches ideal for picnics, fishing, swimming. Whanarua Creek leads to a series of lovely bush waterfalls. (Glow-worms feature on the creek banks at night.) The lofty hill above the bay commands a majestic view of the coast.

Maungaroa, Te Kaha
From Gisborne:
246 km (153 miles)

Beside the roadside between two lovely pohutukawa trees, beneath a guardian angel headstone, are buried Princess Te Rangi Pai and her husband Mr John Howie. Princess Te Rangi Pai was a famous New Zealand singer who performed before royalty.

Te Kaha

A popular vacation area on a headland, surrounded by glorious bays and beaches. Accommodation, general store and garage. Good fishing, swimming. Tukaki, a beautifully carved meeting house, and the remains of the old redoubt and pa may be seen. Once a whaling station and an early missionary settlement. Nowadays, fish processing, crayfishing and game meats are important activities.

Omaio
From Gisborne:
272 km (169 miles)

A wide, fairly sheltered bay. The shingle surf beach shelves steeply, but is still suitable for swimming. Good fishing. Post Office and well-stocked general store.

Whitianga
From Gisborne:
278 km (173 miles)

Deep-water cove, suitable for rock fishing, crayfishing. Some attractive camping spots.

Motu River
From Gisborne:
283 km (176 miles)

From Maraenui the road runs inland, then crosses the Motu River.This mighty river falls 487 metres (1,597 feet) from the mountains along its 110-kilometre (65 mile) run, having a dense virgin forest catchment area, of over 900 square km. (347 square miles). It is one of the most magnificent rafting and scenic rivers in the country.

Maraenui
From Gisborne:
290 km (180 miles)

These coastal flats and the hills behind were the location of numerous pa. During the siege of Te Kaha, this area provided a much-needed food supply for the defenders. Maraenui pa was attacked by the Ngapuhi tribe (from the Bay of Islands.)

Torere

A large semi-circular bay, rocky at each end with a steeply shelving pebble beach. No swimming, but good fishing. Worth visiting is a richly decorated church serving the local Ngaitai tribe.

Opape
From Gisborne:
310 km (193 miles)

The sandy beach ends amid the rocky inlets. Good for launching small fishing boats. The Muruwai meeting house overlooks the sea.

Omarumutu
From Gisborne:
316 km (197 miles)

The interior decoration of the Omarumutu War Memorial Hall, belongs with the finest Maori art in the country. Nearby Tutamere meeting house reveres the ancestral chief of the Ngatirua sub-tribe.

Tirohanga
From Gisborne:
321 km (200 miles)

Sandy beach close to the road. Good surf, fishing, swimming. Note hill-top pa on the seaward side of the road, where old trenches are easily discernible.

Mts Ruapehu and Ngaruahoe Volcanic Plateau. ***(Courtesy Turangi Scenic Flights)***

About 1,800 years ago a massive eruption, greater than Mt St Helens, Karakatoa or Santorini, rocked the earth. Debris was thrown 55 kilometres (34 miles) into the air and the land around for 20,000 square kilometres (7,722 square miles) was devastated. (Mt St Helens threw up a column 23 kilometres (14 miles) high and demolished 550 square kilometres (212 square miles) of forest.).

Look on the vast tranquil Lake Taupo today and it may be hard to imagine that the lake once exploded with one of the biggest volcanic eruptions in human history. But look more closely and evidence of the massive blast lies all around the Volcanic Plateau – in the pumice soils that dominate the plateau, in cliffs of white pumice on the lake's eastern shore, in beaches of white pumice stone, in charred remains of trees protruding from banks on the Desert Road.

This is a region of wild expansive beauty. Lake Taupo covers 619 square kilometres (238 square miles); in the west thick bush and waterfalls edge the isolated bays, in the east the landscape has been tamed with small parklands where deciduous trees provide brilliant colour in the crisp autumn air. At the southern end of the lake, beyond the fishing and tourist township of Turangi, a cluster of volcanic mountains rise to 2,706 metres (8,875 feet) with one, Ngauruhoe (2,290 metres or 7,500 feet), constantly belching steam. These mountains, a mere 3 million years old, are the southernmost link in a volcanic chain that stretches around the perimeter of the Pacific.

Travel around the region and find roadsides edged with purple and white heather or yellow broom, see red-tussock grasslands stretching out to meet pine forests, native beech forest spilling down the Kaimanawa Ranges (mountains that are 300 million years old) and great totara, matai and rimu trees in stands of rainforest.

In a region of startling contrasts, discover the Tongariro National Park encircling the mountains Ruapehu, Ngauruhoe and Tongariro. Within the park's 76,198 hectares (188,000 acres) are glaciers, a hot crater lake, hot springs, barren desert, alpine herb-lands, ski fields.

The neighbouring Kaimanawa Forest Park attracts trampers, rafters, fishermen and hunters seeking red and sika deer, wild pigs and goats.

The Tongariro River which flows between the national park and the forest park, is world famous for the fighting rainbow trout that battle the fast glacier-fed waters. By the Tongariro, visitors can see a trout hatchery and view wild fish through windows cut in the side of a tributary stream. Fry raised at the hatchery are not destined for Taupo or its surrounding rivers but for other parts of New Zealand and other countries.

At nearby Tokaanu there's a small, unspoilt thermal area – paths through manuka scrub lead to hot springs, a small geyser, boiling mud pools and silica deposits.

A great delta of reeds stretches out into the lake around the mouth of the Tongariro, near the township of Turangi and the village of Tokaanu. Birds abound here – black swans, cormorants (known as shags in New Zealand), bitterns, pukekos, white-faced herons, ducks, dab chicks, fernbird.

At the western edge of the delta, where the lake road ends, is Waihi, a Maori village of quiet charm, nestling on the lake edge beneath cliffs that exude steam. On the Taumarunui road that rises above the lake behind Waihi are splendid views of the lake and the Tongariro delta.

The Volcanic Plateau

Another superb lake view may be gained from the Pihanga Saddle Road, leading from near Tokaanu across to the Tongariro National Park. Further over the saddle a short but superb bush walk leads to a tiny bush-fringed crater lake, Rotopounamu.

Head south along State Highway 1 and pass by the mountains, travelling across the desolate Rangipo Desert. Prevailing westerly winds lose their moisture on the far side of the mountains, sweeping around to help create a strange, inhospitable desert of drifting sand and gravel. Out of the desert and tussock lands the road dips and climbs through deep gorges and over high, rolling hills that form large sheep farms.

The Volcanic Plateau is a region for swimming in hot pools or cold lake, water skiing, sailing, boating, fishing for incomparable rainbow trout, rafting, canoeing, climbing, skiing, tramping, hunting; or a place to take a picnic to a quiet lake or riverside spot where bellbirds and tuis sing in the surrounding trees and trout leap in the clear water below.

Travel around best by car. The wildness of the region is its attraction, with its rivers, lake, forests, desert and stark mountains most easily experienced to the full with independent transport. The main Auckland-Wellington railway line runs through the west of the region, with stops made at Taumarunui, National Park, Ohakune. Buses of N.Z.R. Road Services, Newmans and Hawkes Bay Motors serve main points in the region.

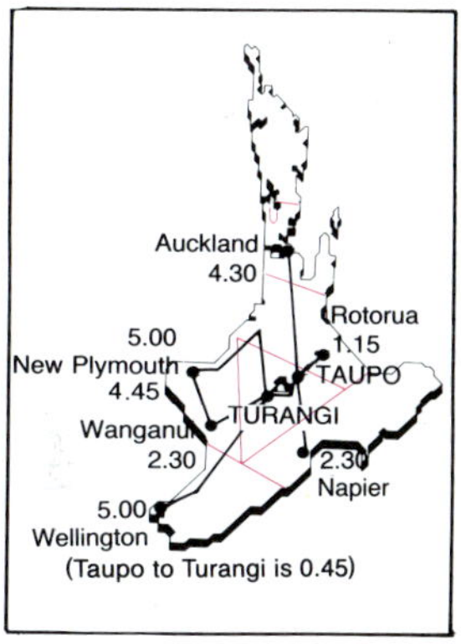

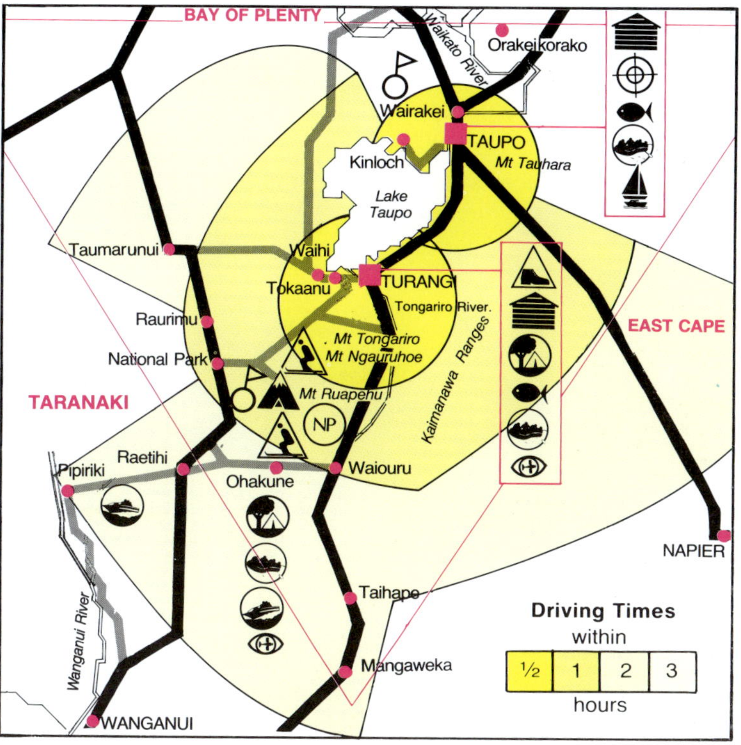

VOLCANIC PLATEAU

National Parks
Tongariro National Park.

Skiing
1. Whakapapa; 2. Turoa.

Climbing

Tramping

Lodges
1. Huka Lodge; 2. Tongariro Lodge.

Outback Safaris

Hunting

Fishing
1. Lake Taupo; 2. Tongariro River.

River Adventures
1. Lake Taupo; 2. Wanganui River; 3. Tongariro River.

Yachting/Cruising

Flightseeing

Golf
1. Wairakei International;
2. Chateau Tongariro.

Taupo

Taupo grew up from a small military outpost in 1869 to a town designed to serve holiday-makers. The warm mineral waters and nearby thermal sights drew nineteenth-century visitors, who stopped over in the town before taking the lake steamer south to Tokaanu. Then came the rainbow trout, released in the late 1880s, and the lake became a mecca for anglers.

Take a cruise on the lake – sightseeing launches and charter boats leave from a pretty river bank jetty where the Waikato River leaves the lake. Hire paddle boats, windsurfers and row boats on the lake front.

Swim in the lake – where hot-water streams enter the lake one can enjoy swimming in hot and cold water. Swim in the large thermal pools at the A.C.Baths or De Brett Thermal Pools.

Take walks of extraordinary variety: through the Waipihihi Botanical Reserve, a mixture of rhododendrons, azaleas, alpine herb garden, and bush walks of rare and unusual ferns and trees; to the Opepe Graves, deep in a sombre stand of bush, where British cavalrymen were ambushed in 1869; to the top of an extinct volcano, Mt Tauhara, 1,099 metres (3,600 feet) high; beside the Waikato River along an official walkway from the Huka Falls to Aratiatia, through wild flowers and grasses.

The Huka Falls have been a tourist attraction since soldiers at the Taupo redoubt cut a rough track through to the river bank. Here the Waikato River surges through a narrow chasm, changing colour from deep green to milky turquoise as it fans out in a churning mass at the base of the falls. Drive to the falls or take a tour, and go on to Aratiatia where the river crashes through a zig-zagging drop of 28 metres in 0.8 kilometres (9 feet in 2,600 feet). The natural drop supplies a power station, and the rapids are switched on twice a day for the benefit of visitors.

Between the Huka Falls and Aratiatia is Wairakei, the site of a huge geothermal power station. Visit the power station on the river edge and the valley of steam and pipes behind. There is also a thermal valley of hot springs and bubbling mud pools. Here too is the famous Wairakei golf course.

Further afield, travel out to the thermal region of Orakei Korako for a concentration of geysers, hot springs, terraces and the amazing colours of sinter and algae. Drive to lakeside bays such as Acacia Bay and Kinloch, to the west of the town, or drive along the eastern shores to discover a string of pretty lakeside picnic places stretching the length of the lake. Get to the remote and beautiful bays at the far west of the lake by boat only.

Taupo Information Centre
Tongariro Street
P.O. Box 865
Taupo
Telephone: (074) 89-002

Wairakei steam bore.
(Courtesy Air New Zealand)

Accommodation. – At Taupo the choice is wide – exclusive, luxury lodges, spartan fishing lodges and cabins, luxury motels and motor inns on the lake shore, older traditional hotels, modest motels with self-catering, or motor camps with space for tents or caravans. Turangi has similar accommodation, but less of it because it is a smaller town. However, Turangi does have an extraordinary budget camp with 144 cabins, basic shelter that served large hydro-electric projects. Ohakune also offers travellers good accommodation, geared especially to house skiers. Youth hostels are at Taupo and Ohakune. Accommodation in the national park is at one grand THC hotel, a motel-lodge, camping ground and park huts on tramping routes; some huts also in the Kaimanawas.

Food. – In Taupo you can dine on Bluff oysters or Australian prawns; but for the best taste treats look for game food – venison, wild pork, pheasant, rabbit. Catch a trout and lodge, restaurant or hotel kitchen will cook it for you. Plenty of fast food includes Chinese, hamburgers, fish and chips. Find a great cup of coffee in an espresso coffee shop in Heuheu Street; get picnic food in the little delicatessen nearby – the range is really surprising; buy local fresh cottage loaves with poppy seed or cheese topping. Elsewhere in the region it can be a matter of taking what you can find – not always disappointing. A humble meat pie, homebaked with layers of flaky pastry, takes on a new look when you are hungry.

Entertainment. – It's an outdoor region – find yacht races, speed-boat races, fishing contests. In the evenings there's dinner-dance or live entertainment at restaurants and hotel bars that range from quietly relaxed to rough and raucous.

Take trout fishing, hunting, rafting, jet-boating or tramping adventures with these professionals. Services have a distinctive style, suited totally to individual requirements and fitness levels. The company offers you the best of the region's attractions; appreciate the surrounding beauty on foot; hire a row-boat; take a trophy-trout fishing helicopter safari; relax on the lake in a luxuriously appointed cruiser, or experience white-water thrills on regional rivers! Everything provided, costs on enquiry.

Simon Dickie Adventures Ltd
Boat Harbour, Lakefront
PO Box 682
Taupo
Telephone: (074) 88-115/ 89-680
Telex: NZ60846 FISHING
Host: Simon Dickie

Fun flights through this volcanic wonderland of geysers, faultlines and mountain craters! Excellent options available from 10 minutes to 3 hours (from $22). Scheduled Auckland/return services from $100; New Zealand-wide and safari charters by arrangement.

Taupo Air Services
Taupo Airport
R.D. 2 Taupo
Telephone: (074) 85-325/ 88-773

This quality retreat is as tasteful as its beautiful lake edge environs. Superior accommodation includes private patios and spa baths in each unit, in-house video and teletext. Breakfasts and picnic lunches by request, full kitchens with microwave ovens. Enjoy the heated swimming pool or safe swimming beaches, yachts available for hire and a convenient boat ramp. Close to restaurants and shopping. From $97 to $250 for lakefront suite.

Cascades Motor Lodge
Lake Terrace FLAG INN
PO Box 894
Taupo
Telephone: (074) 83-774
USA: (800) 624FLAG
Telex: NZ 61206 RETREAT

One of Taupo's newest motels offering luxury accommodation in attractive lakeside setting. Units have whirlpool en-suite, queen-sized beds and full kitchen facilities, plus in-house video. Lake view units available. From $73.

Cottage Mews Motel
Lake Terrace
PO Box 1127
Taupo
Telephone: (074) 83-004
Hosts: Helen and Graham Lewis

Chelmswood Manor
Cnr Lake Terrace and Tremaine Ave
PO Box 1150
Taupo
Telephone: (074) 82-715
Telex: NZ63154
Hosts: The Hancocks

Overlooking Lake Taupo in quiet surroundings, this lovely facility offers Tudor-style, ground-floor units, set in 2 acres of spacious grounds. Accommodation ranges from studio to luxury and executive suites with a variety of hot thermal mineral pools, both ensuite and outdoor. Facilities include sauna, baby-sitting services and children's play area, adjacent licensed restaurant, breakfast by request, in-house video, courtesy car service and kitchen facilities. From $55 to $90.

Turangi

Ruapehu Region Information Centre
Clyde Street
Ohakune
Telephone: (0658) 58-151

A town built to serve the complex Tongariro power projects, Turangi now serves holiday-makers. By the swirling glacier-fed Tongariro, a river with a world-wide reputation for magnificent fighting rainbow trout, and also close to the shores of Lake Taupo, Turangi is a splendid base for anglers.

There's boating and swimming in the lake from nearby beaches, bird watching in the vast marshy Tongariro delta that attracts numerous waterfowl, tramping and hunting in the hills, skiing only 45 minutes away by car on Mt Ruapehu and walks by the lake shore, riverbanks or through deep bush.

At nearby Tokaanu is a small, intriguing thermal area of geysers and mud pools.

If you have any time to spare, don't neglect the excellent tiny museum for information on the geological past, the forests, the Maori history and an explanation of the electric power schemes that use canals and tunnels to divert water around and under the mountains.

Skiers at the Whakapapa skifield, Mt Ruapehu, look out to Lake Taupo in the background. The active smoking volcano is Mt Ngaruahoe. *(Scott Lee)*

The Volcanic Plateau

Tongariro Outdoor Centre
Ohuanga Road (opp. Fire Station)
PO Box 174
Turangi

A friendly, economical base from which to experience regional adventure activities. Cabin accommodation for 200. Excellent licensed restaurant seats 100. Dinner/bed/breakfast from $42. Introductions to white-water rafting, skiing and fishing operators.

The Gamekeepers Loft
Town Centre
Turangi
Telephone: (0746) 8821
Hosts: Jack and Bev Allan

Hunting/fishing decor, note impressive wall-mounted trophies. Comfortable, warm ambiance and delicious food! Specialises in game and seafood (will prepare your catch for you). Licensed; range of New Zealand wines. Children's menu, mid-range prices.

Tauranga-Taupo Lodge
State Highway 1
Turangi R.D. 2
Telephone: (0746) 8385
Hosts: Heather & Michael Sadlier

Just north of Turangi, enjoy friendly country hospitality at this lovely facility. Excellent accommodation from luxury self-contained, fully-appointed motel suites to tourist cabins, van park and camping ground. Amenities include laundries/drying room, paraplegic bathroom, spa pool, games room, trampoline and barbeque. Rowboats, canoes available, plus fishing tackle for hire and sale. Guided hunting, fishing and seasonal skiing safaris organised on request. From $66 (motel/double), $33 (cabins), $7.70 (camp); GST inclusive.

Parklands Motor Lodge & Motor Home Park
Cnr S.H. 1 & Arahori Street
PO Box 142
Turangi
Telephone: (0746) 7515
Hosts: Joy, Don & The Fasher Family

Nestled in acres of grounds close to the Tongariro River with 20 self-contained units (queen-sized beds) plus well-appointed van sites. Superb facilities include spas, sauna, fitness room, putting green, laundry and drying room, tennis court, games room and fish smokehouse. Great base – Don organises trout fishing, hunting, skiing, deer stalking, tramping, flightseeing and other outdoor activities. Sunny, sheltered location with great views, peaceful, friendly atmosphere. From $65 (double), GST inclusive.

South to National Park & Ohakune

Ohakune

Once upon a time Ohakune was known as a timber town that diversified into market gardening, concentrating on carrots; but not any longer. Today Ohakune is known as one of the country's best centres for mountain sports and adventure activities.

With the development of the magnificent Turoa ski field, Ohakune blossomed into a lively mountain village with hotels, motels, lodges, chalets and restaurants. It's not merely a skiers' town but a base for all-year-round activities such as canoeing, rafting, trekking, jet boating and trout fishing.

'The Hobbit' Motorlodge
Goldfinch Street
Ohakune
Telephone: (0658) 58-248
Telex: c/- NZ31377 AHISKI
Host: Philip Jackson

'The Hobbit' caters for singles and groups, offering a variety of excellent accommodation at all price ranges. Facilities include laundry and drying room, spa pool, in-house video, courtesy transport and a great licensed restaurant – open year round. Centrally located in this ski resort town and handy to the many adventure activities, it is an ideal base. Book in advance for winter months. From $13 (bunks), $52 (single), $165 (group of 6).

SEE ALSO:

National Parks: Tongariro National Park.
Skiing: Turoa Ski Area (Ohakune), Whakapapa Ski Field (National Park).
Lodges: Huka Lodge, 'MV Waianawa (RHC) (Taupo), Tongariro (RHC) (Turangi).
Outback Safaris: Rawhide Holdings (Taumarunui), Rinestone Appaloosa Stud (Taupo).
Fishing: Lite-Tackle Tours (Turangi), Simon Dickie Adventures (Taupo), Tongariro Guides (Turangi).
Hunting: Simon Dickie Adventures (Taupo).
Live with NZ: Koha Lodge (Taupo).

The west coast swerves out into the Tasman Sea here, creating a region dominated by the symmetrical shape of Mt Egmont, a lone perfect mountain rising to 2,518 metres (8,260 feet) above the lush dairylands of Taranaki.

From the top of Mt Egmont, an easy walk in good weather, Taranaki spreads out below like a vast trim parkland – an illusion that carries some truth, for the rich volcanic soils created by the dormant mountain form not only gentle green pastures but parks and gardens with ferns, trees and flowers.

In the National Park that encircles the mountain, the wild flora has developed in isolation from other alpine areas, often producing features unique to the region. Below the stark snow-capped summit is a wilderness of mosses, alpine herbs, waterfalls and thick forest with giant rata trees.

At lower levels, find a variety of parks and gardens such as New Plymouth's Pukekura Park, regarded as a superb formal park of Victorian charm with flower gardens, fernery, waterfall, fountain and artificial lakes; or the large Pukeiti Rhododendron Trust, a 360-hectare (890-acre) springtime spectacle of rhododendrons and azaleas mingle with the soft green of native bush; or a very special commercial nursery, Duncan and Davies, with rare plants from all over the world and a huge collection of evergreen shrubs and trees – you don't need to be buying to enjoy the 40 hectares (100 acres) of greenery.

Along the region's sweeping coastline are wild seascapes with surf beaches attracting surfers and fishermen. In the north sandstone cliffs have been eroded into extraordinary shapes, and tiny fishing settlements nestle by river mouths. In the south are beaches of black iron sand.

But it is the gentle pastoral charm of the landscape, spreading out from below the massive mountain, that remains the most distinctive feature of Taranaki. Travel through Taranaki, taking a route that encircles the mountain, and you will discover that this charm belies the past. Many of the tranquil rural towns and villages began life as stockades and blockhouses, as Taranaki endured 12 years of battles and bloodshed from 1860. There are tales of fraudulent land dealings by the colonial government that initiated these years of conflict; and tales of settlers and British soldiers ambushed, shot or tomahawked, of towns under siege.

At New Plymouth's Taranaki Museum, ancient sacred stone sculptures echo the monuments of Easter Island. Former pa sites are found on hilltops throughout the region. Koru Pa near Oakura Beach has shown evidence of occupation stretching back a thousand years.

In the 1880s, with friction between European and Maori at an end, the Taranaki Region developed into one of the richest dairylands in the world – today more cheese is said to leave New Plymouth than any other port in the world. Visit dairy farms and butter and cheese factories in the region. At Eltham some of the best New Zealand cheeses are made in the European tradition – for example, Blue Vein (similar to Danish Blue or Roquefort), Danbo, Havarti, Erbo and Gouda.

In the last 15 years a new wealth has appeared in the region to boost the prosperity – natural gas. Great complexes rise on the rural landscape as the energy is tapped and converted to various uses from fields at Kapuni and the off shore Maui Field, one of the top 20 such fields in the world. Energy projects at Kapuni, Oanui and near Waitara all have information centres.

Lake Rotokare Walk

(4.2 kilometres (2½ miles) – approximately two hours) Location: signposted in Eltham Township. Turn off at Rawhitiroa Road, then Sangster Road. Beautiful and easy walk around Lake Rotokare (Rippling Lake) with native trees named and explained. Also good location for native birds.

Hawera

South Taranaki Information and Promotion Office High Street Hawera Telephone: (062) 86-599

A well-preserved ancient pa site of Turuturu-Mokai (heads on stakes), which was deserted before European settlement following tribal war. A short walk from Turuturu-Mokai is the site of a garrison outpost, sacked by the Maori during the land wars of the 1860s. Take the by-pass (Glover Road) to Turatura Road.

From New Plymouth

Drive inland and onto the slopes of Mt Egmont – it is a mere 25 kilometres (15½ miles) from New Plymouth to the end of a road at North Egmont, 936 metres (3,000 feet) high on the mountainside. From here there are various alpine walks, one leading to the 30 metres (100-foot) Bell Falls. From North Egmont it's also possible to walk to the summit – it takes about four hours from the road end to the top of the mountain. The walk is not difficult, but park rangers always stress the need to be sensibly clad and prepared for weather changes. Guides are available from alpine clubs.

On a sharp, clear day the mountaintop views are extraordinary, across dark bush and radiating mountain streams, over a patchwork of green fields spreading to the coast or towards the high heathlands of the Central Plateau and the cluster of volcanoes, Ruapehu, Tongariro, Ngauruhoe.

Legend suggests that Egmont (its Maori name is Taranaki) once formed part of the Tongariro mountains, but left after an argument with Tongariro, banished to the far coast. At times it is not difficult to believe that Egmont gazes back wistfully toward to the distant group of mountains.

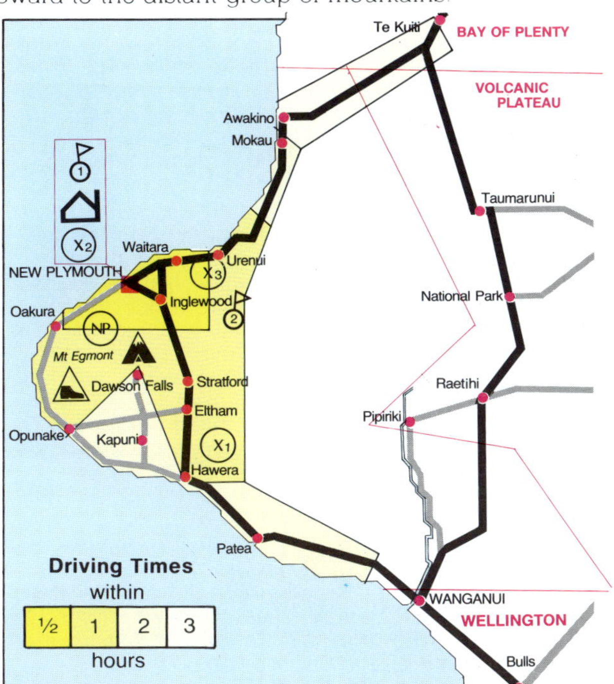

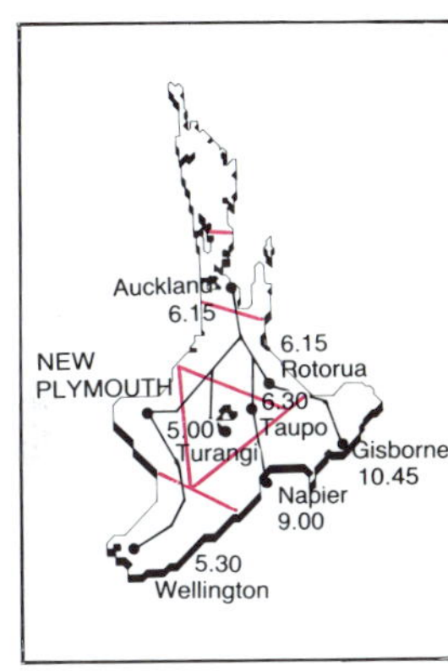

TARANAKI

National Parks
Egmont National Park.

Climbing

Tramping

Golf
1. New Plymouth;
2. Inglewood.

History
1. Hurworth

Local
1. Museum; 2. Pa.

New Plymouth

The main port and service centre of the region, the city of New Plymouth (pop. 44,000), makes an excellent base for touring. a round-the-mountain tour from here makes a leisurely day's travel, with time to pause in the most scenic places.

In the city itself, however, visit the parks – a fifth of New Plymouth's land is devoted to public parks and gardens. First and foremost is Pukekura Park, with paths that lead through mossy arcades to glasshouses of tropical ferns and orchids, through formal flower gardens, beside two artificial lakes and through native bush. At night the fountain provides a multi-coloured, flood-lit, 45-minute performance. Adjoining the park is Brooklands Park, with bush, sweeping lawns, immense trees and a natural amphitheatre where crowds up to 17,000 can enjoy outdoor concerts. From the grassy slopes of Mt Moturoa, rising above a bushy parkland fringe, look out across the city towards Mt Egmont and the distant Tongariro mountains, or along the coast across the North Taranaki Bight.

For the region's most spectacular floral sight, travel out of town to Pukeiti between September and November, when thousands of rhododendrons and azaleas colour the 360-hectare (900-acre) park and bird sanctuary.

At the Taranaki Museum in New Plymouth see an excellent collection of very old and unusual Maori artifacts. The city's Govett-Brewster Art Gallery is one of the most exciting small public galleries in the country, with a superb collection of works by New Zealand-born avant-garde artist and film maker, Len Lye. The gallery contains the two largest Len Lye kinetic sculptures in the world: 'Trilogy' (a flip and two twisters), high-tensile stainless-steel ribbons that whip and scythe the air; and 'Fountain', a great spray of trembling steel rods. Lye, who lived most of his life in New York, explored the power of energy through film and, later, kinetic sculpture. He believed the artist tunes into the human 'old brain' to express emotional truth, unlike the scientist who uses the 'new brain'. He was so pleased with the gallery's 1977 exhibition of his work that he bequeathed to it his collection of papers, works and famous films.

In New Plymouth there's also the charming 'Selwyn' Church of St Mary, the oldest stone church in the country, built in 1842 when the settlement of New Plymouth was only a year old (the settlers came from Devon and Cornwall). The church is as beautiful inside as it is from the outside – don't merely admire the exterior. Also walk through the old churchyard, where many of those first settlers are buried.

At Hurworth, a few kilometres from the city, a young English settler in the 1850s cut and sawed the timber to build himself a simple, elegant cottage and surrounded his new home with trees such as chestnuts and oaks. The settler, Harry Atkinson, later to become Sir Harry, was to be prime minister of New Zealand four times. The house is beautifully restored and some of the original trees remain in an enchanting rural setting.

At Waitara to the north, the Te Atiawa tribe were dispossessed of their land by government troops in 1860, heralding the beginning of many years of bitter fighting. Today visit Waitara to see the Manukorihi Pa, a superbly carved meeting house built in 1936 as a memorial to Sir Maui Pomare, a distinguished and revered politician.

Near Waitara, see also the Pukerangiora Pa site, a dramatic vantage point above the Waitara River for the Te Atiawa people to retreat to in times of tribal warfare.

Continue north to Urenui, once heavily populated with forts on many surrounding hills. Here at Okaki Pa is an impressive memorial to another Maori knight, Sir Peter Buck, politician and internationally acclaimed anthropologist.

New Plymouth Public Relations Office, 81 Liardet Street, New Plymouth. Telephone: (067) 86086

Travel around the region and literally travel around the mountain by car or coach. N.Z.R. Road Services and Newmans provide scheduled bus transport. For flight-seeing around the region and over the mountain, contact aero clubs in New Plymouth.

Entertainment. – One doesn't go to Taranaki for sophisticated night life. However, bands and cabaret singers often entertain in hotels and motor inns. The Egmont Steam Flour Mill (a restored 19th-century building) houses a nightclub. In New Plymouth in summer check what's offering at Brooklands Park outdoor theatre – it could be a pop singer or symphony orchestra. As well as A & P Shows, look out for local horticultural shows.

Food. – In the region of cheese stock up with local varieties. For basic economical sustenance of steak or fish and chips, look in New Plymouth's Devon Street. You can also eat Indonesian, Italian and Chinese in New Plymouth.

Accommodation. – Find the best selection in New Plymouth, with hotels and first-class motor inns. On the slopes of Mt Egmont itself accommodation ranges from a stylish Swiss-inspired lodge at Dawson Falls to spartan bunkhouses and trampers' mountain huts. Youth hostels and camping grounds (some with cabins) provide budget accommodation in New Plymouth and most small towns.

Dawson Falls Tourist Lodge
Stratford
Reservations: NZ Collect (03) 799-127
(Details/Overseas reservations; see p.129)

Recluse at base of Mt Egmont (Mt Taranaki), accommodating 18 persons, Swiss alpine-styled private suites, cuisine traditional Swiss or country NZ. Beautiful scenery, walks, mountain climbs, sauna, spa. From $88 per person. Winner of RHC 1986 Friendly Service Award.

Mountain House Motor Lodge.
Pembroke Road,
Stratford R.D.21
Telephone: (0663) 6100
Hosts: Berta and Keith Anderson

Set on slopes of Mt Egmont in superb surrounds, hotel/chalet retreat with all facilities including sauna and superior licensed restaurant. Handy to skiing, scenic flights, fishing and golf. From $65 (hotel/double), $70 (motel/double).

Pouakai Wildlife Reserve & Zoo Park
590 Carrington Road,
R.D.1, New Plymouth
Hosts: Marea and Gary Faigan

Meet 'Khartoum' (camel), only vervet monkeys in country, plus range of birds and animals in sanctuary. Holds Wildlife Conservation Award. Open daily, escorts for groups/disabled. Wear sensible footwear. From $2.50 (adult), .60c (child). Group concessions.

Pukeiti Rhododendron Trust (Inc.)
Carrington Road
R.D.4
New Plymouth
Telephone: (067) 511-140/513-583

One of world's largest collections of rhododendrons plus thousands of other rare and unusual plants. 360 hectares (890 acres) of well-signposted botanist's paradise, tracks through rainforest, display houses of sub-tropical rhododendrons, orchids and plant sales nursery. A garden for all seasons, open daily (peak flowering September-November). Gatehouse Restaurant and souvenir shops – specialising in Pukeiti memorabilia. Sturdy footwear required/waterproof jacket. Umbrellas etc. available. Bring camera. Facilities for disabled. Admission adults $4, children free. Group discounts.

SEE ALSO:

National Parks: Mt Egmont (Taranaki) National Park.
Outback Safaris: Tuahu Western Horse Safaris.
NZ Historic Places: Hurworth (New Plymouth).

The capital city, Wellington, perches on the windswept southwest tip of this region, its satellite suburbs and towns spreading up the valleys behind.

Travel north from the city, however, and soon discover that the overriding characteristics of the region are distinctly rural, not urban.

Massive ranges of hills, first the Rimutakas and then the Tararuas, run the length of the region, like a mountainous backbone dividing east from west. As you move out of the urban sprawl, the decision must be made to go east or west – straight ahead the rugged Tararuas bar the way, uncrossed by roads for another 130 kilometres (80 miles).

Go west and there are long, pleasant beaches backed by sand dunes, stretching up the coast to the South Taranaki Bight. Here lies the river city of Wanganui, a river that gives access into the interior; its source is in the Tongariro Mountains. Further south, the low-lying coastal countryside, with its market gardens and rich pastures, is peppered with small beach resorts and rural towns. At McKay's Crossing, memorial gates remember a World War II U.S. Marine Corps Camp and there's also a museum of vintage public transport. Otaki is a rewarding stop for those interested in Maori culture and history, in particular for the Rangiatea Maori Church with its superb interior. Levin is a centre of horticulture research and Palmerston North is a city with a university concentrating on agriculture and special research establishments.

The west-east connection can be made from Palmerston North through the Manawatu Gorge. The road follows the tortuous course of the Manawatu River, which rises on the eastern side of the Ruahine Ranges and then turns to flow westward towards the sea. Such are the physical characteristics of the gorge that when the road was cut in 1871 workmen had to be lowered down cliff sides on ropes.

On the east side there's a broad inland valley sweeping the length of the region from Dannevirke (settled by Scandinavians in 1872) through to Masterton and Martinborough. With an eye for geology, you can see fault lines extending through the edges of the valley, defining an area of instability that reaches down to the city of Wellington.

Hills rise again on the east coast, forming high-country sheep and cattle farms that are top dressed by small aircraft. The planes operate from small farm landing strips and perform hair-raising feats, swooping close to hills. On farms too steep for machinery, aerial top dressing has proved the most practical and economical method of spreading fertilisers and lime – a method that is now a vital part of hill-country farming.

Travel up into the Tararuas onto the slopes of Mt Bruce, a native bird reserve in rich native forest, where rare birds are cared for, studied and bred. The primary purpose of the reserve is to provide protection for the birds; some of them, such as the takahe and black stilt, are among the rarest birds in the world. Here too are the kakapo, saddleback, kiwi, blue duck, as well as more common native birds.

The Tararua Forest Park covers 98,400 hectares (243,000 acres) of sharp hills and dense forest, threaded with tracks for trampers and hunters. On the edge of the park the Mt Holdsworth Reserve attracts less-dedicated outdoor folk – those fit enough scramble up a well-marked track to the mountaintop for a superb view of beech forests, valley farms, distant hills and the Pacific Ocean beyond.

In this sheep-farming district of Wairarapa, visit Martinborough, where it all began – the first sheep stations in New Zealand were established around here in 1844. Continue on past Lake Wairarapa to Cape Palliser if you have a taste for wild, savage coastlines.

7

WELLINGTON

Accommodation. – Wellington is a cosmopolitan city, although not large by world standards. It is the centre of government and head office for major commercial businesses. Accommodation can be tight, especially during the week, and it is wise to book ahead in Wellington. There is top-class hotel accommodation and there are also motor inns, and some old hotels for those on a tighter budget. There is a youth hostel in Wellington and also at Kaitoki and Palmerston North. Don't expect to find camping grounds in Wellington, but elsewhere in the region, including nearby Lower Hutt, there are plenty of camping grounds.

Food. – Eat very well indeed in Wellington at some of the country's best restaurants, where high-quality New Zealand food is cooked with the best European skill. Find excellent French, Italian and Greek restaurants; also Asian cooking at Indonesian, Mongolian, Burmese and Chinese restaurants. Pub food at old hotel bars is a bargain institution.

Travel around the region by air from Wellington to Palmerston North on scheduled flights. Hire a car in Wellington or Palmerston North. N.Z.R. Road Services and Newmans provide bus transport to most main points in the region. This is also one region where it is feasible to travel by train, either along the west coast to Palmerston North or along the eastern route towards Napier. Reach outlying suburbs and western-coast beaches on the good commuter rail service.

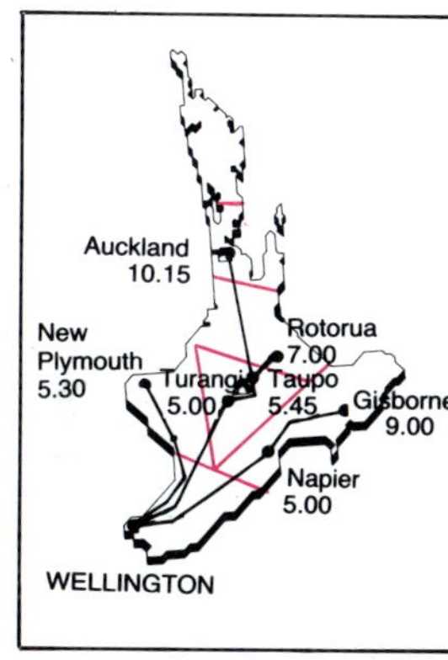

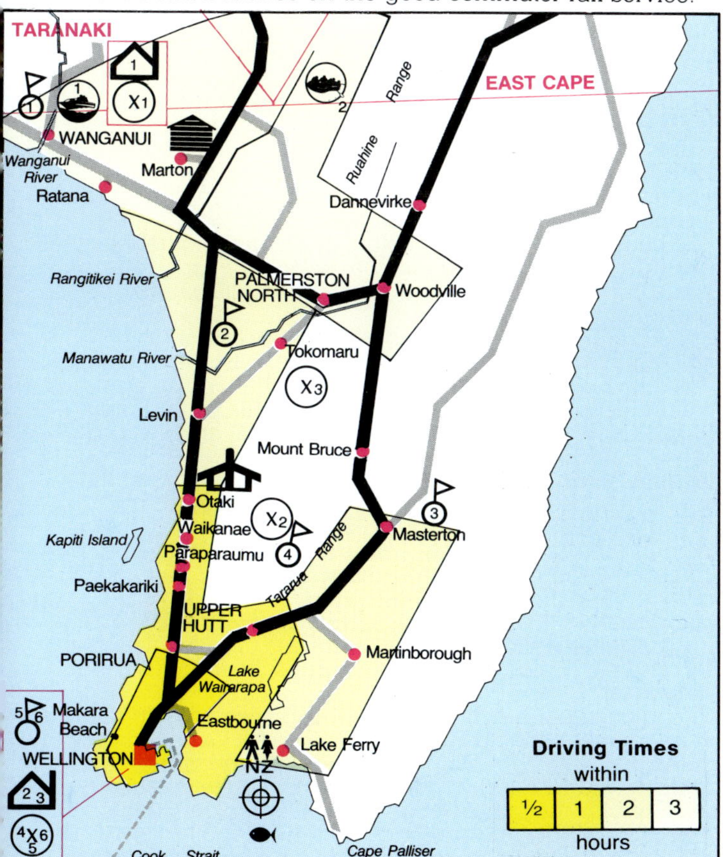

WELLINGTON

Lodges
Maungaraupi Estate.

Hunting

Fishing

River Adventures
1. Wanganui River;
2. Rangitikei River.

Golf
1. Wanganui; 2. Manawatu;
3. Masterton; 4. Paraparaumu;
5. Heretaunga; 6. Miramar.

History
1. Kawana Mill; 2. Antrim House; 3. Old St Pauls.

Live with NZ
1. Wharekauhau Station;

Local
1. Regional Museum;
2. Vintage Car Museum;
3. Steam Engine Museum;
4. Alexander Turnbull Library;
5. Houses of Parliament.
6. National Museum and Art Gallery

Wellington City

Houses perch on hilltops and spill down the steep slopes in tiers towards the high-rise buildings clustered on the harbour shore – look down on the city from Mt Victoria, Tinakori Hill or the hillside suburb of Kelburn on a clear, fine, still day, and the spectacular view of Wellington and its harbour is an exhilarating sight.

Looking up from the boat harbour past St Gerard's to the summit *(Courtesy Air New Zealand)*

Wellington City Council Public Relations Office, 2 Mercer Street, Wellington, P.O. Box 2199. Telephone (04) 735-063

Wellington has a reputation for being the 'windy city', a reputation not unfounded (due to the occasional southerly gales which sweep in from Cook Strait) but which other New Zealanders love to exaggerate. Wellingtonians love their city with its majestic moods, for, in peerless or perilous weather, Wellington is a city of character and contrast.

The harbour, surrounded by a natural ampitheatre of tree-covered hillsides and edged with picturesque bays and beaches, provides a focal point for the quaint old wooden buildings that cling to the slopes and the stark newer buildings that tower beside them.

View both city and harbour from the Mount Victoria lookout by day – or by night, when the lights of the city below are reflected in the waters of the harbour.

The city was the first and most successful of the New Zealand Company's planned settlements. Land was originally purchased in 1839 and the first settlers arrived soon afterwards, building homes in the flat land around what is now Thorndon. The historic Bolton Street cemetery holds many graves of the founders of New Zealand.

Wellington's architectural past still lives. Walk along Tinakori Road and side streets such as Glenbervie Terrace and Ascot Terrace for charming reminders. Visit too the gabled cottage of Plimmer House (now a restaurant), Antrim House (headquarters of the Historic Places Trust) and the Nairn Street Colonial Cottage.

A walk around the vicinity of Parliament buildings provides some interesting architectural contrasts – the dome-shaped Beehive building (designed by Sir Basil Spence), the solemn old stone Parliament House and the gothic-style General Assembly Library. Not far away stand the Government Buildings, the second largest wooden building in the world.

In contrast is the new and stylish Michael Fowler Centre, a superb convention-theatre complex. In the main entrance foyer are twin carved poles known as the 'Pillars of Peace'. These carvings trace the history of the resident Te Atiawa tribe before the arrival of the Europeans.

A ride on the cable car lifts you from the heart of commercial Wellington in just six minutes, past the university and hillside houses and gardens, to the suburb of Kelburn where the panoramic view of city and harbour is outstanding. Stroll back down through the Botanic Gardens and the Lady Norwood Rose Garden.

Get out of town almost as quickly with a drive around the bays and beaches of the Miramar Peninsula. Start from Oriental Bay, less than a kilometre from the central business district, and follow a road that winds around the shoreline, past the airport, by the pleasant beaches at Scorching Bay and Worser Bay and around to Lyall Bay on the far side of the airport. Continue on through Island Bay to Owhiro Bay. From here a shoreline walk of about 6 kilometres (4 miles) leads, in winter, to a seal colony. For the non-driver, scenic bus tours are available.

Wellington offers much to see and do. Those with an interest in art and culture should visit the National Art Gallery, housing collections of British paintings, Italian prints and works by Rembrandt and Dürer in addition to works by New Zealand artists. See also the contemporary art gallery, exhibiting local art, paintings, prints and sculpture, and many galleries dealing in indigenous arts and crafts. The National Museum features Maori and Pacific exhibits, while the Alexander Turnbull

Library holds outstanding collections of books, maps, letters and documents of historical interest.

Serving from 1866 for nearly a century, Old St Paul's is now preserved as a historic place, used for occasional services and as a setting for music and drama. It is a particularly fine timber Gothic church, with superb interior, stained-glass memorial windows and brasses. Open daily (except Christmas Day and Good Friday), 10.00 a.m. to 4.30 p.m. Sundays 1.00 p.m. to 4.30 p.m. Admission free, donations accepted.

Old St Paul's
Mulgrave Street
Wellington
Contact: NZ Historic Places Trust
Private Bag, Wellington.

Entertainment – The city provides more than 300 restaurants and eating places from the elegant to the ethnic, with a wide range of cuisine, from tower-top panoramic and formal establishments to little Chinese cafes. Many restaurants feature live music or dance bands. Late night cafes offer modern jazz, rock and folk music. Visual arts are well catered for, as well as theatre, visit Circa, Downstage or the Depot, or book seats at the Michael Fowler Centre, the State Opera House or the Old Town Hall for world-class entertainment – ballet, opera, stage shows, and orchestral concerts. Check out the night life in Wellington's 'What, Who, When, Where' guides, the 'City' or 'Agenda' magazines.

Time your stay to coincide with the Harbour Capital's Summer City festivities in January, or the biennial Festival of the Arts in March. (See National Events Calendar Page). If shopping is a form of entertainment, Wellington offers some of the country's best: Manners Plaza and Cuba Mall; Upper Cuba Street for curiosities; Willis Street and the ultra modern complexes of Lambton Quay and underground shopping in the BNZ complex.

On a fine day, especially in the weekend, take a walk around Oriental Bay and catch the character of some little city cafes. Further around in Evans Bay is the Shorebird Restaurant and Greta Point Tavern, an unusual corrugated-iron structure.

Looking across the city from the top of Mt Victoria.
(Courtesy Air New Zealand)

Melksham Towers
Cnr Brougham & Ellice Streets
PO Box 10-047
Wellington
Telephone: (04) 851-569
Telex: NZ31446
Facsimile: (04) 733-892

Situated next to the Basin Reserve cricket ground, these stylish and fully serviced apartments provide easy access to both airport and inter-island ferry terminals, and are within easy walking distance to main shopping, business and entertainment areas. Apartments are well appointed; facilities include in-house video, fully equipped kitchens and off-street parking. Cooked or continental breakfasts available with your complimentary morning newspaper. From $75 (single), special weekend rate from $80 for 4 persons.

City Life Apartments
Wellington
Reservations: NZ Collect (03) 799-127
(Details/Overseas reservations; see p.129)

Central city though quiet location, 11 apartments plus diplomat suite. All equipped with full kitchens, television, telephones, ensuite bathrooms. Breakfast delivery and full catering service if required. Organise shopping, tennis, fishing, scenic tours and sailing. From $175.

North to Wairarapa

State Highway 2 through Lower and Upper Hutt flows into the Wairarapa, past the site of the old Fell railway to Featherston. The Fell Engine Museum contains the only remaining Fell engine in the world, in almost fully restored condition. Featherston was the WWI troop recreation centre and the old building has been restored to its original condition. The memorial gardens on Messines Way commemorate the WWI camp sited there. (Messines (Belgium) is Featherston's sister town.) The Cobblestones Museum in Greytown and the old church, built in 1865, are open daily. Divert from the main road to stroll through Martinborough, where in the autumn months two of the largest country fairs in New Zealand are held. These attract over 130 stallholders all selling their wares, from food to batik. See too the Museum, a lovely home built in 1897 and restored to former glory. The Martinborough vineyards (Ata Rangi, Chifney, Dry River, Martinborough and Te Kairanga) from which several award winning wines have lately been produced, welcome visitors.

Continue through Carterton, once a pioneering town and now an industrial centre, to Masterton, first settled in 1854. Visit the Queen Elizabeth Park and the Wairarapa Arts Centre opposite.

Wairarapa Information Centre Inc.
corner Chapel Street & Lincoln Road
Masterton
Telephone: (059) 87-373

28 kilometres (17 miles) north of Masterton, the famous Mount Bruce National Wildlife Centre, is part of a national conservation strategy to ensure that our wildlife heritage is enjoyed by further generations. It contains numerous rare and endangered species of birds and lizards, many of which can be seen nowhere else in captivity. Facilities include a picnic area, restrooms, coffee and souvenir shops, static indoor displays and theatrette, all easily accessible for disabled. North of Mount Bruce at Woodville the Manawatu Gorge road goes through to Palmerston North (State Highway 3); while State Highway 2 continues on to Hawke's Bay.

North to Wanganui via Kapiti Coast & Palmerston North

Wanganui

This rich coastline around Waikanae and Otaki is known for its warm climate, horticulture, local holiday and retirement facilities.

The richness of the area is more than in the soil. Here the arts flourish. One of New Zealand's better-known contemporary artists, Malcolm Warr, lives and works on the coast. The feeling of calm and peace in his work comes from the beach coastline and seabirds found on the coast. Visit Malcom's studio gallery (corner Parata and Kapanui Streets, Waikanae). It's a bonus to find an orchid nursery of 20,000 plants opposite (flowering July to October). Waikanae, with its established homes and beautiful gardens, is also the location of the Nga Manu Bird Sanctuary. Over 50 species of birds use or visit the sanctuary, which combines an impressive array of natural habitats from giant kahikatea to fern-lined walks and ponds (Ngarara Road off Te Moana Road, Waikanae – closed Mondays).

For a collection of a different kind, visit the Southward Museum and Theatre Trust at Otaihanga Road, 2 kilometres (1 mile) north of Paraparaumu on State Highway 1. This is one of the largest privately owned collections of veteran and vintage cars in the Southern Hemisphere.

North in Otaki find Rangiatea Church, in Te Rauparaha Street. One of the finest of the Maori churches in New Zealand, the interior includes carvings and beautiful tukutuku wall panels. (The ashes of Inia Te Wiata, international opera star, are buried in the grounds.)

Hospitality Wanganui Public Relations Assn
Cnr Hill & Guyton Streets
Wanganui
Telephone: (064) 53-286

Te Rauparaha was a famous chief of the area, and his war parties were responsible for the nineteenth-century Wairau Massacre near Blenheim. Kapiti Island, whose distinctive form is ever present along this coast (often featuring in Malcolm Warr's prints), was his stronghold. The island is now a bird sanctuary, which can only be visited by special arrangement with the Forest and Bird Society, 26 Brandon Street, Wellington.

For those interested in geology, Kapiti Island has another significance. The island is the northernmost land of the tectonic plate on which the South Island rests. Like other areas in the Pacific Basin, for example the San Andreas Fault in California, which delineates two tectonic plates, the North and South Island are on two separate plates. Moreover, the plate on which the South Island lies is moving under the North Island at an estimated 6 centimetres (2½ inches) per year and is one of the causes of the region's 200 plus earthquakes per year.

Along the coast, stop and 'pick your own' (P.Y.O.) fruit and vegetables, berries, stone and pip fruits of all varieties, beans, peas, tomatoes, zucchini, aubergine, capsicum, and artichoke – a veritable garden of Eden.

Tokomaru Steam Engine Museum
Tokomaru
Telephone: (063298) 867
Owner: Colin Stevenson

This unique museum has New Zealand's largest collection of working steam engines. Includes country's oldest engine, a ship-winching engine (Appleby Bros, London 1869); 70-ton Filer & Stowel engine driving a Balls 1916 compressor; Shand Mason horse-drawn steam fire-engine; 1929 Marshall Tandem steam roller; plus operating railway. Static displays open daily (9.00 a.m. – noon and 1.00 p.m. – 3.00 p.m.). Closed Good Friday and Christmas Day. Working days held public holiday Sundays (1.30 p.m. – 4.00 p.m.) or by arrangement.

The New Zealand Parliament

Parliament buildings are prominent on a knoll in downtown Wellington.

Beside the neo-Gothic General Assembly Library is the central building of Takaka marble, completed in 1922. It contains the rimu-wooded legislative chamber, laid out in the British tradition. Visitors can sit in the gallery and watch parliament in action. You can join a guided tour and learn how parliament works or visit by yourself. A guard may ask who you are, but there'll be no grilling by a hefty watchdog bristling with weapons. Even this is relatively recent. In 1979 the media nostalgically noted the introduction of staff IDs and 25 uniformed guards to replace the elderly messengers affectionately known as 'dad's army'.

The legislative building is dwarfed somewhat by the 72-metre (236-foot) high Beehive. Designed by Sir Basil Spence, it lives up to its name with its circular construction and appearance of many tiny cells. It is here that cabinet meets, ministers have their offices and state receptions are held. On the way to the reception hall you pass Joan Calvert's huge woven wall hangings in the foyer. Holes cut through the vivid orange, turquoise and yellow wool reveal the soft grey marble of the building's interior walls.

Glory of the Beehive is the John Drawbridge mural, which wraps itself round the curved wall of the reception hall, covering 42 metres (140 feet) in length and rising to 5 metres (16 feet). Drawbridge won a national competition for this commission. He wanted to show the atmosphere of New Zealand – the strong light-blue skies, the sea, the weather. He designed a three-dimensional aluminium mural with fin-like extrusions echoing the surface treatment of the building's exterior. Each surface is treated as a continuous theme so that the mural reveals itself to the viewer differently from different angles. Drawbridge himself suggests walking up the main stairs, through the reception hall doors and continuing in this direction. It cannot all be taken in at once except when viewed from the street outside while spectacularly lit at night.

For New Zealanders, Parliament buildings are often a gathering place for demonstrations and a focal point for protest marches. Groups have even slept on the steps or camped in the grounds, as one group did at the end of the historic Maori land march from the far north in 1975.

Parliament Buildings and the Beehive. *(National Publicity Studios)*

7

WELLINGTON

Every three years New Zealanders over 18 years old turn out to elect the new government. Even the pubs stay shut to encourage a sober choice. For decades they've chosen between the conservative National Party and the traditionally union-oriented Labour Party, but in the 1970s and 1980s new parties – Social Credit, Mana Motuhake, New Zealand Party – have emerged.

New Zealanders can be on familiar terms with their member of parliament. Many MPs hold regular 'meet the constituents' mornings and it's often possible to phone an MP direct, especially a back bencher or opposition member, without having to foil a battery of secretaries.

For 24 years from 1852 New Zealand had a kind of federal system with a national parliament drawing representatives from six provincial councils. Canterbury is the only province that has preserved its provincial chambers, a stone and wood Gothic-styled cluster of buildings square around a courtyard in central Christchurch.

From the abolition of provincial governments until 1950, parliament, based on the British Westminster system consisted of the House of Representatives, members from designated regions and areas, and an elected upper house, the Legislative Council. However, the upper house was stacked with elected supporters of the ruling party, so its only function, in effect, was to rubber-stamp the government. From 1951 New Zealand has had a one-house system, headed nominally by the Governor General as Queen's representative.

New Zealand has no written constitution, nor bill of rights, making, some say, citizens' rights uncomfortably vulnerable to the whim of whoever is in power. Major law changes can be made by the governing party no matter how slim its majority. Fears have been expressed too that the increasing power of the cabinet of government ministers takes decision making away from public scrutiny. The possibility of constitutional reform has been widely discussed.

Although New Zealand was the first country to grant the vote to women only a fraction of the 95 members of parliament are women; few women have ever risen to cabinet rank. The four Maori seats in parliament are traditionally Labour and linked to the Ratana church. Maori voters may register as Maori or on the European roll.

'Social security' has been of central concern to New Zealand governments since the turn of the century, leading to New Zealand being at one time seen as the 'social laboratory of the world'. Premier 'King Dick' Seddon introduced one of the first old-age pension schemes in the world in 1898; widows were provided for in 1906. The first Labour Government, coming into power in 1935 during the Depression, built on this base to introduce a national health service, a universal old-age pension (the first in the world), state rental housing and free milk for all school children (this continued till 1967). Today coal mining, bulk electricity, postal and telegraph services, education and rail transport are just some of the services and industries controlled by the state. Of course this requires an enormous bureaucracy, making the New Zealand Government the largest single employer in the country. Around 190,000 New Zealanders are in the civil service, 38 per cent of the workforce.

Parliament in session is indicated by the New Zealand flag flying; at night by three white lights on the flag pole. A visit to Parliament should not be missed.

Palmerston North Public Relations
Civic Complex,
The Square
PO Box 474
Palmerston North
Telephone: (063) 85-003

Palmerston North city lies in the heart of the green and prosperous Manawatu, home of New Zealand's major agricultural university, Massey. Tours may be arranged through the Public Relations Office to thoroughbred stud farms, deer farms, pedigree Friesian stud dairy farms, Angus cattle studs, Santa Gertrudis farms, Perendale sheep studs, the Levin Horticultural Research Centre, The New Zealand Dairy Board Artificial Breeding Centre, the Department of Scientific and Industrial Research and the New Zealand Dairy Research Institute.

Visit 'Westoe' or 'Pukemarama,' historic homesteads; the Manawatu Museum; take a local tour with 'Gadabout Tours'. Follow the walking track down Fitzherbert Avenue over the bridge alongside the university campus and around Bledisloe Park. Just north of the city find Leisureland and the adjacent Golf City, a 9-hole course and mini-golf park. A variety of accommodation and restaurants is available.

A thriving area of early Maori settlement before the Pakeha arrival, Wanganui is one of the country's earliest settlements and today proudly maintains its historical links.

At Wanganui's Regional Museum, find an excellent collection of Maori artefacts presented with style and imagination, plus one of the finest collections of greenstone artefacts and Lindauer paintings in the country.

St Paul's Church (Naua Street, Putiki), is noted for its magnificent Maori carvings and tukutuku wall panels. At Operiki Pa, on the left bank of the Wanganui River, find the remaining earthworks of a great pa with commanding views of the river.

Now the centre of a wealthy farming community, Wanganui (population 40,000) is the entry point to the wild beauty of the newly formed Whanganui National Park.

Once a main trade waterway to the central North Island, the Wanganui River today is accessed as far as Taumarunui by riverboats and jet boats, canoes and rafts, all enjoying some of the 250 rapids and many contrasts of this waterway.

Many places along the river have biblical names from early Catholic Missions, for example, Jerusalem; others are amended to Maori, like Atene (Athens) and Koriniti (Corinth).

With its temperate coastal climate, the area is developing as a horticultural region – in fact Wanganui was the first area to grow kiwifruit, planted more than 100 years ago! Beautiful trees and public gardens abound, such as Kowhai Park, Moutoa Gardens, Basin Reserve and Virginia Lake (north to Hawera). Drive to the summit of Durie Hill for a view of the city, stroll along Castlecliff Beach and absorb the magnificence of the Raukawa Falls from the Parapara highway in the Valley of a Thousand Hills.

Kawana Mill, near Wanganui. *(Historic Places Trust)*

Kawana Mill
Matahiwi
Wanganui Valley
Contact: NZ Historic Places Trust
Private Bag, Wellington.

This flour mill was the longest operating, most successful of those on the Wanganui River in the 1900s. Machinery was given to the Poutana people by Governor George Grey, who practiced a policy of self-sufficiency and education for the Maori people. Operational from 1855, production later became spasmodic, finally closing 1912-13. Reconstruction saw the mill reopened in 1980. The interior can be seen at all times through viewing windows.

At your service! Located centrally, the Visitors Information Centre offers a range of complimentary services, from accommodation bookings to organising scenic tours, jet boat rides, river cruises, etc. Check for interesting events happening during your visit. Open daily (except Christmas Day) Monday to Friday, 8.30 a.m. to 5.00 p.m; Saturday/Sunday, 9.00 a.m. to 2.00 p.m. Hospitality Wanganui books all the following services.

Hospitality Wanganui Visitors Information Service
100 Guyton Street
PO Box 637
Wanganui
Telephone: (064) 53-286

Just 20 minutes' drive from Wanganui, leave Pungarehu by jet boat, experiencing the beauty and excitement of the Wanganui River as it winds through the Whanganui National Park. Visit the splendid Maranganui meeting house or historic Kawana flour mill. Service offers half-hour, 1-hour, 2½-hour, 6-hour or full-day trips (to the famous 'Bridge to Nowhere'). Bring refreshments or a barbeque and have fun! Bookings essential. From $14 (Half-hour).

Te Awa Kaitangata
Jet Boat Tours
RD 2
Wanganui
Telephone: (064) 27-796
Telex: NZ27796
Host: Eric Hammond

A historical celebration of the Manawatu region. Includes many rare and beautiful Maori objects, some dating back 1000 years or more. See historic buildings ('Totaranui' Cottage and old school-house). No charge, donation box at door.

Manawatu Museum
321-325 Church Street
Palmerston North
Telephone: (063) 83-951

Service guarantees friendly professionalism. Fascinating tours arranged in the Wanganui area; historic/Maori sites; scenic city trip; skiing, fishing, white-water rafting, Whanganui National Park safaris. Rent a mini-bus or charter a complete tour.

Wanganui Tours Limited
6 Indus Street
PO Box 685
Wanganui
Telephone: (064) 55-860

Experience 5 days of fascinating wilderness on 253 kilometres (152 miles) of a most scenic and historic river. Trips depart Taumarunui skippered by Winston (with 20 years' river experience), travelling to Wanganui on a powerful boat especially designed for maximum comfort/viewing. See superb historical sites, traverse rapids, camp out in tents and lodges, dine fireside style; enjoy the adventure of a lifetime. Great for all ages. From $440 (adult, GST inclusive) $275 (child).

'MV Wakapai' Adventure
Wanganui River Trips
R.D. 6 Raetahi
Telephone: (0658) 54-443
Host: Winston Oliver

Largest regional museum in New Zealand. Famous Maori Court contains 23-metre (75-foot) war canoe and extensive collection of rare greenstone artefacts. The natural history section includes an extinct American passenger pigeon. Open weekdays 10.00 a.m. to 4.00 p.m.; weekends/holidays, 1.00 p.m. to 4.30 p.m. Admission: $1.75 adults, .60c children.

Wanganui Regional Museum
Corner Watt Street & Maria Place
Wanganui
Telephone: (064) 57-443

You are guaranteed a friendly reception and a happy smile when you visit Wanganui's leading greenstone and paua specialists. Located next to Hurley's Grand Hotel in the town centre. Fine range includes: lapidary supplies, quality New Zealand souvenirs and many novelty gift lines. Open weekdays, 9.00 a.m. to 5.00 p.m. Moana will be happy to open the shop after these hours, by arrangement, for tours and conferences.

The Rock Shop
93A Guyton Street
Wanganui
Telephone: (064) 57-502
Owner: Moana Henry

A unique opportunity to stay in a grand old mansion, in 98 hectares (242 acres) of glorious parkland, scenery, birdlife and splendid solitude. Enjoy log fires in the lounge, well-appointed kitchen, reading room/library. View the stables, the museum, and walk through the surrounding forest. All that is missing is the servants – you look after yourself! Bring your own food. Close to Wanganui. From $45 (double, nightly).

'Bushy Park Lodge'
Royal Forest & Bird Protection Society
Kai-iwi
Wanganui
Telephone: (064) 29-879
Manager: Alan Johnson

The Riverside Inn
2 Plymouth Street
Wanganui
Telephone: (064) 32-529
Host: Sylvia Power

Enjoy olde worlde hospitality (at olde worlde prices) at this grand two-storied inn, built prior to 1895 as a home and used in the early 1900s as a hospital. Now this homely guest house offers comfortable accommodation, in-house video, child-minding facilities, off-street parking, guest lounge and dining room. Two restaurants are adjacent. A short walk to city centre, Kowhai Park or major historic attractions. Bookings essential.

Aramaho Park Motor Camp
460 Somme Parade
Wanganui
Telephone: (064) 38-402

One of New Zealand's 'Top 10' camps. First class facilities include well-appointed tourist flats, sheltered van sites in parklike surrounds, cooking and ablution amenities, children's play area and adjacent shop. Enjoy a round of golf on the Gonville Domain golf course, and in summer visit the two heated outdoor swimming pools at Gonville and Wanganui East (where there is a superb water slide).

Bryvern Motor Inn
321 Victoria Avenue
PO Box 7046
Wanganui
Telephone: (064) 58-408
Facsimile: (064) 52-295

Tastefully comfortable accommodation includes family units (sleeping to 6) and waterbed suites; providing in-house video, off-street parking, three excellent restaurants, spa pool, cocktail bar and kitchen/laundry facilities. From $63 (single, GST inclusive).

Rangitikei River Adventures Ltd
Main Road
Mangaweka
Telephone: (0658) 25-747
USA: (307) 733-9408
Manager: Tom Kemper

Located S.H.1 at Mangaweka, on the banks of the Rangitikei River (between Hunterville and Taihape), you'll find this company's adventure headquarters. Complex includes Flairport service station and historic DC 3 aircraft, log cabin accommodation, cafe serving light meals and refreshments and office for white-water rafting, helicopter rides, jet boating, camping trips and guided trout-fishing safaris.

SEE ALSO:

National Parks: Whanganui National Park.
Lodges: Wharekauhau (RHC) (Featherston).
River Adventures: Rangitikei River Adventures (Mangaweka).
Live with NZ: Farmhouse Bed & Breakfast (Palmerston North), Mairenui Holidays (Mangaweka).
NZ Historic Places: Antrim House (Wellington).

South Island Touring

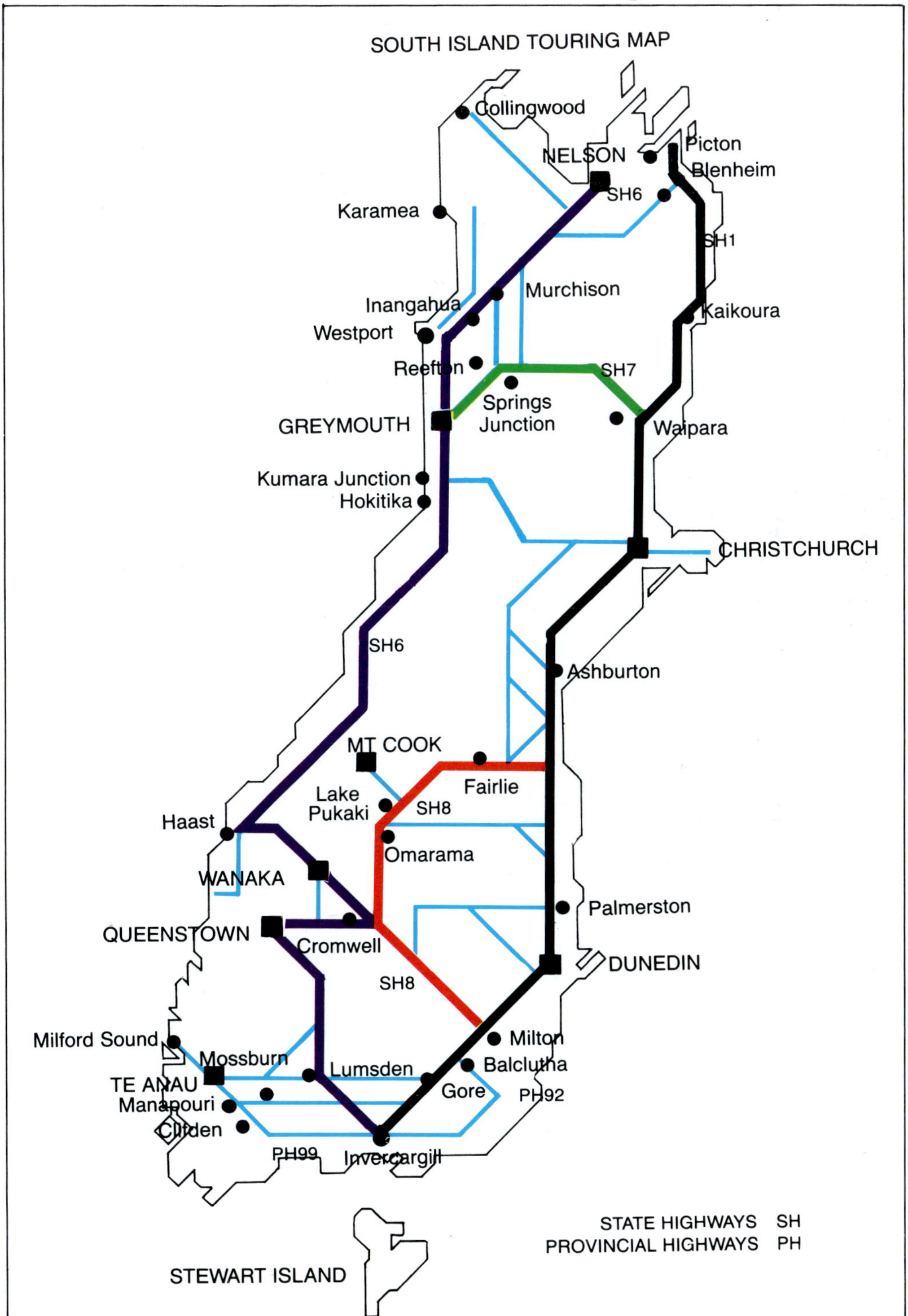

Yachts at anchor, Queen Charlotte Sound. *(National Publicity Studios)*

Arrive in the region by sea, as many do, sailing up the deep, green waters of Queen Charlotte Sound. The coastline unfolds before you, with bush-covered hillsides plunging down into the sea.

From Picton you can travel straight to Canterbury along the Kaikoura coast, with a rugged chain of mountains to the west and a wild, rocky shore to the east; or you can linger awhile in the Nelson-Marlborough region and discover that this is the place to 'get away from it all'.

From Picton and Havelock, boats leave for all parts of the sounds – charter yachts, line-fishing boats, game-fishing boats, water taxis, mail boats, sundowner cruises, luncheon cruises, picnic cruises. Arrange for a boat to take you to a remote bay for a day or a week of Robinson Crusoe living; or to a beach-front lodge with all the comforts but none of the hassles of modern life.

The whole northeastern tip of the region is gashed with deep inlets and dotted with white sandy bays, coves and islands in a vast system of drowned river valleys – there's a total of 1,000 kilometres (620 miles) of coastline in the sounds, most of which can only be reached by boat.

You can see some of the splendour of the sounds from the road. Travel from Picton to Havelock and detour along the Queen Charlotte Drive that rises above the Queen Charlotte and Pelorus Sounds.

The intricate, beautiful sounds are only part of the region. Elsewhere, mountains and high hills frame warm slopes where apples, pears, grapes, hops, tobacco and garlic grow. Small towns are surrounded by towering hills, which are threaded with tracks and walkways leading to high lakes, deep caves, fast rivers and forests of mountain beech, splashed in summer with the red-flowering southern rata.

In the Nelson Lakes National Park, tracks lead near the glacial Lakes Rotoroa and Rotoiti and over alpine passes. Roads encroach briefly into the area to the lake-side townships of St Arnaud and Rotoroa. At St Arnaud is the headquarters of the park, and there are plenty of picnic places on the beech-fringed shores, and a backdrop of mountains that rise sharply on every side.

Bordering on the western shores of Tasman Bay is another national park, the Abel Tasman National Park. Take off by boat from Takaka or Kaiteriteri to explore the sandy bays and granite headlands of the park; take short walks or take a three- or four-day trek along the coast above lagoons, white-sand beaches, and estuaries crowded with wading birds.

In the west there's another large wilderness area, the Northwest Nelson Forest Park, with 376,000 hectares (930,000 acres) of mountains, forest and alpine meadows. The many tracks include one of the country's best known, the Heaphy Track, a five-day trek linking Golden Bay and the West Coast.

The curve of Golden Bay originally bore the name Murderers Bay, when Abel Tasman, the first European to see the coast of New Zealand, anchored here in 1642. After four of his crewmen were murdered by Maoris, he gave the bay its name and hurriedly left. The physically descriptive name of Golden Bay suited later settlers better.

Here, golden sand beaches lead out to Farewell Spit, a slim bar of sand 35 kilometres (22 miles) long, which turns inward sheltering the bay. From Collingwood, four-wheel-drive tours take visitors along the treacherous sands where seabirds gather.

You don't need to be an outdoors person to revel in the scenic variety of Nelson-Marlborough, but if you are, the region offers extraordinary opportunities – climbing, skiing and ski touring, caving, hunting, fishing, trekking, sailing, diving; and this is New Zealand's sunniest region as well.

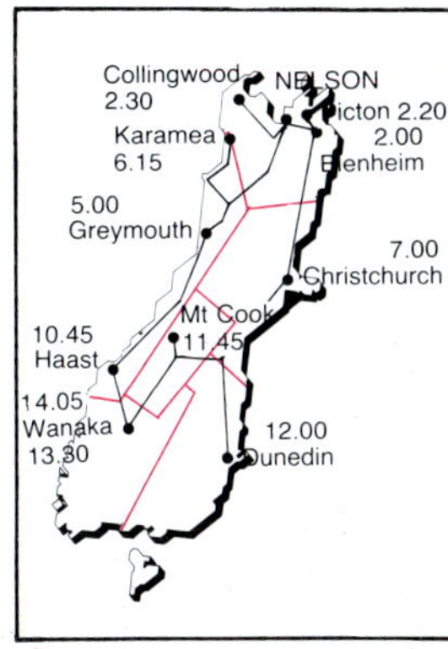

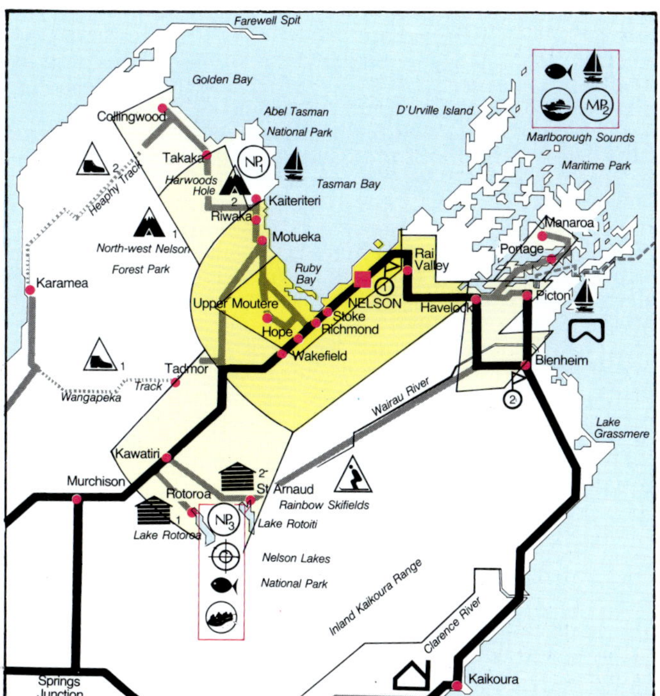

MARLBOROUGH

National Parks
1. Abel Tasman National Park; 2. Marlborough Sounds Maritime Park; 3. Nelson Lakes National Park.

Skiing
Rainbow.

Climbing
1. Mt Arthur; 2. Harewoods Hole (caving).

Tramping
1. Heaphy Track;
2. Wangapeka Track.

Lodges
1. Lake Rotorua Lodge;
2. Alpine Lodge.

Hunting

Fishing

River Adventures

Yachting/Cruising

Diving

Golf
1. Nelson; 2. Marlborough.

History
Fyffe House.

Driving Times
within

½	1	2	3

hours

Backed by bush-covered hills, the city of Nelson is a city of walks – walk up hill and down dale, through parks, along walkways and tramping tracks. There are dozens of walks to choose from.

Nelson Public Relations Office
Corner Trafalgar & Halifax Streets, Nelson
P.O. Box 194
Telephone: (054) 82-303

Nelson City

For a stunning view over Tasman Bay, walk to the top of Flaxmoor Hill. Another city walk leads out of town, through open country and native bush to Dun Mountain. Around Nelson there are gentle family walks and walks for the dedicated tramper.

In the city there are even walks that focus on grand colonial houses – they can, of course, be reached by car or coach tour as well. Early settlers built elegant houses, filled them with stylish furniture and planted splendid gardens to remind them of England. See especially Isel House, a solid timber and stone Victorian house set in 5 hectares (12 acres) of exotic trees, rose gardens, rhododendrons and azaleas. Behind the house is Nelson's Provincial Museum, which emphasises the early European settlers. See also Broadgreen, an 1855 two-storey cob farmhouse, nostalgically modelled on the style of farmhouses in England's West Country. The house is elaborately furnished in period. Wander through the sweet-smelling Lavender Hill Herb Garden, a traditional herb garden set around a century-old cottage.

Arts and crafts obviously thrive in Nelson – the city is crammed with shops selling quality pottery, ceramics, glasswork, woodcraft, weaving and jewellery, all made locally. The high-quality Nelson clay and the pleasant quality of life have led to flourishing cottage industries. Everywhere you turn there's a shop, studio or gallery. On the outskirts of the city, potteries with showrooms attached are prolific – drive out through Hope, Brightwater and Wakefield in particular to visit potteries and perhaps see craftspeople at work.

To the west of Nelson, the rich agricultural land spreads in a patchwork of apple orchards, then fields of tobacco and hops – in spring, fruit trees blossom against a background of snow-capped mountains. Village names have a suitable charm; names such as Redwoods Valley, Pigeon Valley, Spring Grove, Dovedale and even Pretty Bridge. Picturesque old churches and cob cottages nestle in the valleys, and each place seems to have a different, intriguing history. Hope began its life as a German Lutheran settlement called Ranzau. Brightwater was the birthplace of Rutherford, the first person to 'split' the atom. In the less idyllically named Pig Valley, find the South Island's oldest church, built in 1846.

Visit vineyards at Redwoods Valley, Ruby Bay and Upper Moutere. At Ruby Bay there's a pleasant sandy beach and several picnic places, and from the nearby Observation Point there's a superb view of Tasman Bay out to D'Urville Island. Upper Moutere was originally a German Lutheran community and the valley once bore the name Schachtstal.

For New Zealand's largest spread of vineyards, travel through to Blenheim, where thousands of hectares of vines reach out in straight lines toward the surrounding high, grass-covered hills, which turn a contrasting yellow-brown in dry summer weather.

For those who want to stay close to town in Nelson, there's a well-signposted circular drive that takes in some of the best sights the city has to offer: the Cawthron Institute Museum, with excellent scientific and agricultural displays; the Botanical Reserve, with views over city and bay; the pretty Queen's Gardens and Suter Art Gallery; the simple elegant building of Bishopdale, Isel House and its parkland, Broadgreen; Tahunanui Beach, with a foreshore promenade; Princes Drive, with remarkable views; and the Cathedral, which dominates Nelson's city centre.

Nelson — Marlborough

Not to be missed is Founders Park, an ambitious entertainment, leisure and historical centre 5 minutes' drive from the town centre. Started in 1977, it is a vast project; Stage one is open and Stage two well underway. Historic buildings have been relocated to the park and along with replicas now comprise some 20 buildings in landscaped surroundings. Each houses exhibits and the village is a setting for a variety of feature programmes and festivities.

Visit also Betsy Lou Dolls Ltd. in Bridge Street for reproductions of exquisite porcelain dolls.

Entertainment. – Summer beach carnivals at popular beaches. Arts and crafts festivals, wine and food fairs, fishing contests, yacht races, horse racing, stock-car racing, motorcycle speedway, A & P Shows, horticultural shows. The Suter Gallery has a restaurant, film screenings, plays and recitals.

Food. – With rich seas, soil and climate, the produce of Nelson-Marlborough is superb. From the sea come scallops and mussels; for white fish try the sweet-flavoured butterfish. Apples, pears, boysenberries, blackberries, loganberries, cherries, kiwifruit, tomatoes and broccoli all grow to perfection here. Roadside stalls sell garden-fresh produce for do-it-yourself meals. In Rai Valley, local cheese and bread are famous. A wide range of ethnic cuisines is available.

Accommodation. – Modern first-class hotels, motor inns, motels, private hotels, guest houses, camping grounds; lodges and cabins in secluded bays reached by sea; youth hostels at Nelson, Havelock, Kaikoura; camping, caravan sites, park huts in Nelson Lakes National Park; casual camping in remote bays of Marlborough Sounds, also camping in Titirangi Farm Park in the sounds. Forest Service huts in Northwest Nelson Forest Park and Mount Richmond Forest Park.

Travel around by car, renting a car in Nelson, Picton or Blenheim. Nelson suburban buses service the town and immediate countryside. Newmans buses cover Nelson to Picton, Blenheim, Golden Bay, Motueka. Flight-seeing and charter aircraft are available from Nelson, Blenheim and Motueka. Charter an amphibian taxi for flight-seeing from Picton. Boat charter and cruises from Nelson, Havelock, Picton, Kaiteriteri and Motueka.

North to Takaka

More a lively arts centre than a gallery. Dine elegantly while overlooking the gardens and enjoy a cuisine with a national reputation. Browse through the shop which sells pottery, weaving and fine reproductions. View the continuing programme of exhibitions, films and live performances. Gallery is renowned for its New Zealand watercolours, especially works by John Gully. From .20c (child under 16), $2.20 (family group) GST inclusive.

Bishop Suter Art Gallery
Bridge Street
Queens Gardens
Nelson
Telephone: (054) 84-699

SEE ALSO:

Outback Safaris: Off Road Tours (Nelson).
Fishing: Nelson River Guides.
Live with NZ: Bed & Breakfast NZ, The Friendly Kiwi (Nelson).

Golden Bay
Information Centre
Willow Street
Takaka

Goat Bay, Abel Tasman National Park, Nelson. *(Andris Apse Ltd)*

Sixteen kilometres (10 miles) past Motueka, turn off and see the Riwaka River source, where the river flows out from a limestone cavern in bush surroundings. Picnic downstream at the Moss Reserve before setting off across the 'Marble Mountain' to Golden Bay. At 20.6 kilometres (13 miles) from Motueka, turn right along the Canaan Road and drive through a blasted landscape to a 40-minute bush walk leading to the edge of Harwoods Hole. Experience the best vertigo in the Southern Hemisphere as you gaze down 370.6 metres (1,215 feet). From Takaka itself explore the springs at Waikoropupu, where 2,160,000,000 litres of water well out of the ground daily – one of the largest freshwater springs in the world.

Motueka Garden Motel
71 King Edward Street
Motueka
Telephone: (054) 89-299
Hosts: Jan and John Cramond

Two acres of lovely parklands and gardens provide a restful setting for your stay in Motueka. Centrally located for day trips to Nelson, Golden Bay, Kaiteriteri Beach and Abel Tasman National Park. Well-appointed, roomy suites are complemented with a spa and swimming pool, golf putting and children's play areas. Ample off-street parking. Off-peak rates from $44. Heavily booked November-January. Normal tariff from $48 (Double).

SEE ALSO:

Tramping/Trekking/Walking: Abel Tasman National Park Enterprises (Motueka).
National Parks: Marlborough Sounds Maritime Park.

Marlborough Public Relations Assn. Inc.,
Market Place,
Blenheim,
P.O. Box 199.
Telephone: (057) 84480

South to Christchurch via Picton, Blenheim & Kaikoura

Drive east from Nelson to Havelock and take the scenic Queen Charlotte Drive across to Picton. If time permits, use Havelock as a base for exploring the Sounds by mail-boat, or take the Kenepuru road from Linkwater past the Portage, around the shores of Kenepuru Sound across to Manaroa on Pelorus Sound. Wild swans and wading birds live in profusion along the estuaries.

The last 20 kilometres (12 miles) of the road from Linkwater to Picton winds along the coast of Queen Charlotte Sound through bush with spectacular views of the deep blue waters of the Sound.

Blenheim Wairau Valley

Blenheim's original name of Beaver, because of a flood experienced by an early party of surveyors, belies its position as the 'sunshine capital'. However, local vintners aim to capitalise on this climatic advantage. The most extensive acreage of grapes in New Zealand is planted in the Wairau Valley. This valley is part of the earthquake-faulted landscape that extends north across Cook Strait to Wellington. Before the big earthquake of 1848, the area at the river mouth was noted as birding ground by the Maoris.

Picton

Once the rival of Blenheim for capital of the old Marlborough Province, Picton is a quiet, picturesque village, a centre for water-based recreation at the head of Queen Charlotte Sound. A summer yachting and cruising paradise for New Zealanders, Picton is also the rail head into the South Island from the inter-island ferries.

SEE ALSO:

National Parks: Marlborough Sounds Maritime Park.
Sailing: Charter Link NZ Marlborough Sounds.
Lodges: Lake Tamira Estate (RHC) (Blenheim).

Nelson – Marlborough

Lake Grassmere

Before reaching the wild seascape of the Kaikoura coastline, the eye is struck by the pale pink and red ponds of Lake Grassmere. These are evaporation ponds for salt-making; the brine becoming strained reddish-pink by microbes as it concentrates.

Around Kaikoura stop and enjoy freshly cooked crayfish, advertised 'at the gate' on the roadside.

SEE ALSO:

NZ Historic Places: Fyffe House (Kaikoura).

South to Christchurch or Westland via Nelson Lakes

The Nelson Lakes' National Park area (see the National Parks section) is one of New Zealand's undiscovered scenic jewels. The beautiful alpine lakes of Rotoiti and Rotoroa, the source of the Buller River, nestle at the foot of the northernmost reaches of the Southern Alps. Both summer and winter activities are available. Good walking tracks and huts are serviced by the park board. A range of activities are possible, though few are commercially developed – it's mainly a do-it-yourself area. Fishing, hunting (permits to be obtained from park headquarters), tramping, mountaineering, white-water rafting and also skiing. There is a choice of two small ski fields: Mt Robert – August/September, weekends and school holidays (check with park headquarters, St Arnaud, Phone 806); Rainbow Valley – a new field, partially developed, offers a wide range of terrain and magnificent views over the Rainbow Valley, Lake Rotoiti, the Waimea and Wairau Valleys.

SEE ALSO:

Lodges: Alpine Lodge (St Arnaud), Lake Rotoroa Lodge (Rotoroa).
National Parks: Nelson Lakes National Park.

Murchison

The small town of Murchison nestles amongst rugged escarpments and steep rainforest-clad ranges. With a population of 700, the town is service centre to the travelling public and local farming community. Great earthquakes in the earlier half of the century have wrought this land of beautiful lakes and jagged skyline profiles. Old Man Mountain can be seen from the Upper Buller Gorge, the reclining figure of a man in the mountain skyline. Walks close to Murchison attest to the gold mining history of the area and provide views of abundant birdlife and cascading waterfalls.

Contact the Conservation Department (Telephone: 106) for information on the many walkways in the area and the Information and Adventure Centre (Telephone: 350) for the recreational activities available. Hunting, tramping, fishing, horse treks and water sports are all organised. Visit the Museum (next to the service station), see original commercial stables in operation, ride a Clydesdale horse at the Newton Livery or take a water taxi for a scenic excursion on Lake Rotoroa. A range of accommodation is available around the township from hotels to a well-equipped motor camp.

SEE ALSO:

Outback Safaris: Lake Matiri Horse Treks (Murchison).

Westland is a region apart, a wild land separated from the rest of the South Island by high mountains. A climate of heavy rainfall creates distinctive dense forests and the freshest air and water.

Nikau. *(Dept of Lands & Survey)*

Huge waterwheel used for machinery operation in the Reefton Quartz Mine. ***(Courtesy West Coast Historical Museum)***

The winter is relatively mild with clear fine days and settled weather. As the rain falls mostly at night, the coast matches Auckland for sunshine hours. But don't forget your raincoat. The mood, the manner, the style of Westland are distinctly its own. Learn that many of the early settlers were Irish, bringing their own national characteristics to the coast, and you will understand that the idiosyncracies and charm of the coast are more than geographical.

Between the mountains and the sea, the habitable land is never more than 50 kilometres (30 miles) wide. Towns and villages that lie by river mouths have often diminished in size from boom towns of gold – or coal-mining days – see deserted, once-thriving gold towns at Charleston and Barrytown, former coal-mining towns at Denniston and Stockton. Gold changed this countryside. In three years after 1864, the population climbed to 30,000 and Hokitika became the busiest port in the colony.

In limestone country at the north of the region the erosion of wind and sea has created weird coastal shapes at Punakaiki. Ashore, startling gorges of deep green forest sweep inland where there are deep and often unexplored caves.

All along the coast, low-level forest with nikau palms, tree ferns, toi toi grasses and flax alternates with areas of pasture and wasteland known as pakihi, a local peculiarity created by the interaction of decomposing vegetation and the high rainfall. Behind lie rain forests with rimu, miro, beech and southern rata, rising to forests of mountain beech that reach up into the snowcapped peaks of the alps.

It is a land of grey mists, ink-dark rain clouds, white snow, fresh green forests and ice-blue glaciers. The Franz Josef and Fox Glaciers, in the Westland National Park, plunge from heights of 2,600 metres (8,530 feet) to near sea level, fringed by green tree ferns in the lower reaches.

There are beautiful small lakes all along this West Coast, all abundant with brown trout and salmon – Lakes Mapourika, Paringa, Ianthe, Wahapo. Bird life is also abundant – fantails, tuis, greywarblers, bellbirds, weka, wood pigeons – and includes a variety of sea-birds – black-backed and black-billed gulls, blue and black shags, oyster catchers and occasionally Australian gannets and caspian terns.

At the one-time boom town of Charleston, there's an operating goldmine, still using an original stamp battery, but the town's 80 hotels have long gone. Visit Shantytown to the south of Greymouth for a splendid reconstruction of a gold-mining town.

In Hokitika, visit the West Coast Historical Museum, which emphasises gold-mining history, and nearby see the old Blue Spur Gold Mines with hand-dug shafts reaching deep into the hillsides.

Greenstone, the local name for nephrite jade, was sought by Maori tribes, who risked perilous journeys over the alps from all parts of the country to gather greenstone around Hokitika. It was used to make adzes, chisels, weapons and ornaments. Today, boulders of greenstone are brought out of the rugged mountain valleys by helicopter to factories in Hokitika. Visitors can watch the process that turns rocks into jewellery.

In a region of fast mountain rivers, high alps, thick forests and tranquil lakes, there are countless opportunities for climbing, tramping, fishing and hunting.

Westland

9

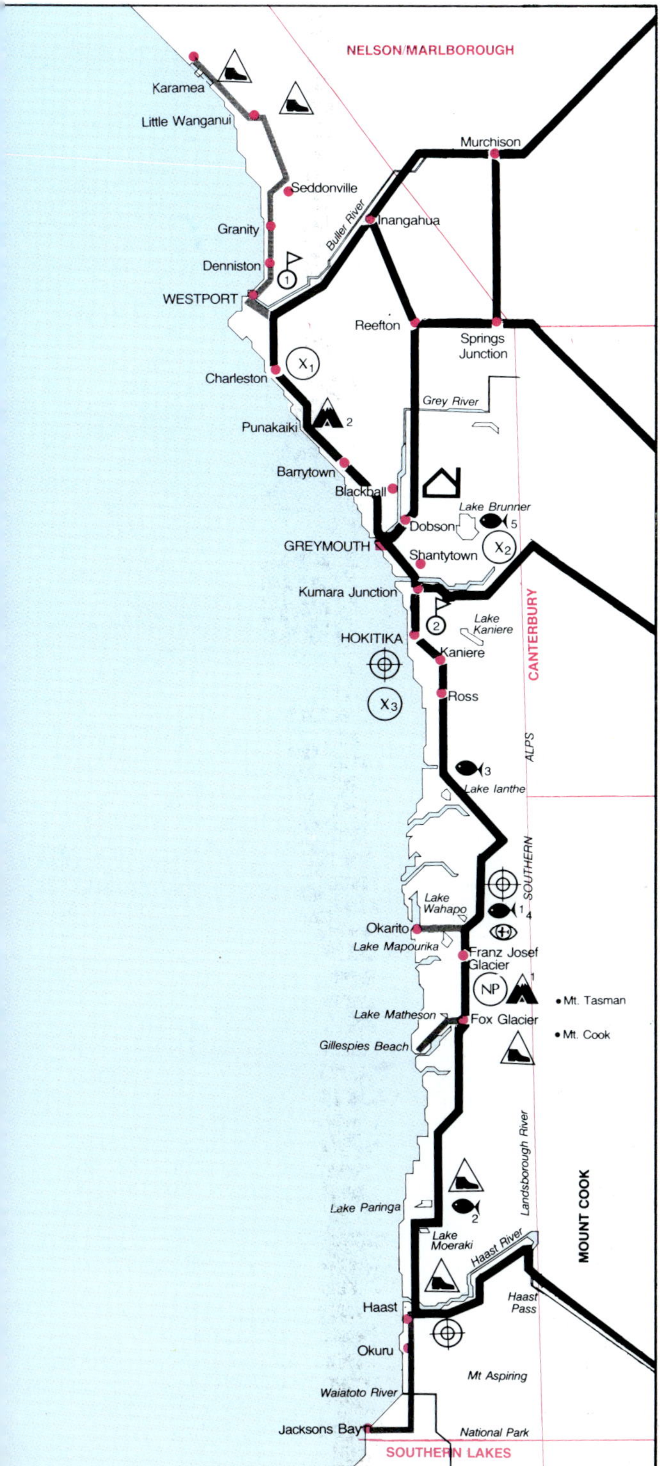

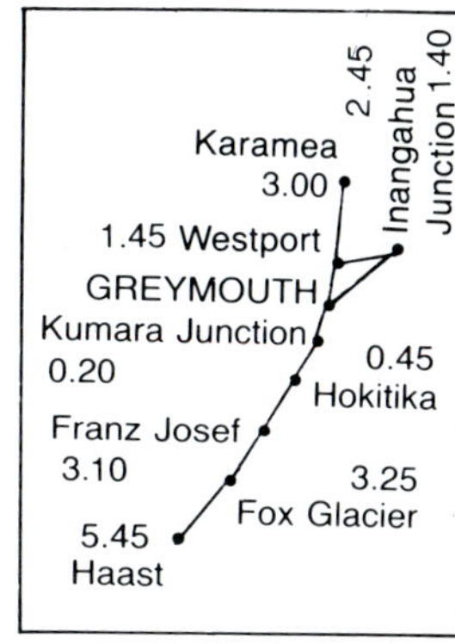

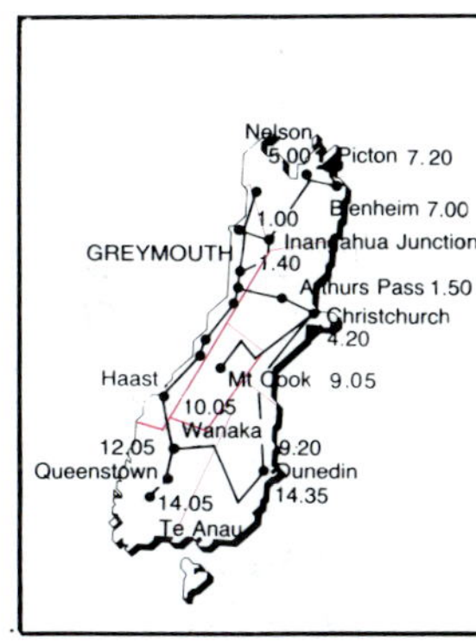

WESTLAND

(NP) **National Parks**
Westland National Park.

Climbing
1. Westland National Park;
2. Punakaiki.

Tramping

Hunting

Fishing
1. Lake Mapourika; 2. Lake Paringa; 3. Lake Ianthe; 4. Lake Wahapo; 5. Lake Brunner.

Flightseeing

Golf
1. Westport; 2. Hokitika.

History
Brunner Industrial Site.

(X) **Local**
1. Mitchells Gully Gold Mine;
2. Shantytown; 3. West Coast Historical Museum.

West Coast

Banking: Before leaving Hokitika, ensure you have good cash reserves. There are no banks at Fox Glacier or Franz Josef and other small areas. Petrol: Available only at main service villages (Haast, Fox Glacier, Franz Josef Glacier) and towns (Hokitika, Westport, Karamea).

Greymouth, Hokitika and Around

The town of Greymouth is not large, although it is the most populated centre on the west coast. Squeezed between hills, sea and river, it began as a government depot for surveyors, and developed into a river port as gold, coal and then timber were brought down from the hills. It's a functional town that grew to serve the needs of gold miners, coal miners and bushmen in an area where life can be harsh.

From the end of the breakwater at the southern mouth of the Grey River, the surf can be seen crashing along the curving coastline with the alps sweeping into the distance behind. The Grey and its surrounding rivers, streams and lakes, such as the beautiful bush-fringed Lake Brunner, offer superb fishing for brown trout.

Travel up the Grey Valley to the former coal town of Blackball – on a misty day the town has a bleakness that accentuates the hard life of miners on the coast. Buy a gold-pan in Greymouth and head off up the Grey Valley at Moonlight Creek and up the Moonlight Valley for picnics, stream swimming and gold panning. At Reefton, an old gold-mining town surrounded by wooded hills, walks lead to old mines along former packhorse trails and by boulder-strewn streams where old batteries lie rusting. In Reefton's town museum, in an old church, the history of the town and its quartz mines are detailed. At Reefton's School of Mines Museum there's an excellent exhibition of the coast's mineral wealth – gold, coal, garnets, uranium, mica are all found in Westland.

West Coast Historical Museum
Tancred Street
PO Box 155
Hokitika
Telephone: (0288) 58-321 58-322

Excellent display of authentic gold-mining equipment and West Coast goldfields history dating from 1864-5. A superb 20-minute audio-visual programme has been installed in a seated theatre, bringing this era to life. Friendly and knowledgeable staff welcome your questions. Allow 40 minutes' viewing time to appreciate this facility. Open weekdays 9.30 a.m. – 4.30 p.m.; weekends, 10.00 a.m. – 4.00 p.m. Reduced winter hours apply from June to August. From $2.50 (adult), .50c (child). Group discounts.

Lake Brunner, Westland. *(Andris Apse Ltd)*

West Coast Public Relations Information Centre,
Corner MacKay & Herbert Streets,
Greymouth,
P.O. Box 95.
Telephone: (027) 5101

Westland

Just 11 kilometres (7 miles) from Greymouth is Shantytown, a unique replica of a West Coast gold-mining town at the turn of last century, complete with sluicing claim and full-scale working sawmill. As you approach the entrance and reception building you'll see the massive 30-foot, overshot water wheel. An 0-6-0 side tank locomotive and an American geared 'Climax' steam engine operate on a railway line threading its way through the surrounding beautiful native forest. On 'Memory Lane' (the main street), see interesting historical buildings, plus licensed restaurant and tearooms. A horse-drawn vehicle operates most fine days, but the stage coach operates only in school holidays. Fun for all the family. Entry fee from $4 (adult), $2 (child), plus special family rates available. Gold panning $4 per head; train rides from $1.20 (adult), .60c (child), (prices valid to 30/6/88). Open every day except Christmas Day.

Shantytown
C/- Post Office Shantytown
Via Greymouth
Telephone: (02726) 634
Hosts: The West Coast Historical and Mechanical Society Inc.

Local crafts and artwork displayed in an upmarket environment. Meet one of 17 members of the gallery rostered on duty and gain first-hand knowledge of their work. Woodwork, weaving, pottery, patchwork, native flora trinkets and stationery, native timber furniture, knitwear, gold nugget jewellery, plus fine and varied artwork. Members ply their art/craft at the rear of the shop.

Hokitika Craft Gallery
25 Tancred Street
Hokitika
Telephone: (0288) 58-802

For that memento of your West Coast experience, this shop specialises in friendly and helpful service. From selections of teaspoons to sheep-skin products, costume jewellery, paua, greenstone and weaving, you are bound to find a treasure which reflects the unique aspect of this lovely ocean- and mountain-bordered town. Jill is a colour-coding consultant so take time out to discover the colours that bring out your best! Open Monday – Saturday, Sundays by request.

Hokitika Gifts and Souvenirs
29 Weld Street
PO Box 181
Hokitika
Telephone: (0288) 58-115
Host: Jill Hazeldine

Privately owned and operated, this motel offers a tradition of friendly and warm hospitality. Centrally situated to town facilities, yet set apart in quiet surrounds. Units are large, clean and comfortable. Additional facilities include off-street parking, colour TV, in-house video, full kitchen facilities and ample heating.

Kiwi Lodge Motels
214 Weld Street
PO Box 164
Hokitika
Telephone: (0288) 58-161
Hosts: Veronica and Mac McLean

Hokitika Public Relations Office
29 Weld Street, Hokitika
P.O. Box 171
Telephone: Hokitika 1101

Most of the land on the west coast is publicly owned (except for the fertile river valleys and coastal plains). Entry permits are not required for public land unless you want to hunt.

Mist can descend quickly on this plateau; take care when exploring. As well, do not go out on to the glaciers without a guide.

North of Greymouth to Karamea

Again, this is a land apart – forest-clad mountains, extensive basins of lowland forest rich in native bird life, swamp lands, desolate coal plateau, plummeting gorges and endless sandy beaches; and the area around Karamea has a subtropical micro-climate. Take the Heaphy Track, one of New Zealand's most popular walks, 70 kilometres (45 miles) long, towards Collingwood. This is a four-day walk, which begins along the beaches and luxuriant subtropical, lowland forest.

In the fertile, sheltered basins near Little Wanganui, find some of the largest rimu, kahikatea, matai and beech trees in the country (well over 5 metres or 16 feet in girth).

Denniston, located 600 metres (1,969 feet) above sea level on the distinctive coal plateau, is good base for exploring the old coal workings. Of particular note is the Denniston 'incline', now being restored. An engineering feat in its time, this almost perpendicular rail track delivered coal to the coast. Once a thriving town of 3,000 people in 1910, it is now almost a ghost town.

The Granity-Millerton area combines the working Stockton mine with the history of past efforts. The drive to Millerton passes a burning mine covering 81 hectares (200 acres), which has resisted all attempts to extinguish it over 70 years.

For Summer Guided Walks programmes (January), contact Department of Lands and Survey, Government Buildings, Palmerston Street, Westport. Telephone 7869.

Charming Creek Walkway (32 kilometres (20 miles) north of Westport): follow an old bush-railway through bush between Ngakawau and Seddonville and see some of the finest scenery in the North Buller – rugged country, high bluffs, immense boulders and the spectacular Mangatini Falls. This is part of the National Walkway system, suitable for family groups. About 3 hours.

SEE ALSO:
NZ Historic Places: Brunner Industrial Site (Grey Valley).
National Parks: Westland National Park, Mount Aspiring Park.
Lodges: Lake Brunner.

Accommodation. – Some hunting and fishing lodges; THC hotel at Franz Josef; motor inns, motels, old hotels (and West Coast old hotels often look battered as well as aged), guesthouses; youth hostels at Greymouth, Franz Josef and a shelter hostel at Okarito (a swamp reserve renowned for nesting white herons and royal spoonbills); camping grounds.

Food. – If you are in Westland between September and November, feast on whitebait – tiny delicacies caught at river mouths, generally served in a fritter. Also try local venison. With few exceptions, meals on the coast are likely to be old-fashioned grills or roasts, not cordon bleu.

Entertainment. – On the coast you go to the pub. The pubs of Westland are a legend – in the days of 6 p.m. closing the licensing laws were blithely ignored. The laws have changed but the atmosphere of the pubs hasn't.

The Glaciers – Westland National Park

Fox Glacier

Note: It is dangerous to walk onto the glacier without a guide.

Dominating the valley – a breathtaking panorama of mountains and snowfields towering above the deep green bush – is the huge white tongue of the Fox Glacier. There is easy access by road, though stop and take time. Take a guide and walk onto the glacier – one of the few opportunities in the world to do this so easily. Try the 10-minute heli-flight, which leaves from the village, over the glacier.

A glow-worm grotto – a short 10-minute walk just south of the village – and Gillespies Beach, where gold and gemstones are to be found in the black sands; seals add to the bevy of natural attractions. For other activities, try hunting, fishing and mountaineering.

THC Trips & Tramps
Franz Josef Glacier
Telephone: Franz Josef Glacier 719 ext 590

Go glacier walking! Over 130,000 people have enjoyed these professionally guided trips, from short glacier walks and heli-hikes, to 10-day Alpine expeditions. Tours to suit requirements through this uniquely beautiful area. Headquarters incorporate Glacier Guides, Coffee Shop/Lunch Bar (serving delicious meals), restrooms and well-stocked shop. All equipment is provided. Glacier walks depart 9.30 a.m. and 2.00 p.m. – from $20 (adult), $10 (child). Other trips and costs on enquiry. Bookings essential for multi-day trip.

Alpine Guides (Westland) Ltd
Main Road
PO Box 38
Fox Glacier
Telephone: Fox Glacier 825
Chief Guide: Mike Browne

Owned and operated by descendants of early New Zealand pioneers, this historic hotel offers real 'home away from home' comfort. Beautifully appointed with open log fires, central heating, and electric blankets and situated in the stunning rural beauty of this glacier area. The dining room serves a delicious and substantial traditional New Zealand 4-course, home style meal and casual diners are most welcome. From $27 (single), $50 (double).

Fox Glacier Hotel
PO Box 2
Fox Glacier
Telephone: Fox Glacier 839
Telex: NZ4356

FLAG INNS

A variety of walking tracks around Fox Glacier introduce glacial phenomena and Westland's rain forest. Lake Matheson offers outstanding forest walks and the most famous of reflections. Some of the major peaks of the Southern Alps – including Mt Cook and Mt Tasman – are captured in the mirror of the lake's black waters. Walk around the lake in 1 hour 20 minutes. ***(Andris Apse Ltd)***

The great ice floe of the Franz Josef Glacier appears an almost impenetrable barrier to those wishing to walk onto the glacier itself. However the three-hour THC guided walk to this grand glacier, climbing up the valley floor, is most rewarding for those of reasonable fitness. The thrill of walking on the glacier is well worth the climb up the valley.

Excellent walks from 5 minutes to 4 hours include: Sentinel Rock – 5 minutes to a spectacular view of the Glacier Valley Terrace; Tatare Track – an hour walk climbing the terrace behind the village to visit a sluice face and gold-mining relics; Alex Knob – 4 hours, 1,290 metres (4,230 feet), a moderate climb through lowland and subalpine forest to alpine grasslands and herb fields. Superb views of glaciers, mountains, forest and sea coast.

Personal Car Tours
PO Box 23
Franz Josef Glacier
Telephone: Franz Josef Glacier 721
Host: Derek Williams

A great way to discover spots only locals know about is by personal car tour. These can include the stunning grandeur of the Franz Josef and Fox Glaciers, the famed Lake Mathieson, the Gillespies Beach seal colony and Okarito Beach with its protected lagoon – home to the beautiful and unique white heron. These important ecological areas will add a fascinating dimension to your West Coast visit. Costs on enquiry.

DA's Licensed Restaurant
Franz Josef Glacier
Westland
Telephone: Franz Josef 721
Host: Derek Williams

For the hungry traveller with time to stop and relax, or no time to waste, DA's Restaurant is open until late every day. It offers full meals – with specialities such as venison and succulent seafood – in addition to a wide range of take-out foods and a coffee shop. Select from the extensive wine list or bring your own. Reasonable prices and informal atmosphere make DA's a must when you are visiting Franz Josef Glacier.

Glacier Store and Tearooms
PO Box 8
Franz Josef Glacier
Telephone: Franz Josef Glacier 731
Hosts: Ralph Fegan and Lynne Wyber

These lovely alpine-style tearooms offer ideal refreshments: fresh-brewed tea and coffee, hot soup, pies, savouries, cakes and deliciously different sandwiches. The general store caters for all requirements: food, outdoor clothing (woollen and wet-weather gear), hardware supplies, stationery, haberdashery, fresh seasonal fruit, vegetables. Clean toilet facilities available. Open every day (along with souvenir shop), all year through, from 7.45 a.m. to 6.30 p.m.

T.H.C. Franz Josef Resort Hotel
(2 kilometres, 1.2 miles, north of Village)
Franz Josef Glacier
Telephone: Franz Josef Glacier 719

This Tourist Hotel Corporation hotel offers quality accommodation in a luxurious native rainforest setting. Featured highlights are the splendid viewing gallery (for coffee-breaks) and the Fern Room, a fully licensed restaurant renowned for its excellent cuisine, specialising in legendary West Coast whitebait, mussel chowder, venison steaks and other delicious dishes. Rooms from $65 to $90 (double), young children free. Book through Southern Pacific Hotel Corporation, Travelodge, Hotelex, travel agent or direct.

Rata Grove Motels
Cron Street
Franz Josef Glacier
Telephone: Franz Josef Glacier 741
Hosts: Elaine and Ray Barron

Caters for the weariest of travellers with the best of home comforts and traditional West Coast hospitality. Well-appointed units are warm and close to all amenities – centrally situated in the village. The scenery is beautiful with magnificent views of snow-clad mountains from each unit. Elaine and Ray provide glacier and other sightseeing trips in a vintage car! From $54 (double) per night.

SEE ALSO:

Skiing: Alpine Guides (Westland) (Fox Glacier).
Outback Safaris: Alpine Guides (Westland) (Fox Glacier), South West Saddle Safaris (Ross), Waiho Stables (Franz Josef).

Westland

From the Glaciers to Wanaka via Haast Pass

South of Haast settlement is the west coast 'in the raw'. Along each side of a flat, treeless, straight road, between sand dunes and a swamp, is a classic exhibition of recent ramshackle architecture – none of it spoiled by footpaths or kerbs. Bleached peeling wood, iron, desolate yards, the odd upturned can

This is not a 'ghost town'. Stop and talk to the garage manager (who left university to return to the family business) and he will introduce you to the store manager, Ian, who left the Orkney Islands 22 years ago. If you're interest in staying, Ian will tell you where and how to fish, surf cast or whitebait. And note: Haast is famous for whitebait (see food section).

The commercial fishermen at Jacksons Bay may even take you out crayfishing. It's a harsh pioneering area, with a history of past settlers, like the German and Polish families whose dreams were lost in the Smoothwater River Valley in 1878 (now a walking track 1 kilometre (½ mile) before reaching Jacksons Bay).

Seal, blue penguins and Fiordland crested penguins inhabit rocky portions of the coast. Rimu and kahikatea dominate the forest around Haast, giving way to silver and mountain beech in Jacksons Bay. The exception to the scrubby vegetation of the pakihi flats is a forest of kowhai just south of the Haast Hotel – masses of yellow flowers each spring.

Haast Motor Camp
Haast
South Westland
Telephone: Haast 860
Hosts: Brian and Phillippa Glubb

Offering friendly West Coast hospitality and inexpensive accommodation in lovely surrounds, this facility has 34 van sites, 15 cabins of differing grades, one fully equipped 'tourist' flat plus bunkroom. Clean and comfortable facilities include TV lounge, two communal kitchens, shower blocks, automatic laundry and camp store. Fishing tackle/whitebait nets available and bed linen available for hire. Jet boating and tramps organised on request. Competitive costs available.

SEE ALSO:

Hunting: Westland Guiding Service (Fish).
NZ Historic Places: Brunner Industrial Site (Grey Valley).

When visiting National Parks, always report to the park headquarters for information and inform them of your plans to go into the park; check road conditions also. For further information contact: Lands and Survey, Westland District Office, Sewell Street, P.O. Box 123, Hokitika, Phone 585. Forest Service, Central District H.Q., Weld Street, P.O. Box 138, Hokitika, Phone 1224.

Waitangi River, near Haast, Westland.
(Andris Apse Ltd)

Wide plains of wheat, high snow-capped mountains, broad rivers – the Canterbury region is New Zealand on a grand scale.

Trampers pause to admire the "Devil's Punchbowl", Arthur's Pass National Park. *(Andris Apse Ltd)*

Across the plains travel roads that run straight, as far as the eye can see, over long bridges crossing tumbling, braided rivers, through crop fields and pasture land where lambs are fattened for market, the fields defined by the dark green of pine shelter belts.

Travel on into the golden-brown tussock-covered foothills of the alps. Here are the sheep stations – much larger than most other New Zealand farms and often isolated with a self-contained way of life. Visit Mt Peel, where the grand homestead is set among spreading 100-year-old English trees – the stone family church is open to visitors. Nearby is Peel Forest Park, an unusual pocket of forest in a tussock landscape, with ferns growing thickly under the shelter of matai, totara and kahikatea. Also close by is Orari Gorge Station, a cluster of restored station buildings including an impressive 1862 homestead, 1859 cottage and smithy.

Molesworth, the largest of the stations, spreads for 1,800 square kilometres, (450,000 acres) straddling the northern boundary of the Canterbury region and the Nelson-Marlborough region. On the station's southern perimeter is Hanmer Springs, a nineteenth-century spa that today offers visitors horseback riding, jet boating, skiing, trout fishing, golf, tennis, walks in a magnificent forest of deciduous trees, as well as hot-spring bathing and crisp mountain air.

The mountains of Canterbury offer far more than spectacular alpine scenery – there's superb skiing at Mt Hutt and several less-developed ski fields, and there's excellent climbing and tramping in the Arthur's Pass National Park. The park falls across both sides of the alps, with rainforest to the west, beech forest, tussock and scree to the east. There's tramping tracks suitable for beginners or family groups and there's serious climbing for dedicated 'alpinists'. Find the park's headquarters in the mountain village of Arthur's Pass on the road that crosses to Westland.

The towns of the Canterbury plains and foothills are essentially market towns, serving the outlying farming districts. Filled with English trees – elms, oak and planes – planted last century, these leafy towns also serve the visitor. Towns such as Ashburton, Geraldine, Oxford, Waimate and the small coastal city of Timaru are all surrounded by rivers and streams that offer trout and salmon fishing, jet boating and canoeing. The farming centre of Methven also now serves as the base for the ski fields on Mt Hutt, as well as the centre for the summer and autumn activities of fishing, trotting and rodeo.

The rivers plunge down from the alps, often through dramatic gorges such as the Waimakariri Gorge or the Ashley Gorge, and then fan out across the alluvial plains in ribbons through the stones, shingle and sand of the river beds. The Rakaia River reaches 1.6 kilometres (a mile) wide on the plains, crossed by the country's longest bridge.

Huge hydro-electric power stations harness the energy of the rivers high in the tussock hills – on the Waitaki, see the immense Benmore Dam, 109 metres (357 feet) high, creating the country's largest man-made lake. Jet boats make sightseeing and fishing trips on the lake.

Other natural lakes in glacial bowls ringed by mountains offer rainbow trout and land-locked salmon for anglers and remote lake and mountain scenery for others.

Canterbury 10

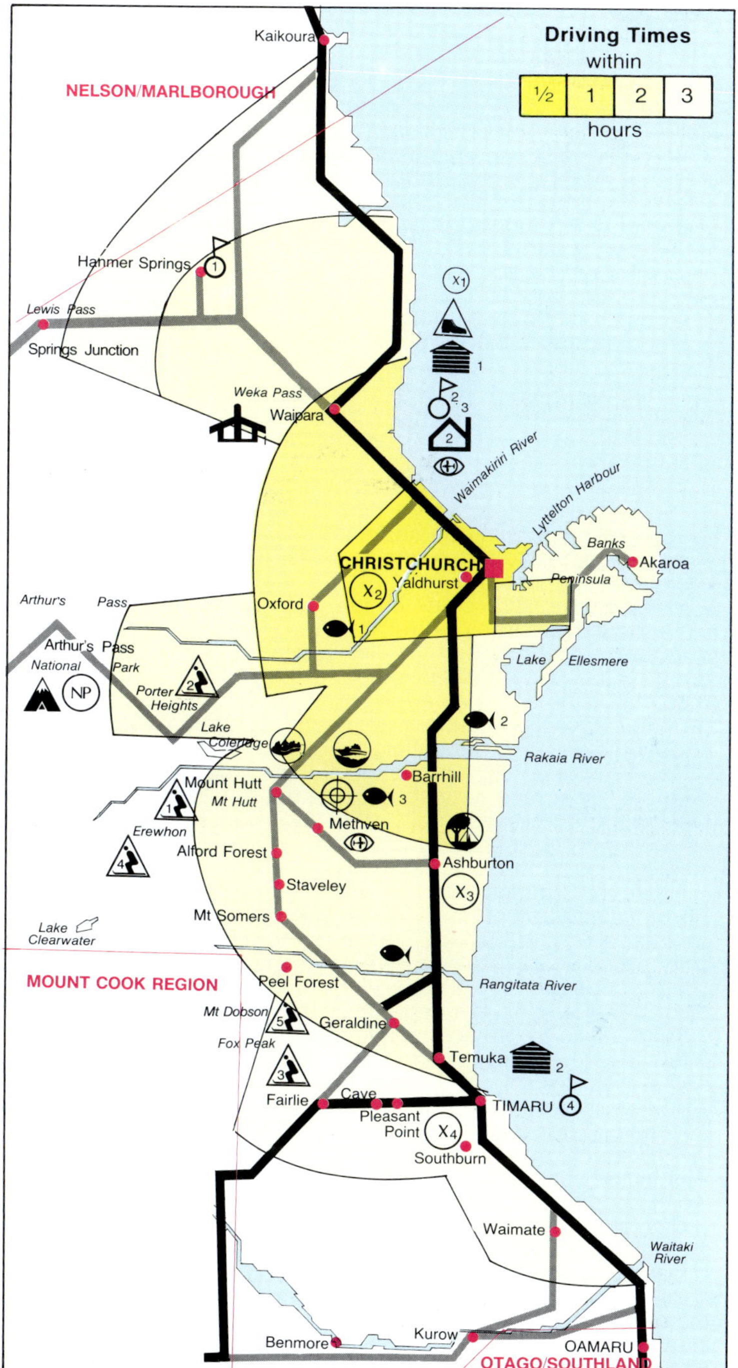

CANTERBURY

National Parks
Arthur's Pass National Park.

Skiing
1. Mount Hutt; 2. Porter Heights; 3. Mount Dobson; 4. Erewhon; 5. Fox Peak.

Climbing
1. Arthur's Pass Nat. Park.

Tramping

Lodges
1. Eliza's Manorhouse; 2. Milcroft Lodge.

Outback Safaris

Hunting

Fishing
1. Waimakiriri River; 2. Rakaia River; 3. Rangitata River (nr Rangitata).

River Adventures

Flightseeing

Golf
1. Hanmer Springs; 2. Shirley; 3. Russley; 4. Timaru.

History
1. Weka Pass; 2. Time Ball Station.

Local
1. Ferrymead Historic Park; 2. Transport Museum; 3. Plains & Vintage Car Museum; 4. Museum and Railway.

Christchurch

Christchurch, the third largest city in New Zealand, is imbued with a surprising tranquillity, rare even in many smaller cities or towns. The pace is so gentle you must remember to watch for traffic and office workers. Take picnic lunches to the grassy banks of the meandering Avon River.

It is often said that Christchurch is the most 'English' city outside of England, an impression easily gained from the dominance of stone Gothic-style buildings, the willow-fringed Avon and spring daffodils flowering under the oaks in Hagley Park. Catch sight of uniformed Christ's College schoolboys wearing straw boaters, and the impression is enhanced.

The planners of Christchurch began with high aspirations for a model Church of England settlement with a carefully structured social system. Not all their hopes were realised as egalitarian ideas progressed and prevailed. However, the city still remains very aware of its origins.

Christchurch's best-known landmark is the cathedral, dominating the central square. You can't miss seeing the decorative stone Gothic-style building, inside which panels commemorate early missionaries, bishops and members of the church. Take the increasingly steep stairway up to the balcony of the bell tower for a view that reaches over the city to the distant mountains.

Traffic has now been banned from the square around the cathedral. Instead, it has become a lively area where people gather – it's the favourite haunt of the city's resident wizard. (Christchurch also has a reputation for tolerating, even encouraging, eccentricity.)

Other Gothic-style stone buildings to see include Christ's College and the Arts Centre. The Arts Centre buildings originally formed part of the University, but the University outgrew its space and moved out of town. Now the medieval-style complex arranged around two quadrangles provides accommodation for a theatre, cinema, ballet, crafts shops, restaurants and gallery.

The Provincial Government Buildings enjoy a ponderous title that gives little indication of their architectural delights – a fascinating combination of Gothic-style buildings including stone, timber and brick, and inside, ornate ceilings, stained-glass windows and mosaic walls.

However Christchurch isn't all Gothic stone. The city's Roman Catholic community branched into 'high renaissance' for their splendid basilica built at the turn of the century. In the city centre, solid Victorian buildings line up alongside modern office buildings, and on the banks of the Avon the modern town hall complex is a delightful tribute to architectural flair.

Take lunch in the Town Hall's restaurant by the Avon River – few town halls anywhere could offer a more pleasant setting and stylish design. Other examples of modern Christchurch architecture include buildings at the university and the Queen Elizabeth II Park.

Walk in Hagley Park, under the lofty trees by the river. Within the vast park are playing fields, riding tracks, woodlands and the city's botanic gardens.

Catch up with cultural pursuits at the McDougall Art Gallery, by the botanic gardens, where there are excellent exhibitions of painting, sculpture and ceramics. Next door is the Canterbury Museum – as well as Maori and pioneer history there is a splendid section devoted to Antarctic exploration and studies, in fact, the only Antarctic exhibition gallery, library and theatrette in the world. Special items on display are Scott's

Canterbury Information Centre,
75 Worcester Street,
Christchurch,
P.O. Box 2600.
Telephone: (03) 799629

sledge, a ski used in his 1904 expedition and Shackleton's 1914 motor sledge. The world-renowned botanic gardens also deserve particular mention. Established in 1863, the 30 hectares (75 acres) accommodate a wide variety of exotic and native species. Guided tours are run daily at 12.00 p.m. and at 4.00 p.m. in fine weather. In wet weather, visit the five conservatories housing tropical plants, cacti, ferns, succulents, native and exotic alpine and insectivorous plants.

Drive southeast out of Christchurch and over the Port Hills, or through the long road tunnel to Lyttelton (the energetic can walk the Bridle Path over the hills from Heathcote). The town spills down the steep hillside to the port below. Of special interest is the Time-ball Station, a fort-like building used until 1935, now restored and open to visitors.

Further on explore an unusual village, Akaroa. Founded in 1840, the country's only French settlement echoes its origins in French colonial buildings, place and street names. Visit particularly the Langlois-Eteveneaux House and Museum.

Entertainment. – In a city that prides itself on culture, find lively music, theatre, dance and art. Check what is offering at the Town Hall's theatres and visit the Arts Centre. Watch a cricket match, go to the races, or go to the night trotting races.

Travel around Christchurch on a rented bicycle – or try the bus service. Buses for many destinations leave near the main square. Several car-rental agencies provide sturdy four-wheel-drive vehicles for back-country touring. Flight-seeing, air charter and scheduled flights leave from Christchurch airport. Trains run north to Picton, west to Greymouth and south to Dunedin. Long-distance bus transport is by all major companies: N.Z.R. Road Services, Mt Cook Landlines, Newmans, Guthries, H & H. Plenty of organised tours available, from conventional sightseeing to high-adventure tours.

Christchurch city surrounds beautiful Hagley Park, seen here against a backdrop of the Southern Alps. ***(Andris Apse Ltd)***

Christchurch

Food. – Excellent restaurants in Christchurch, both licensed and B.Y.O. Range includes French, Italian, Chinese, Greek and British (roast beef and Yorkshire pudding). Pub meals can be pleasant, low-cost eating. In Canterbury look for Canterbury lamb, cooked to pale-pink perfection. If lamb can't be found, don't ignore the rich flavour of hogget. (When everyone lives on lamb and hogget down on the farm, restaurants are less inclined to serve it.) Try the salmon, fresh or smoked. Discover tearooms serving delicious large afternoon teas, including scones thick with jam and cream.

Accommodation. – In Christchurch there are luxury to modest hotels, motor inns, motels, budget private hotels and two youth hostels. Comfortable traditional hotels and motels serve towns of the region.

Geocraft Tours
12 Ngaio Lane
PO Box 3229
Christchurch
Telephone: (03) 61-937/ 661-937
Host: Mark Yetton B.Sc M.Sc (Hons).

Go sightseeing with a difference! Take this combined geology, archaeology and natural history tour around spectacular hill and coastal fringes of Christchurch and tranquil Lyttelton Harbour (submerged extinct volcano crater). Half and full day tours include home workshop visits with leading regional craftspeople (selling bargain-priced, top quality work). A stimulating, entertaining tour and a definite highlight. From $27 (half-day), $60 (lunch inclusive, full-day). Educational materials provided.

Ferrymead Historic Park
269 Bridle Path Road
Heathcote
Christchurch
Telephone: (03) 841-970

An historic theme park sited in 16 hectares (40 acres) and situated 10 minutes by car from the city centre (take Ferry Road out to the turn-off). The park offers an historic slice of Edwardian New Zealand, including an operating bakery, print shop, blacksmith and other miscellaneous crafts people. The park demonstrates in an operational setting, various forms of vintage transport. These include an electric tramway system and horse-drawn vehicles (weekdays), accompanied on weekends by an operating railway system, including steam locomotives each Sunday.

There is an excellent collection of vintage cars and motorcycles, items of Edwardian technology, military and naval museums, a sound museum and an aeronautical museum. Being developed are: an operating vintage sawmill from 1915, a working model railway layout (reputedly one of Australasia's largest) and the ongoing development of an Edwardian township. This facility has been developed by the Ferrymead Trust on behalf of some 15 voluntary organisations, with a strong input from local regional authorities. The area is historically important as the site of the ferries which took the Canterbury Pilgrims (walking over the Bridle Path from Lyttelton) across the Heathcote River. Drive yourself or catch a Number 3 bus from Cathedral Square. Admission from $5.50 (adult), $2.75 (child). Special discounts for groups of 20 or more.

MTR Ranch
PO Box 35
Oxford
Telephone: (0502) 24-737
Host: Brian Stanley-Jackson

One day photo Safari walks and country tour: In one day – be driven to the mountains, walk through lush forest; photograph magnificent scenery, see deer, elk, peacocks, geese, goats and boar – all in the wild, enjoy lunch in the outdoors, tour a sheep/cattle farm and visit an arts/crafts centre. Departs Christchurch on 160 kilometre round trip, be collected and returned. Maximum 9 persons. Bring sturdy footwear. From $85 (per person, lunch, GST included).

Walks around Christchurch

Riverside Walk (90 minutes). Cathedral Square, Avon River and Victoria Square – numerous historical buildings and city features. (For guided walks, phone 68-243.)

The Bridle Path (90 minutes one way). Take the path first used by settlers travelling from Port Lyttelton to the Canterbury Plains. Start from the Christchurch end of the Lyttelton Tunnel and walk over the hills.

Coronation Hill (30 minutes). Begin at the Sign of the Kiwi, and follow the harbour around until Marleys Hill, or continue to Kennedys Bush (2 or 2½ hours return).

Quail Island in Lyttleton Harbour. A half loop (1 hour) or full (2½ hours) across grassland, wooded areas and basalt cliff tops. Once a quarantine station, it is now a pleasant retreat in this dramatic harbour landscape.

For excellent detailed information on city walks and other regional attractions, visit the Canterbury Information Centre, corner Worcester Street and Oxford Terrace. Telephone 799-629. Hours: Monday-Friday 8.30 am.-5.00 p.m.

Beachcomber Restaurant
25 Esplanade
Sumner, Christchurch 8
Telephone: (03) 26-6592
Hosts: Jeff Dalley and Mary Holloway

Sumner's lovely seaside village enjoys a relaxed atmosphere envied by the city close by. First opened in 1911 as Pier Tearooms and Bathhouse, 'Beachcomber' is acclaimed as one of our finest seafood restaurants. The ocean laps under the windows – creating the perfect ambience for lovers of innovative cuisine. Fresh local seafoods, Canterbury venison, lamb, other game and vegetarian dishes. Mary will prepare your own catch by arrangement! Open from 6 p.m. plus Sunday brunch. Closed Christmas.

Meadow Park Holiday Park
39 Meadow Street
PO Box 5178
Christchurch
Telephone: (03) 529-176
Hosts: Daphne and Ian Gamble

This motor park is situated in a rural setting in the heart of Christchurch's northern side, close to shops, restaurants and bus services. Accommodation varies from tent and van sites to cabins, tourist flats and a lodge. Facilities include dining rooms, adventure playground, automatic laundries, games room, indoor heated pool, spa pool, TV lounge, video games, weight training, conference room plus full visitor information on local attractions. From $13 (tent) to $35 (tourist flat).

The George Hotel, Christchurch
Reservations: NZ collect (03) 799-127
(Details/overseas reservations; see p.129)

New, small and exclusive hotel, designed to highest international standards and offering superior service. Luxurious and spacious suites, beautiful views, 3 restaurants, cocktail and piano bars plus full amenities, central to city. From $150.

Vacation Inn
776 Colombo Street
PO Box 1896
Christchurch
Telephone: (03) 795-880
Telex: NZ4523
Facsimile: (03) 792-374

This hotel is situated in the heart of the 'Garden City' of Christchurch, overlooking beautiful Victoria Square and the tranquil Avon River. Each of the 86 guest rooms and 5 suites are appointed with all facilities including in-house video. Two fine restaurants, cocktail bars and a lounge offer excellent relaxation, wining and dining. Staff are renowned for their friendly service. Conference facilities available. From $110 (single). Major credit cards accepted.

SEE ALSO:

National Parks: Arthur's Pass National Park.
Tramping: Karavan Adventure Treks, New Zealand Treks (Christchurch).
NZ Historic Places: Lyttelton Time-ball Station.
Outback Safaris: Overleigh Horse Treks (Banks Peninsula).

South via the inland route through Methven & Mount Hutt

Ice skating on a frozen mid-Canterbury lake. *(Courtesy Four Seasons Scenic Tours)*

Nestling at the foothills of the Southern Alps, this area is rapidly developing as an all-year-round recreation area.

Access is gained by Provincial Highway 72, which runs parallel to the alps – an alternative scenic route from Christchurch, through to Mackenzie Country and Mt Cook.

Once a coach stop between Alford Forest and Rakaia, Methven doubles as the service centre for local agriculture and the summer and winter activities.

Its recent development has been assisted by the growth of the Mt Hutt Ski Field, internationally recognised as having the longest season in the Southern Hemisphere.

Within 1½ to 2 hours of Methven, there are seven other smaller club ski fields: Erewhon, Mt Dobson, Mt Olympus, Porter Heights, Mt Cheeseman, Broken River and Craigieburn.

There is, however, more than skiing. The Rakaia River, with its spectacular gorge, provides not only thrilling jet-boat rides but also some of the best salmon fishing in the country. Each February a fishing competition with $30,000 in prizes is held.

At Easter a marathon begins in Methven and finishes at Ashburton. Spring is time for the floral festival (October) and the rodeo (September), both in Methven. As the area is known for breeding some top trotting horses (many exported to the U.S.A.), enquire whether your visit coincides with one of the local trotting meetings.

Being part of the Canterbury Plains means villages and the influence of England. See little villages like Alford Forest and Staveley (where there are interesting bush walks across a swing bridge to the Sharplin Falls, skating and curling). Barrihill Village (20 kilometres (12 miles) from Methven) nestles amongst beautifully established English trees.

Methven and Mount Hutt District Promotion Assn
P.O. Box 77
Methven
Telephone: (053) 28-605

Barkers Wines Ltd
Geraldine-Mount Cook Highway
Geraldine
Telephone: (056) 38-969

Well signposted, 8 kilometres (5 miles) from Geraldine, this reputable boutique winery offers fresh, fruity surprises – a range of totally natural berryfruit wines and liqueurs. Tastings are invited; sample delicious natural blackcurrant juice, 'Mountain Thunder' mulled wine, or Spritzig Strawberry wine! Hostess available to discuss wines and assist. Casual tastings are free, open Monday through Saturday, 9.00 a.m. to 6.00 p.m. Group tours of winery with cheese and biscuits to accompany tasting, from $2.50 per person.

The Sunflower Centre
31 Main Road
Fairlie
Telephone: (0505) 8258

Natural wholefood restaurant, open daily for delicious take-away foods or stop to eat in pleasant surroundings. Giant vegie-burgers, quiches, salads, fruit-salads, sandwiches and soup. Full range health products, herbal formulas and general information centre.

Rimuwhare Motel and Restaurant
53 Mt Cook Road
Fairlie
Telephone: (0505) 8058
Hosts: Stephanie and Jon Hellmrich

Rimuwhare (House of red pine) – a welcoming haven to travellers since 1896, situated at the gateway to the Mackenzie Country. Enjoy olde worlde charm of this beautifully appointed accommodation and restaurant complex, staying in private and comfortable units (swimming pool, laundry facilities, room service) and delighting in gourmet treats like 'Chicken Aorangi', – blended taste sensation of apricots, chicken, brandy and cheese. Shameless indulgence this – warm fires, intimate bar, lunches amid sunshine and roses. Motel from $50 (double).

SEE ALSO:

Lodges: Mt Hutt Station Resort.
Hunting: Mt Thomas Resources.
Skiing: Mt Dobson Ski Area, Mt Hutt Ski Area.

South via the coast – through Ashburton and Timaru

Once a stark featureless arid land of shingle fans spreading to the east from the Southern Alps, Ashburton is now the centre of one of the country's most prosperous agriculture areas. Irrigation, wheat, sheep, cropping and determination have led to prosperity, all achieved in the past 130 years.

For the traveller, this quiet garden town offers a good base for exploring the area. The northern and southern boundaries of the county, the Rakaia and Rangitata Rivers, are nationally important angling rivers, especially for quinnat salmon (season, February and March).

In total there are 24 species of fish in these rivers. A rarity in New Zealand, American brook trout, can be found in the Hinds River, 20 minutes to the south. Try fishing for rainbow trout or land-locked salmon in Lake Clearwater.

The rugged alpine grandeur of the hinterland, up the Ashburton Gorge, past mineral-rich Mt Somers and Lake Clearwater, provides a marked contrast with the massive patchwork of paddocks and farmhouses of the plains.

Ashburton is also another trotting and horse-racing centre of considerable note.

Fishing for trout at the Rakaia River-mouth, near Ashburton. ***(Andris Apse Ltd)***

Luxury, reasonably priced motor inn, close to town centre, set in 5 hectares (12 acres) of landscaped grounds. Fifty-four well-appointed units (colour television), some with kitchens; paraplegic facilities; excellent a la carte and bistro restaurants plus full range of bars; heated pools, sauna, spa, games room, trampoline, golf course, all-weather tennis court; conference facilities; ample parking. From $70 (single), off-season rate. Book through travel agents, Instant Freeline, Best Western or direct.

Hotel Ashburton
Racecourse Road
PO Box 70
Ashburton
Telephone: (053) 83-059
Telex: NZ 4598

Re-live the past – see an old working steam railway, plus (up Maronan Road) a vintage car museum. The 'Washington' locomotive (built U.S.A. 1879) was dumped in a river in 1927. Restored, it now runs on a section of what was the original Mount Somers branch line. See old locomotives, fire engines, vintage horse-drawn agricultural machinery and tractors, printing presses and steam cranes. A rare N.Z. exhibit is the sole remaining Kemp Electric tractor (built Ashburton 1930s). Museum is operational every second Sunday from October – May.

Plains and Vintage Car Museum
Tinwald Domain
C/- PO Box 5051
Tinwald

Ashburton Public Relations Committee
56 Johnston St
P.O. Box 85
Ashburton
Telephone: (053) 6690

Pastoral scene near Fairlie, South Canterbury. *(National Publicity Studios)*

Timaru

One of New Zealand's more scenic cities, set around a harbour. Close to the city centre is Caroline Bay, a safe, sandy beach with extensive gardens, play areas, tennis courts, aviary and restaurant and the Aigantighe Art Gallery.

The Lovelock Oak can be seen in the grounds of Timaru Boys' High School; this specimen is the only tree still standing of those given to gold medallists by Adolf Hitler at the 1936 Berlin Olympics.

A drive should include Pleasant Point Railway and Museum, as well as the old rock drawings of the moa hunters, signposted on the road between Cave and Southburn. The Public Relations office has details.

Aorangi Public Relations Assn
corner Stafford and Sefton Streets, Timaru
Telephone: (056) 86-163

DB South Island Brewery Ltd
Sheffield Street
Washdyke
PO Box 841
Timaru
Telephone: (056) 82-059
Telex: NZ40087
Facsimile: (056) 82-225

Don't miss this opportunity to see how our great New Zealand beer is made, just 5 minutes' drive north of Timaru at Washdyke. Conducted complimentary tours of this modern brewery take place at 10.30 a.m. and 2.30 p.m. daily (except Saturdays, Sundays and statutory holidays). Suitable for all ages, enclosed footwear is a necessity. May be closed during June and July so please check first by telephone. Bookings unnecessary.

Cedar Motor Lodge
36 King Street
Timaru
Telephone: (056) 44-084
Hosts: Pam and Stewart Frew

This motor lodge guarantees the traveller a peaceful night's sleep in well-appointed units, with kitchen facilities. Sightseeing, skiing and factory tours arranged. Relax in the spa pool and enjoy in-house video movies. From $55 to $70.

The northern inland route to Westland or Nelson

Hanmer Springs has long been known for its thermal springs, its invigorating climate and its magnificent setting enhanced by man-made forests.

In 1859 William Jones of the St Leonard's Station found several hot springs in thick scrub near the Jollies Pass Track. The waters are saline and alkaline, and the temperature varies from 36 to 40°C. In 1883 Hanmer was declared a Government Resort and a Government Sanitorium was built in 1897, at the same time as the original Lodge Hotel. In 1916 the Queen Mary Hospital was opened.

There are many walks to choose from, in both exotic and native forest. A track leads to the top of Conical Hill, where there are excellent views of the surrounding countryside. The Mt Isobel Track is of special interest for its magnificent subalpine plants and fine panoramas. The Nature Trail and the Waterfall Track take visitors through mountain-beech forest, while the Woodland Walk and the Forest Walk are located close to the Information Centre on Jollies Pass Road, from which further information on all these walks, and a Forest Drive, may be obtained.

Waimakiriri River and the Southern Alps, North Canterbury *(Andris Apse Ltd)*

Post Office Champions Trophy Hockey	Christchurch	*Canterbury*
South Island Championship Indoor Bowls	Ashburton	*Canterbury*
University of Otago Capping Week	Dunedin	*Otago*
Southland Winter Show	Invercargill	*Southland*

JUNE

Queens Birthday (1st)

New Zealand Agricultural Fieldays	Hamilton	*Waikato*
Wellington Half Marathon	Wellington	*Wellington*
Takaka – Nelson Annual Road Race	Nelson	*Nelson*
Nelson Racing Club Winter Trotting Carnival	Nelson	*Nelson*
South Island Snooker and Billiards Championships	Dunedin	*Otago*
Regent 24-hour Books Sale & Entertainment	Dunedin	*Otago*

JULY

International Cinema Film Festival	Auckland	*Auckland*
Tulip Queen Contest	Kaponga	*Taranaki*

AUGUST

NZ Billiards/Snooker Championships	Auckland	*Auckland*
Garden Week	Auckland	*Auckland*
New Zealand Craft Show	Hamilton	*Waikato*
Waikato Open Golf Tournaments	Hamilton	*Waikato*
Tauranga City Festival	Tauranga	*Waikato*
NZ Cross-country Runner Championships	Taupo	*Volcanic Plateau*
World Protea Conference	New Plymouth	*Taranaki*
Potters Club Exhibition	New Plymouth	*Taranaki*
NZ Round the Ranges Road Relay	Palmerston North	*Wellington*
International Cinema Film Festival	Wellington	*Wellington*
Conservation Week Urban Park Promotion	Nelson	*Nelson*
Nelson Road Running Race	Nelson	*Nelson*
Music Festival	Greymouth	*Westland*

SEPTEMBER

Antique Fair	Auckland	*Auckland*
Champion of Champions Indoor Bowls Singles	Auckland	*Auckland*
Bollé NZ National Skiing Championships	Whakapapa	*Volcanic Plateau*
World Trade Fair or New Zealand Trade Fair	Wellington	*Wellington*
National Bull Sale	Hamilton	*Waikato*
Spring Blossom Festival	Alexandra	*Central Otago*

OCTOBER

Labour Day (26th)

70km Road Relay Fun Run	Paihia	*Northland*
Government Life Amateur Golf Tournament	Whangarei	*Northland*
Hamilton Festival	Hamilton	*Waikato*
Hamilton International Runners Marathon	Hamilton	*Waikato*
Joggers Club Half Marathon	New Plymouth	*Taranaki*
Mobil Nissan 500 Saloon Car Race	Wellington	*Wellington*
Waterfront Road Run	Wellington	*Wellington*
'Isel in Bloom' Park Festival	Nelson	*Nelson*
10k National Mutual Fun Run	Nelson	*Nelson*
Rhododendron Week	Dunedin	*Otago*
NZ Road Runners Championships	Invercargill	*Southland*
Annual Spring Exhibition	Invercargill	*Southland*
Southland Country Music Awards	Invercargill	*Southland*

Continued on page 231

Mt Tasman, Southern Alps. ***(Andris Apse Ltd)***

Mt Cook the region is mountains and more mountains. Mt Cook, the highest mountain in New Zealand at 3,764 metres (12,349 feet), and Mt Tasman are the focal points of a national park in the west of the region, and is surrounded by a further 140 peaks over 2,300 metres (7,550 feet) – a lot of mountains.

Between the mountains of the park are glaciers, great walls of ice with permanent snow covering, remnants of a time when glaciers gouged out the great valleys through the region. These glaciers include the Tasman, the largest outside the Himalayas or Antarctica, 29 kilometres (18 miles) long, 3 kilometres (1.8 miles) wide.

Outside the park there are still more mountains, great rounded mountains reminiscent of Scotland, and classic alps rising above glacial valley floors.

Travel into the region from the north and drive through long U-shaped valleys of the Mackenzie Country, named after a legendary sheep-stealer who first passed this way. It is country where hardy Merino sheep withstand the rigours of winter, beef cattle graze, and great steel pylons carry electricity across country from hydro-electric schemes.

It is also country where the lakes have a startling beauty. From the north one suddenly arrives at Lake Tekapo and the burst of colour is a visual shock – a brilliant opaque turquoise, edged with grey shingle and red-brown tussock with a backdrop of snowy mountains sprawling across the horizon.

On the shore of the lake the tiny Church of the Good Shepherd stands alone between the road and the lake, looking out across the serenity of water and mountains. Enter the church and find the window behind the altar is clear glass, a recognition that nature here provides more than stained glass could ever achieve. To appreciate the effect at its best, visit the church in the early morning or late afternoon when the interior is shadowy but the lake and mountains etched in brilliant light.

It is an area of clear light and cloudless skies, so much so that at nearby Mt John high above the lake there is an international observatory and also a United States satellite-tracking station.

Whether approaching from the north or from the south, the road to Mt Cook village takes the traveller by Lake Pukaki, another milky blue-green lake. From the eastern end of the lake the view leads up the glacial valley along the lake to the Southern Alps, rising in a cluster around Mt Cook – at times the mountains are mirrored perfectly in the lake waters. The lakes Pukaki, Tekapo and Ohau all occupy the end of glacial valleys, drawing their water from the glaciers above. Fine dust, ground by the action of the glaciers and held in suspension by the lake waters, is responsible for the remarkable colours.

Whilst the State Highway 80 between Lake Tekapo and Lake Pukaki meanders across the tussock grasslands of the Mackenzie, it is often out of sight of the main alpine views and the lakes. The canal road, a sealed road which is in fact a shorter route and virtually level for the entire distance to Lake Pukaki, is much closer to the riverbeds, the lake and the Main Divide. This is a popular route for tour buses, campervans and cyclists.

Skiing is one of the region's major attractions, with diverse skiing possibilities. At Mt Cook there's glacier skiing, ski planes, heli-skiing, alpine ski-mountaineering, downhill ski touring and, especially in spring, Nordic ski touring.

Aorangi – Mt Cook

Lake Ohau offers a conventional field looking down on the incredible blue waters of the lake and heli-skiing in the long Ben Ohau mountain range. The Tekapo slopes above the northwest end of the lake provide an excellent family field, with heli-skiing from the adjacent ridges for the more adventurous.

Mt Dobson is one of the newest fields, with wide slopes looking out across lakes to Mt Cook and the Southern Alps. Runs are excellent, facilities as yet limited but improving with every season – the learners' area is one of the best. Fox Peak offers plenty of variety, with long exciting runs, but it lacks sophisticated equipment and facilities – rewarding for skiers who don't mind good rope tows instead of high speed lifts.

Travel around by air (flight-seeing and charter ski plane, light aircraft or helicopter are a regional feature); by car (rental car can be arranged by major hotels); by bus, especially Mt Cook Landline services; by tour – take conventional coach tours or four-wheel-drive safaris that go to 'the back of beyond'. Tours can be arranged from Christchurch through Guthreys.

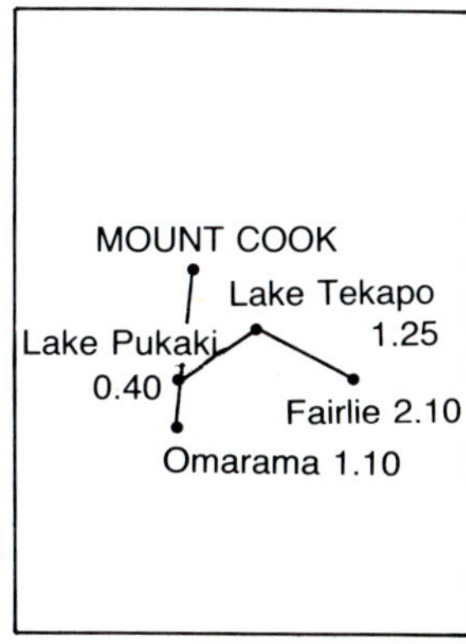

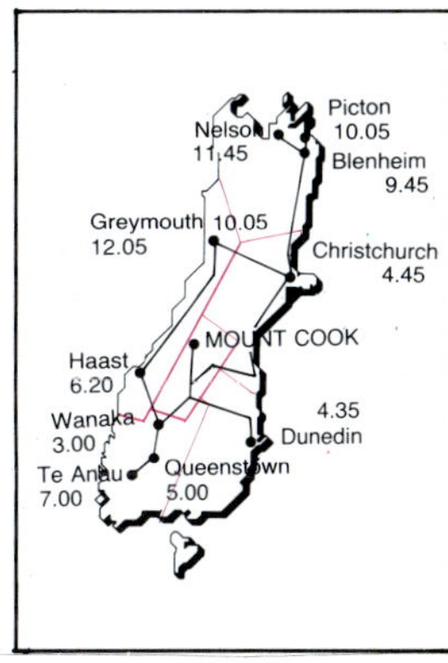

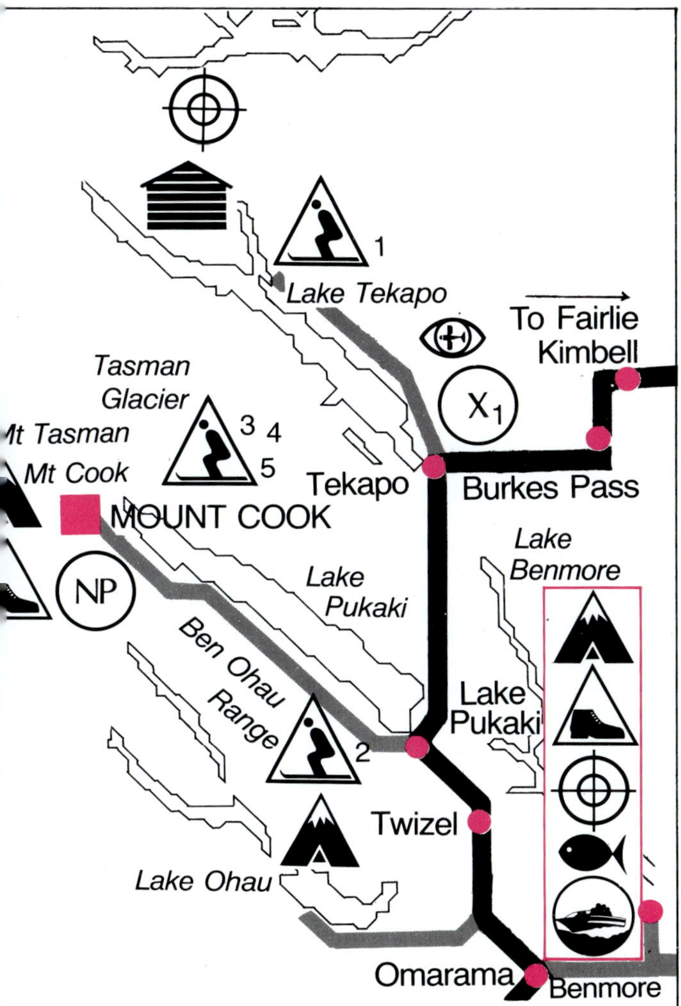

MOUNT COOK SKI

(NP) **National Parks**
Mount Cook National Park.

Skiing
1. Tekapo; 2. Lake Ohau.

Heli/Cross Country Skiing
3. Tasman Glacier;
4. Murchison Glacier;
5. Mannering Glacier.

Climbing

Tramping

Lodges
Lilybank Safari Lodge.

Hunting

Fishing

River Adventures

Flightseeing

(X) **Local**
1. Ice Rink.

Aside from Twizel, the major service town, other villages in the region are really outposts, devoted to the tourist, the adventurer, the climber, tramper, skier and angler.

Tekapo is a village devoted to the holiday-maker, catering for skiers, trampers, campers, boaters and anglers and offering flight-seeing over lakes, mountains and glaciers. The tiny settlements of Burkes Pass and Kimbell also serve skiers at Tekapo, Fox Peak and Mt Dobson fields. (Burkes Pass is little more than a hotel, motel and tiny church on the border of green rolling hills and wild tussock country). Fairlie, on the eastern perimeter of the region, is the service centre for surrounding sheep runs but also offers a base for skiers and other holiday-makers.

Deep in the mountains of the southern Alps is Mt Cook village. The village groups itself around the sprawling splendour of The Hermitage, a luxury hotel overlooked by towering mountains.

There's a school of mountaineering, guides for climbing, tramping, glacier skiing, heli-skiing, ski touring and ski mountaineering. Those who don't wish to ski or climb can be whisked into the heart of the mountains by ski plane to land on the perpetual snows of the Tasman Glacier. In winter the emphasis here is on the skiing, in summer on climbing, but all year round there is some of the most spectacular, most accessible alpine scenery in the world. At the park headquarters, find detailed information on the many walks, from the 10-minute Bowen Track through alpine shrubs to the three-day alpine crossing over the Copland Pass to Fox Glacier in Westland.

Twizel was built in 1968 to house construction workers on power projects that redirect water from Tekapo, Pukaki and Ohau in a series of dams and canals.

Lake Ohau Lodge serves anglers in summer and skiers in winter. It is also the base for tramping into the Hopkins, Hunter and Dobson mountains.

Omarama, on the southeastern edge of the region, is a centre for excellent trout fishing (the Ahuriri River is world famous), jet boating, skiing, flight-seeing and gliding – every summer pilots and gliders congregate at Omarama where ideal gliding conditions exist, away from sea breezes.

Accommodation – Hotels, motels and camping ground with cabins are available at Fairlie; limited hotel and camping ground accommodation at Burkes Pass; first-class hotels and motor inns at Tekapo, Mt Cook village, Twizel, Lake Ohau and Omarama. Tekapo also has camping ground with cabins, cottages and a youth hostel. At Mt Cook there is also a moderately priced lodge, motel, chalets and a youth hostel. All Mt Cook accommodation should be booked well in advance – it's a long way back if there's nothing available! Nearby Glentanner Park has a camping and caravan park and cabin accommodation. Twizel offers hotel, motel, and camping ground with cabins; Omarama has a modern caravan park and cabins.

Food. – First-class restaurants attached to the top hotels and inns. Otherwise food tends to reflect the needs of outdoors enthusiasts – hearty and filling. You won't go hungry with meals in traditional country hotels.

11

Aorangi – Mt Cook

This was the giant Upper Waitaki power scheme. The town was saved from being bulldozed to the ground in 1985 after a long political battle by its residents. While the population has declined from the peak of 6,000 in 1977, to 1,250, Twizel retains the major service functions for the power scheme and the Mackenzie Basin, and is now developing into a tourism centre. Find out about Twizel's history and obtain regional information from the Information Centre.

Twizel
Mt Cook-Queenstown Tour Route
Twizel Development Inc.
PO Box 4
Twizel

The town of trees in the high country's heart – providing a great holiday base! Nearest town to Mt Cook – 63 kilometres (40 miles). Regional centre for the Mackenzie Basin (pop. 1250) and focal point of the major Mackenzie Lakes – Tekapo, Pukaki, Ohau, Benmore and Ruataniwha. Centre of Mt Cook ski region – Ohau, Tekapo, Dobson areas, glacier ski Mt Cook, heli-ski Ben Ohau Range. FACILITIES: Trading bank (foreign exchange), post office, service station, food and shopping complex. Library, sports hall, squash and tennis courts, heated swimming pools and hydro-slides. ACCOMMODATION: 350-bed hotel, 180-bed lodge, lakeside camping ground with cabins, van and tent sites. INFORMATION CENTRE: Open daily adjacent S.H.8 – films, excellent displays, maps, general information. ACTIVITIES: Fishing (canals year round), swimming, yachting, windsurfing, hang-gliding, trailbike/horse riding, camping, picnics, tramping, climbing. International rowing course, power-boat racing on Lake Ruataniwha.

Entertainment. – In the evening activity centres on the nearest bar, whether in a smart modern hotel, a rough-and-ready dam-workers' bar or a hotel that began life as a coaching stop last century.

Lake Tekapo skifield, Mt Cook ski area, with Lake Tekapo in the background.
(Andris Apse Ltd)

Lake Ohau Motor Lodge
Lake Ohau
PO Box 51, Twizel
Telephone: (02984) 885
Telex: NZ5297
Hosts: Lyn & Iain Mehrtens

This complex of 72 units, comprises both luxury and budget accommodation. Most rooms have ensuite facilities, tea/coffee making equipment and superb views over Lake Ohau and surrounding mountains. Additional facilities include fully licensed house bar and restaurant, cots for children, drying rooms, plus a 7-day service station with mechanical workshop. If you have a caravan or campervan, there are power-appointed sites available. Situated 20 minutes drive from State Highway 8, between Twizel and Omarama, set amid the splendid isolation of this idyllic lake and mountains. Enjoy friendly hospitality and a range of outdoor activities; snow-skiing (just minutes away at Ohau Ski Area), tennis, para-gliding, walking, climbing, water-skiing, jet-boating, swimming and scenic flights. From $66 (double, GST inclusive). Special rates for children.

Glenburn Caravan & Campervan Park
State Highway 83
PO Box 90
Omarama
Telephone: (02984) 411
Hosts: The Wardell Family

Situated on a high country sheep station just minutes from Omarama, this tranquil park overlooks Lake Benmore and offers very modern camping. Each spacious van site has its own personal ensuite bathroom – shower, toilet, heated towel rail and basin! Comfortable self-contained motel units and farm cottages also available. Experience farm life, four-wheel drive safaris, lake and river activities, skiing, trout-fishing. Costs on enquiry. Discounts for extended stays.

SEE ALSO:

National Parks: Mount Cook National Park.
Skiing: Tekapo Ski Area, Ohau Ski Area.
Climbing: Alpine Guides (Mt Cook).
Hunting: Lilybank Safari Lodge.
Flightseeing: Air Safaris & Services (Lake Tekapo).

Droving sheep on the Mt Cook Rd, Mackenzie Country. *(Andris Apse Ltd)*

NZ Photographic Exhibition	Invercargill	*Southland*
NOVEMBER		
National Top Hospitals Competition	Paihia	*Northland*
Government Life Golf Tournament	Whangarei	*Northland*
NZ Champion Runners Marathon	Auckland	*Auckland*
Air New Zealand/Shell Open Golf	Auckland	*Auckland*
International Trout Fishing Competition	Rotorua	*Bay of Plenty*
Rose Festival Week	Hamilton	*Waikato*
Hawkes Bay Anniversary (1st)		*Hawkes Bay*
Waitara Golf Club Open Hangi Tournament	Waitara	*Taranaki*
Holiday and Leisure Show	Wellington	*Wellington*
Rose Week 'Broadgreen House Rose Display'	Nelson	*Nelson*
Marlborough Anniversary (1st)		*Marlborough*
Marlborough Agriculture/Produce Show	Blenheim	*Marlborough*
Operatic Society Show Week	Greymouth	*Westland*
Christmas Parade	Greymouth	*Westland*
Agriculture/Produce Show	Christchurch	*Canterbury*
Trotting Cup Week	Christchurch	*Canterbury*
Winstone Marathon: Riverton-Invercargill	Riverton	*Southland*
DECEMBER		
Christmas Day (25th)		
Masters Tennis Tournament	Auckland	*Auckland*
Nissan Mobil Air NZ Golf Open	Wellington	*Wellington*
New Zealand Golf Open	Wellington	*Wellington*
Nelson City Mardi Gras	Nelson	*Nelson*
Westland Anniversary (1st)		*Westland*
West Coast Marathon	Greymouth	*Westland*
Canterbury Anniversary (16th)		*Canterbury*
Whare Flat Folk Festival	Dunedin	*Otago*
Riverton Annual Carnival	Riverton	*Southland*

Note: Some sporting events are held in different centres each year. For specific information, contact the local Public Relations Office in each area. For specific golf dates and venues, contact The NZ Golf Association, telephone (04) 722-967.

Mitre Peak, Milford Sound, Southland. ***(National Publicity Studios)***

This is 'champagne' scenery, the region that contains New Zealand's best-known, most-photographed tourist destinations – Milford Sound, Queenstown, Lake Wakatipu, Lake Wanaka, Lake Te Anau. The scale, the colours, the juxtaposition of mountains, lakes, rivers, forests and fiords combine to create unsurpassed, unforgettable scenery.

It is a region where visitors come to absorb the scenery, to tramp, climb, hunt, ski, raft, canoe or fish. Then they come back to do it all again, returning to the region each year, not merely from other parts of New Zealand, but from all over the world.

Lakes and mountains dominate the area. See mountains sharply etched against the skyline, rising from wide valley floors, abruptly from the edge of lakes or sheer from the sea, in the deep fiords. Here you can see, or travel on, rivers such as the Shotover, which rushes in a wild torrent through steep, barren canyons, or the Landsborough, which flows through a trackless wilderness approachable only by expert trampers or by helicopter transport.

In the Southern Lakes Region you can walk the famous Milford, Hollyford or Routeburn Tracks or any of the hundreds of lesser-known tracks.

The Milford Track is acclaimed as 'the finest walk in the world', a five- or six-day trek from the head of Lake Te Anau to Milford Sound, leading alongside and across clear green rivers, over an alpine plain, across a high mountain pass, by the Sutherland Falls (third highest in the world at 580 metres or 1,900 feet) and down to the sea at magnificent Milford Sound.

The Hollyford walk begins in the Hollyford Valley at the road's end and follows the blue Hollyford River through to Lake Alabaster, Lake McKerrow (once a fiord) and the sea at Martins Bay, where there is a colony of fur seals. The experience is varied, with jet-boat travel on river and lake, and transport out by light aircraft.

The Routeburn is a high track leading from the head of Lake Wakatipu over the Harris Saddle Pass, by tiny mountain lakes, through red-beech forest, over alpine meadows full of flowers in late spring and early summer and with spectacular views down glacial valleys.

The coast of the region is deeply indented with immense gashes gouged out by glaciers that finally disappeared as recently as 15,000 years ago, leaving behind sheer granite walls that drop hundreds of metres into the dark-green sea. At Milford Sound, Mitre Peak rises in serene splendour straight from the mirror-calm waters of the fiord – a scene that has become a symbol of New Zealand. Reach Milford Sound the energetic way, on the Milford Track, by road from Te Anau along one of the world's great alpine drives, or by air on what is probably the most spectacular scenic flight in the world.

Milford Sound is the focal point for most visitors to the 1.2 million-hectare (3 million-acre) Fiordland National Park, but it is only one aspect of an amazing area. Here, there is not only one of the world's highest waterfalls, but also one of the world's highest rainfalls – up to 7,600 millimetres (300 inches) in places. With this rain come forests that seem almost magical; giant totara, rimu, matai, red and silver beech grow in precarious places, clinging to humus gathered on rocks; ferns, mosses and vines engulf the trees and lichens hang in drifts, like immense lace curtains; shafts of sunlight glance through the forest in muted colours; glow worms display their

Kea.

12

Southern Lakes

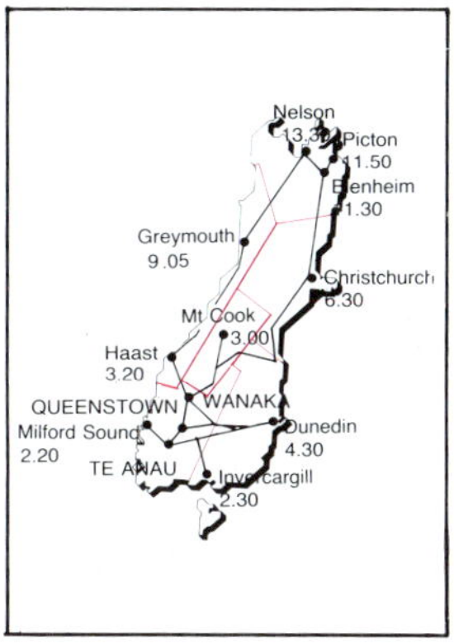

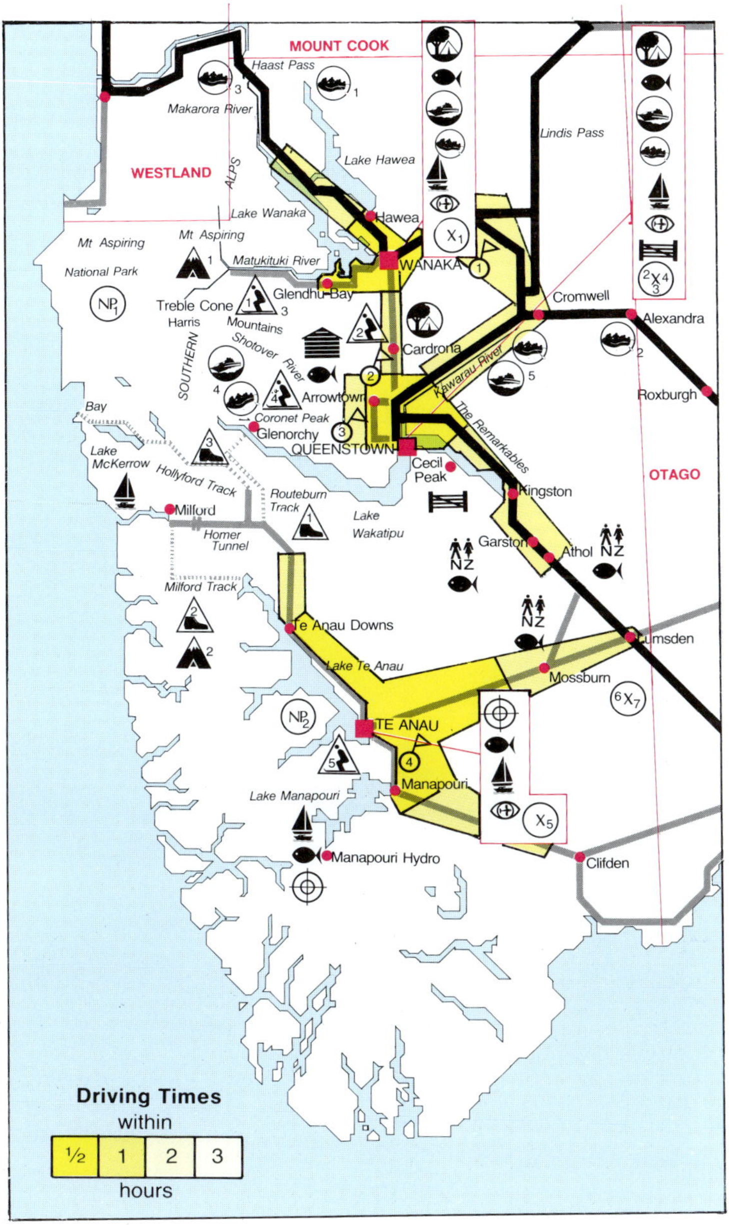

SOUTHERN LAKES

National Parks
1. Mount Aspiring National Park; 2. Fiordland National Park.

Skiing Heli/Cross Country
1. Treble Cone; 2. Cardrona; 3. Harris Mountains; 4. Coronet Peak. 5. Mount Luxmore.

Climbing
1. Mount Aspiring National Park; 2. Fiordland National Park.

Tramping
1. Routeburn; 2. Milford Track; 3. Hollyford Track.

Lodges
Crown Lodge.

Outback Safaris

Hunting

Fishing

River Adventures
1. Hunter River; 2. Clutha River; 3. Landsborough River; 4. Shotover River; 5. Kawarau River.

Cruising

Flightseeing

Golf
1. Wanaka; 2. Arrowtown; 3. Queenstown; 4. Te Anau.

Down on Farm

Live with NZ

Local
1. The Maze & Puzzle Centre; 2. Motor Museum; 3. Sound & Light Museum; 4. Art Gallery; 5. Milford Track Audio-Visual; 6. Matuku Engine Museum & 7. Bee Bazaar.

tiny lights on damp, mossy banks.

Bush life includes forest birds such as tuis, bellbirds, cuckoos, kakas, and robins. The park is also home to the rare takahe and kakapo. There's wapiti, red deer, chamois, rainbow and brown trout; on the shores, seals and penguins.

In the north of the region, Mt Aspiring National Park draws dedicated mountaineers, trampers and adventurers to an area that includes classic alps, more than 50 glaciers, the headwaters of seven major rivers, rainforest, beech forest, alpine meadows and wide, tussock river flats. It is wild, difficult, intensely beautiful terrain, sought out by experts, unchanged from the days when the mountains earned names such as Mt Awkward, Mt Awful, Mt Dreadful and Mt Defiant. See the park in comfort on flight excursions.

The gateway to Mt Aspiring National Park is through Wanaka (the park's headquarters are in Wanaka). On the edge of the long twisting Lake Wanaka, the town is a centre for skiing, trout fishing, boating, canoeing, rafting, flight-seeing and horse trekking.

A similarly wide range of activities awaits visitors to Queenstown, the top South Island tourist destination on the shores of Lake Wakatipu. On the edge of Lake Te Anau, the largest South Island lake, there is the town of Te Anau, yet a third excellent base for exploring the region, and gateway to dramatic Fiordland.

Mt Talbot and reflection, Fiordland National Park. *(National Publicity Studios)*

Southern Lakes

Accommodation. Excellent quality accommodation in hotels and motor inns at Queenstown, Wanaka and Te Anau. Milford Sound has one high-class THC hotel and one hostel (prior booking advisable). Also find excellent accommodation in exclusive hunting and fishing lodges and on high-country sheep stations. Plenty of motels. Queenstown has seven camping grounds with cabin accommodation within reasonable distance of town. Camping grounds also at Wanaka, Glendhu Bay, Te Anau, Hollyford Valley, Manapouri. Find budget accommodation in bunkhouse lodges, guest houses and youth hostels.

Food. Queenstown offers a full range, in fact the highest number of restaurants per capital of any New Zealand town, of stylish licensed restaurants, informal bistros and plenty of snack bars for people in a hurry. Less to choose from in Wanaka and Te Anau, but excellent quality. Look for New Zealand specialities such as lamb, venison and salmon. For something different, try some locally made fruit wines – apricot, elderberry, plum, cherry – at the Key of the Lakes near Te Anau.

Entertainment. Queenstown is small but one of the liveliest towns in the country. Excellent restaurants, convivial bars, good live entertainment. Most night life centres on the hotels with music, cabaret or dancing. In Te Anau or Wanaka, after an enjoyable outdoors day a relaxing dinner and early night are usually the rule. Good hotels have spas or saunas to soothe weary limbs.

Travel around the Southern Lakes region with the most spectacular alpine flight-seeing in the world. Light aircraft, float planes, amphibians and helicopters leave from Queenstown, Wanaka, Te Anau. Travel by car, remembering that mountain roads off the beaten track may test your motoring skills. (Rental car insurance does not cover travel on the Skippers Canyon road, so take a tour bus.) All major bus companies serve the region well – buses to Milford coincide with launch tours. Plenty of tours are available to suit all tastes, from outback four-wheel-drive to conventional sightseeing.

Wanaka

From Wanaka, the gentle township on the edge of Lake Wanaka, explore the lake's bays and beaches, fringed with willows, maples, kowhai and poplars.

A successful day's fishing on Lake Wanaka. ***(Courtesy Paul Miller)***

A favourite boating lake with little road access, Wanaka is long and twisting, winding its way through peninsulas and islands with mountains often mirrored in the lake's calm surface. Take a launch cruise on the 390-square-kilometre (240-square-mile) lake, leaving from the Wanaka waterfront and stopping off at lake islands, perhaps for a barbecue or picnic lunch. Go jet-boat touring, water skiing, para-sailing or windsurfing on the lake. Hire a sail boat, power boat, row boat or canoe and explore the bays independently.

Go swimming too, if you enjoy a dip in ice-cold mountain water (the town beach, Sunshine Beach, is one of the best for swimming). Swimmers find the lake's water refreshingly welcome on a hot summer's day. Summer in Wanaka can be very hot indeed, with cloudless sunny days, in a suntrap valley where temperatures soar to 38°C.

There's superb fishing in Lake Wanaka, neighbouring Lake Hawea and surrounding rivers. Local guides ensure visitors find the best spots for brown trout, rainbow trout and land-locked salmon, and provide all the necessary equipment. Even if you're not going fishing, visit the trout hatchery in Stone Street, where trout and salmon make a fascinating study.

Other around-town diversions include a one-kilometre maze, an elaborate mini-golf course, a puzzle centre, hire bicycles and tandems.

But it is the recreational variety of lake, hills, mountains and valleys that draws thousands of visitors to Wanaka each year. As well as the magnificent boating and fishing, holiday-makers come to play golf, take high-country safari tours, go tramping, climbing, hunting, horse trekking along old mining trails, rafting and canoeing on fast rivers; all these activities are based at Wanaka.

In winter, Wanaka becomes the centre for skiing at the Treble Cone and Cardrona ski-fields. Both fields have fabulous views over distant lakes and with new facilities are one of the country's fastest growing ski areas. For heli-skiing try the Harris Mountains, where over 30 runs provide intermediate and expert slopes of 600 to 1,200 vertical metres (2,000 to 4,000 feet). There's also ice skating on Diamond Lake, a small sparkling lake set in the hills above Lake Wanaka's Glendhu Bay.

Take flight-seeing excursions from Wanaka's airfield or lake front, over the lakes and the wilderness of Mt Aspiring National Park or further afield to Milford Sound or Mt Cook; there are chicken and champagne breakfast flights over mountains and lakes.

Enjoy the splendour of Wanaka's scenery from boat or plane, but also travel out from town by road; drive along the fringe of Lake Hawea to The Neck, and then to the Makarora Valley by Lake Wanaka, through to the edge of Mt Aspiring National Park. Continue through to Haast Pass for constantly changing alpine views.

Travel west from Wanaka township to Glendhu Bay, with the dramatic landscape softened by willows and poplars.

Confident drivers who enjoy mountain roads can take the Cardrona Valley – Crown Range Road. (On a map it looks like a short cut between Wanaka and Queenstown – it's not.) This is exciting mountain territory, an old gold-mining route where

Horse-trekking by the Cardrona Hotel ***(Courtesy Gin & Raspberry Stables)***

12

Southern Lakes

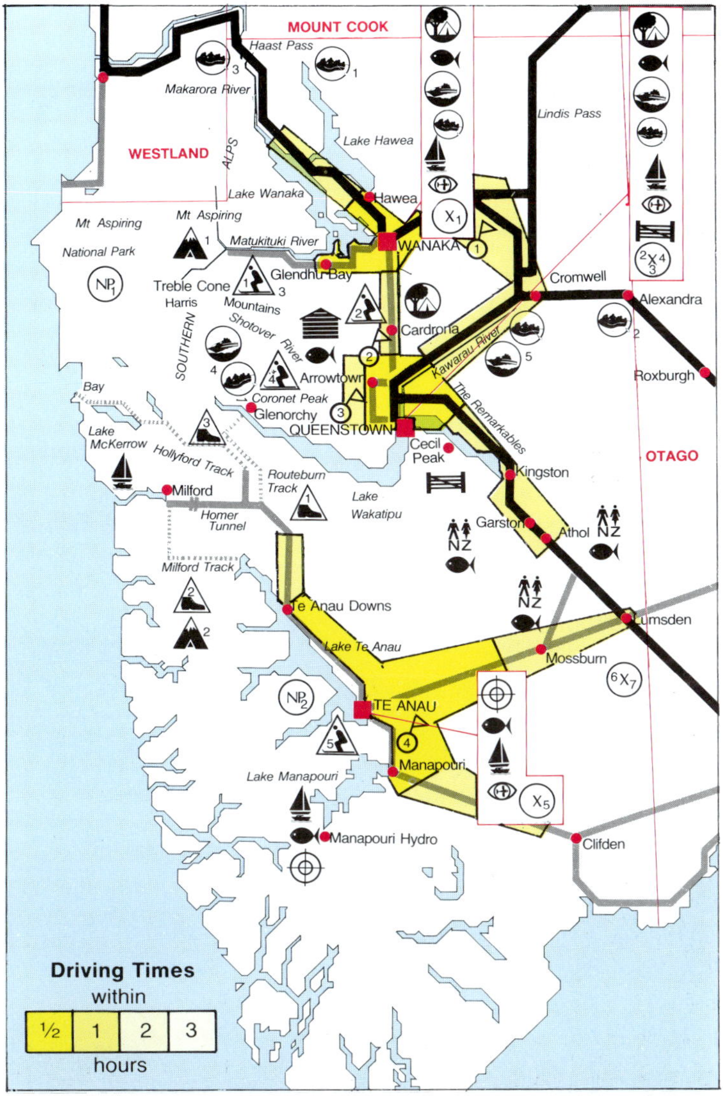

SOUTHERN LAKES

National Parks
1. Mount Aspiring National Park; 2. Fiordland National Park.

Skiing Heli/Cross Country
1. Treble Cone; 2. Cardrona; 3. Harris Mountains; 4. Coronet Peak. 5. Mount Luxmore.

Climbing
1. Mount Aspiring National Park; 2. Fiordland National Park.

Tramping
1. Routeburn; 2. Milford Track; 3. Hollyford Track.

Lodges
Riverview Farm Lodge

Outback Safaris

Hunting

Fishing

River Adventures
1. Hunter River; 2. Clutha River; 3. Landsborough River; 4. Shotover River; 5. Kawarau River.

Cruising

Flightseeing

Golf
1. Wanaka; 2. Arrowtown; 3. Queenstown; 4. Te Anau.

Down on Farm

Live with NZ

Local
1. The Maze & Puzzle Centre; 2. Motor Museum; 3. Art Gallery; 4. Milford Track Audio-Visual; 5. Matuku Engine Museum & 6. Bee Bazaar.

decaying stone cottages stand as reminders of bygone days. At Cardrona, find an old gold-mining pub and the quaintly named 'Gin-and-Raspberry Stables', offering guided horse-treks deep into the mountains.

Take walks beginning with tracks leading from the town's waterfront around the shore of the lake. From the Glendhu Bay Road you may take a walk to the top of Mt Roy for spectacular views of sharply ridged ranges spreading out into Lake Wanaka. Drive on up the Mt Aspiring Road to Raspberry Creek, and from there take walks up the Matukituki River valleys, with forests, mountain and glacier views; the road can be grim but the tracks are well worth the drive. Intrepid walkers should visit the Mt Aspiring National Park Headquarters in Wanaka for all information on the mountain wilderness of Mt Aspiring.

Wanaka

The Wanaka Maze and Puzzle Centre
Wanaka-Cromwell Highway
(2 kilometres, 1.2 miles, from Wanaka)
Telephone: Wanaka 7489
Hosts: Jan and Stuart Landsborough

This maze has won national awards for enterprise – find out why! The first of the world's mazes, it is a three-dimensional maze with 1.5 kilometres (1 mile) of confusing over-and-under passageways, through which you must make your way to the lovely Rose Garden terminal. This is great fun for adults and children alike, and there are emergency gates for those with limited time or energy!

The other major attraction not to be missed is the Puzzle Centre, which contains one of the largest displays of puzzles and puzzling things in the world.

For those of you interested in the art of maze design, talk with Stuart, who has designed mazes around the world, including the United States and Japan, and is known as a foremost authority in the field.

Lake Hawea Hotel
Lake Hawea
Central Otago
Telephone: (02943) 8224
Telex: NZ5502

Ten minutes drive from Wanaka, superb hotel unit accommodation plus fully-serviced, ensuite motor home facilities, overlooking this beautiful lake. Close to shops, the hotel features open fireplaces and an atmosphere of warm comfort. Facilities include laundries, dining room, bistro and garden bars, children's playground and facilities. Minigolf, fishing, boating, water-skiing, hunting and pony treks all available, plus seasonal skiing. From $75 (double) unit, $25 campervan. Off-peak rates available.

SEE ALSO:
National Parks: Mount Aspiring National Park.
Outback Safaris: Gin & Raspberry Stables (Cardrona).
Skiing: Ski Guides (NZ) (Wanaka), Treble Cone and Cardrona Ski Areas.
Flightseeing: Aspiring Air (Wanaka).

Looking across from Scar Burn area to Lake Wanaka and beyond to Mt Gold, Central Otago. *(National Publicity Studios)*

Paragliding in Queenstown *(Photo Express Ltd, Queenstown).*

Queenstown

In Queenstown the emphasis is on action, whatever the season, whatever the time of day. Yet the town also has a dream-like quality, a faultless setting of mountains and lake; a charm based on the days when it catered to miners seeking their fortunes on the Shotover, Arrow and Kawerau Rivers. All these qualities combine to make Queenstown the perfect place for a complete holiday.

From hotels and motels you can look out on the splendour of the glacial Lake Wakatipu. To further savour the view, take a gondola ride straight above the town, a four-minute ride to the top of Bob's Peak (466 metres, 1,530 feet), through dark pine woods; at the top is a glass-walled restaurant and magnificent views. Take a walk up Queenstown Hill, from York Street to the top of a 900-metre (3,000-foot) hill overlooking the town.

On the wooded peninsula that forms the west side of Queenstown's almost square bay (formed by a glacial moraine), find a garden reserve, rimmed with fir trees concealing wide lawns, rose gardens, lily ponds, skating rink and tennis courts. Stand on the peninsula looking back on the town with Bob's Peak looming above. Look in the other direction to the Remarkables, unfolding into the distance along the lake shore.

See further views by travelling a little out of town to Deer Park Heights, a game reserve near Frankton, where wapiti, red deer, chamois, thar and mountain goats surround you and the lake spreads out below. Ride a chairlift to the top of Coronet Peak – in winter one of the country's top ski fields with some of the best facilities and skiing in the Southern Hemisphere.

Experience more views and excitement with flight-seeing; there are 10-minute flights over mountains and lake; half-hour flights that can encompass several mountain ranges, rivers, lakes and high-country sheep and cattle stations; flights further afield reach Milford Sound quickly and spectacularly. Take a helicopter ride to the top of the Remarkables.

Queenstown is a town eminently suited to wandering; stroll through tiny, narrow streets where shops, boutiques, restaurants and century-old buildings of timber and stone cluster. At the corner of Ballarat and Stanley Streets, the flavour of old Queenstown is encapsulated in the 1876 courthouse and library buildings.

Present-day Queenstown centres on the mall at the lake end of Ballarat Street. Here find quaint shops selling hand-knitted woollen garments, jewellery, crafts and leatherwork. The Wakatipu Trading Post is an arcade of small shops created out of historic buildings.

There are also information and tour offices, offering dozens of excursions in and around town and further afield into the region. Find out all you want to know about jet-boat trips on the Shotover River, white-water rafting and canoeing, horse trekking along old mining trails, safaris into the back country, or tours to the spectacular Skippers Canyon.

On the lake front, have a drink at Eichardt's Hotel, a pub that's been in business since 1871, and contemplate a lake excursion.

Pride of the lake is the *Earnslaw*, a steamer that has been plying the lake since 1912. At one time its prime purpose was to carry supplies to sheep stations around the lake. Today its interior is more sophisticated, with a licensed restaurant and room for 1,000 passengers. Luncheon cruises serve chicken and champagne while steaming by the Remarkables mountain range. Other *Earnslaw* cruises include visits to high-country

12

Southern Lakes

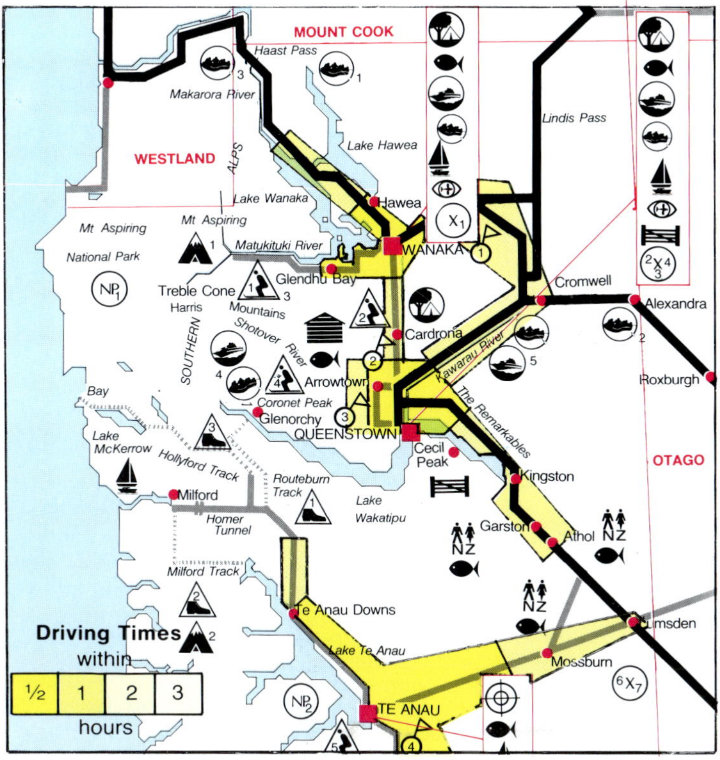

SOUTHERN LAKES

National Parks
1. Mount Aspiring National Park; 2. Fiordland National Park.

Skiing Heli/Cross Country
1. Treble Cone; 2. Cardrona;
3. Harris Mountains;
4. Coronet Peak.
5. Mount Luxmore.

Climbing
1. Mount Aspiring National Park; 2. Fiordland National Park.

Tramping
1. Routeburn; 2. Milford Track;
3. Hollyford Track.

Lodges
Riverview Farm Lodge

Outback Safaris

Hunting

Fishing

River Adventures
1. Hunter River; 2. Clutha River; 3. Landsborough River; 4. Shotover River; 5. Kawarau River.

Cruising

Flightseeing

Golf
1. Wanaka; 2. Arrowtown;
3. Queenstown; 4. Te Anau.

Down on Farm

Live with NZ

Local
1. The Maze & Puzzle Centre; 2. Motor Museum; 3. Art Gallery; 4. Milford Track Audio-Visual; 5. Matuku Engine Museum & 6. Bee Bazaar.

sheep and cattle stations and dinner-dance cruises.

Lake excursions also include hydrofoil, hovercraft and jet-boat cruises, and launch tours to sheep and cattle stations; watch sheepdog, shearing and spinning demonstrations; walk through historic farm buildings and enjoy a high-country morning or afternoon tea. In the fishing season the options extend to charter boats and fishing guides for rainbow-and brown-trout fishing.

Back on dry land, visit the Cattledrome on the Arrowtown Road for a stage show featuring live beef cattle and dairy cows. (There's the chance, too, for you to try hand-milking a cow.)

For journeys into the past, visit the motor museum, an excellent collection of vintage touring cars, racing cars and motor cycles; or visit Colonial Sounds, an audio-visual display of gold-rush days, which recreates the past superbly.

Relive the gold-mining days further at a recreated village, Golden Terrace Mining Town, near Frankton, which includes 1860s-style general store, sweet shop, book shop, mining company office, bank, stables, barber shop and, of course, the pub; or travel to nearby Kingston to take a memorable journey on the Kingston Flyer, a picture-book steam train that travels to Fairlight and back.

When is the best time to visit Queenstown? The answer is in summer, when the town and lake are caught in a hot, dry, sun trap; in winter, when it turns into a skiers' town with the liveliest aprés-ski life in the country; in spring, when wildflowers, hawthorn and may trim the roadsides; in autumn, as the crisp mountain air turns leaves bright yellow and red.

Queenstown

Visitor Activity Centre
Corner Beach and
Shotover Streets
PO Box 453
Queenstown
Telephone: (0294) 27-966

VISITORS ACTIVITY CENTRE

Where to go, What to do and How to do it in Queenstown! Make this your first port of call on arrival in Queenstown. The Visitors Activity Centre provides information on all activities, accommodation and restaurants in the area. They will book everything for you or simply give you their considered advice and assistance. For your convenience, a free shuttle bus runs from the centre to main hotels and motels hourly. The centre is open from 7.00 a.m. to 11.00 p.m. every day of the week. Relax in comfort in the coffee shop, use the free local telephone, have your precious films developed quickly, watch free and informative videos, browse in the souvenir shop. A 24-hour tourism information machine, plus restrooms complete this comprehensive facility, created to help you to make the most of your visit.

Kiwi and Birdlife Park
Brecon Street
Queenstown
Telephone: (0294) 28-059
Hosts: The Wilson Family

Close to town is a haven for native New Zealand birdlife! Guides show you some of New Zealand's most active kiwis feeding and fossicking. Amongst native plantlife and streams, view common, rare and endangered birdlife, both in and outside aviaries and enclosures. Restrooms, coffee shop, souvenir shop (under construction). A spectacular, unique experience you won't forget! Umbrellas available. Open daily except Christmas Day, 9.00 a.m. to 5.00 p.m. From $4 (adult), $2.50 (child), GST inclusive. Group rates.

Queenstown Motor Museum
25 Brecon Street
Queenstown
Telephone: (0294) 28-775
Hosts: John & Glenys Taylor

Just 5 minutes walk from the town centre, this beautiful display of vintage, veteran and classic vehicles dating from 1861, is reputed to be one of Australasia's best. Included are cars, motor bikes, aircraft exhibits plus wonderful motoring memorabilia. A souvenir shop specialises in motoring themes. From $3.50 (adult), $1.50 (child). Have a sepia photograph taken of yourself in 19th-century period costume, for old time's sake (cost additional).

Kawarau River, near Queenstown. *(Andris Apse Ltd)*

Southern Lakes

'Wakatipu Gold'
Precious Metal Dealers
Wakatipu Mall
Beach Street
PO Box 135
Queenstown
Telephone: (0294) 29-223
Manageress: Betty Ward

You are warmly invited to visit this unique shop and discover the beauty of gold. Mined locally, this is the same gold which brought immigrants in their thousands to this region in the 1800s to seek their fortunes, now leaving in their wake a wealth of history and – the remainder of the gold. Special to this range are the nuggets, retained in natural state – as found, with others being crafted into fine, handmade jewellery. The natural nuggets are between 94-96% pure (approximately 22 carats) and are mounted on various settings. All the gold jewellery is produced locally as in few other areas in the world does gold have as high a purity. Thus it retains a high investment value in addition to its ornamental beauty and its interest as a talking point. The range of gold pieces includes earrings, tie-pins, rings, charms, pendants and brooches. Also available are 9-, 14- and 18-carat crafted gold chains.

The shop also trades and sells bullion, plus stocking gold coins: Quarter-Kiwis, Full-Kiwis, Krugerrands, Maple Leafs and ingots. Other ranges include handcrafted greenstone (jade), silver and paua jewellery, polished stones, pottery and woodcarvings. Open daily September through May; Monday to Saturday morning (10.00 a.m. – 2.00 p.m.) June through August.

Queenstown under snow. *(Ray Dustow)*

A1 Queenstown Motel
13 Frankton Road
Queenstown
Telephone: (0294) 27-289
Host: Peter Garrett & Co.

In peaceful surrounds, near Botanical Gardens and town centre; this motel offers 10 self-contained, spacious units, including kitchens. Excellent facilities include inhouse video, central heating and electric blankets, outdoor pool for hot summers, plus a private spa for year-round enjoyment. Courtesy transport available. Enjoy friendly service plus activities and sightseeing arrangements. From $65 (two persons). Bookings heavy at peak times. PRESENT THIS BOOK AND RECEIVE A 10% DISCOUNT OFF USUAL TARIFF!

Nugget Point Resort
Queenstown
Reservations: NZ collect (03) 799-127
(Details/overseas reservations; see p.129)

Exclusive new luxury resort with spectacular mountain and lake views. Thirty-three one- and two-bedroomed apartments, lounges, bars, restaurants, conference room. All facilities: close to 4 ski areas, watersports, hunting, fishing, climbing and tramping. From: $165.

Hillside Holiday Motel
35 Gorge Road
PO Box 513
Queenstown
Telephone: (0294) 29-280
Host: Anne Henley

Overlooking forest-clad hills, just 5 minutes walk from central Queenstown, this motel welcomes families. Telephones, colour TV and full kitchen facilities in each unit plus ample heating. Off-street parking with convenient level access from carparks to units. Be assured of a warm and friendly welcome plus helpful advice with things to do in and around Queenstown. Book well in advance during winter months and Christmas period. From $45 (double), off-peak rates.

Queenstown Motor Park
Man Street
PO Box 49
Queenstown
Telephone: (0294) 27-252

Beautifully sited on lakeside with lake/mountain views. Offers 300 serviced and tent sites (set among trees). Ten fully-serviced motel units, 4 tourist flats (occupants supply linen and blankets), tourist lodge (18 rooms – private facilities/communal cooking), 26 units (own equipment necessary). Excellent facilities – bedding for hire, automatic laundry, television room, children's playground, store. Close to towncentre. Reasonable rates scale. Off-peak discounts on stays over 3 nights. Bookings heavy holidays and ski-season.

The Lodges
6 Lake Esplanade
PO Box 244
Queenstown
Telephone: (0294) 27-552
Telex: NZ5464 TRAVQNZ
Hosts: Carol and Tony Royds

This new, award-winning condominium complex overlooks Lake Wakatipu and the mountains from a lakeside situation, close to town and facilities. Fully self-contained units provide 3 bedrooms, lounge (with colour TV) and private balcony, bath or spa bath, garage or carport, laundry and kitchen with dishwasher and other amenities, (beautifully finished in natural wood panelling). Central to all regional activities which Carol and Tony are pleased to arrange for you.

SEE ALSO:

Skiing: Coronet Peak and The Remarkables.
Lodges: Riverview (Athol).
Fishing: Riverview (Athol).
River Adventures: Alpine Safaris, Danes Back Country, Heli-jet, Twin Rivers Jet, Value Tours (Queenstown).
Sailing: Charter Link NZ (Queenstown).
Down on the Farm: Expo Cattledrome.

Southern Lakes

12

Jet boating. *(Andris Apse Ltd)*

ARROWTOWN

Arrowtown is a trip into the past, a town that once bustled with life when thousands of miners from all over the world converged on the area to seek their fortunes in gold. Gold fever diminished, the town's heyday was over, but the town didn't die. It remained to become one of the prettiest villages in the country, with old wood and stone cottages lining the street, nestling beneath great sycamore trees, a brilliant display of yellow in autumn. The pub and the shops that served the miners are still open for business.

Cobb cottage, Central Otago. ***(Ray Dustow)***

There's a splendid museum outlining the gold-mining history of the area and an old stone jail with heavy iron doors. If you wish, take a gold pan and try your luck in the nearby Arrow River. Flash floods on this river caused many miners' deaths, evidence of which survives in the tombstones in the local cemetery. Chinese tombstones show the cultural diversity of the area.

From Arrowtown, follow the trails of miners across country on four-wheel-drive, horseback or walking tours, to Mace Town, a mining town that didn't survive – old mining equipment, stone walls, garden trees and hedges mark the site.

Gold mining.

In 1862, when two prospectors panned up a large amount of gold from the Shotover River at Arthurs Point (near Queenstown), swarms of fortune hunters surged and flooded into the towering mountains and unexplored creeks. The solitude of a few run holders was lost as numbers mushroomed when the stories of fabulous rich finds spread – daily finds reckoned in pounds weight rather than mere ounces.

Makeshift canvas towns of miners' tents, stores and grog shops sprang up overnight, establishing Queenstown and Arrowtown and many small encampments on the lower reaches of the swift-flowing Shotover River.

The way to the source of the Shotover was impossible because of the sheer precipitous rocks that hemmed it into a long gorge. Undaunted by this, the miners invaded the mountain ranges that confined the river. The way was rough and often in deep snow.

To reach the upper part of the 'richest river in the world', the most spectacular and dangerous Skippers Road winds around precipitous bends, following the bridle track that the miners carved through this wild empty landscape. This is tussock country with huge rock outcrops. Chimneys and stone walls remind tourists of the numerous hotels that lined the road.

After the descent from Long Gully, the Shotover lies deep between its canyon walls. Marvel at the engineering ingenuity at Pinchers Bluff, where Chinese workers armed with hammer and chisel were lowered down a cliff face to forge this part of the road. There are parts of the road where, even today, cars have to reverse back and have two attempts, so sharp are the bends.

The gentle sloping terrace of Maori Point once held a busy mining population of over 2,000 people, complete with bakery, several shops, bank, courthouse to curb lawlessness, library and police camp and even a race track.

Though gold mining still goes on in the river below using sophisticated techniques, the town has totally disappeared. Nearby Skippers, once the largest town on the river, is now a ghost town with a cemetery full of those who lost the battle for gold through hardship, disease, severe winters and flash floods.

Life on the Shotover was excessively hard for miners, and by the 1870s large companies' dredges replaced the prospectors, but without the same dramatic success.

Walks around Queenstown

Sawpit Gully: (Three hours return). A looptrack rising out of the Arrow Gorge and returning via Bush Creek.

Big Hill to Macetown: (Nine hours return). Old high-level route to Macetown Historic Reserve, then return via Arrow Gorge.

Check details at the local Land and Survey Information Office, Stanley St, Queenstown, telephone (0294) 27-933. In Arrowtown, visit the Lake District Centennial Museum which contains an excellent gold mining section and comprehensive displays detailing the history of the Southern Lakes Region.

The Stone Cottage
PO Box 10
Arrowtown
Telephone: Arrowtown 860
Host: Shelley Witchalls

Built in 1876, provides mouth-watering foods; from cooked American/English breakfasts, delicious Devonshire cream teas, luscious lunches, pastries, cakes, salads, pates and quiches – all homemade and served in the gracious atmosphere of yesteryear. Open Friday and Saturday evenings (skiing/summer season only) for informal dining (blackboard menu: crepes, rack of lamb, seafood). See the display of early blue and white china. On the historic avenue of trees (opposite museum), and open daily. Great prices!

SEE ALSO:

Live with NZ: Royalburn Farmstays (Arrowtown).

Jet boating on the Shotover River, near Queenstown. *(National Publicity Studios)*

Te Anau

The *Milford Haven* passing the Stirling Falls, Milford Sound, Southland. *(National Publicity Studios)*

The lakeside township of Te Anau declares itself 'the gateway to Fiordland' and, as such, is the obvious base for more than a passing glimpse of the great Fiordland wilderness.

Make your first stop at the Fiordland National Park Headquarters at the southern end of the lake-front road for information on the park, its tracks and trails and outdoor activities. The park's rangers also organise summer field trips and special evening programmes. There are displays of the park's unusual plant and birdlife and explanations of the geological history.

Get your first hint of Fiordland's beauty with a cruise on the lake. Surrounded by bush and mountains, Lake Te Anau offers isolated coves, bays and islands; to the west, the lake branches into three land-locked fiords of its own. Take a launch trip to the Te Ana-au Caves, discovered only in 1948. At the limestone caves, visitors transfer to a punt that glides along on an underground river, where the cavern ceilings are covered with glow worms.

Other launch trips offer scheduled excursions to bays and islands for picnics, swimming and bushwalks. There are jet-boat rides, fishing charters and a water-taxi service for sightseeing, tramping, hunting and fishing. Arrange for a boat to drop you at a remote bay and return at a pre-arranged time; or hire a sail boat, outboard-motor boat, row boat, canoe or pedal boat. For travel on fast water, arrange for rafting or jet boating on the Waiau River.

Take walks – Te Anau is the base for the grand walks, the Milford and Hollyford Tracks, but less energetic, short walks are within easy distance of the township. Nature and lake-shore walks lead away from the centre; or combine lake travel and short bush walks with lake cruises to Glade House and Brod Bay.

In town, hire bicycles for pleasant around-town travel. Visit the wildlife museum – a display of stuffed animals and native birds. At an underground trout observatory, get a side view of rainbow, brown and brook trout – trout food is available for visitors to feed the fish.

Drive further afield to Milford Sound (2½ – 3 hours), by way of the Eglinton and Hollyford Valleys and Homer Tunnel, through red-beech forest with mountains looming closer on every side. En route, visit the Mirror Lakes, so calm and reflective that you may never know which is the right way up in subsequent photographs. Stop off at other lakes along the way – Lake Gunn, Lake Fergus and Lake Lochie. At Gunn's Camp on the Hollyford Road, find an intriguing little museum of mementoes and relics from the days when hardy pioneers tried, and often failed, to carve out an existence in this wild land.

On a day visit to Milford from Te Anau, take a cruise on Milford Sound right by Mitre Peak, rising 1,695 metres (5,560 feet) straight from the sea, past waterfalls that plummet from sheer mountainsides and past colonies of fur seals basking on the rocks.

Southwest from Te Anau is Lake Manapouri, often regarded as New Zealand's most beautiful lake – high praise in this land of beautiful lakes. It is also the country's deepest lake at about 450 metres (1,500 feet). The dark, still surface of Manapouri reflects the dense forest that grows down to the water's edge, tiny sandy bays appear as a flash of white, 36 forested islands dot the lake and three immense coves take the water deep into the mountains. Take a launch tour from Pearl Harbour. The

Fiordland Promotional Assn (Fiordland Travel) Telephone: (0229) 7416

most spectacular tour takes you to West Arm to visit a hydro-electric power house, 184 metres (600 feet) deep down in a granite mountain. From there a bus takes visitors to the sea at Doubtful Sound.

The sounds of Fiordland are one of the most remarkable areas of New Zealand. It was here in Dusky Sound in 1769-70 that Captain James Cook of the *Endeavour* stopped for provisions and exploration. In this untouched wilderness you can still see where he cut spars for the ships. The earliest drawings of the Maori were made in this area, which lead in later years to the myth of the Lost Tribe of Fiordland.

Tragedy is also recorded. In the 1760s a ship also called *Endeavour* sank in the sound after being driven off-course on a Sydney-London voyage. One hundred and ninety survivors, including five women, built the first house in New Zealand while some men built a boat and sailed thousands of miles to Sydney for help. In a land that time forgot, their survival was no mean feat. Today the launch cruises capture magic without misery.

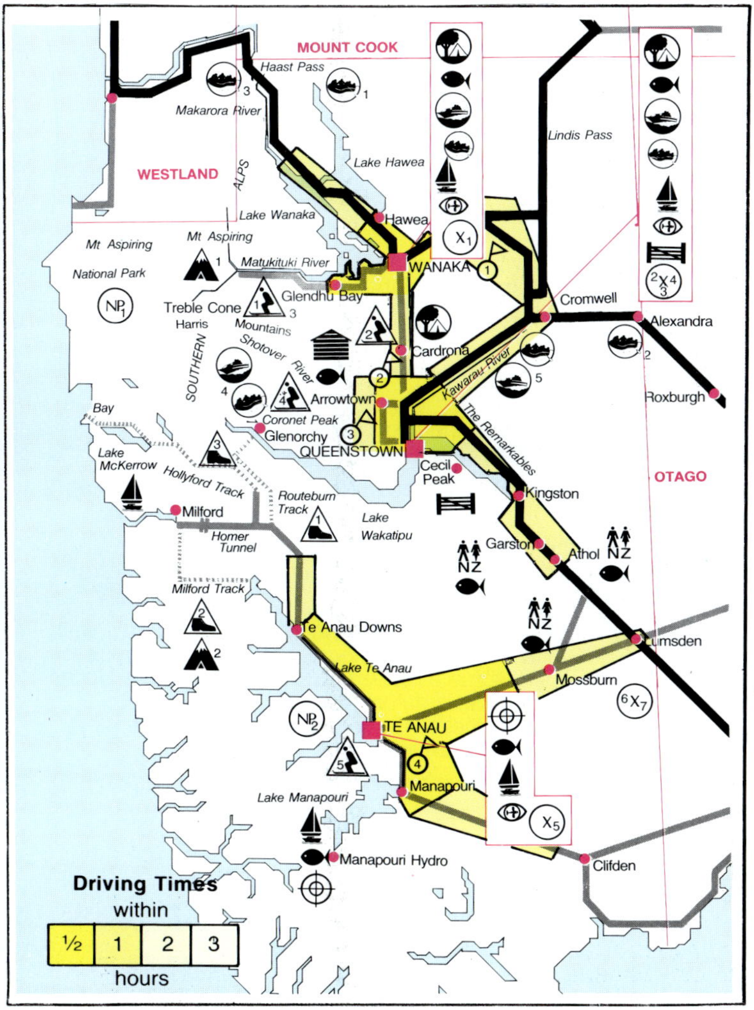

SOUTHERN LAKES

National Parks
1. Mount Aspiring National Park; 2. Fiordland National Park.

Skiing Heli/Cross Country
1. Treble Cone; 2. Cardrona;
3. Harris Mountains;
4. Coronet Peak.
5. Mount Luxmore.

Climbing
1. Mount Aspiring National Park; 2. Fiordland National Park.

Tramping
1. Routeburn; 2. Milford Track;
3. Hollyford Track.

Lodges
Riverview Farm Lodge

Outback Safaris

Hunting

Fishing

River Adventures
1. Hunter River; 2. Clutha River; 3. Landsborough River; 4. Shotover River; 5. Kawarau River.

Cruising

Flightseeing

Golf
1. Wanaka; 2. Arrowtown;
3. Queenstown; 4. Te Anau.

Down on Farm

Live with NZ

Local
1. The Maze & Puzzle Centre; 2. Motor Museum; 3. Art Gallery; 4. Milford Track Audio-Visual; 5. Matuku Engine Museum & 6. Bee Bazaar.

The Milford Road

One of the most dramatic scenic drives in New Zealand – with a lot to do on the way if you make time. Start early (7.30-8.00 a.m.) from Te Anau, taking insect repellent, warm clothes and a raincoat. Don't despair if it's wet. Milford in the rain is at its most spectacular.

Ten-mile Bush	Typical beech forest – red, mountain and silver beech with a few podocarps – rimu, miro and kahikitea
Te Anau Downs	Departure point for Milford Track trampers. Meals, accommodation, film and petrol available here.
Mirror Lakes	Popular photography point for mountain reflections in calm weather. Boardwalks provided for convenience of viewers.
Knods Flat	Named after the scattered hillocks left by a receding glacier.
Lake Gunn	Good fishing for land-locked Atlantic salmon and trout. Low boat speeds of 8 km/h (5 mph) help protect the floating nests of the great crested grebe.
Lake Gunn Nature Walk (30 minutes)	A variety of mosses and native birds including New Zealand's smallest bird, the rifleman, are usually seen on this loop track.
Lake Fergus	Discovered in 1889 and named after a member of parliament.
The Divide	Lowest east-west pass in the Southern Alps (534 metres; 1,751 feet). Start of Routeburn and Greenstone overland routes to Lake Wakatipu.
Key Summit (3 hours return)	Tarns, shrubland and alpine bog are a feature of the viewpoint appropriately named for three major river systems originating on its flanks.
Marian Corner	Avalanche gates enable the road to be closed when there is any danger to motorists.
Lake Marian (3 hours return)	Depart from Marian swingbridge 1 kilometre (0.6 miles) down the Lower Hollyford road from the Marian Corner. A steep walk through west-coast bush into the Marian Valley to a lunch spot beside Lake Marian, with superb alpine views.
Gunns Camp	Cabins and limited supply of stores. An early settlers museum here is well worth visiting.
Gertrude Saddle (4 hours return)	A steep steady climb from the head of the Gertrude Valley to a point overlooking Milford Sound.
Homer Tunnel	7.4 metres (approximately 24 feet) in diameter, the tunnel descends at a grade of 1 in 10 to the Cleddau portal on the Milford side.
Homer Walks	At both ends of the tunnel walks lead through natural alpine gardens with named species of native plants, which are a delight to view, particularly in the flowering period December/January.
The Chasm (15 minutes return)	A short distance down to Milford, find the spectacular Chasm walk. Here the Cleddau River has cut its way down through the rock to form a narrow chasm, some 22 metres (72 feet) deep at the Upper Fall. It plunges again under a natural rock bridge to another spectacular fall some 16 metres (52 feet) lower. It is dangerous to venture outside the safety barriers.

Southern Lakes

Situated on peaceful shores of Lake Te Anau, just 10 minutes walk to shops. Features private spa pool facilities and a warm, friendly atmosphere. Renowned restaurant and bar. From $105 (single). Major credit cards accepted.

Vacation Inn Te Anau
Te Anau Terrace, Te Anau
Telephone: (0229) 7421
Telex: NZ4379
Facsimile: (0229) 8037

Amazing collection of old American, English, New Zealand agricultural engines/equipment, many still working; the Ideal petrol engine – designed 1895 (only known one remaining); a huge 1925 Aveling/Porter 5hp coal-fired steam roller, one of the world's 4 working models remaining. Janet also spins/weaves natural wool into rugs etc., items for sale. Try the honey and see the working hive on display. Open 7 days – 9.30 a.m. to 5.00 p.m., May-August – weekdays only.

Matuku Engine Museum
and Bee Bazaar
York Street
PO Box 36
Mossburn
Telephone: Mossburn 6282

On the Milford Track,
Southland. *(National Publicity Studios)*

Scenery ranges from dramatic to picturesque through this region.

Inland, great dry valleys barely support even the hardy tussock grasses that cling tenuously to life, seeking meagre moisture in areas ravaged by climate, by moa-hunters long ago and by rabbits introduced last century. Here there are hot, dry summers and bitter winters, an inhospitable, harsh landscape with its own distinctive beauty.

There are also broad green rolling hills and long plains thick with sheep and dairy cows, a landscape of soft bucolic charm. In gentle river valleys the willow-edged streams and rivers wind their way through meadows, anglers seek monster brown trout in quiet pools and, in spring, the green gives way to the fresh pinks and white of spring blossom in apricot, apple, peach and cherry orchards.

Old stone fences edge fields. Old cottages or farm buildings made of stone or sod, some derelict, some restored, stand by the roadside. In the back-country hills run holders built great stone homesteads in times of prosperity.

Travel into the heart of Otago, to the old goldfields in the barren hills. Take the road known as the Pigroot from Palmerston near the coast and travel past old stone buildings – inns and stables that served miners, sheep-station homesteads and farm buildings.

Throughout this southern region stone and brick dominate the small towns and villages that grew up alongside rivers and railway. Many communities began as gold towns in the 1860s and then prospered after the gold rush as farming centres or used river waters for the development of paper mills, oat mills, wheat-flour mills, woollen mills.

Naseby, in the northwest of the region, is one of the prettiest former gold towns, filled with trees in an otherwise treeless, dun-coloured landscape. Holiday cottages surround the village, nearby there are relics of gold-mining days in the stark Kyeburn Diggings, and horsetrails lead over old miners' routes. In winter tiny Naseby becomes a centre for outdoor ice skating and the Scottish ice sport of curling.

The Scots influence in the region is readily apparent in place names such as Dunedin, Duntroon, Mosgiel, Bannockburn, Balclutha, Invercargill, Lochiel, Balfour. The cities of Dunedin and Invercargill began as essentially Scottish settlements, their early prosperity based on gold, wool, wheat and meat. Predictably perhaps, this is the only New Zealand region to have ever grown significant crops of oats; and in the Hokonui Hills behind Gore early highland settlers manufactured a heart-warming reminder of home – illicit whisky. This activity continued up until World War II, with the distillers making elaborate attempts to conceal their still from the customs men. (One of the illicit stills can be seen in Invercargill's Southland Museum.) Today whisky is made, legally, at a distillery in Mosgiel.

The Southland Museum in Invercargill is a gem. There are relics of sealing and whaling days around the coast, curiosities from early shipwrecks and a tuatarium containing two live tuataras, reptiles that are close relatives of dinosaurs that lived 200 million years ago. At the door of the museum is a section of fossilised forest 160 million years old.

Settler homestead, Otago Peninsula. ***(National Publicity Studios)***

Otago — Southland

13

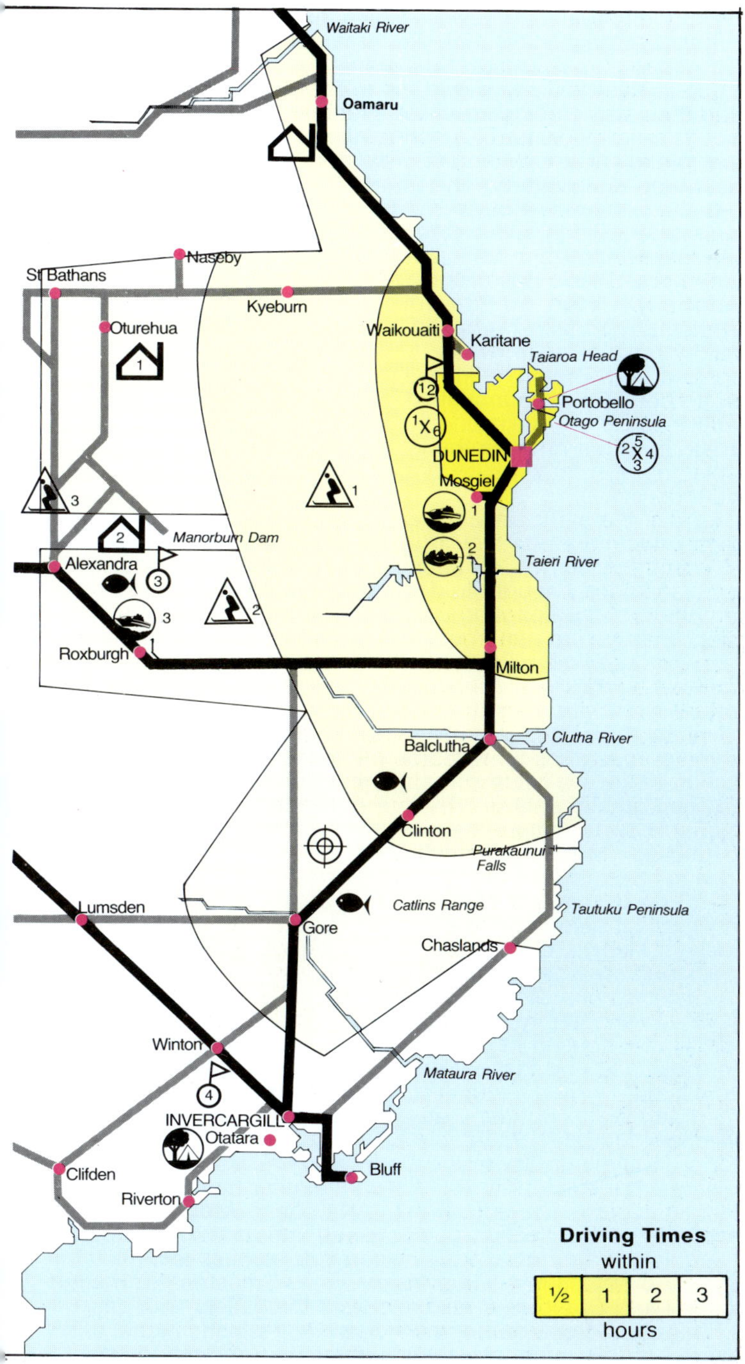

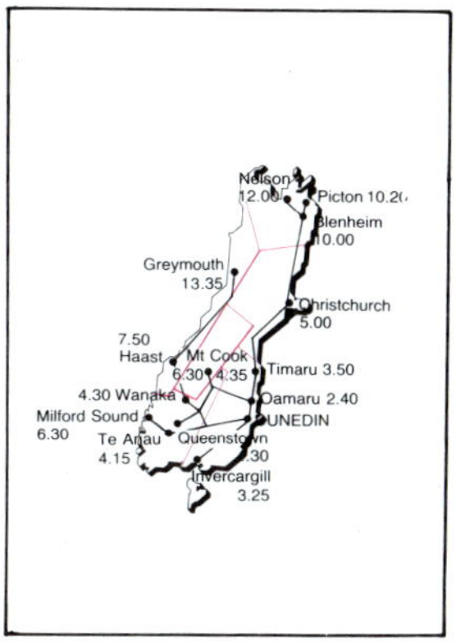

OTAGO/SOUTHLAND

Heli/Cross Country Skiing
1. Rock & Pillar Range; 2. The Old Man Range; 3. Pisa Range.

Outback Safaris

Hunting

Fishing

River Adventures
1. Taieri River; 2. Clutha River; 3. Lake Roxburgh.

Cruising

Flightseeing

Golf
1. Balmacewan; 2. St Clair; 3. Alexandra; 4. Invercargill.

History
1. Hayes Engineering Works; 2. Totara Estate.

Local
1. Olveston; 2. Glenfalloch Woodland Gardens; 3. Larnach's Castle; 4. Penguin Place; 5. Albatross Colony; 6. Art Gallery and Museum.

Dunedin

A city of turrets, spires, gables and gargoyles, Dunedin is rich in decorative Victorian and Edwardian stone buildings built by wealthy merchants when the city was the country's most prosperous. The times of prodigious growth and great wealth have gone, but the legacy is a city of splendid, elaborate architecture.

Visit the railway station, even though you may have no intention of catching a train – the building is a marvellous construction in bluestone, emblazoned with heraldic lions. Inside there are ornate stone scrolls, stained-glass windows, gleaming brass fittings, elaborate plastered ceilings and intricately contrived mosaic floors. See the three main churches: the Presbyterian First Church, built with creamy Oamaru stone with delicate stone carving in the interior; St Paul's Anglican Cathedral, also of Oamaru stone with huge vaulted ceiling; and St Joseph's Roman Catholic Cathedral with beautiful stained-glass windows and stonework.

Other public buildings to admire include the Municipal Chambers, the Law Courts, the brick Victorian police station, old bank buildings, old hotels, the Otago Museum, the slate-roofed bluestone university buildings and the bluestone buildings of Otago Boys High School. There's a grand mansion, Olveston, an Edwardian house built in Jacobean style, crammed with European antiques and art collected by its wealthy businessman owner. Many of the materials were imported from Britain, even the joinery, and the banqueting hall and gallery were modelled on those at Chequers, the country estate of British prime ministers. More modest houses remain from the nineteenth century – terraced brick cottages displaying iron fretwork decorations uncommon in New Zealand.

Many of the early settlers were people with a background of liberal education; into their trunks they crammed their classics and paintings. As well as keeping in touch with European arts, they also eagerly sought to document, understand and collect the culture of the fledgling colony. Some were rich, some had vision; many were generous, and evidence of Dunedin's early prosperity survives in the art gallery and museum, richly endowed by these culturally aware patrons. Dr Thomas Moreland Hocken gave the Dunedin public an extensive collection of books, maps, paintings and manuscripts. One of the major resources for research into New Zealand history, the Hocken Library is housed in the arts block of the University. It has been greatly enlarged by further bequests including the Charles Brasch contemporary painting collection.

The Otago Museum profited from the turn-of-century wealth of the community, and today possesses one of the best collections in this part of the world of art and sculpture from the Classical periods in Greece and Rome. There are also excellent Maori artifacts from the Otago region, including greenstone ornaments and weapons.

A historian and Member of Parliament of great foresight, Robert McNab avidly collected books, and his extensive collection is housed in the Dunedin Public Library. There, also find the Alfred and Isabel Reed collection of early bibles and manuscripts, which feature handwritten works of the the great American, Walt Whitman. The vast and valuable Reed collection can be found on the third floor of the new library in the Octagon.

Several benefactors have swelled and enriched the collections of the Dunedin Public Art Gallery. Archdeacon Smythe gave a collection of eighteenth and nineteenth-century watercolours, a number of Gainsborough portraits and an impressive selection of Old Masters. Peter Smeaton, Sir Percy Sargood and Dr Norcroft also endowed the gallery with gifts and bequests. Look out for the magnificent Claude Monet and Claude Lorrain paintings recently given by Edmund de Beer.

Otago – Southland

The early fathers placed great store by education and today Dunedin boasts one of the finest seats of learning in the country. Otago University not only attracts interest for its beautiful architecture, but takes an active role in the city's life. The residents regard their student body fondly, indulging the annual pranks and festivities inherent to university life, such as the bizarre and beautiful floats created by the students for the Procession held during Capping Week. A wide range of extension courses are held for non-students, (see listing this section).

Take the Golden Arrow scenic drive through the city and gardens, starting from the Chief Post Office. The green Town Belt fringing the city centre is 200 hectares (494 acres) of native and introduced flora and fauna, punctuated by signposted walks. Visit the Botanic Gardens, noted for the rhododendron dell in the upper gardens and the new aviary. See too Queens Gardens and Chingford Park and Stables. Further north are the Mt Cargill-Bethune's Gully walkway to the summit of Mt Cargill, the prime city viewing point along with nearby Signal Hill and the Pineapple-Flagstaff walkway. See also the Tunnel Beach walk.

A city by the sea, Dunedin's beaches range from the powerful surf of the Pacific (where at St Kilda and St Clair's white sand beaches, surfers will brave even the coldest temperatures to ride the waves), to the peaceful bays of the Otago Peninsula. The city is built around the harbour, known for its clean waters and wildlife.

There is much by way of activities offering around the city from fishing, fine golf courses, and harbour cruises to specialist guided tours of the city and its environs. Inland from Dunedin is Mosgiel and the beautiful Taieri River area, offering a variety of adventure excursions and scenic tours. Take the 'Taieri Gorge Limited' train ride from the city railway station for a view of this unique area.

Entertainment
Theatre, arts and music flourish in the city. Advocates of contemporary music will find a range of great pub bands around the city at night and regular festivals and theatre entertainment are offering. Check the Annual Events Calendar and contact the Dunedin Visitor Centre for current 'happenings'.

Robert Burns statue and St Paul's Cathedral, Dunedin. *(National Publicity Studios)*

Dunedin

The Otago Peninsula

Leave the city and head for the Otago Peninsula for an extraordinary variety of special sights. You can whizz round the peninsula on a 64-kilometre (40-mile) round trip, but it's possible to spend several days exploring all that it has to offer at a leisurely pace.

At the very tip of the peninsula is Taiaroa Head, a special reserve that includes a rare mainland nesting site of royal albatrosses, among the world's largest birds with a wing span over 3 metres (10 feet). Visits to the colony are under careful control and occasionally prohibited at critical times. From a look-out the birds may be seen taking off on the wind or returning to feed their chicks with regurgitated fish and squid. Nearby is a penguin nesting place, where yellow-eyed penguins rush ashore on the tide to waddle home through coastal grasses. On the rocks a few metres off shore seals may be seen basking.

Travel around Otago and Southland by rental car from Dunedin or Invercargill. Explore the back country with a self-drive rental four-wheel-drive from Dunedin or Invercargill. Flight-seeing from Dunedin, Invercargill, Mosgiel, Winton. Travel by train through Invercargill and Dunedin along the east coast. N.Z.R. Road Service buses run throughout the region.

A formal driveway and shaped trees lead to Larnach's Castle, the dream house of a Dunedin businessman and politician, created in 1871. There's very little that's 'New Zealand' about the house. It was designed in Scotland (with turrets and battlements), built by workmen brought especially from Europe for the task, using materials sought world wide, such as cedar, mahogany, ebony, oak, ceramic tiles from France, glass and marble from Italy, including massive Italian marble fireplaces.

At Glenfalloch is a garden idyll, with trees and shrubs from all over the world planted over a hundred years. Paths lead around the gardens and the original 1871 homestead, peacocks roam the lawns and doves flutter in the trees.

The peninsula is indented with bays, with many good picnic places. Above the bays the hills, criss-crossed with old dry stone walls, offer constantly changing views, and at Lovers' Leap and The Chasm, cliffs drop 200 metres (650 feet) and 130 metres (426 feet) sheer to the rocky shore.

Larnach Castle
Camp Road (off Highcliff Road)
PO Box 1350, Dunedin
Telephone: (024) 761-302
Facsimile: (024) 761-574
Owners: Mr and Mrs Barry Barker

Stay at the Castle Lodge overlooking Otago Peninsula and harbour, set in beautiful gardens and grounds beside the famous castle. Your choice of share or private, well-appointed facilities. Bunkroom accommodation is also available in an historic coach-house. The Castle Cafe provides lunches and teas, breakfasts and dinner in the Castle Dining Room. From $46 to $89 (bunkroom from $20).

Food. – Dunedin is a university city and has a good range of low-key, inexpensive restaurants and take-away food. Pub eating can also be good value. In up-market restaurants, look for fresh crayfish, Bluff oysters (in season March to August), blue cod, venison, lamb, salmon, pheasant. A local speciality mutton bird, probably won't appeal but adventurous palates might try it. Mutton birds are the young of the sooty shearwater, pulled from burrow nests on clifftops and stuffed with salty fish. The oily, fishy flesh is an acquired taste. Throughout the region old hotels are likely to serve traditional roasts of mutton or beef. Morning and afternoon teas remain substantial.

Accommodation. – Ranges from hunting and fishing lodges in the countryside down to camping grounds by coast or river; in Dunedin there are hotels, motor inns, motels, old hotels, private hotels, guesthouses; youth hostels at Oamaru, Palmerston, Waikouaiti Beach, Dunedin and Invercargill.

Otago — Southland

Dunedin Visitor Centre
48 The Octagon
Dunedin
Telephone: (024) 743-613/4/5
Telex: NZ5231
Facsimile: (024) 743-594

The Dunedin Visitor Centre is conveniently located in the heart of the city, in the greenspace known as the Octagon, near the Cathedral and under the clocktower of Dunedin's beautiful Victorian Municipal Chambers.

Visitors may relax in the spacious lounge, watch a video on Dunedin or browse through the extensive range of information available to visitors. The staff will personally assist you to plan your stay with information on tour bookings, local attractions, accommodation, cultural, arts and recreational events plus dining out. Maps, books and souvenirs are available for purchase. All attractions listed below below can be booked here.

The Visitor Centre stays open seven days a week, all year around, with extended hours in summer.

Newtons Coach Tours
City pick-up

See many of Dunedin's major attractions and sights in coach comfort, pickup/return to city hotels. Includes Larnach Castle, Glenfalloch Gardens, Royal Albatross Colony (December-April), the historic 'Olveston', and the Disappearing Gun at Taiaroa Head.

Penguin Place
McGrouthers' Farm
Otago Peninsula
Telephone: (024) 780-286/780-478
Hosts: Elizabeth & Howard McGrouther

At the farthest end of the Otago Peninsula, sign-posted from Taiaroa Heads. From the carpark, enjoy a short walk to this sanctuary, viewing marine life at Penguin Bay and Seal Island. Seals bask on a rocky islet close to the shore, and yellow-eyed penguins emerge from the surf to climb to their nests. These penguins are unique to New Zealand, and as is often the case with rare species, threatened with extinction. This haven has been created to save these birds. Best viewing time: last 3-4 hours of daylight, when they are returning to their nests from fishing. Nesting commences September. Binoculars available for use. Open year round, camping facilities/powered van sites available on request. Access: private car, or bus to Portobello and a 9.6 kilometre (6 mile) walk. Telephone for further information and best viewing times.

Larnach's Castle, Otago Peninsula. *(National Publicity Studios)*

Ardachy Trail Rides
Taieri Gorge

Guided horse-rides – spectacular Taieri Gorge and farmland. Farmstays available. Experience unnecessary. From $12 per hour.

Otago Harbour Cruises Ltd.
Dunedin Harbour Basin

A Monarch cruise is the way to see the city of Dunedin; the peninsula, the wildlife (including albatrosses), the beautiful harbour, an historic landing and a great deal more! Departs Rattray Street wharf 1.30 p.m. (November-April) and 7 p.m. (January/February).

Carnegie Art Centre
Central Dunedin

Superbly restored Victorian building houses shopping complex, exhibitions of New Zealand artists and crafts, galleries and restaurant.

Fortune Theatre
Central Dunedin

World's southernmost professional theatre, ensures visitors the best of live entertainment, year through. Call for programme.

Guided Inner City Walks
Central Dunedin

Two hours leisurely walking, enjoying Dunedin's beautiful Victorian architecture and rich history, with experienced guides.

Leith Valley Touring Park
North Dunedin

Excellent van park, close to town but in lovely forest/stream setting. Excellent facilities, friendly atmosphere, good rates.

Silver Peaks Tours
Taieri Gorge

Exhilarating white-water/family rafting, jet-boating, hunting/fishing safaris – all in Taieri Gorge; plus ski tours.

Otago Excursion Train Trust
Dunedin Railway Station

Bring your camera aboard 'The Taieri Gorge Limited' – a great 100-seater train. Thread through spectacular gorge, tunnels and lofty viaducts – far from highways. Excellent facilities plus snack bar. Departs daily – 3.30 p.m., October through March only.

South Pacific Odyessy Ltd

Inbound tour operators specialising in highly-personalised itineraries with the accent on clients' specific interests.

Motor Holdings Air Services
Dunedin Airport

Scenic adventure flights around Dunedin's environs, and to all major tourism centres of the magnificent South. From $60.

Otago Museum
Central Dunedin

Superb facility: see extinct moas, rare takahe, tuatara, albatrosses; Polynesian/Melanesian culture; finest Oceanic art.

Hereweka Pony Treks
Otago Peninsula

See the beautiful Otago Peninsula from horseback. Guided treks for riders of all ages, sizes and abilities. Closed June-August.

Royal Albatross Colony
Taiaroa Head

Internationally famous as the world's only mainland breeding ground for these giant birds (wing span up to 3.3 metres (10 feet)). The first egg was discovered in 1920 and by 1930 the first Taiaroa-hatched chick had flown. This magnificent and legendary seabird mates for life, rearing young only once every 2 years. Colony is heavily protected: viewing is permitted from a specially-constructed lookout, closed between May and October. From $8 (GST inclusive).

Armstrong Disappearing Gun
Taiaroa Head

Installed in 1882, the 6-inch gun and associated tunnel complex have been restored to working order – well worth viewing.

Glenfalloch Woodland Gardens
Portobello Road

Ten hectares of woodlands: rhododendrons, azaleas, fuchsias, peacocks, and working potter and tea house.

Otago Peninsula & Inland Guides
City pick-up

Experienced local guides for small group wildlife tours; afternoon and evening, half- and full-day specialist options.

Otago – Southland

Provides week-long stimulating, live-in courses throughout New Zealand, for the over-55's. Topics – New Zealand history, literature, ecology, social issues. Learn through informal lectures and field trips – a friendly, social atmosphere with experienced directors/hostesses. Optional evening activities and entertainment provided. Previous knowledge/experience not required. Overseas visitors particularly welcome into predominantly New Zealand groups. Everything provided, including accommodation. From $500 (all inclusive, even celebration dinner). Courses late January-early February. Check for discount travel available.

New Zealand College for Seniors
Continuing Education Unit
University of Otago
PO Box 56
Dunedin
Telephone: (024) 770-345
Australia: (042) 270-531
Secretariat: Brian O'Rourke

Tells the story of the 1840 pioneers who settled Otago and built Dunedin – renowned for its noble architecture and excellent educational facilities. Originally called 'New Edinburgh', Dunedin reflects the Scottish influence from those settlers. Colonial supper and museum tour organised by arrangement. Restrooms, a book/souvenir shop and refreshments complement this excellent facility. Genealogical information and research service available, plus children's holiday programmes. From $3 (adult), .50c (child). Group, family rates.

Otago Early Settlers Museum
220 Cumberland Street
Dunedin
Telephone: (024) 775-052

A stately home built between 1904 and 1906, designed by Sir Ernest George (a famous English architect), this Jacobean styled, brick and stone building mirrors the lifestyle of the Theomin family, for whom it was built. Olveston created a stir among the locals of Dunedin then, and captivates thousands of visitors today. It has been retained exactly as it was in the 1920s and reflects the grand style of yesteryears, complete with conveniences like heated towel rails, interphone system and full central heating. The 35 rooms reflect a scale of entertaining belonging to elegant times. View fine art treasures from around the world, including paintings by leading New Zealand artists. Reservations essential for guided tours. Open daily (except Good Friday and Christmas Day). Sunday tours, afternoons only. Telephone for reservations and costs.

Olveston
42 Royal Terrace
Dunedin
Telephone: (024) 773-320

Southland Promotion Inc
82 Dee Street
Invercargill
P.O. Box 705
Telephone: (021) 86-091

One of Dunedin's newest motor inns, tastefully built around a tranquil courtyard garden, close to the University and central city. Relaxation is guaranteed in ultra-modern luxurious suites, complete with 24-hour room service. Close to tennis courts and golf courses, facilities include waterbeds, spa baths, in-house video and off-street parking. Cargills Licensed Garden Restaurant, specialising in French cuisine opens from 7.00 a.m. until late. From $90 (single) to $180 (suites).

Cargills Motor Inn
678 George Street
PO Box 6063
Dunedin
Telephone: (024) 777-983
Telex: NZ5606

North to Waikouaiti and Oamaru

A jagged spectacular natural pa site, the peninsula walls rise sheer from the sea, providing resistance in the past against warring Maori tribes. Huriwawa peninsula has three foaming blowholes and offers fine coastline views.

Leave Dunedin on State Highway 1 to reach Waikouaiti, one of the South Island's oldest European settlements. A few kilometres from Waikouaiti are the old Matanaka farm buildings. Well kept and sturdy after 136 years, the granary, barn and stables are a memorial to their builder, Johnny Jones.

Fishing boats mooring in the estuary of the charming seaside village of Karitane are sheltered by the Huriwawa peninsula.

SEE ALSO:

NZ Historic Places: Hayes Engineering Work (Oturehua), Totara Estate (Oamaru).

Brydone Hotel
115 Thames Street
Oamaru
Telephone: (0297) 49-892
Telex: NZ5625

Old-world charm, warmth and comfort, modern facilities include sauna and inhouse video. Owned by the Oamaru Licensing Trust and well-known for excellence in service and dining. Great conference facilities. From $56 (single), $73 (double).

South to Invercargill via the Catlins

The coast road from Balclutha to Invercargill climbs over hills of lush grass, which encroach on the primeval Catlins Hills, dressed in beech forest, crimson rata, kahikatea and rimu.

The transition from virgin bush through to well-cultivated tidy farms in the space of a few kilometers is startling. Although the timber trade is long past its heyday, milling is still depleting forests.

A perfect crescent of curving golden sand leads to the Tautuku Peninsula, a magical place of lush grassy slopes and tiny secluded coves, which sheltered the earliest inhabitants during their moa and fish feasts, the whalers resting from voyages, and, more recently, holiday-makers and bach owners.

Just south, another glorious beach may be reached through a bush track; at the northern end of Waipati beach are the grand Cathedral Caves, eleven lofty caverns and echoing tunnels carved by the sea. Discover at low tide a second set of caves around the point.

The road weaves on to Invercargill through the Chaslands coast, famous for many shipwrecks and loss of life.

Southland Progress League Inc.,
Oreti House,
120 Esk Street,
Invercargill,
P.O. Box 311.
Telephone: (021) 84538

Ascot Park Motor Hotel
Cnr Racecourse Road & Tay Street
Invercargill
Telephone: (021) 76-195
Telex: NZ5255
Fax (021) 77-002

Superb facility set in quiet, landscaped parkland; 50 hotel rooms, 2 deluxe suites and 23 self-contained motel units, plus indoor heated pool, spa, saunas, solariums, inhouse video and a la carte dining. Great convention venue. From $70 (motel), $115 (single, hotel).

Grand Hotel
Dee Street, PO Box 89
Invercargill
Telephone: (021) 88-059
Telex: NZ5774

An older-styled very comfortable hotel, tastefully refurbished and offering a range of well-appointed accommodation, all with private facilities. Located centrally to shopping (car parking close by), with restaurant and lounge bar. From $40 (small single).

Kelvin Hotel
Cnr Kelvin and Esk Streets
Invercargill
Telephone: (021) 82-829
Telex: NZ5774

This highrise hotel offers 50 deluxe twin rooms/suites with inhouse video, the excellent signature restaurant 'Highlights' and a carvery restaurant. Recently renovated, conveniently located to all facilities, city centre. From $60 (single). Weekend/children's rates.

Southern Air Ltd
(Invercargill Airport)
PO Box 860
Invercargill
Telephone: (021) 89-129

Less than 20 minutes by air from Invercargill, Stewart Island awaits your discovery – accessed by at least three return flights daily in twin-engined 'Islander' aircraft. Southern Air arranges package tours, including accommodation, fishing trips and sightseeing. Walk through native forest, or just browse in the unique museum. Don't miss meeting this historic and timeless island and its friendly people.

West to Alexandra and Clyde

Citizens Advice Bureau
Telephone: (0294) 87-771

'Heart of Gold' Information Centre
Central Otago
Citizens Advice Bureau
Centennial Avenue
Alexandra
Telephone: (0294) 86-472

In Alexandra, a walk over the Shakey Bridge (sign-posted from Tarbert Street) can lead to the Graveyard Gully Memorial and up the hill for a closer inspection of the largest illuminated clock in the world. Note the thyme thriving amongst the rocks, another inheritance from gold-mining days. A stroll about the streets of Clyde will evoke something of the atmosphere of its hustling mining-town past. West of Clyde is the Clyde Dam, the country's largest concrete dam under construction. Take a jet-boat trip to explore the gold diggings and settlement below Alexandra, on the shores of Lake Roxburgh.

In Alexandra, a walk over the Shakey Bridge (sign-posted from Tarbert Street) can lead to the Graveyard Gully Memorial and up the hill for a closer inspection of the largest illuminated clock in the world. Note the thyme thriving amongst the rocks, another inheritance from gold-mining days. A stroll about the streets of Clyde will evoke something of the atmosphere of its hustling mining-town past. West of Clyde is the Clyde Dam, the country's largest concrete dam under construction. Take a jet-boat trip to explore the gold diggings and settlement below Alexandra, on the shores of Lake Roxburgh.

Ice skating

Summer tranquillity at the Manorburn is shattered in the winter, June to August, when the lake behind the dam freezes (becoming the largest natural ice skating rink in the Southern Hemisphere). Ice skaters and curlers revel in the freedom of 28.3 hectares (70 acres) of singing ice. Skates can be hired.

Gold

Drive to the gold dredge tailings at the end of McPherson Road, off Earnscleugh Road, just a few minutes from Alexandra or Clyde. Although the last gold dredge stopped in 1964, there were 27 dredges working within 8 kilometres (5 miles) of Alexandra in 1900. The often dramatic scars can still be seen, though softened by time and vegetation. For longer day trips to historic spots such as St Bathans and Oturehua, consult information on the Goldfields Park, available from the Lands and Survey Department. Museums in both towns display memorabilia of this colourful past.

Festivals

Alexandra's Blossom Festival (held fourth weekend in September). Thousands throng to this festival (recognised nationally as the major spring festival in the Otago-Southland area), which is highlighted by the colourful and artistic procession of floats.

Easter Arts Festival displays work created by the many local professional and amateur craftspeople in the region, including potters, spinners, weavers and painters.

Lombardy poplars line an irrigation canal near Cromwell, Central Otago. *(National Publicity Studios).*

A fisherman on Cook's Arm with the granite peaks of Gog and Magog in the background. ***(Courtesy Stewart Island Pictorial Promotions)***

Imagine an island covering 1,680 square kilometres (648 square miles), twice the size of Singapore, with an indented coastline of 755 kilometres (470 miles), only 20 kilometres (12 miles) of road, 220 kilometres (124 miles) of walking tracks and a permanent population of about 500.

For those who love wildnerness, seclusion, unique dense forests and exciting birdlife, who enjoy the experience of living totally removed from the modern world, Stewart Island offers extraordinary opportunities.

Even in Oban, the island's only village, in Halfmoon Bay, the pace of life isn't exactly speedy – action centres on the island's one hotel, the southernmost hotel in the world, and on the Oban wharf, where ferry and fishing boats berth. Near the shore there's a tiny museum and a shop selling ferns propagated from the island's wild ferns. Small though the museum may be, it is well worth a visit, with seafaring relics from shipwrecks and the island's days as a sealing and whaling base. There's an emphasis on the rich plant, bird and marine life too, alongside early Maori settlement artefacts.

To find out more about the island, visit the Forest Service headquarters. This is of interest to day visitors, and essential for anyone planning to take off into the remote parts of the island. The Department of Conservation administers much of the island, maintains tracks and huts (accommodation free) and will provide all the information needed.

Stewart Island becomes an adventure the moment you leave the mainland by boat (two or three times a week) from Bluff, or by air (several times daily) from Invercargill. You can make the journey for a day's outing, see Halfmoon Bay where houses hide in the enveloping bush, explore some of the island on a brief mini-bus tour – with only 200 kilometres (12 miles) of road there are obvious limitations – or perhaps take a launch trip to out-of the-way bays.

Stay for a day or two, or more, in Oban and make the same excursions or venture on foot to points within easy reach – to hilltops with views over forests, coasts and rocky islands, along coastal paths that lead to sandy bays or rugged promontories. Take off for days on end into that wilderness of virgin rainforest, golden beaches, steep hills and cliffs that rise starkly from the sea – tramping, bird watching, fishing, boating, beachcombing, deer hunting, diving.

For such 'backwoods' expeditions, participants naturally need to be well equipped and experienced – it is not territory for the novice, nor anyone who objects to an encounter with mud.

Although so far south, the climate is surprisingly mild, never very hot or cold, with frost a rare winter occurrence. But it is damp – frequent light rain is a fact of Stewart Island life. The result, however, is forest thick with vines and ferns, with tiny native orchids hiding in the lush jungle-like growth under a canopy of totara, southern rata, miro, rimu.

At times the forest fills with birdsong – a rewarding sound for those interested in New Zealand's unique birdlife. The forest and scrub are home to tuis, bellbirds, wood pigeons, fantails, kakas, wekas, kiwis, parakeets, brown creepers, moreporks, welcome swallows and fernbirds. It is also the last-known natural home of the kakapo, the flightless night parrot, although visitors are unlikely to stumble upon this rare bird in the wild. On the shore birds include blue penguins, yellow-eyed penguins, mollymawks, sooty shearwaters, gannets, skuas, shags, white-faced herons, oystercatchers, New Zealand dotterels and terns.

Stewart Island

14

The young of the sooty shearwater are the 'muttonbirds', taken from the cliff-top burrows on the nearby Titi islands. The perilous occupation of muttonbirding is the traditional right of local Maori tribes.

Accommodation. – One hotel, camping ground with cabins, sometimes cottages available in Half Moon Bay. Forest service huts strategically placed through northern part of island – the rest is even more wild, no tracks, no huts.

Food. – Apart from mutton birds, fresh fish is available, especially blue cod and crayfish caught by the fishing fleet based at Oban. Country-style cooking can be sampled at the South Seas Hotel; Robinson Crusoe types live off land and sea, catching fish; gathering paua and mussels, hunting deer. Food supplies can be bought at Oban with friendly and welcoming locals well able to entertain with many a tale!

Stewart Island Travel Ltd
PO Box 26, Halfmoon Bay
Stewart Island
Telephone: (021) 391-269

Your first stop for information and bookings. Arranges entertaining island sightseeing bus tours around all the beautiful bays, with a full commentary. Booking agents for Southern Air and all of the following services.

Horseshoe Haven Lodge
PO Box 75, Halfmoon Bay
Stewart Island
Telephone: (021) 391-266

Set in native rain forest with panoramic view of the bay, the 'Haven' features accommodation chalets and a licensed restaurant.

Stewart Island Lodge
PO Box 5, Halfmoon Bay
Stewart Island
Telephone: (021) 391-085

Relax in comfort with superb view, enjoying fully licensed hospitality, fresh seafood, fishing and scenic trips. (See listing Lodges section.)

South Sea Hotel
PO Box 52, Halfmoon Bay
Stewart Island
Telephone: (021) 391-059

Situated in the heart of Oban, the hotel is a comfortable social base for visitors, with an excellent cuisine and warm hospitality.

SEE ALSO:

Flightseeing: Southern Air.

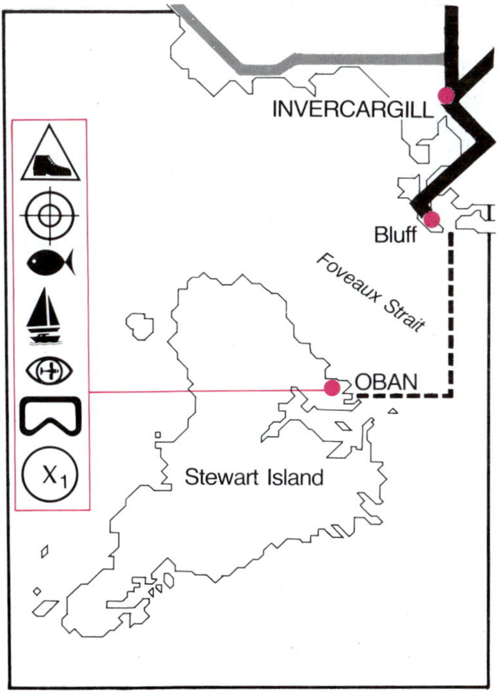

STEWART ISLAND

Tramping

Hunting

Cruising

Fishing

Flightseeing

Diving

Local

1. Museum.